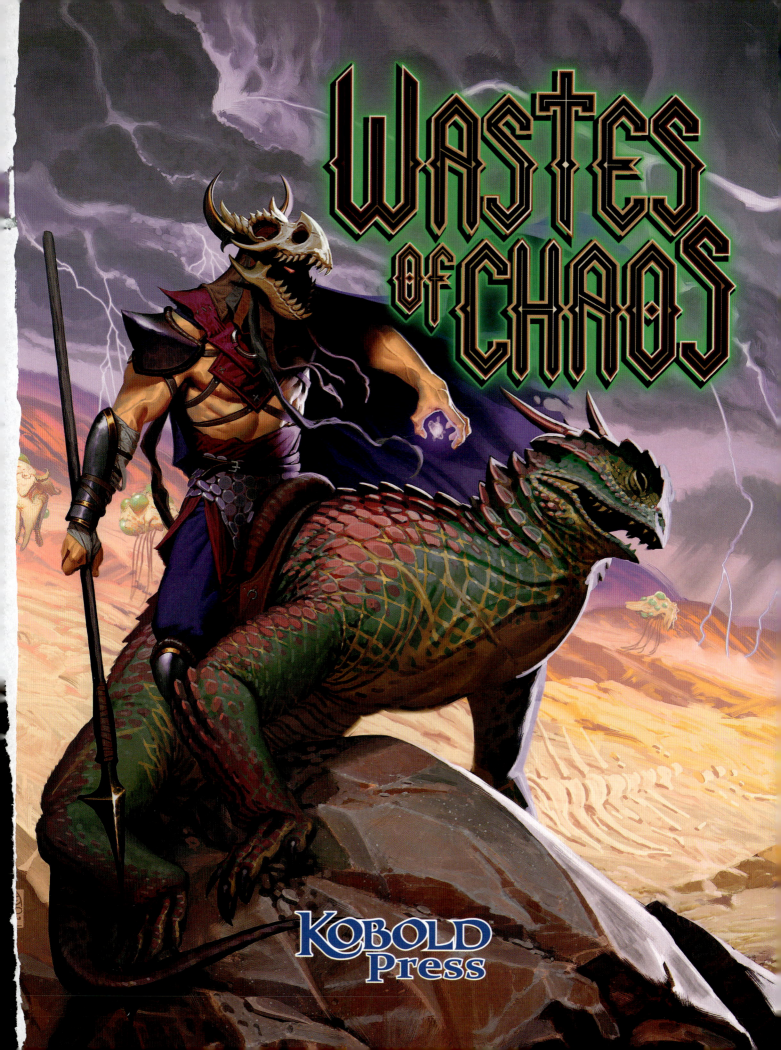

CREDITS

Lead Designers: Richard Green, Tim Hitchcock, Sarah Madsen

Designers: Dan Dillion, Phillip Larwood, Jeff Lee, Ben McFarland, Carlos & Holly Ovalle, Kelly Pawlik, Brian Suskind

Editor: Kim Mohan

Proofreader: Thomas M. Reid

Cover Artist: Marcel Mercado

Interior Artists: Gustavo Dias, George Johnstone, Marcel Mercado, William O'Brien, Roberto Pitturru, Kiki Moch Rizki, Bryan Syme, Egil Thompson

Graphic Designer: Marc Radle

Cartographer: Jon Pintar

KOBOLD WARRENS

Publisher: Wolfgang Baur

Chief Operations Officer: T. Alexander Stangroom

Director of Digital Growth: Blaine McNutt

Art Director: Marc Radle

Art Department: Marc Radle, Amber Seger

Editorial Director: Thomas M. Reid

Editorial Department: Scott Gable, Meagan Maricle, Jeff Quick, Thomas M. Reid

Senior Game Designer: Celeste Conowitch

Marketing Director: Chelsea "Dot" Steverson

Project Manager: Amber Seger

Community Manager: Zachery Newbill

Sales Manager: Kym Weiler

In Memoriam: Kim Rudolph Mohan 1949–2022; friend, mentor, and valiant champion of the game.

SPECIAL THANKS

To the 2,770 backers who made this book possible and the dozens of playtesters who helped refine it!

Product Identity: The following items are hereby identified as Product Identity, as defined in the Open Game License version 1.0a, Section 1(e), and are not Open Content: All trademarks, registered trademarks, proper names (characters, place names, new deities, etc.), dialogue, plots, story elements, locations, characters, artwork, sidebars, and trade dress. (Elements that have previously been designated as Open Game Content are not included in this declaration.)

Midgard and Kobold Press are trademarks of Open Design LLC. All rights reserved.

Open Game Content: The Open Content includes the circle of dust druid, dust goblin, and wasteland dragon. All other material is Product Identity, especially place names, character names, locations, story elements, background, sidebars, and fiction.

No other portion of this work may be reproduced in any form without permission.

©2023 Open Design LLC. All rights reserved.
www.koboldpress.com
PO Box 2811 | Kirkland, WA 98083
Printed in China / FSC Paper
ISBN: 978-1-950789-51-1
Limited Edition ISBN: 978-1-950789-53-5
2 4 6 8 10 9 7 5 3 1

CONTENTS

Introduction 6	Fighter: Doombringer...............................30
What's In This Book? 6	Monk: Way of Chaos................................31
Chapter 1: Dangerous Lands.......................7	Ranger: Wasteland Rover........................33
Downfall and Causes of Wastes 7	Rogue: Bandit Priest................................ 34
Magic in the Wastelands..............................9	Rogue: Chaos Cultist 35
Types of Wastes 10	Warlock: Demonic Tutor 36
Badlands 10	Backgrounds...37
Battlefields...13	Chaos Child 37
Deserts...14	Wasteland Reaver 39
Flinty Hills 16	**Chapter 3: People, Tribes, & Cults**.............40
Haunted Marshlands............................18	Chaos Reavers 40
Polluted Blights 21	Chaos Reaver 42
Chapter 2: Heroes of the Borderlands 23	Wasteland Barnstormer........................43
Races 23	Oracle of the Wastes 43
Automaton...23	Cult of the Black Goat 45
Dust Goblin 25	Prophet of the Black Goat 48
Wasteland Dragonborn 26	Red Moon Bandit Gang 49
Wasteland Orc.......................................27	Mimsy Biteflower 51
Subclasses 28	Lapis Begonia Nightshade 52
Barbarian: Path of the Demon 28	Tolf Toadlashes 52
Druid: Circle of Dust............................29	Spider Face Goblin Tribe 53

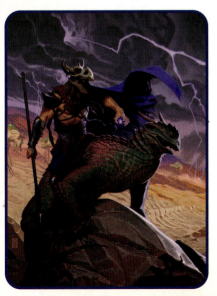

ON THE COVER
A riding lizard and a chaos warlord await the arrival of a storm in this art by Marcel Mercado.

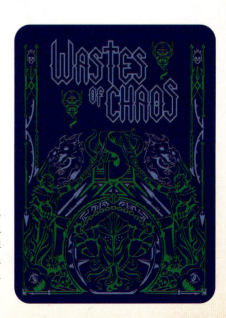

ON THE LIMITED EDITION COVER
Horned warriors, chaos drakes, and skulls adorn the limited edition in this art by Addison Rankin.

Spider Face Goblin Warlord 56	**Chapter 5: Monsters of the Wastes............109**
Chaos Goblin Priest 58	Anathema Locust..109
Wasteland Wanderers 58	Bat, Saber-Toothed 110
Djerl Huskel's Abomination 59	Black Goat Cultist... 111
Mad Wizard 60	Black Goat Priestess 112
Void Lord 62	Chaos Orb 113
Chapter 4: Places of Chaos 65	Child of the Silver Sphere 113
Bleakspire, Tower of the Lich King 65	Demon, Mire Fiend 114
Rustspike, Castle of the Lord of Ruin 69	Doom Champion..116
Cathedral of the Black Goat 73	Doom Champion Overlord 116
Mother's Milk Sidebar 76	Drake, Chaos 117
Ghost Light Marshes 77	Drake, Ruins..118
Goblin Town of Nichenevin 80	Dread Mouther 119
Tangleside, Chaos Wastes Village 83	Dread Colossus Flesh Golem 120
Maze Caverns of the Wasteland Drake.......... 87	Eldritch Horror 121
Nygethuaac, the Dread Colossus 91	Eonic Loner 122
Raw Chaos Portal 94	Gellimite 122
River of Alchemy 99	Goblin, Chaos... 123
Vault of the God-King 103	Goblin, Nomadic 124

Goblin, Dust..125	Wasteland Dragon 145
Dust Goblin Archmage 126	Wasteland Monarch 148
Insatiable Brood 127	Wasteland Priest 149
Robot, Drone...................................... 127	Wasteland Swarms 150
Robot, Warden 128	Swarm of Warp Rats 151
Satarre Infiltrator 129	Swarm of Zoogs 151
Slitherjack 130	Wasteland Trollkin 152
Spider, Song..131	Wasteland Worm 153
Tentacled Crab...................................132	Xotliac 154
Tiefling Diabolist 133	
Troll, Chaos 134	**Chapter 6: Spells and Magic......................155**
Troll, Necromancer 135	Ancient Magic 155
Vile Looter 136	Chaos Magic 158
Vile Reconstructor 137	Doom Magic 162
Void Witness 138	**Chapter 7: Gear & Ancient Treasures 167**
Void-Bound Warlock 139	Ancient Treasures 167
Warped Behemoth 140	Chaos Items....................................... 181
Warped Treant 142	Vril Items 191
Wasteland Lizard 143	Other Lost Technology Items 195
Warpling... 144	**Appendix: Midgard Lore........................... 197**

INTRODUCTION

Welcome to the wastes.

Windswept badlands, fetid marshes, battlefields blasted by magical corruption . . . all beckon to the intrepid—some say foolhardy—adventurer seeking wealth, lost secrets, or unparalleled magical power. The wastes are no place for the timid or unpracticed. The inhospitable land guards its treasures jealously. Strange, chaotic forces of nature and ferocious, twisted inhabitants rebuff all who dare pass through. Nihilistic cults and roaming tribes fight savagely over the few meager resources to be found.

For those with the mettle to barve such onslaughts of rage, magical corruption, and weird, alien energies, renown and wealth are possible. Mighty artifacts and indescribable technological marvels lie hidden within the ruins of fallen empires or beneath the surfaces of foul, alchemically poisoned waterways. It's all there for the taking. As is a lonely death.

Welcome to the Wastes of Chaos.

WHAT'S IN THIS BOOK?

Wastes of Chaos provides Game Masters and players a wealth of new options for use in any campaign. Players can find options that tie their characters to these dangerous and devastated lands, while the book offers game masters everything they need to add the wastes to their adventures and campaign settings. The Wastes of Chaos are unpredictable and deadly, and those who dwell there are hardy people that struggle for their daily survival. These perilous lands also offer amazing opportunities and heroic adventures for those willing to brave their hazards.

Chapter 1: Dangerous Lands describes causes that might create the Wastes of Chaos in your world. The chapter details what events might cause wastes to form, some of their unusual characteristics, and what types of environments you might find as wastes.

Chapter 2: Heroes of the Borderlands presents several new options for character creation, sharing new races, subclasses and backgrounds appropriate for characters that originate from the wastes or for those who wish to tie themselves to such lands.

Chapter 3: People, Tribes, & Cults provides examples of individuals and groups that characters may encounter in the wastes, including engaging NPCs characters can interact with.

Chapter 4: Places of Chaos presents unique locations for exploration and adventure. Each locale has a map and description to make it immediately ready for game master use when adventuring in the wastes.

Chapter 5: Monsters of the Wastes provides statistics for creatures found in the wastes of varying Challenge Ratings, ranging from its nomadic goblin inhabitants to the dread colossuses that themselves may have caused the cataclysm that created the wastes.

Chapter 6: Spells and Magic denotes some of the magical traditions unique to the wastes, waiting to be unleashed on the wider world. This chapter includes the dark spells that can only be taught by the cults of the wastes, lost ancient spells ready to be rediscovered, and the secrets of chaos magic.

Chapter 7: Gear & Ancient Treasures describes the riches that can be found in the wastes, including ancient magics and lost Vril technology.

Chapter 1
Dangerous Lands

This section describes different causes that might create the Wastes of Chaos in your world. The chapter details what events might cause wastes to form, some of their unusual characteristics, and what types of environments you might find as wastes.

Downfall and Causes of Wastes

Wastes begin as an area like any other. A significant and often tragic event heralds their creation, a cataclysm that warps the land beyond recognition. The results of these devastating changes are often juxtaposed with the surrounding, unharmed areas, the barren lands serving as a warning to bordering civilizations. While pockets of unspoiled nature may remain in the wastes, one of the wastes' defining characteristics is their general unsuitability for life.

CAUSES OF WASTES

While this book generally assumes a magical element to the wastes, the formation of such lands can be caused by any of the factors presented here.

DIVINE INTERVENTION

The gods can make their displeasure known in specific and devastating ways when angered. The people have turned away from their deities, breaking their laws and earning their powerful wrath. An angry cult partially succeeds in their rituals to bring about the end of the world, summoning the avatar of their vengeful deity. Rival gods take their battle to the mortal plane, shattering the land unwillingly hosting their combat. Of course, sometimes the gods are merely petty and bored, their motives inscrutable to their worshippers, who must suffer their pernicious actions.

ELDRITCH HORRORS AND EXTRADIMENSIONAL BEINGS

Terrible things exist outside the Material Plane, beyond mortal comprehension. These unknowable entities seek access to the world, and mad cults and secret societies do all in their power to realize their desires and reach through the Void to summon them. The very presence of these beings can warp the land and those within. Those people that remain in the wastes hide in the mists, desperately avoiding the baleful attention of these unnatural creatures.

MAGIC

In realms of fantasy, powerful and uncontrolled magic is often the catalyst that brings destruction and ruin to the land. A battle between cities of mages invokes treacherous powers. A massive arcane experiment spirals out of control, bringing ruin and leaving magical effluent to further taint the earth. An ancient curse corrupts the land, slowly growing the borders of the wastes. Spells may draw their power from surrounding life. The consequences of these insidious magical forces are often felt in other ways, forever affecting the living things that still grow there, natural phenomena, and even the fabric of magic itself.

MONSTERS

Creatures from fantastic worlds have the power to rain destruction on the land, making it barren and unhospitable to normal life. Dragons incinerate the forests, spreading fire and desolation. An apocalyptic beast rises, destroying the countryside before it is sent back to its hidden slumber once again. The dead rise from their graves, slaying everything that lives and changing the land into an unholy shadow of what it once was. Such creatures roam their claimed lands, resisting those who enter from outside the wastes.

NATURE

Wastes can be the result of natural disasters or extreme weather phenomena. Uncontrolled fires devastate the area and nothing can grow in the once-verdant lands. Powerful earthquakes destroy civilizations, raising mountains and toppling towers. Catastrophic tsunamis sweep away cities, leaving flooded lands and underwater structures. A meteor crashes into the earth, the resulting destruction leaving the area in ruin for centuries. Such occurrences can regularly level the land, again destroying whatever attempts are made at rebuilding, hiding secrets and treasures beneath the wreckage that remains.

TECHNOLOGY

Use or misuse of technology can wreck the land as assuredly as magic can. Byproducts of dangerous experimentation pollute the land and air, leading to burning rivers, acid rain, and skies darkened by ash. Chemical or nuclear disasters of the past have left the land barren, with resulting radiation and mutated creatures a constant danger. The remnants of these technologies may persist in the wastes, even if the secrets of these technologies are long forgotten. Robots continue to patrol their premises. Laser turrets spring to action when a potential enemy comes into range.

TIME

The passage of time brings the end of all things. The sun flickers as its slow death approaches. Civilizations have all but collapsed, and those people who remain lapse into decadence and squabbling over remaining resources. In these lands, the wastes are the rule rather than the exception. Pockets of civilization may exist or even thrive, but ultimately all the inhabitants of these worlds await their inevitable doom.

WAR

Nations battle over nationalistic pride, religious zealotry, or to expand their borders. Hordes of barbarians sweep aside civilization, destroying everything in their path. Armies consume the countryside to fuel their continuance, salting the earth in their retreat to ensure that their enemies cannot use the lands again. The lands ravaged by constant war become lifeless and barren. Raiders and scavengers are constant threats to those who attempt to travel those lands.

AGGREGATE CAUSES

Wastes often result from a combination of these causes. Midgard's Wasted West, for example, was once home to prosperous kingdoms of mages that eventually succumbed to warring among themselves. The destructive magics of the magocracies of Midgard turned the land into a twisted and unnatural desert beset by chaotic magics. The eldritch abominations summoned in their Great Mage Wars lie frozen in time throughout that landscape, a constant danger worshipped as gods by the goblin tribes that now call the wastes home.

FALLEN KINGDOMS

In many situations, the wastes serve as the tomb of once-thriving kingdoms, their ruins a testament to the hubris of the fallen people who caused or were victims of the land's destruction. Intrepid explorers who survive the dangers of the wastes may discover these civilizations' mighty secrets. Treasure, secrets, and lost magic or technology wait in these shattered remnants of once prosperous empires.

The cataclysm that created the wastes can alter the survivors beyond recognition, mutating their physical forms or driving them to insanity. The descendants of these unfortunate few may have since banded together for survival in the harsh lands, forming barely recognizable clans that are strongly protective of their lost history. They may dwell in and protect the collapsed edifices that remain. Other peoples or beasts may move to the existing structures as well, taking advantage of their construction to create protective settlements against the horrors of the wastes. Adventurers may need to negotiate or battle with these groups, whose knowledge and claimed ownership of the land make them deadly enemies.

The calamity may not have destroyed everything. Entire cities may have been spared the brunt of the catastrophe, points of civilization isolated by the desolate wastes. The cities may be havens for those traveling the wastes, offering sanctuary to those who can make their way to the walls. Alternatively, such places may be home to xenophobic peoples who mistrust and respond with violence to anyone coming from the world outside. In any case, these peoples may see themselves as the inheritors of the kingdoms of the past, struggling to restore or at least grasp their former glory.

Magic in the Wastelands

Magic itself is warped in the abnormal environs of the Wastes of Chaos and in turn may further alter the land and its inhabitants. Using magic in the wastes presents risks and opportunities absent elsewhere, and the magic that infuses the wastes offers rewards for those who risk its dangers.

CHAOS MAGIC AND WARPED RESOURCES

Casting spells in the wastes can lead to unpredictable results unless the caster takes precautions. All spells cast in the Wastes of Chaos are treated as if they are chaos magic. Unless a spellcaster uses a bonus action to concentrate to manipulate the twisted magical energies, the caster must roll a d20 to determine if a chaos magic surge occurs (see **Chapter 6**). Casters cannot use this bonus action to remove the surge chance for spells that are normally chaos spells. The chaotic magic of the wastes permeates the land itself, warping everything within. Plants that survive

CHAOTIC MAGIC

GMs may wish to forego this randomness entirely, or conversely increase the chances of these unexpected occurrences. See the Midgard Worldbook's Wasted West for an example of still riskier spellcasting, where the odds are much greater for magic to fail entirely or to have another unexpected effect, such as attracting a wandering creature or triggering a dangerous magical storm.

the wastes become twisted versions of their natural counterparts and may be valued for their magical properties. When using plants harvested from the wastes as spellcasting components, the caster may choose to consume the component to invoke a chaos magic surge as if the spell were a chaos spell, even when used outside of the wastes. These ingredients are highly sought after by chaos mages and others who use wild magic to their advantage. Such components always have a cost of 5 gp or twice the material component cost of the spell, whichever is higher.

Stone and other substances gathered or mined from the wastes hold similar properties when used as spellcasting components. Additionally, artisans and crafters can create distinctive gear and equipment using these materials. Even the residue of mining activities can be used to create Warp Dust, a fine powder with magical properties that unpredictably transforms those exposed to it (see **Chapter 7**).

CHAOS SEASONS

Seasons may exist in the Wastes of Chaos, but they are often defined by extended periods of similar weather rather than distinct predictable times. Summer may be followed by winter which may in turn be followed by another summer before seeing a spring. The people and creatures that live in the wastes are quick to take advantage of any periods of relative calm to explore, forage, or grow food, knowing that such a lull may not soon occur again. Weather in the wastes is nearly always at its most extreme. When a random weather generation system is used to determine the weather, treat light or gentle outcomes as heavy versions of the weather event. When a result shows wind, rainfall, or snowfall, for example, these occurrences are always at their strongest. This punishing weather exposes the creatures of the wastes to extreme hazards, including the risk of flash flooding.

CHAOS WEATHER

In addition to the severe weather characteristics of the wastes, supernatural storms with deadly side effects occasionally sweep the land. Arcane weather known as spawning storms occur at random intervals, typically no more than twice in a year. These dangerous and life-bringing thunderstorms unleash torrents of rain from clouds flickering with multi-colored lightning, twisting and transforming those creatures caught in the downpour or swept away by resulting floods.

Some effects of the storm help the creatures of the wastes survive. Plants nourished by their waters grow unnaturally rapidly even in these barren lands, maturing in days before suddenly dying. The resulting vegetation is strange, often sporting colors and features not otherwise found in nature: moving of its own volition, expanding and contracting as if breathing, or releasing glowing spores or clouds of pollen. The plants are usually safe for consumption despite the landscape's eldritch appearance. People and creatures of the wastes compete and fight to gather this rare harvest before the land is claimed by the wastes once again.

Other effects are not so benign. A creature exposed to the rains of the spawning storm for at least 10 minutes or that is caught in a spawning storm's flash flood must roll on the Spawning Storm Exposure Effects table. Most exposure effects are temporary, lasting for 2d12 hours with initial exposure and an additional 2d12 hours for every hour the creature is exposed to the storm. The effect has a 5% chance of becoming permanent at the end of this time.

The exception to these temporary effects is body warping. If the result of the exposure effect is body warping, roll on the Body Warping table for additional results. These changes are permanent and can only be removed by a *wish* spell or similarly powerful magic.

TYPES OF WASTES

There are many types of wastes environments.

BADLANDS

Epitomized by steep, dry hills and rocky expanses with little brush, this hostile terrain favors prepared ambushes and cavern lairs. Wind-carved sandstone pinnacles claw the sky, marking sharp-edged slot canyons gouged by flash floods and ancient deluges and barren parallel ridges revealing brightly hued layers of raw earth and clay. Quiet, shaded valleys with small pools or trickling creeks garnished with sparse, hardy, often poisonous greenery are juxtaposed by steaming geothermal springs encrusted with sulfur crystals. Straight-edged buttes and stripped volcanic cores loom overhead, while broad plains of salt-dusted, sun-baked mud stretch out to the horizon, concealing sinkholes that open their uncaring maws without warning. Twisted cedars and juniper trees, thorny creosote and sagebrush, and tall cacti dominate the plantlife. Constant winds tirelessly grind, resulting in curious formations, with some resembling mushrooms. Locals regularly name these winds, attributing personalities to them. Whether this causes a genius loci to manifest or is simply the recognition of an existing spirit remains unclear.

The fauna is discreet and shy, doing its best to remain hidden or attack with the element of surprise. Horned sheep, antelope, mountain lions, and bobcats, as well as jackrabbits, coyotes, and raptors roam the region. Smaller creatures fare better with reduced needs.

WEATHER

While arid, badlands do not compare to the extreme dryness of deserts. Rainfall is extremely sparse, and often borders on near-drought, but it happens. The true danger lies in those times when something more than a brief shower falls. Any moderate downpour threatens to create a flash flood in the badlands' confined ravines and passes, where the narrow spaces cause the water to suddenly become deadly (see sidebar next page).

Strong winds whip up dust storms, which limit vision to no more than 50 feet, or cause relatively small tornados of great strength. Medium or smaller creatures caught in such a whirlwind must make a DC 13 Strength check or be thrown 5+2d6 feet, suffering 1d6 damage and landing prone.

TRAVEL

Aside from the weather and hostile inhabitants, the other subtle hazard to travel in badlands is the region's unpredictable terrain. Some slot canyons may be too narrow for mounts or Large creatures, and impassable chasms might open as a result of sudden erosion, both of which require time-consuming backtracking to find alternative and potentially more dangerous routes. Additionally, the chaotic nature of the terrain makes attempting to travel by flying over it difficult if travelers need to land and rest, as the maze-like landscape easily hides those on the ground, waiting to attack newcomers.

Common routes through badlands may even be clearly marked, but the concealing nature favors bandits looking for easy places to hide and easier places to ambush travelers. Truly safe roads require constant patrolling and maintenance by an established government or dedicated community, and they are certain to demand a price for safe passage.

CREATURES

Of all types of wastelands, communities most often grow in badlands. Natural forces usually shape the landscape, rather than a constant, ongoing effect, and while the climate is very arid and windy, water exists. The people choosing to live in a badlands are usually bandits, escaping refugees, or other groups trying

SPAWNING STORM EXPOSURE EFFECTS

d100	EFFECT
01-15	Creature increases in muscle mass, becoming stronger but clumsier. Its Strength increases by 2 and its Dexterity decreases by 2.
16-30	Creature's body swells, causing pain, discomfort, and lack of motion. It has disadvantage on Strength, Dexterity, and Constitution checks.
31-45	Creature suffers from headaches, minor hallucinations, or other mental maladies. It has disadvantage on Intelligence, Wisdom, and Charisma checks.
46-60	Creature's flesh grows especially dense. It gains resistance to bludgeoning, piercing, and slashing damage from nonmagical sources, but its speed (for all modes of movement) is reduced by 10 feet, and it loses any swim speed for the duration.
61-70	Creature's body produces growths and tumors. It gains a +1 to its natural armor and gains advantage on Charisma (Intimidation) checks, but it has disadvantage on other Charisma checks.
71-80	Creature experiences growth of claws, horns, and teeth, and it deals +2 damage on such attacks.
81-85	Creature experiences a painful but swift period of growth. It is treated as if enlarged by the *enlarge/reduce* spell for the duration. This effect can be negated by a *dispel magic* or *greater restoration* spell.
86-90	Dormant spores and seeds on the creature begin to sprout, covering it in fungal or plant growth, adding a +1 bonus to AC and providing advantage on Stealth checks made to hide in areas of thick plant growth. If this effect becomes permanent, the plants begin to subsume the creature. It loses 1 point of Charisma each hour. When the creature's Charisma reaches 0, it is fully subsumed, and the creature becomes a shambling mound.
91-95	Lightning strikes the creature, dealing 35 (10d6) lightning damage. The creature must succeed on a DC 16 Dexterity saving throw to take half damage. In addition, roll again for a second effect.
96-100	Body warping. Roll again on the **Body Warping** table.

BODY WARPING

d10	BODY WARPING
1-2	Unsightly pustules grow from the creature's skin. If the creature takes piercing or slashing damage, all creatures within 5 feet take 3 (1d6) poison damage per point of the warped creature's proficiency bonus and are poisoned for 1 minute. An affected creature must roll a Constitution saving throw (DC 10 + warped creature's Con modifier + warped creature's proficiency bonus). On a successful save, the creature takes half damage and is not poisoned.
3-4	Creature gains +2 to natural armor. The source of this armor can be thickened skin, scales, bony growths, or any other similar warping effect.
5-6	Creature grows an extra limb. It can take an extra attack with that limb as a bonus action.
7	Creature grows extra eyes, gaining advantage on all sight-based Wisdom (Perception) roles.
8	Creature gains resistance to one of the following types of damage: acid, cold, fire, lightning, or thunder.
9	Creature is infused with magic. It gains resistance to nonmagical damage of one of the following types: bludgeoning, piercing, or slashing damage. Its natural attacks are considered magical.
10	Creature gains magic resistance, giving advantage on all saving throws against spells and other magical effects.

to remain hidden; they may be the most dangerous thing travelers encounter as they have no desire to be discovered by the outside world.

Successful residents who keep their location secret have found or created an underground warren safe from floods, easily secured against intrusion, and with easy, but non-obvious, access to food and water. They probably use commonly found creatures like drakes, harpies, or manticores as both unwitting sentries and alarms; the creatures' attacks alert a community that trespassers are nearby. Truly arable land remains rare and precious; threats to that resource immediately mobilize an overwhelming response.

NOTABLE SITES
Badlands locales that might draw a traveler's attention include the following examples.

Pillars of the Gods
This valley sports a field of over a hundred natural stone pillars ranging from a mere 50 feet tall to over 200 feet tall and of varying circumference. A few have slumped at an angle, some rest against neighbors, and at least a dozen have toppled to the valley floor.

Many show fully articulated skeletons of people, dragons, and giants, partially or fully visible in rocky sides. They stand trapped in poses that suggest the creatures were falling or flying, but the volcanic basalt implies temperatures capable of vaporizing anything living. One hosts a titan facing outward, flush with the pillar's surface and arms stretched upwards reaching through the stone. Divination spells indicate the creatures have names, but no scholar has yet learned them.

Drakes' Graveyard
Interspersed in a broad region of dark jagged ridges lie the bleached and yellowing bones of a thousand drakes, dragons, and dragonkin, alongside the moldering corpses of dozens of more relatively recently dead. Some rest curled like cats, others are stretched across the peaks of stone formations, their blank eye sockets staring out over the landscape of death. Many creatures make several pilgrimages to the site, taking great care to not only select a proper resting place, but in some cases, to bring servants or followers to craft memorial stelae or lay protective enchantments ensuring their remains are not disturbed. A few guardian constructs patrol the whole area, looking for scavengers, alchemists, or spellcasters who might desecrate the bodies out of greed, necromancy, or revenge.

Sinkhole Ritual Site
More than 300 feet across and plunging down into darkness, this gaping maw in the earth is ringed with standing stones and seven low dolmens. Engraved symbols on the stelae seem to change, depending on the particular stellar conjunction observed overhead. On new moons and at midnight, stars appear to float within the shadows of the sinkhole's well. Claimed by no less than four different cults as a profane and magically significant location, this sinkhole has been destroyed several times, only to reopen again a year later, complete with engraved stone formations. Strangely, the site usually appears overcast, but on rare, clear middays, the bright sun overhead shows the bottom filled with crystal-clear water, devoid of the expected corpses or rubble.

WILDERNESS HAZARD: FLASH FLOODING

Ditches, ravines, and other low-lying areas can be dangerous to travel in heavy precipitation. Massive amounts of water released at higher elevations quickly find their way downstream, rushing to fill in these areas without notice to sweep away anything in their path.

A creature must succeed on a DC 14 Wisdom (Perception or Survival) check to notice the oncoming flood. The wall of water and debris arrives 1d4+1 rounds later. If unable to escape, creatures in the path of the water must succeed on a DC 20 Dexterity saving throw or take 22 (4d10) bludgeoning damage and be swept away. A creature that braces itself or grasps a boulder, cliff face, or similar feature must succeed on a DC 15 Strength (Athletics) check to take half damage and avoid being taken by the waters.

Creatures move 80 feet and take 5 (1d10) bludgeoning damage at the beginning of each round they are caught in the flood as they are battered by detritus and other obstacles. A creature attempting to pull itself out of the water by swimming to the closest edge or grabbing hold of an object unaffected by the flood must succeed on a DC 20 Strength (Athletics) check. The creature is ejected from the flood after 5d4 rounds, either tossed aside or as the waters subside.

STORY SEEDS

Adventures in badlands regularly involve navigating geographic hazards or dealing with hostile residents.

Get To the Temple

A character's relative has become betrothed to a fiancé in a nearby town. The relative's parents cannot escort them to the wedding ceremony due to age and health, and custom demands both members of the wedding party meet at a regional temple. The only route capable of delivering the relative in time passes through the badlands, and they ask the characters to escort them through the dangers. Can the party keep not only the relative, but their dowry and personal items, safe as the group completes the hazardous journey?

Lost and Found

Recent storms flooded a canyon shrine, damaging it, killing many of the attendant priests, and washing away an important relic as the head priest attempted to usher it to safety. The party arrives on the storm's heels, expecting sanctuary but finding a crisis. More storms are imminent; can the party assist with necessary repairs, defend the site against marauding creatures seeking to violently occupy the structure, and discover the fate of not only the head priest, but possibly recover the relic they'd initially set out to protect? What do they do if they learn the priest summoned the storms?

BATTLEFIELDS

Battlefields are vast expanses of terrain left ruined in the wake of ancient conflicts. Though the details of such devasting combats are often lost to time, the scars of magical warfare leave the land permanently warped. Such sites are typically devoid of life but still stalked by living spells and machines of eldritch destruction left to rampage across the field without anyone left to command them.

A magical battlefield is likely full of scorched earth, craters, partially melted stones, smoldering tree trunks, and the terrible, broken remains of the unfortunates who lost their lives in the fight. Mists might creep over the land, undead rising from those who left tasks incomplete, and dangers likely still lurk amidst the wreckage.

WEATHER

Cataclysmic arcane warfare often leaves the environment of a battlefield warped beyond recognition. Travelers are likely to experience a gambit of bizarre magical weather driven by surging waves of chaos. Sunny weather may suddenly shift into a downpour of flaming meteors, or the rocky ground might split open into literal jaws as violent quakes rattle the earth. The only predictable thing about weather in this type of terrain is that it always defies prediction.

While the characters travel through battlefields, frequently refer to the Magic in the Wastelands section of this chapter. The effects of chaos weather should create routine obstacles in this type of environment.

TRAVEL

Unpredictable hazards make travel through battlefields nearly impossible for common wanderers, and hopeful explorers require an array of arcane protective measures to guarantee survival. Despite the danger, there are always a handful of skilled guides ready to lead treasure-hunters or salvagers into the heart of such places, but their services always come with an exorbitant fee.

CREATURES

Natural life as it exists in most regions of the world is entirely absent from battlefield wastes. Flora and fauna that existed in these areas before they were ravaged by war was long since obliterated or mutated by rampant surges of magic. New life is quickly snuffed out by ancient war constructs and furious undead doomed to eternally haunt the fields where they died.

Though long-term survival on the surface is nearly impossible, rumors of flourishing underground communities occasionally circulate through the outside world. Lucky creatures who discover a sure-fire way to avoid the magical storms that ravage the land can find safety amid ancient bunkers, the buried carapaces of gargantuan war machines, or ruins of blasted cities swallowed by the poisoned earth.

NOTABLE SITES

Though the original factions have long since passed from the world, the relics of their warfare remain, waiting to be discovered by enterprising salvagers.

Green Field

Red rocky hills hide one of the wastes' most curious fields of battle, a 50-square-mile stretch of labyrinthian trenches built by an unidentified battalion before living memory. The trenches' jagged metal walls, mechanical traps, and riveted metal bunkers have oxidized over the long centuries, forming a bright green patina that has even stained the ground. While passage through the trenches is generally regarded as a fool's errand, survivors whisper of incredible magical technologies hidden deep within its twisting passages.

R0v3r

Deep in the heart of the wasted battlefields, amidst the shattered ruins of a once-glittering mage city, a massive treaded construct collects the remains of its fallen fellows. Seeing the looming shadow of the hulking junker is enough to send any observer into immediate panic, but the creature reportedly ignores travelers who don't interfere with its never-ending work. Some say R0v3r's interior hosts an entire city of robotic workers that keep the construct functioning, others claim it is occupied by a cabal of undying sorcerers who pilot the titan, but neither claim has yet to be proven.

STORY SEEDS

Adventures in battlefields routinely center around retrieving abandoned technology and dealing with fallout from a distant past that refuses to stay buried.

Lost Redoubt Route

As a famous general called a retreat and attempted to fall back to a nearby, hidden mustering point, living spells overwhelmed their forces. The whole unit was lost after being turned to stone and partially melted by acid. Adventurers discovered the fractured remains of the statues uncovered by a storm and brought them to a sage for identification. Verified as the general's soldiers, the sage wants the characters to recover the chest of documents that divinations suggest lies within that ruined landscape. With those papers, the general's hiding place and important relics could be discovered. Living spells still dominate the area, making any attempt extremely dangerous. However, the general was trying to evacuate precious national heirlooms. Finding them would bring great renown.

Rude Awakening

After centuries of inactivity, hundreds of soldier constructs suddenly power on and launch brutal attacks against nearby settlements. The energy source keeping the creatures awake must be located and destroyed before all life in the region is stamped out.

DESERTS

Several types of terrain constitute most temperate and tropical desert ecosystems. These include ergs, the broad sandy expanses of swirling, shifting dunes; hamadas, the broad, irregular regions of bare rock and odd stone formations; and salt flats, the vast open swaths of hard, bone-dry plains. High deserts might include scorched hills of thorny yucca or cactus and rare patches of hardy, low scrub brush and occasional acacia trees. Rain-fed wadis are hidden gems known by the wildlife, and permanent oases, even small mud-choked holes, are bloodstained treasures held only as long as the current occupant remains vigilant. Grit and dust coat everything after any length of time, making comfortable rest an elusive, distant memory. Creeping dunes gradually swallow most structures, or regular conflicts leave them unworthy of the scant protection they provide from the unyielding wind and scorching gaze of the sun. Rock shelters and shallow caves can be as valuable as water, offering respite from sweltering midday heat.

Consummate survivors, this region's creatures manage survival in an unceasingly, actively hostile environment. They never pass a perceived easy meal or unnecessarily challenge an obviously powerful foe. The resources used might mean the difference between life and death later.

WEATHER

In deserts, the weather is notable specifically for the non-existent precipitation. Unless magically conjured, rainfall is limited to no more than two or three annual storms, falling on hard-packed ground and finding its way to ancient, bone dry waterways and causing flash floods. Water from rare storms collects for brief periods in depressions called wadis. These are different from oases, which are fed from springs.

This makes sandstorms the most commonly encountered phenomenon. These swirling tempests of wind, silt, and sand obscure vision, draw the moisture from bodies, and reshape the landscape. Checks made during a sandstorm have disadvantage to navigate overland, find food or water, or endure water deprivation. Particularly strong storms impose disadvantage on overland navigation checks until the travelers have journeyed for a full day.

Additionally, the heat of the desert environment greatly impacts those physically exerting themselves. Anyone attempting an Strength (Athletics) check or participating in combat longer than five consecutive rounds while wearing heavy armor must make a DC 15 Constitution check each subsequent round or gain the poisoned condition until they take a short rest.

TRAVEL

Journeys across deserts remain punishing, potentially fatal endeavors without magic or special preparation. Sand dunes migrate with the winds, potentially overrunning paved or marked causeways, further complicating navigation. The heat and lack of water can easily kill those who aimlessly wander. Most follow established trade routes, which journey between known sources of water. Each leg may require many days or even weeks before arriving at the next water source, with no guarantee that nothing hostile is waiting.

A traveler who has spent the whole day marching in the hot sun must make a DC 12 Constitution save or be unable to regain any spent Hit Dice during their long rest. Travelers who have had sufficient water and supplies as they traveled make this check with advantage.

CREATURES

Growing food in the desert requires either an oasis, underground water aquifers called foggaras, or magic. Crops must either be shaded or tolerant of extreme sunlight. Date palms, citrus trees, olives, figs, and wheat do best but require a great deal of water.

Likewise, building with sun-baked mud bricks is possible, but also requires water. Other options include subterranean dwellings, clay bricks, cut slabs of salt or raw stone, and caves. Temporary tents of cloth or hide are feasible but provide little defense against anything but the sun and wind.

Communities that attempt to thrive in deserts always take advantage of nearby natural resources. Some build circular walled communities with residences built into the walls or keep interior structures close enough for fabric awnings to stretch across the passages between buildings, providing shade but not hindering air flow. Ambitious merchant houses carve caravanserai out of large rock formations, sometimes resulting in complexes three to six levels deep.

Undead are a common threat when unfortunates die in the dunes or get caught by **ghouls**. **Gnolls** roam in packs, and **bulettes, purple worms,** and **ankhegs** look for prey. Without dedicated sentries, a community shouldn't make long-term plans.

NOTABLE SITES

There are several interesting locales potentially found in the desert.

Ancient Acacia Grove

Rising out of the sandy dunes stretching for miles around, a jagged plateau of dark basalt hosts a swift, cool spring and a community of acacia **treants** and two olive **treants,** who insist on keeping a small herd of goats. Each treant has at least a four-part name; the youngest is 600 years old, while the oldest has seen several millennia. The treants rarely move, scattered across hillsides, observing the paths of the stars every night.

A small complex of caves shows evidence of habitation at some point in the past, but now only stacks of votive weapons lie here. Many bent or twisted in evidence of their sacrificial donation, but a few magical implements grace special carved niches, awaiting prophesied reclamation.

Overhanging Petroglyphs

Along the inside curve of a towering wind-hewn arch of faded, blood red sandstone stretches an enormous treatise of arcane petroglyphs. The symbols detail dozens of spells, etched in rock and accented with deep rubbed ochre. The work of generations, this artwork documents histories, folklore, bargains with strange spirits, and the true names of potent wizards and demons alike.

No springs or trees exist within a week's journey, but the fire rings near its northern base hold the cold cinders of countless visits and a single deep well at the southern base always holds clear, cool water. Angry daemons of scorching winds appear to desiccate any plants brought in hopes of establishing a garden. A wasteland dragon sometimes visits but refuses to pass beneath or through the arch, claiming it is "an unspeakable gate."

Sand-Choked Fort

Once the outpost of a long-dead empire or principality, this walled structure lost its gates long ago, and now sand dunes fill the inner courtyard. Its towers remain in various states of disrepair, from nearly pristine to dangerously crumbling, but inside its foundations lie several levels of abandoned catacombs and chambers.

Shades of the last defenders rise on new moons to reenact their final night, battling any they find. The deepest vaults remain untouched, guarded by an ancient guardian bound by forgotten terms. The ghost of a cowardly deserter lingers nearby. Unable to sneak past the creature, they cannot rest until their bones are submerged in the cistern's waters or covered in whatever treasures lie behind the vault doors of hammered bronze.

STORY SEEDS

Stories in deserts often revolve around life-giving resources, or lost, valuable sites.

Water of Life

Characters arrive at an oasis nearly out of water, only to discover two groups at a standoff, unwilling to allow one another to access the meager excess available. However, neither group wants the water, but to harvest strange, multicolored crustaceans living in the pond. When ground into a paste and consumed, the heliotropic substance halts the aging process and cures all wounds, but the shrimp-like insects only appear approximately every five years. How long until the detente descends into violence, and will the characters participate, especially when they realize they recognize some members of both groups?

Missing Mystics

When the party reaches the gates of a hidden desert monastery, they find it strangely and recently abandoned. From the site's perch on a spring-fed butte above the sands, it's clear the residents didn't walk away, and still-burning cookfires and partially eaten meals suggest the residents left not long ago. It seems one of the ascetics may have accidentally triggered a magical device kept at the site, which caused the monks to become trapped in a ghost-like state, only able to write messages in sand. Can the PCs determine what happened and reverse the effect?

FLINTY HILLS

Rough, rocky hills with sparse vegetation, sharp ridges, and unforgiving weather dominate this terrain. Grass and even soil seem nearly non-existent, although grime and mud feels universal under the freezing rain. Raw chasms occasionally open into narrow caves serving as hidden lairs or poor, leaky shelters. Fuel for campfires remains difficult to acquire and burns poorly, offering scant warmth and sputtering, dim light. Most scraggly plants are bitter, thorny specimens ill-suited for grazing. Water seems to fall deep into the earth in weeping flows or sad rivulets, rather than form pools or creeks. Structures are often ramshackle, leaky, and drafty, or dangerously ruined. The splintering stone is better at causing rockfalls and debris fields than yielding well-cut blocks for construction.

Here, the miserable beasts often hide throughout the daylight hours and forage for subsistence or stalk travelers at night. Scavengers and predators live desperately from meal to meal, leaving them willing to cooperate or hunt in larger packs than they might otherwise. Sometimes, this turns fatal for the weak or injured when a hunt ends unsuccessfully. In the case of a dominant and capable creature or band, the area surrounding their lair becomes a boneyard littered with the bleached remains.

WEATHER

In regions like flinty hills, the difficulty arises not from the constant miserable drizzle, but the fact little exists to break the impact of the weather. While shallow overhangs remain easy to find, they do not block the misty rain, and true caves serve as the lairs of regional predators. No substantial plant life grows to serve as firewood, and what does grow is perpetually soaked and unusable as fuel. The rocky, nearly dirt-less ground makes planting stakes and securing tents a hard-fought chore, drawing the attention of those regional predators or bandits with the noise of hammering spikes into stone. Any Wisdom (Survival) checks made to acquire food have disadvantage, Wisdom (Perception) checks to hear creatures' activity have advantage, and characters must make a DC 13 Constitution (Survival) check to regain spent Hit Dice after a long rest, unless they enjoy the benefits of suitable natural or magical shelter.

TRAVEL

Routes through flinty hills often benefit from clearly defined paths; the unforgiving nature of the land serves to keep roads in fairly good repair, though

difficult to build initially. The only exceptions to this tend to be natural stairs or bridges, which may suffer from the extremes in temperature, cracking and spalling as wet stone freezes or bakes, potentially creating areas of dangerous terrain with landslides or a bridge's unexpected failure, capable of inflicting life-threatening falls or landslides. Characters who make a successful DC 13 Wisdom (Perception or Survival) check to spot such a hazard gain advantage on any check to navigate the area or saves against its effects. Construction of any infrastructure tends to be simple and sparse, just augmenting the existing landscape whenever possible, due to the minimal amount of resources and the difficulty in transporting or maintaining large work crews in the environment.

Clear routes also unfortunately mean hunting monsters know where to best find traveling prey. Creatures like **stone giants, bulettes, cockatrices,** or **basilisks,** capable of ignoring the region's worst effects, tend to be aggressive and bold within defined territory. They can become known threats in local folklore, as favorite bribes or distractions spread through survivors' tales.

CREATURES

In such a rocky environment, those trying to build a community face adjacent challenges to those in desert environments, but instead of lacking water, they lack basic, mutable terrain. Being forced to cut cisterns and growing beds from the raw stone is daunting, dangerous, and time consuming. Injuries are common, and members may even trek to areas beyond to haul in fresh soil, bag by bag.

Livestock's value must be weighed against the resources necessary to maintain it, the products it produces, and the chances it may draw monsters or predators looking for an easy meal. Ducks and chickens are common favorites, as they can be easily transported and kept out of sight without too much effort, as are goats. Larger animals offer a great source of fertilizer but need prohibitive amounts of water and fodder.

Homes either utilize existing caves or work with the terrain to keep a low profile. Communities need to stretch from lower elevations, where water collects, to higher points, where sentries can maintain observation points without drawing attention. Competition for appropriate sites between people, predators, and supernatural monsters makes for a constant source of tension.

NOTABLE SITES

Remote and unforgiving terrain, like flinty hills, sometimes serves as exactly the setting desired to keep a location remote and undisturbed. These are some examples.

Hidden Monastery

Perched on the wall of a switchback canyon and built of dark slate stone, this imposing edifice is the home and training facility of the Way of the Whisper, an order of monks who take vows of near silence. Never speaking above a hushed tone, and never saying more than a word at a time, they learn feats of extreme acrobatics and hand-to-hand martial arts. Those who wait three weeks at the foot of the monastery, unmoving, suffering the thrown rocks of the acolytes above, receive an invitation to study the monastery's little-known style. The structure is said to extend deep into the stone, its passages carved by students testing their punches, and its leader is rumored to never speak except to people they intend to kill.

Lost Monument Tomb

Located at the foot of the flinty hills, where they meet the edge of a snow-capped mountain range, stands the black iron spire marking the entrance to this massive crypt, dedicated to the emperor of a forgotten realm. Constructs guard the door but only open the heavy, soot-colored gates when approached by those with swords drawn. Inside lies a madhouse of chambers occupied by a guillotine-headed golem, pools of frozen blood, and an extended representative map of the old empire's lands, crafted from silver, jade, and sapphire. The map supposedly reflects the true world outside the sepulcher, and survivors indicate opening doors or disabling the contents of tiny replicas within the map's space supposedly performs the same action at the represented site.

Old Quarry

Broad and labyrinthine, this ancient pit quarry extends for half a league in several directions, following the veins of nearly completely harvested blue-green marble. A few remaining lodes show the marble to be shot through with streaks of white and bearing strange fossils. The marble is never wet, regardless of the weather; the fossils in it change location and type but always show extinct marine creatures. Three separate stories report seeing various figures within the marble, who have never been seen twice, never engaged verbally, and never properly documented. One tale indicates the figures fought a pitched battle, with a strangely attired corpse being ejected from the stone before turning into a puddle.

Waterskins left on a block of the marble never go empty, and keeping a marble shard supposedly helps finding potable water.

STORY SEEDS

Adventures in flinty hills focus on survival elements or the investigation of specific sites.

Giant's Toll

A stone giant has commandeered an ancient imperial aqueduct, which once gathered the mists of the region into a reasonable water source, enabling a community's survival. The usurper now demands regular tribute, or it will strangle the residents with thirst. Additionally, the giant has sent its cave bear companion to a relative's stronghold deeper in the area, inviting cousins to join them in this new endeavor, creating a fortress and imposing their reign on the nearby innocents and their meager trade route. Can the party resolve the situation before the giants make a tough situation worse?

Forbidden Fruit

A small mining community established next to a rich marble quarry has been engaged by a group of derro claiming to be dwarves. The derro have begun trading a delicious and addictive mushroom to the encampment, which will eventually leave them so addled over time that the derro can simply capture them without a fight and sell them into slavery. The party arrives before this plan is complete; interaction with the town makes derro machinations clear. The characters must enter the tunnels, infiltrate the derro stronghold, and reveal the mushroom's effects while acquiring the antidote.

HAUNTED MARSHLANDS

Unlike those wastelands wrought by slow erosive decay of passing eons, the haunted marshlands give neither pause nor mercy in their conquest. Waters rise and seep into the lands, swallowing the ground and decomposing remains. Marshlands lack patience and consistency, instead capriciously shifting form as their meandering channels creep across the land, continuously reshaping passages and leaving behind voracious and all-consuming mire.

The haunted marshes engulf a vast tract of land well over a hundred miles long and fifty miles wide that spans the vales of a once-lush river valley at the foothills of an extensive mountain range.

Throughout the marshes flow slow-moving channels of black water that skirt through an endless shifting maze of islands of rock, mud, and silt blanketed in dense tangles of reeds, sedges, cordgrass, cattails, and bulrushes. Black waters saturate the surrounding land, weakening the sediments, leaving the ground unstable and filled with natural hazards such as quicksilts, quaking bogs, and strange creatures that make travel extremely dangerous.

There are few landmarks and the topography shifts as channels carve new passages that lead into unknown waterways and strangled trails so overgrown with reeds and rushes that they obscure all landmarks. Luring ghostly wisps drift through these mazes, preying upon lost travelers. Dead reeds and other detritus lying only a few feet below the surface deceptively cover chasms of silt that drop deep enough to drown the unwary. In other sections, channels hit dead ends where they dry up, forming small brackish pools lined with silty saturated soil spotted with corpse cabbage. Even the fauna seems strange and foreboding. Eerie marsh birds with slender legs and long curved beaks whose crowing resembles the haunted cries of frightened children scavenge the shallows for leeches. As the sun sets, the air fills with the wild croaking of circuses of frogs. Moisture from the sodden lands results in dense blankets of rolling fog while thickets of reeds, cattails, and bulrushes block both passage and sight. When the seasons are warm, the air fills with thick black clouds formed from thousands of tiny biting insects.

WEATHER

Marsh weather is chaotic and unpredictable. Excess water keeps the surroundings humid, inciting rapid changes that accompany sudden shifts in temperature. Within minutes clear skies may fill with a sudden rush of clouds that quickly boil over into violent rains. Drizzle and mist can last for days, creating drops in temperature as clouds block the sun. When clouds break, a lack of tree coverage allows the burning sun to scald the lands. As a result, waters recede, drying up in some places, and fields of cracked mud and meandering paths of unstable sediment conceal quicksand pools.

TRAVEL

Those seeking passage through the marshes typically travel larger channels using flatbottomed rafts or barges to compensate for inconsistent depths created by eroding substrate and other structures lying beneath. The two most effective methods of transport include paddles or poling against the bottom. Keel-boat travel is only possible in the deeper channels and their sweeping erratic curves make piloting a wind-driven craft nearly impossible.

d6	Random Weather
1	Washes of clouds block the sun, the temperature drops, and it begins to drizzle.
2	Dense fog rises over the waters, completely obscuring the ground.
3	Sudden downpours unleash sheets of rain that rip across the endless sea of rolling marsh grass.
4	Heavy mist rolls across the marsh grasses, turning the world into amorphous shadows.
5	A burning sun rips across the marshland, striking the still water and reflecting the glare in all directions.
6	Shifting temperatures force the hot, muggy air to condense on every available surface.

Boats frequently scrape bottom in the shallows or become stuck, forcing travelers to step into the surrounding murk to push their crafts. Those wading in the shallows risk wandering into deep patches of loose silt and mud, becoming trapped, making easy prey for marshland predators.

Characters traversing marshlands on foot face different challenges and run into different types of creatures than those using boats. Thick banks of woody reeds and tall bulrushes obscure all sight. Marsh water saturates even the most stable ground, blanketing it in several inches of mud that slows travel and quickly breaks the ankles of draft animals. Along the perimeters, makeshift trails traverse the shallows, though few of these last very long before the marshlands reclaim them. Piles of rock and planks span patches of murk or floating logs bound together with old ropes and dried marsh rat gut. In other spots, only lengths of ropes or chains serve as handholds or guides. Constructed paths rarely last longer than a few weeks before greenish splotches of moss and dangling strands of algae swallow them.

Over the years, various travelers placed marking posts throughout the marshlands, at least in those areas where folk travel. These consist of long wooden poles jammed deep into the mud and notched or carved to denote depth, location, or other warnings. Unfortunately, the markings are infrequent, and their specific meaning is often indecipherable.

Marsh Hazards

Corpsecabbage. These leafy, yellowish-green cabbage-like plants grow in patches in loose murky silt. When touched, fragile pods rupture, emitting a putrid stench similar to a rotting corpse. Any creature within a 30-foot radius must make a successful DC 12 Constitution save or become poisoned for 1d4 minutes. The pungent stench clings to living creatures and remains virulent for 1d4 days. For the duration, or until the stench-befouled characters bathe thoroughly, they have disadvantage against any Charisma-based ability checks, and smell-based Perception checks made to locate them have advantage.

Razor grass. Razor grass is a short cordgrass species like other common marsh grasses. Its thin-bladed leaves can cause fine cuts to the unprotected. Unarmored characters attempting to move through razor grass must travel at half speed or take 1d4 points of slashing damage each minute of travel.

Silt Sinkholes. Silt sinkholes form along the muddy bottoms of deeper wet marshes when loose sediments fill eroded pockets camouflaged with detritus such as dead reeds and leaves. A typical sinkhole is five to fifteen feet in diameter and five to ten feet deep. Characters stepping in a sink must make a DC 12 Dexterity saving throw to avoid falling in. The fall does no damage; however, the sinking creature disturbs all the silt, heavily obscuring anything in the water. Individuals weighted with gear or armor may find it difficult to swim and may be at risk of drowning. Intelligent marsh predators frequently hunt near silt sinkholes and strategically use them to ambush prey.

CREATURES

While the interiors of the marshland are largely uninhabitable, throughout the decades, a handful of small villages of subsistence fisherfolk have cropped up along the perimeter. Despite their best efforts, most attempts to settle the marshlands prove short-lived. The isolated marshes hold few resources. A worthy alchemist may successfully harvest rare marsh plants. The occasional prospector may dredge for lumps of iron with magnets, but villages typically lack viable sources of commerce and fail to attract outsiders. As a result, abandoned ghost villages litter the marshlands, providing local folk tales with their haunted histories. Still, an even greater number of these settlements lie forgotten entirely.

NOTABLE SITES

Mysterious sites of once-glorious purpose are hidden among the brackish water and sunken pits of the marshlands.

Sunken City

Near the very center of the haunted marsh, the ruins of the ancient city of Kalthros-Shi poke their crumbling spires through the glistening surface of still, black waters. The chunks of rough-cut stone jut at odd angles like the broken teeth of a fallen god. Impenetrable mists hover and weave through the mire while clusters of bulrushes crowd the edges of small rocky islets. Legends of the city's sinking are older than recorded history. However, it is believed an ancient dragon recalls the ages when its sorcerer-empresses summoned demonic consorts and raised armies of undead slaves to serve their bidding. The city warriors believed the highest honor lay in sacrificing themselves to dark gods, who bound their souls to their undead flesh so they might fight in honor of the city for all eternity. Legend describes Kalthros-Shi as one of the wealthiest cities of the lost age, and these tales lure treasure hunters and explorers to seek their fortunes deep in the heart of the marshlands.

Spire of Ten Thousand Bones

Two larger channels feed into a section of the east marshland emptying into a deep lake. A towering pillar of skulls and bones rises from the murky waters at the center. Strange vines with brightly colored flowers coil up the pillar, burning the surrounding air with their cloying fragrance. Short, rusted iron posts encircle the pillar's base, each fitted with a single ring. Worn remains of rope and chain dangle from several of the rings. Those watching the lake for more than a few minutes notice the entire area is curiously silent and devoid of birds or frogs. Every 10+1d10 minutes, a curving trail of ripples breaks the surface, hinting that something swims in the depths below.

Ghost Villages

Those traveling along the edges of the marsh eventually come across the rotting remains of small, abandoned villages. A typical ghost village has five or six structures—tilted frameworks of sagging, water-rotten timber buried beneath moss and overgrown with thickets of sawgrass and coiling catbriers. At night, strange, flickering lights drift through the broken frames.

Aunty Gremblewick

A massive barge of detritus and bone glides slowly through the marshlands, its wierdling crew a motley assortment of deformed humanoids who serve a foul and powerful ancient hag known as Auntie Gremblewick. Some refer to her as the Hag Queen, though others believe she holds greater power and might even be a demon or demigod. Aunty Gremblewick is a renowned oracle, and both hags and superstitious locals leave her offerings and tribute in exchange for her prophecies.

Twisted Grove

A trio of large islets marks an intersection where two of the marshland's wider channels converge. Here, currents slow, depositing a thick bed of rich sediment. Atop the islets grow copses of mangroves with hard serpentine roots that probe hundreds of feet into the surrounding marsh. Above the water, the roots form grand swooping arches while they create dense knotted tangles below. The mangroves create a vast natural maze from which few explorers ever return. Webs of vines and creepers shroud the passages, blotting out sunlight and trapping humidity. Those lucky enough to escape describe the ominous feeling of being watched by unknown sentience and claim the roots and branches of the mangroves shift, reworking the maze, trapping the unwary.

Colossus Graveyard

A strange forest formed from the petrified skeletons of unknown colossal creatures emerges from a desolate swath of murk. Patches of glistening oils slick the surfaces of small, brackish pools throughout the colossus graveyard. In some areas, mud covers pools of hot sticky tar, which occasionally ignite gas bubbles beneath the surface, causing sudden gas flares.

Over the centuries, the monstrous graves have attracted looters and cultists seeking to harvest the bones for magical properties. Similarly, more than a handful of powerful necromancers have attempted to reanimate the remains, but thus far, there are no recorded successes.

ADVENTURE SEEDS

Adventures in the haunted marshlands focus on hidden secrets and lurking beasts.

Dark Rituals

The locals of a tiny village hold a pact with a revolting marsh creature they call the Eelmonger. The creature feeds off small animals and other things it scavenges in the wilds. Fearing its anger, the villagers appease the creature by throwing their dead in the nearby marsh until visitors from the outside world give them a better option. Characters poking around the village grounds discover totems topped with bones, feather fetishes and human skulls that warily mark a pathway leading deep into the marsh.

Missing Fisherman

An apothecary sends the characters to pick up some rare salts from a small fishing village at the edge of the marsh. Shortly after their arrival, an older fisherman returns from his work early in the afternoon, fearfully shaken. He claims he found the rowboat of his friend Jobriah Scud half sunk in the marshes. He called out a few times but got no answer. He then heard a loud rustling in the reeds and got scared, so he rushed back to the village seeking to rally others to organize a search before the sun sets.

The Bloodgate Assassins

Authorities offer a bounty to track down and capture members of a secret order of psychopaths wanted for the gruesome assassinations of five clergypersons. Instead, the cultists fled into the marshes ushered by the whispering call of a powerful demon thing called Thraxis-Kra, dragging the hearts of their victims with them. Witnesses say they overheard the cultists discussing fleeing for a portal called the Bloodgate.

POLLUTED BLIGHTS

The noxious potions, failed alchemical experiments, and magical malfunctions left to spill into the currents of local waterways leave greasy, iridescent slicks while bubbling vents emanate from slag piles consisting of accidental heaps of poorly combined reagents. This inconsiderate, mystical trash warps the creatures and alters the plants and the very terrain of the region, tainting everything with aspects of the arcane experiments dumped here. If left untouched or even perpetuated, such places might become the lair for even more powerful and terrible creatures. Disease runs rampant, and the awful stain befouls more of the countryside with every sunrise.

WEATHER

Centuries of chemical pollution create a perpetual smog over the blighted lands, trapping noxious humidity and heat close to the ground. Since little vegetation survives in such befouled conditions, there is little to no rain to feed the parched ground despite perpetually muggy conditions. When temperatures rise, lightning storms surge in frequency, along with the occasional sprinkle of toxic run off.

TRAVEL

Travel through polluted blight lands is made perilous by the huge variety of monsters well-adapted to poisonous environments. Visitors are scarce due to the myriad of mundane and magical diseases common to such locales, which require extensive countermeasures to avoid.

CREATURES

All manner of monstrous denizens lives in the polluted blight. Some migrate to the lands because they are naturally adapted to the harsh conditions, but the majority are creatures mutated or created by alchemical run-off. Expect to find chimeric beasts, oversized and aggressive flora with a taste for travelers, living spells, and an increased frequency of hazards like slimes, molds, and various ravenous oozes.

NOTABLE SITES

Generations of people have dumped their shameful secrets into the polluted blights and many such secrets have mutated into even more troubling forms.

Menagerie Vault

Hidden deep within the polluted blights is an expansive complex of laboratories that house the unnatural experiments of a shadow organization known as the Chimera Society. Few have ever been inside the remote complex, but the alchemists and mages who keep council there occasionally extend invitations to renowned academics interested in viewing their research. Stories about the purpose of the Chimera Society—and of the experiments conducted in their vaults—are often contradictory accounts of monstrous creations, bioterrorism, and efforts to cure various diseases.

Swamps of Alchemy

The perfumeries, laboratories, and workshops of a noted alchemists' guild have dumped their mistakes and accidents into the swamps surrounding the city since a mages' council forcibly teleported the alchemical district away from the rest of their city into the wetlands. The alchemists and artisans knew how to spin gold from dross, though, and ignored the slight, exulting instead in the sudden access to a rich variety of ingredients and proceeding to shore up their structures and rebuild their community. However, their incessant magical runoff has resulted in regular chimeric creatures simply emerging from the wilds. **Harpies, manticores, giants, oozes,** and **owlbears** all roam the area. The centuries-long behavior has created a city as accidental and as chaotic as the fruits of its residents' labors.

STORY SEEDS

Adventures set in polluted blights often deal with themes of environmental devastation and the dangers of unchecked magical experimentation.

Race for the Cure

Citizens in a major metropolis suddenly start to mutate *en masse* when a circle of druids dump toxic runoff into the city's drinking water. As the situation devolves, it becomes a race against time to find the original source of the contaminants so an antidote can be created.

Wandering Front

An acquaintance of the party comes to them, delirious and upset. He keeps finding himself in random places, injured and disheveled, and two different people assaulted him on the way here. He begs the group to restrain him and monitor him for the next three nights. During the night, he breaks free and travels by great leaping bounds to a small spring in the nearby swamp. Despite the difficulty in tracking him, his destination becomes apparent: a modest shrine on a hill. Inside, a strange creature of living, flowing wax and oil holds its court, infusing the acquaintance with a greasy black substance and whispering directions before the enthralled acquaintance leaps away. What is this thing, and what sway does it hold over their friend?

Chapter 2
Heroes of the Borderlands

This chapter presents several options for character creation—new races, subclasses, and backgrounds for characters who are native to the wastelands or those who have a connection to such places.

RACES

The wasteland is a desolate place, but it is far from lifeless. Members of many races live here in conditions that others find inhospitable. Perhaps the most distinctive natives of the wasteland are the automatons, who owe their existence to lost magic or advanced technology. A special breed of goblins has learned to thrive in these lands, as have offshoots of naturally hardy races such as dragonborn and orcs.

AUTOMATON

An automaton is an artificial life form—not a construct, but a living organism. Though superficially an automaton resembles a human, having the same general physical characteristics, the perfection of its form is a clue to their its nature. Its facial features are just a bit too symmetrical, its skin too unblemished, its body shape just a shade too robotic. Inside, their muscles, bones and organs resemble those of typical humans, but an artificially created crimson liquid flows through their veins instead of blood.

HUMANLIKE BUT NOT HUMAN

Automatons have the same build as most humans, with no size difference in height or weight between males and females. Because they move with mechanical precision, automatons appear slightly odd to members of many other races.

Automatons' coloration encompasses the normal human range and includes metallic shades such as silver and zirconium. Their hair and eyes can be of any hue, including white.

GROWN, NOT BORN

Virtually every automaton came into being in wasteland ruins or some other forgotten place in the world. Unlike most other races, automatons are not born, nor are they built as a construct is. Each one is grown in a pod filled with nutrient-rich fluids and enzymes designed to accelerate its maturation until it reaches the age programmed into its pod and is ready to be released. This process can take as little as a few weeks or as long as a year. A pod that contains an ungrown automaton embryo remains functional for centuries or longer until the pod initiates the growth process. Once it produces an automaton, a pod becomes nonfunctional. These dormant pods might be found languishing in a crumbling technological ruin (possibly the remains of a starship, an ancient culture, or a trans-dimensional colony) until a pod completes the growth process and a new automaton stumbles out into the world.

BLANK SLATES

Automatons emerge from their pods with no knowledge of who or what they are or how they came to be. Obeying a subconscious directive from its pod, an automaton ventures away from its birthplace as quickly as possible. Its first days of independent life are spent in a barely sentient haze while the automaton's mind struggles to adapt to its new environment. Many automatons fall prey to monsters

or other hazards during this time. Those who survive experience a moment they call the "Awakening" approximately five days after their emergence from their pods. They abruptly become clear-headed and self-aware, ready to make decisions about how to spend their lives. Some automatons have an insatiable curiosity about every aspect of existence, often venturing far and wide in search of new experiences. Others become fixated on a particular subject and devote all their time to increase their knowledge or aptitude in their chosen obsession.

AUTOMATON NAMES

When an automaton becomes self-aware after emerging from its pod, it realizes it needs a name to identify itself. Most automatons adopt names used by the first race or culture they encounter after their Awakening. Some take a more imaginative approach, inventing monikers that reflect how they perceive themselves, or they choose names derived from the strange dreams they sometimes experience. Due to some quirk of their minds, once an automaton takes a name, they never change it. This has sometimes led to odd name choices as newly awakened automatons don't understand the cultures and societies they find themselves in.

> ### DREAMS OF BEFORE
> During a long rest, automatons have a 5% chance of dreaming about the culture or race who created them. These dreams could be remnants of the programming infused into the automatons during their maturation in their growth pods, forgotten directives from a long dead race, or messages sent from other stars or dimensions. The automatons themselves do not know the truth behind the dreams and generally chalk them up to yet another oddity of their existence. However, there are some automatons who call themselves "Seekers" who actively try to follow these dreams. Though many of their searches are fruitless, following the dreams has led some seekers to lost technological ruins in the wastelands, so perhaps there is something more to these visions.

Some automatons are content with a single name, while others prefer to have both a name and a family name. Little distinction exists between male, female, object, and family names; the order of things depends on the preference of the automaton.

Male Automaton Names: Bob, Erdan, Merric, Pouch, Rhogar, Seebo, Sold, Thokk, Unit Zero-One

Female Automaton Names: Althaea, Cat, Kathra, Heskan, Model 15j, Janet, Merla, Spoon, Sutha, Zanna

Automaton Family Names: Brawnhammer, Dinner, Galanodel, Hunter/Seeker, Kerrhylon, Pillow, Nackle, Smith, Tealeaf

AUTOMATON GLYPH

Each automaton is distinguished by a unique, glowing, coin-sized glyph somewhere on its body. The importance of this symbol is unknown, and it resists all attempts to decipher it, whether mundane or magical. You can choose the location of your glyph or use the following table to determine where it is. You can decide whether to display your glyph openly or cover it with a piece of clothing.

AUTOMATON GLYPH LOCATION

d8	Location	d8	Location
1	Forehead	5	Back
2	Chest	6	Foot
3	Leg	7	Hand
4	Arm	8	Back of the head

AUTOMATON TRAITS

Your automaton character has the following traits.

Creature Type. You are a Humanoid.

Ability Score Increase. Automatons are produced for a variety of different functions. One ability score of your choice increases by 2, and another score increases by 1. Optionally, three scores of your choice each increase by 1.

Age. Automatons do not visibly age and do not suffer the effects of aging, but they are not immortal. Unless violence or tragedy claims its life before then, an automaton's body simply shuts down exactly 150 years after the moment it emerged from its pod.

Alignment. Most automatons tend to have a polarized view of the world. Creatures and their deeds are either good or bad, orderly or chaotic. A few deliberately shun this way of thinking, embracing the concept of neutrality.

Size. Your size is Medium.

Speed. Your base walking speed is 30 feet.

Darkvision. You can see in dim light within 60 feet of you as if it were bright light, and in darkness as if it were dim light. You can't discern color in darkness, only shades of gray.

Artificial Life Form. You were created to resemble humans, but because you are an artificial life form, you gain the following benefits:

- **Enhanced Physiology.** You need to breathe, eat, and sleep, but you can go without breathing for a number of hours equal to your proficiency bonus, and you can go without eating or sleeping for a number of days equal to your proficiency bonus.
- **Disease Immunity.** You are immune to disease, whether natural or magical in nature.
- **Accelerated Healing.** Once every 24 hours, when you recover hit points by finishing a short rest or from magical healing, you recover twice the normal amount.

DUST GOBLIN

Of all the humanoid races that live in the blighted lands of the world, perhaps the most successful are the dust goblins. Their ability to survive in almost any environment and the prolific rate at which they breed enables them to face nearly any challenge that comes their way. Indeed, in a land populated by otherworldly horrors, unhinged cultists, and rampaging dragons, that they not only survive but prosper is something of a miracle.

MALNOURISHED AND TWISTED

Dust goblins appear to be perpetually underfed because of their thin limbs and swollen bellies. Their skin is dry and cracked from exposure to sun and wind, and their hands and feet are heavily callused. Dust goblins are roughly the same size as others of their ilk, with dusky gray to dark green skin and dark red, black, or green hair. Their eyes are invariably yellow or red and seem close to bulging out of their sockets. Some dust goblins are born with deformities such as an extra (but useless) limb or ugly boils covering their bodies, but these defects have no impact on their abilities.

FEARLESS TINKERERS

Dust goblins are driven by two universal characteristics: a lack of fear, even in the face of overwhelming odds, and an insatiable interest in anything ancient and magical, particularly if such a thing can be made to blow up or otherwise harm another individual. Why dust goblins are so different from their cowardly cousins has long been a cause of conjecture among sages and scholars. Some believe their minds have been warped by prolonged exposure to aberrations or foul magic, others that the race has been blessed by a mad god, and a few maintain that they were specifically bred long ago to enhance their fearlessness and curiosity.

Although dust goblins are not the equal of gnomes or dwarves when it comes to craftsmanship, they have a knack for activating and using technological devices that others might find perplexing or distasteful. For instance, they have no qualms about making use of any vril technology or chaos devices they might find in an abandoned ruin or in a lich's tower.

DUST GOBLIN TRAITS

Your dust goblin character has the following traits.

Creature Type. You are a Humanoid.

Ability Score Increase. Your Dexterity increases by 2, and your Constitution increases by 1.

Age. Dust goblins are short-lived, reaching adulthood at age 10 and living approximately 40 years.

Alignment. Dust goblins lean toward neutrality and evil, though an individual's alignment is heavily dependent on where it lives. Dust goblins who have grown up in more stable environments are often lawful in alignment despite their somewhat twisted perspectives.

Size. Dust goblins range between 2 and 4 feet in height and weigh between 20 and 80 pounds. Your size is Small.

Speed. Dust goblins are extremely fast for creatures of small stature. Your base walking speed is 30 feet.

Darkvision. You can see in dim light within 60 feet of you as if it were bright light and in darkness as if it were dim light. You can't discern color in darkness, only shades of gray.

Chaotic Mindset. You have advantage on saving throws against being charmed or frightened.

Sneaky and Wily. You have proficiency in the Dexterity (Stealth) and Wisdom (Survival) skills.

Heinous. When you attack a creature that is unaware of your presence, the target must make a Wisdom saving throw with a DC of 8 + your Dexterity modifier + your proficiency bonus. On a failure, the target is frightened of you until the end of its next turn.

Languages. You can speak, read, and write Common and Goblin.

WASTELAND DRAGONBORN

Dragonborn who are native to the wastelands can trace their lineage back to dragons that might have ruled over vast stretches of ruins or other places made desolate by magical forces or eldritch corruption. They bear the evidence of their connection to lands that have been warped by catastrophe in their rust-colored scales and in the bright energy of their breath weapons.

All wasteland dragonborn have an instinctive distrust of wizards and other users of arcane magic. After generations of dwelling in the wastes, they are keenly aware of the destruction that magical corruption can cause and have developed an innate sense of when it begins to affect the land. Some wasteland dragonborn spend their lives patrolling the borders of their blasted domains in an effort to keep away any who might further despoil the land. Others actively explore their environment, looking for treasures to enrich the land or themselves.

WASTELAND DRAGONBORN TRAITS

Your wasteland dragonborn character has the following traits.

Creature Type. You are a Humanoid.

Size. You are Medium.

Speed. Your base walking speed is 30 feet.

Breath Weapon. You can use your action to exhale a bright beam of force energy in a 30-foot line that is 5 feet wide. Each creature in the area of the exhalation must make a Dexterity saving throw. The DC for this saving throw equals 8 + your Constitution modifier

+ your proficiency bonus. A creature takes 2d6 force damage on a failed save, or half as much damage on a successful one. The damage increases to 3d6 at 6th level, 4d6 at 11th level, and 5d6 at 16th level.

After you use your breath weapon, you can't use it again until you finish a short or long rest.

Bite. You have a fanged maw that you can use to make unarmed strikes. When you hit with it, the strike deals piercing damage equal to 1d6 + your Strength modifier, instead of the bludgeoning damage normally dealt by an unarmed strike.

Draconic Resistance. You have resistance to force damage.

WASTELAND ORC

At first glance, the orcs of the wastelands seem little different from their mountain- or forest-dwelling brethren. But they are in some ways more predictable and less savage than other orcs and will sometimes interact with other humanoids for trade or companionship. Of course, when circumstances permit, wasteland orcs enjoy bloodshed and war just as much as their kin.

LEAN AND LANKY

Wasteland orcs are noticeably thinner and taller than other orcs, with wiry, muscular frames. Their skin tone also tends to be of different hues, with tan, orange, or yellowish skin being common and grayish or greenish skin rare. Their hair is coarse and typically dark brown or black, though bone-white or ashen hair is not unheard of. Wasteland orcs have the general facial features of other orcs, with jutting tusks and flat, broad noses. Unlike regular orcs, however, their eyes are slanted and surrounded by thick folds of skin that protect them from stinging dust and airborne pollutants.

LEARNING THE LAND

Few humanoids are more adept at surviving in the wastes than wasteland orcs, because of their ability to locate fresh water, sniff out potential danger, and resist the effects of chaotic magic. Young wasteland orcs are taught all the skills they need to survive in a harsh world, and they know from an early age that failure to learn these lessons leads to a quick death.

Though dealing with wasteland orcs can be challenging, they have been known to guide travelers through dangerous areas or serve as guards for merchants passing through the badlands. Some wasteland orc tribes engage in primitive protection rackets, protecting caravans that travel through their territory from attacks by bandits or dust goblins in return for a suitable "donation."

WASTELAND SETTLERS

Wasteland orcs live in heavily fortified camps where they engage in practices that other orcs would see as ludicrous or unbecoming, such as vegetable farming and the raising of goats and other livestock. While this way of life might seem strange to onlookers, wasteland orcs understand that relying on hunting and raiding for sustenance in the desolate wastes is a surefire way to risk starvation.

Almost every wasteland orc encampment features a fighting pit or similar location where young orcs can test their mettle against prisoners, fierce animals, and monsters such as owlbears. A visitor to one of these strongholds can earn the orcs' respect by stepping into a fighting pit and coming out alive.

WASTELAND ORC TRAITS

Your wasteland orc character has the following traits.

Creature Type. You are a Humanoid.

Ability Score Increase. Your Strength increases by 2, and your Constitution score increases by 1.

Age. Wasteland orcs reach adulthood at the age of 14. Most wasteland orcs rarely reach 30 years of age because of the threats that exist in the barren lands. Wasteland orcs who take up residence in more civilized settings typically survive twice as long.

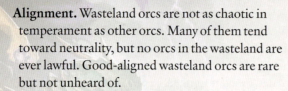

Alignment. Wasteland orcs are not as chaotic in temperament as other orcs. Many of them tend toward neutrality, but no orcs in the wasteland are ever lawful. Good-aligned wasteland orcs are rare but not unheard of.

Size. Wasteland orcs tower over most other humanoids, most reaching upward of 8 feet in height, but are still considered Medium creatures.

Speed. Your base walking speed is 30 feet.

Darkvision. You can see in dim light within 60 feet of you as if it were bright light and in darkness as if it were dim light. You can't discern color in darkness, only shades of gray.

Aggressive. You can use a bonus action to move up to your speed toward a hostile creature that you can see.

Chaos Resistance. You have advantage on saving throws against spells and other magical effects that have the chaos descriptor and against the special attacks and spell-like abilities of chaotic aberrations and fiends.

Wasteland Awareness. You have proficiency in the Wisdom (Survival) skill. In addition, you apply double your proficiency bonus to checks for this skill when you try to locate fresh, unpolluted drinking water or when you want to determine whether an area is free of dangerous creatures or hazards.

Wasteland Resilience. You can survive for extended periods without sustenance. You can go without food or water for a number of days equal to 6 + twice your Constitution modifier before you begin to suffer the effects of exhaustion. In addition, the heavy folds of skin around your eyelids grant you advantage on saving throws against the effects of airborne dust particles and similar substances that could cause blindness or otherwise impair your vision.

Languages. You can speak, read, and write Common and Orcish.

SUBCLASSES

This section provides new subclasses appropriate for characters who are native to wasteland environments or who travel frequently in such places.

BARBARIAN: PATH OF THE DEMON

In times lost lived ancient races whose ambitions drove them to seek pacts with fiends and demons of the lower planes. Offering themselves as vessels and conduits, they forged artifacts that allowed them to channel demonic entities, unleashing their terrible power into the mortal world. In their arrogance, they believed they could control the demonic lords, that their mortality might temper them, and that they might use their will to force them to save the world. While sane folk condemn these dark pacts and would banish the secret rituals of the ancients, there are always those driven by the desperation of merciless fate that continue to walk the Path of the Demon.

AWAKEN RUNEBLADE

When you choose this path at 3rd level, you forge a ritual pact with a demon lord. The demon grants you the weapon that becomes your bonded runeblade. A runeblade typically appears as a rune-covered sword forged from an unidentifiable black metal, but you can have it take the form of any melee weapon you desire. Once summoned, you are bound to the runeblade. The runeblade is a magic weapon and requires attunement before you can use its special features, which are described below.

RUNEBLADE'S SONG

Whenever you enter a rage, the demon channels a measure of its power through your runeblade. It pulses as if it were alive, and if you score a critical hit on an attack with it, the weapon begins to sing softly. All creatures, friend or foe, within a 10-foot radius must make a successful Wisdom save (DC 8 + your proficiency bonus + your Strength modifier) or become frightened of you until the end of your next turn. The song ends when your rage ends.

At 6th, 10th, and 14th level, the radius of your runeblade's song increases by 10 feet to a maximum of 40 feet.

LIFE SIPHON

Any creature you slay by using your runeblade during a rage surrenders its life essence to the demon, and the demon shares the benefit with you. The first time during a rage when you use your runeblade to kill an opponent, you gain 2d8 temporary hit points. At 6th level and every four levels beyond that, the number of temporary hit points you gain increases by 1d8 to a maximum of 6d8.

At 10th level and higher, this feature also activates the first time you score a critical hit against an opponent, regardless of whether the creature dies.

SLAKE THIRST

Starting when you reach 6th level, the runeblade demands that you slake its thirst for life energy. The first creature the sword damages takes an extra 3d6 necrotic damage. The runeblade then transfers some of the target's energy to you, healing an amount of hit points equal to the necrotic damage dealt.

At 10th level, this feature affects the first two successful attacks you make with your runeblade.

At 14th level, this feature deals an extra 5d6 necrotic damage, and it affects the first three successful attacks you make with your runeblade.

SOUL DRINKER

When you attain 10th level, your runeblade begins demanding souls. Each time you enter a rage, the sword tries to capture a soul for itself. Whenever your attack with the weapon scores a critical hit, the opponent must make a Wisdom saving throw (DC 8 + your proficiency bonus + your Strength modifier). On a failed save, the runeblade begins leeching out the target's soul. If the opponent drops below 0 hit points, the runeblade consumes its soul, permanently slaying the creature. After the runeblade consumes a soul, it cannot do so again until you finish a long rest. A consumed soul grants the runeblade a +1 bonus to attack and damage rolls, which lasts until you finish a long rest. A runeblade can consume a number of souls equal to the wielder's Path of the Demon character level, after which it becomes temporarily satiated. For every five souls the runeblade consumes, its bonuses increase by an additional +1 to a maximum +4 bonus at 20th level.

TEMPER BLADE

At 10th level, you learn to temper the effect of your Runeblade's Song feature. Each round, you can choose a number of allies equal to your Strength modifier that are not affected when the feature activates.

DRUID: CIRCLE OF DUST

Groups of dust goblin shamans, druids, treasure hunters, and explorers once banded together, united by their lives spent crawling the wastes. These canny survivors eked out a living among the dust and unpredictable magic as they searched for lost relics from empires long buried. The Circle of Dust is the result of their study. Most members of the Circle of Dust are dust goblins, but druids of other races who are brave or foolish enough to venture into the wastes, hoping to earn the circle's trust, have joined their ranks.

Druids of the Circle of Dust use their magic to offset or better understand the unpredictable nature of the wastes. They draw sustenance from their spells, protect themselves against otherworldly creatures, and seek lost knowledge hidden beneath the sands.

CIRCLE SPELLS

The magic of the wastes that infuses your being grants you knowledge of certain spells. At 3rd, 5th, 7th, and 9th level, you gain access to the spells listed for that level in the Circle of Dust Spells table. Once you gain access to one of these spells, you always have it prepared, and it doesn't count against the number of spells you can prepare each day. If you gain access to a spell that doesn't appear on the druid spell list, the spell is nonetheless a druid spell for you.

CIRCLE OF DUST SPELLS

Druid Level	Spells
3rd	levitate, locate object
5th	create food and water, magic circle
7th	banishment, death ward
9th	hallow, legend lore

WEAPON AND ARMOR OPTIONS

When you choose this circle at 2nd level, you gain proficiency with martial weapons, and you can wear and use armor and shields made of metal.

RESONATING SHROUD

Starting at 2nd level, you gain the ability to create a field of magical energy around yourself that warps ambient magic. As an action, you can expend a use of Wild Shape to create an aura, which fills the area within 10 feet of you. While this aura is active, you gain the following benefits:

- Your melee weapon attacks deal an extra 1d6 force damage to any target they hit.
- Your AC increases by 2.
- When you cast spells with a range of touch, your reach extends to anywhere within your shroud. Other aspects of the spells are unchanged.
- When you or an ally within your shroud cast spells in the wastes, you don't risk unstable results from your spells.

The aura lasts for 1 hour or until you use your Wild Shape again.

OTHERWORLDLY RESONANCE

At 6th level, your mind transforms due to the twisting energies of the wastes. While your Resonating Shroud is active, you can no longer be charmed or frightened, and aberrations must succeed on a Wisdom saving throw against your spell save DC to attack you. An aberration that fails this save can choose a new target, or it wastes the attack.

MYSTIC ABSORPTION

At 10th level, you have advantage on saving throws against spells and other magical effects.

Additionally, when you take damage from a spell, you can use your reaction to absorb some of the energy. You can expend Hit Dice to regain hit points as if you finished a short rest. The maximum number of hit dice you can expend is equal to half your druid level. Once you use this feature, you can't use it again until you finish a short or long rest.

SHROUD DISRUPTION

At 14th level, your Resonating Shroud now extends to the area within 30 feet of you, and your foes treat the area within your shroud as difficult terrain. A creature hostile to you that ends its turn in your shroud takes 1d8 force damage.

FIGHTER: DOOMBRINGER

The doombringer is violence personified, a fighter who revels in bloodshed and the terror they cause in their enemies and who constantly seems to be on the verge of exploding into furious action at the slightest provocation. Most of the doombringer's abilities are associated with causing fear in their opponents.

While not necessarily evil, doombringers are typically bitter and moody individuals who only seem to really enjoy themselves while in battle or terrifying others. This is not to say that doombringers cannot forge loving friendships or form lasting bonds with others, but such circumstances are rare, and most must prove their worth to the doombringer in battle.

HELM OF DOOM

When you take this martial tradition at 3rd level, you gain possession of a helm that fully covers your face, leaving only holes for your eyes and nose. While wearing this helm, you gain several special abilities that you can use in combat. While not technically a magic item, the helm is a quasi-mystical symbol of your fury and bloodlust and does not work if worn by another creature. Additionally, you cannot wear any other helm while wearing this helm, though it does not count toward your attunement slots.

If you should lose your helm or if it is destroyed, you cannot use the class features tied to it until you have procured a new helm to replace it. This process can be completed during a long rest and does not cost any resources.

TERRIFYING VISAGE

At 3rd level, while you are wearing your helm, you can settle your gaze on a target within 30 feet of you as an action. The target must then make a Wisdom saving throw or become frightened of you for 1 minute. If you have already damaged the target in combat, it has disadvantage on its saving throw. A creature can make a new saving throw at the end of each of its turns to end the effect, and once it makes its saving throw, it is unaffected by your gaze for 24 hours.

The saving throw for this ability is equal to 8 + your Strength modifier + your proficiency bonus, and you can use the ability a number of times equal to your Strength modifier (minimum 1). You regain all uses of this ability once you have taken a long rest.

FUELED BY FEAR

Starting at 3rd level, when you strike a creature suffering from the frightened condition, you deal an extra 1d6 damage to the target.

This extra damage increases to 2d6 at 10th level and 3d6 at 18th level.

MENACING ADVANCE

At 7th level, your movement speed increases by 5 feet, and whenever you move toward a target while wearing your helm and you end your turn no more than 15 feet from them, you can activate your Terrifying Visage feature against them as a bonus action.

This counts toward the total number of times you can use Terrifying Visage.

VICTOR'S ROAR

Beginning at 10th level, while you are wearing your helm, you can unleash a bloodcurdling screech as a reaction whenever you score a critical hit against a creature or reduce a foe to 0 hit points, allowing you to target all enemies within 15 feet of you with your Terrifying Visage feature.

This counts towards the total number of times you can use Terrifying Visage.

DOOM APPROACHES

Starting at 15th level, your movement speed increases by an additional 5 feet, and when you target a creature with your Menacing Advance feature, you can target

an additional target within 10 feet. If you only target a single creature with your Menacing Advance feature, the target has disadvantage on its saving throw.

PERSONIFICATION OF DREAD

At 18th level, you become a living paragon of fear and bloodlust. Creatures normally immune to the frightened condition are not immune to your Terrifying Visage and whenever you take the Attack action against a creature affected by the frightened condition and successfully hit it, the target automatically fails its next saving throw to end the frightened condition or resist your Terrifying Visage.

MONK: WAY OF CHAOS

While most who seek perfection of the mind and body espouse the virtues of temperance and discipline, others argue that such fruits are only temporary. Balance, order, and law are feeble attempts to stave off the inevitable spiraling dissolution of entropy. Chaos is the stuff of creation, the creativity of the gods, and the birth of the universe. These individuals preach that nothing can withstand pure chaos and

d4	Result
1	A blast of chaos rips through your opponent's mind. They must make a successful Wisdom save, or your attack deals psychic damage and staggers the opponent, forcing them to make their next action or save at disadvantage.
2	Your blow disrupts a chakra in your opponent's stomach, forcing them to make a successful Constitution save or take poison damage, drop their weapon, and spend their next turn vomiting.
3	You trigger an entropic ripple which forces the opponent to make a successful Dexterity save or take force damage as the ripple knocks them back 10 feet.
4	Your opponent must make a successful Wisdom save to avoid being affected by a hideous laughter spell.

Optional Rule. If you want more chaos, your GM may also allow Chaos Strike to trigger whenever you roll a critical hit with a monk weapon or unarmed strike. The triggered effect replaces dealing double damage on a critical hit.

DRIVEN BY CHAOS

Starting at 3rd level whenever you channel your ki, you must transform the energy into pure chaos. This action is incredibly strenuous and causes your eyes to cloud over. Your eyes become pupilless milky orbs, effectively blinding you of normal vision in order for you to see the swirling entropy of pure chaos. Whenever you use ki to activate one of your monk abilities, replace your normal sight with blindsight 90 ft. Your normal sight returns after a long rest; however, many who follow the way of chaos channel pure chaos so frequently that the condition is effectively permanent.

ENTROPIC JAUNT

At 6th level, you learn to trigger rifts within the realms of chaos. Whenever an opponent strikes you in combat, you can spend a ki point as a reaction to cause a chaos rift that triggers one of the following spell effects as cast by a 6th-level spellcaster. After taking damage from the attack, roll 1d4 to determine which spell effect you trigger.

d4	Result
1	blur
2	darkness
3	mirror image
4	misty step

therefore to embrace this reality opens the gate to the truth of the multiverse. On the other hand, those who train in chaos fuse their minds and bodies to pure chaos, entropy, and constant change. They forget what they know. They dream immortal dreams. They step beyond reality and let their thoughts and actions be driven only by each fleeting moment they exist.

CHAOS STRIKE

Starting when you choose this tradition at 3rd level, you can transform ki into pure chaos to create powerful random effects when you attack opponents with an unarmed strike or monk weapon. You can spend 1 ki point to imbue your fists or monk weapon with chaotic energy. When your strike hits, you roll 1d4 to determine which effect the chaos triggers. To avoid its effect, your opponent must make the appropriate save against your attack (DC 8 + your proficiency modifier + your Wisdom bonus). On a successful save, your attack deals its normal unarmed strike damage.

CHAOS CONDUIT

At 11th level, your body transforms into a natural conduit for pure chaos energy. The type of damage you deal shifts randomly whenever you attack an opponent with a monk weapon or your unarmed strike. Roll 1d12 to determine the type of damage you inflict.

d12	Result	d12	Result
1	acid	7	piercing
2	cold	8	poison
3	fire	9	psychic
4	force	10	radiant
5	lightning	11	slashing
6	necrotic	12	thunder

You can spend a ki point to stabilize the energy, preventing it from shifting. If you stabilize the energy, each round you do not release it with an attack, the chaos accumulates in your body.

On the 1st round, any attack you make with an unarmed strike or monk weapon deals an additional 2d8 points of the damage type you have stabilized. Alternately, you can shape the energy into a ball and hurl it at an opponent as a ranged attack with a range of 30 ft. Each additional round, the damage increases by 1d8 to a maximum number of rounds equal to your monk proficiency bonus + your Wisdom modifier. You must release the energy before it reaches maximum capacity. If you do not make an attack on or before the maximum number of rounds, the chaos explodes, dealing 8d8 points of the accumulated damage type to you and every creature in a 20-foot-radius blast centered on you.

WILL OF CHAOS

At 17th level, the chaos monk can bond themselves and others to the whimsically capricious energies of pure chaos, causing extreme chaos warps, ripping of time and space, and surges of entropy. You can spend two ki points to activate Will of Chaos, then roll 1d4 to trigger one of the following random effects.

RANGER: WASTELAND ROVER

Some rangers revel in the thriving regions of the world surrounded by nature's bounty. Wasteland rovers put this aside, preferring to test themselves in lands reduced to desolation by falling civilizations, natural disasters, or magical cataclysm. They believe life is all the sweeter when it is threatened every day by the land itself. These rangers develop ways to survive in desolate environs, using the fragments of fallen civilizations and the remnants of ancient conflicts in ways the creators never envisioned. Wasteland rovers are sometimes born out of necessity, rising to heroism in hard-scrabbled settlements trying to claw a home out of the wastes. Others come to the badlands later in life, drawn by the promise of discovering ancient treasures, the thrill of combating strange creatures, or to protect the so-called "civilized lands" from the menace of the wastes.

WASTELAND ROVER MAGIC

Starting at 3rd level, you learn an additional spell when you reach certain levels in this class, as shown in the Wasteland Rover Spells table. The spells count as a ranger spell for you, but it doesn't count against the number of ranger spells you know.

WASTELAND RANGER SPELLS

Ranger Level	Spell
3rd	*purify food and drink*
5th	*spider climb*
9th	*tiny hut*
13th	*dimension door*
17th	*telekinesis*

VIGILANT SCAVENGER

Beginning at 3rd level, when you are in any terrain you routinely pick up baubles: bits and pieces of ancient artifacts, magically imbued objects, or other seemingly worthless ephemera. When you finish a short rest, you can prepare a number of these baubles equal to half your proficiency bonus. Prepared

d4	Result
1–2	**Chaos Transformation.** On a roll of 1, you force your opponent to make a successful Wisdom saving throw or polymorph into a random creature as per the *polymorph* spell cast by a 15th-level spellcaster. On a roll of 2, you polymorph yourself.
3–4	**Entropic Shift.** On a roll of 3, you force a number of opponents equal to 1 + your Wisdom modifier to shift into an alternate plane as if affected by the *planeshift* spell cast by a 15th-level spell caster. On a roll of 4, you planeshift yourself and up to 5 additional allies.

baubles can be used in your various ability features, detailed below. Once a prepared bauble is used, it crumbles to dust.

ADAPTIVE TINKERER

At 3rd level, as an action you can use a prepared bauble to function as any type of artisan's tool for 1 hour. You have proficiency with that tool during the duration.

IMPROVISED BAUBLE

At 7th level, you learn a wider variety of uses for your prepared baubles:

- **Anoint Weapon.** As a bonus action, you can pour a liquid from the bauble over your weapon, giving it 1d6 of your choice of damage (acid, cold, fire, lightning, poison) on the first successful attack before your next turn.
- **Detonation.** As an action, you can throw the bauble at a point up to 60 feet away from you. It explodes on impact, dealing 2d6 fire damage plus your proficiency bonus to all targets within 5 feet.
- **Enhancement.** As an action, you can touch the bauble to a creature and give it advantage on its next ability check.
- **Healing.** As an action, you can touch the bauble to a creature and heal it a number of hit points equal to 2d8 plus your proficiency bonus.
- **Sensor.** As an action, you can hold the bauble up to your eye to see through a number of feet of solid objects equal to your proficiency bonus.

TERRAIN BOMB

At 11th level, you can cobble a few of your baubles together to magically change the land around you. As an action, you can combine two or more of your prepared baubles and throw the resulting combination at a point up to 60 feet away. The area 15 feet around that point immediately changes into one of your favored terrains and is considered difficult terrain for 1 hour. Moreover, each creature that enters the area or begins its turn there must succeed on a Dexterity saving throw (DC equal to your spell save DC) or take 2d6 damage of a type appropriate to the terrain you've created. For example, an arctic terrain bomb deals cold damage.

For each additional prepared bauble you add to the terrain bomb, the damage increases by 1d6.

ANIMATED BAUBLES

At 15th level, as an action you can scatter all your prepared baubles onto the ground within 5 feet of you. The baubles immediately come to life as Tiny-sized animated objects (as the spell *animate object*), with the following statistics:

Size	Tiny
HP	20
AC	18
STR	4
DEX	18
Attack	+8 to hit, 1d4 + 4 bludgeoning damage

The animated baubles' attacks are considered magical, and they obey your mental commands. Controlling the baubles does not require concentration on your part. After 1 minute, the baubles crumble into dust.

ROGUE: BANDIT PRIEST

Sometimes even bandits need divine aid to fall back on to heal their injuries or tend to their spiritual needs. In lieu of having a cleric or druid perform the function, one of the bandits might take it upon themselves to fulfill the role. Bandit priests are rogues who have a connection with a particular deity, typically one whose portfolios revolve around robbery or other larcenous pursuits. However, this is not set in stone, and bandit priests can worship just about any deity under the right circumstances.

MINOR SPELLCASTING

At 3rd level, you gain the ability to cast *bless* and *healing word* from your chosen deity. You can cast each spell once per long rest. At 9th level, you can add an additional 1st-level, 2nd-level, or 3rd-level spell of your choice to the spells above, and at 13th level, you can add an additional 4th-level, 5th-level, or 6th-level spell of your choice to the spells above. You can cast the chosen spells once each per long rest.

Wisdom is your spellcasting ability for determining your spell prowess, and you use Wisdom whenever a spell refers to your spellcasting ability. In addition, you use your Wisdom modifier when setting the saving throw DC for a cleric spell you cast and when making an attack roll with one.

Spell save DC = 8 + your proficiency bonus + your Wisdom modifier

Spell attack modifier = your proficiency bonus + your Wisdom modifier

LARCENOUS BENEDICTION

Starting at 3rd level, whenever you or an ally within 10 feet of you fails a Charisma (Deception), Dexterity (Sleight of Hand), or Dexterity (Stealth) check, you can utter a minor blessing as a reaction to allow the target to reroll the result. The target must take the result of the new roll.

You can use this ability a number of times equal to your Dexterity modifier (minimum 1), and you regain all uses of the ability once you have finished a long rest.

FORTIFYING CUP

Starting at 9th level, you can use an action to bless a single piece of food or cup of wine or similar liquid in the name of your chosen deity. The food or beverage remains blessed for 1 minute or until it is consumed, and you can bless a number of such items equal to your proficiency modifier.

A creature that consumes the food or liquid gains 10 temporary hit points and advantage on its next attack roll or saving throw. It also gains resistance to poison damage and immunity to the poisoned condition for the duration. The temporary hit points and the other benefits of this blessing last for 1 hour or until used.

You regain all uses of this ability once you have finished a long rest.

HEART OF THE BAND

Beginning at 13th level, your attacks embolden your allies. Whenever you successfully gain the benefit of sneak attack against a target, you can use a reaction to reduce your sneak attack damage by 2d6 to grant all allies within 30 feet of you a bonus of 1d6 to their next attack roll, saving throw, or skill check. This benefit lasts for 1 minute or until used.

You can use this class feature a number of times equal to your proficiency bonus, and you regain all uses of the feature once you take a long rest.

SWIFT BLESSINGS

Starting at 17th level, you can use your Cunning Action class feature to cast any spell you know from your Minor Spellcasting feature as a bonus action. You gain no additional benefit if the spell could already be cast as a bonus action (such as *healing word*).

ROGUE: CHAOS CULTIST

Where some rogues specialize in delving into ancient ruins, anointing their blades in deadly poison, or skillfully picking the most difficult lock, the chaos cultist forms a mystical connection to the swirling cacophony of chaos itself. These rogues embrace randomness, reveling in probability as they dance through the ever-changing possibilities of reality. Chaos cultists make for unpredictable companions as their powers occasionally go awry, but open-minded adventuring parties relish in the seeming impossibilities they harness for their own ends.

CHAOTIC MANIFESTATION

Those who are touched by chaos seldom remain unaffected by its influence. When you choose this archetype at 3rd level, choose one of the manifestations of chaos described below, or roll randomly on the following table.

d6	Chaotic Manifestation
1	Your eyes change color randomly.
2	Sometimes furniture is afraid of you.
3	You befriend a small sphere of chaos and talk to it like a pet. It has tentacles.
4	Every morning, you change your name and details about your past.
5	You often find random things in your pocket.
6	Any cloak you wear becomes a swirling mantle of chaotic shadows and disturbing images.

UNLIKELY INSIGHT

When you choose this archetype at 3rd level, your connection to chaos provides occasional flashes of knowledge. For 1 hour, you gain proficiency with one skill or tool of your choice (including any in which you are already proficient), and whenever you fail a check with that skill or tool, you can reroll the result, but you must take the new result regardless of its outcome.

You can use this ability twice, and you regain any expended uses when you finish a long rest.

MARK OF CHAOS

Your attacks mark your foes with the touch of chaos itself. When you deal sneak attack damage to a creature on your turn, that target is mystically marked. As a reaction, before the start of your next turn, you can force that target to reroll a single attack roll, damage roll, or saving throw. You make this decision after you see the result of the marked target's initial roll. The target must use the result of the second roll.

DODGE THE ODDS

Starting at 9th level, you unconsciously shift the skeins of probability to protect yourself. As a reaction when you fail a saving throw, or when you are struck with a successful attack, you can choose to make the saving throw or for the attack to miss. Manipulating chaos comes with a cost, however. Until the end of your next turn, you have disadvantage on all rolls.

IMPLAUSIBLE HINDERANCE

Beginning at 13th level, when you deal your sneak attack damage to a creature on your turn, you can reduce the number of d6s of damage you deal. When the target makes an attack roll, ability check, or saving throw before the start of your next turn, roll the d6s you excluded from your sneak attack damage. The target reduces its roll by the result (to a minimum of 1).

AGENCY THIEF

Starting at 17th level, you understand how to steal from probability itself. When you deal your sneak attack damage on a creature on your turn, you can reduce the damage by half and force the target to make a Constitution saving throw (DC 8 + your Dexterity modifier + your proficiency bonus). On a failed save, the target can't take an action on its next turn. Moreover, one ally you can see within 30 feet of you can take an extra action on its turn.

WARLOCK: DEMONIC TUTOR

Some warlocks make pacts with entities of immense power that dwell on distant planes or in other dimensions. For the demonic tutor, the connection is more personal, as their fiendish lord is much closer at hand. You have made a pact with a fiend and, as part of the agreement, you have agreed to house the spirit of the fiend inside your own body. This grants you power, even if you work at goals anathema to the fiend's objectives.

EXPANDED SPELL LIST

Your demonic tutor lets you choose from an expanded list of spells when you learn a warlock spell. The following spells are added to the warlock spell list for you.

DEMONIC TUTOR EXPANDED SPELLS

Warlock Level	Spell
1st	bane, inflict wounds
2nd	augury, flame blade
3rd	clairvoyance, haste
4th	freedom of movement, polymorph
5th	arcane hand, telekinesis

FIENDISH HOST

Beginning at 1st level, you become the host for your demonic patron's spirit. While the fiend is within you, it is immune to magical detection and scrying. It can communicate with you telepathically, whispering in your ear with its observations, comments, and directions. You also have advantage on saving throws to resist being charmed.

HELPING HAND

At 1st level, your demonic tutor can manifest a shadowy hand and arm out of your chest at your command. The helping hand lasts for 1 hour and does not require concentration to maintain. This third hand obeys your mental commands as if it were a natural appendage. It can carry an object you could normally carry in your hands, freeing your normal hands for other tasks. The helping hand can carry weapons and items but can't wield them or activate them. Transferring an item to or from your helping hand does not require an action. If it is not actively holding an item or performing a task, the fiend can occasionally use the helping hand as it wishes.

Once you use this feature, you can't use it again until you finish a short rest or long rest.

WHISPERED INSIGHT

Starting at 6th level, your demonic tutor uses its own senses to observe the surroundings. You can no longer be surprised and can always act during the first round of combat. Moreover, you can see invisible creatures out to a range of 30 feet.

PASSENGER'S ACTION

Starting at 10th level, your fiendish passenger allows you some limited control over its own actions. On your turn, you can take one additional action as the fiend makes use of your abilities, traits, and features.

Once you use this feature, you can't use it again until you finish a short or long rest.

PUPPETEER'S TOUCH

Starting at 14th level, when you hit a creature with an attack, you can use this feature to force the target to make a Charisma saving throw against your warlock spell save DC. On a successful save, the target resists your efforts, and you can't attempt to use this feature on it again for 24 hours.

On a failed save, the target's soul temporarily leaves its body and is replaced by your demonic tutor. Once in possession of the target, the demonic tutor uses the creature's statistics, abilities, and features. The tutor is friendly to you and your allies, unless directed otherwise by you.

The possession lasts for 1 hour or until you will the effect to end as a bonus action.

If the possessed body is killed while the demonic tutor is possessing it, your patron flees back to your body, and you take 5d10 psychic damage.

BACKGROUNDS

The following backgrounds are suitable for playing a character native to the wastes.

CHAOS CHILD

You were born in an area tainted by the forces of chaos, whether that be a demon-blighted wasteland, twisted, alien forest, or region of badlands marked with the ruins of an ancient fallen civilization. The taint subtly infests your soul, drawing you toward corruption and madness, but that does not mean you have to give in to it, and more than one child of chaos has become a symbol of order and righteousness in the world.

Skill Proficiencies: Any two of your choice

Tool Proficiencies: One of your choice

Languages: Void speech (this alien tongue comes naturally to you)

Equipment: A set of traveler's clothes, a waterskin, a knife, and 2 days of rations.

FEATURE: TAINT OF CHAOS

Regardless of where your life has taken you, you still bear traces of your chaotic ancestry in your appearance and mannerisms. For example, you could possess eyes that are mismatched in color or size, strangely rubbery limbs, an odd shuffling gait, extra webbing between your fingers and toes, or even just a chronic twitch. Because others find your appearance strangely unsettling, they have disadvantage on Wisdom (Insight) checks made against you.

Aberrations can sense the taint of chaos within you more than other creatures and are less likely to be hostile toward you. You have advantage on Charisma (Persuasion) checks made when conversing with a neutral or friendly aberration.

SUGGESTED CHARACTERISTICS

Your time spent growing up in the wastes has shaped your perceptions of the people and world around you. You accept things that others might find bewildering or disturbing and rarely shy away from the eldritch or fantastical, especially objects, people, or places touched by the forces of chaos. You may choose from any of the following characteristics.

d8	Personality Trait
1	I find the sound of slithering tentacles oddly comforting.
2	I am incredibly messy.
3	I know what it's like to struggle. I shall never travel down that road again.
4	I accept my friends for who they are. Who am I to judge them?
5	I get anxious in holy places dedicated to gods of law and order. Do the gods hate me?
6	I like foods that others might find disgusting, like pickled yak eyes.
7	I do not show respect to those who do not respect me.
8	I am careful to conceal my true nature around those who might take umbrage with my past.

d6	Ideal
1	Stoicism. I will not give in to the chaos that infests my blood. (Lawful)
2	Friendship. My friends are what keep me sane in this chaotic world. (Neutral)
3	Anarchy. Rules and laws are made to be broken. True freedom can only be obtained when you toss away these impediments. (Chaotic)
4	Kindness. I have known suffering in my life. I hope that through my deeds, others will not suffer as I have. (Good)
5	Wrath. Violence is the only response to a world governed by wars and madness. (Evil)
6	Aspiration. One day I will be renowned throughout the land. (Any)

d6	Bond
1	My mother left me this strange idol. I shall cherish it always.
2	My life is shrouded in mystery, yet the note I found by my bed that night tells me to travel east.
3	A kindly paladin rescued me from cultists. I must repay the debt.
4	These wastes may not seem like much to you, but they are my home. I must protect them.
5	The birthmark on my arm burns whenever creatures of chaos draw near. Somehow I must find out why.
6	My brother wandered into the wastes one day and never returned. I will not rest until I have found him.

d6	Flaw
1	I sometimes talk to myself in public. Does something whisper back?
2	I am prone to sudden outbursts of emotion.
3	I giggle inappropriately at things that others find disgusting or terrifying.
4	Some people call me flighty. I often change my mind in an instant.
5	I have a horribly raspy voice. Some people say listening to me is like walking over shredded glass.
6	I sometimes creep people out by staring at them for too long.

WASTELAND REAVER

You grew up prowling the wastes as a member of a bandit gang, orc tribe, or similar warlike group. You spent much of your early life raiding and pillaging, plundering villages and merchant caravans. Then, at some point, you turned your back on this life to pursue the path of an adventurer.

Skill Proficiencies: Stealth, Survival

Tool Proficiencies: Choose any one of the following: cook's utensils, leatherworker's tools, thieves' tools, or woodcarver's tools

Languages: Any one of your choice

Equipment: A set of traveler's clothes, a waterskin, a simple weapon, and a pouch filled with 10 gp

FEATURE: A REAVER'S LIFE

Your life as a brigand or outlaw has brought you a certain notoriety. You have advantage on Charisma (Intimidate) checks against those aware of your past, and most criminals and bandits will have a starting attitude of indifferent toward you. On the other hand, people like lawmakers and town guards will initially be hostile toward you until you can prove yourself to be trustworthy.

You also know the location of various places within the wastes where you can hide or seek shelter. These locations should be relatively well hidden and free of monsters, hazards, and traps. You can choose up to three such locations when you take this background.

SUGGESTED CHARACTERISTICS

You lived a life of violence and excess, your only loyalty (if you had any) to your fellow reavers. You can either embrace your sordid past or free yourself from it. Ultimately, the choice is yours. You may choose from any of the following characteristics.

d8	Personality Trait
1	I live every day to the fullest because it could be my last.
2	I take what I want when I want, laws be damned.
3	I'm no coward, but neither am I a fool. I will not risk my neck unless there is a profit to be made.
4	Allies are useful commodities. I even like some of them.
5	The wastes rewards those who are prepared.
6	I know every tavern between here and the eastern sea.
7	I am always looking over my shoulder for danger.
8	Profanities slip effortlessly from my lips. I have a comeback for every situation.

d6	Ideal
1	Honor. I left my past behind me to take on the role of protector rather than predator. (Lawful)
2	Fame. I left the reavers to make a name for myself. (Neutral)
3	Freedom. I will not let laws or kings tell me what I can and cannot do. (Chaotic)
4	Charity. I must pay society back for all the ill I have inflicted upon it. (Good)
5	Might. Those weaker than me deserve no mercy or respect. (Evil)
6	Fun. Life is to be enjoyed. (Any)

d6	Bond
1	I would be dead in a ditch if it were not for my fellow reavers. I owe them everything.
2	A noble took pity on me and freed me from the gallows.
3	My fellow reavers left me for dead in a ditch. I will have my vengeance.
4	A cleric raised me from the dead to serve the cause of good. I will not let them down.
5	A pack of chaos trolls devoured every last member of my band. I will hunt down every last one of them until they are dead.
6	They are waiting out there for me somewhere: the person I will devote my life to.

d6	Flaw
1	I am slow to trust and quick to anger.
2	I habitually curse and spit even in polite company.
3	I am a compulsive liar. I can never be trusted to tell the truth.
4	I think there is an enemy around every corner. It leaves me constantly feeling nervous and twitchy.
5	I betrayed those close to me. Their screams still haunt my nightmares.
6	I carve my name into those I kill.

Chapter 3
People, Tribes, & Cults

People, Tribes, & Cults provides examples of individuals and groups that characters encounter in the wastes, including interesting and engaging NPCs the characters can interact with.

Chaos Reavers

Chaos reavers are disorganized bands of thugs and hooligans that threaten wasteland wanderers and settlements alike. People who are unfortunate enough to encounter the reavers more than once in a lifetime often make the mistake of thinking each encounter is with the same group, but it is just as likely they have encountered a different, unaligned group. The error in perception is easy to make, as each band of chaos reavers looks and acts in largely the same manner, and each group is led by a hulking, helmeted **doom champion** (see **Chapter 5**). Unlike other bandits and ne'er-do-wells, which proliferate in the wastes, attempting to survive and find their profits wherever they can, chaos reavers aren't motivated by coin or even by their own survival. They are akin to a force of nature that is most concerned with its own good times, as long as the good times are accompanied by an excess of violence, liquor, and noise.

The Chaos Reavers spend daylight hours traveling the wastes. Viewed from a distance, their course looks like a ragged, disorganized parade of people, wagons, and beasts. Clouds of dust, kicked up by the movement of the throng, often presage their arrival at a settlement. Even if there is no dust, the approach of the horde is announced by the sound of dozens of magically amplified instruments and voices mixed with the baying of hounds and the cries of more dangerous beasts. The Chaos Reavers don't sneak into a settlement, they announce their approach and dare those in authority to deny them entrance.

Once the reavers encamp themselves around a settlement, they incite the residents to join them, either as participants in their violent debauchery, or more often as the unfortunate victims of their excesses. The presence of the reavers amplifies the aggressive tendencies of otherwise unassociated creatures, driving them to pick fights and destroy property. Homeowners burn down their houses. Hounds maul their masters. Farmers slaughter their flocks and ruin their crops. Townsfolk drag their reeves and mayors from their homes and bludgeon them in the dusty streets. Creatures that spend more than an hour immersed in the reavers' anarchy are likely to pick up and leave with them when they move on, becoming reavers themselves.

Due to the anarchic nature of the organization, the Chaos Reavers are difficult to quantify. Their numbers swell each time they leave a settlement, and contract again as reavers fall to wasteland dangers and their own foolhardy fearlessness.

Members of the troupe commonly practice body modification. Most reavers display piercings of the ear, nostril, septum, lip, or brow, or they have received small, crude tattoos from another reaver. Longtime reavers often endure extensive scarification or branding, which is frequently centered on injuries that refuse to heal without a mark.

A doom champion strides at the head of the raucous procession, unmistakable among the rest of the rabble. Some of the reavers see this individual as a messianic figure, a hulking bastion of disorder, offering them the freedom to live a life without rulers and laws in exchange for tribute and obeisance. Others of the riotous gang see the overlord as the architect of an approaching new world order, offering freedom to the toiling masses. The rest of the Chaos Reavers view the doom champion as the host of an always-moving, never-ceasing party. The doom champion's whim sets the reavers on their course, and they invite everyone they come across to join the festivities, one way or another. The overlord never claims leadership of the reavers nor issues orders or edicts, expecting nothing of these followers. The doom champion doesn't congratulate them on their successes, doesn't urge them on, and doesn't mourn their deaths.

NOTABLE FIGURES

The true leader of a band of chaos reavers is Judethel's Crown, the helmet each doom champion wears. The crowns are all copies, linked to the original artifact that houses the malevolently intelligent spirit of Judethel, its creator and first bearer. The artifact seeks to corrupt benign souls into chaos and depravity for reasons known only to itself. If a doom champion falls, the absence of leadership for the associated band of chaos reavers is short lived. Anyone who claims Judethel's Crown is transformed into a new doom champion within a week of placing it on their head. If a crown goes unclaimed, it telepathically entreats nearby beings with enticements of power and strength. With the simple modus operandi employed by the chaos reavers—to travel the length and breadth of the wasteland, creating havoc and destruction every time a settlement finds itself in their path—leadership is a relative and rarely onerous thing. Judethel's Crown is rarely forced to wait too long before a new wearer comes under its influence.

Before he became the longest-running overlord to hold the title, Gravis Kindt was a pious knight of a neighboring realm. Concerned with the complaints of raiders and vandals on the borders of his fief, he rode out to find a band of chaos reavers despoiling one of the farming villages and coercing its residents to join them on their madcap travels. After handily dispatching the overlord of that band, he thought to dishearten and scatter them by wearing the fallen overlord's helmet, proving to his followers that their leader was dead. Instead, the act sealed his fate, transforming him into a doom champion and making him the rabble's new leader. From time to time, Gravis' original honorable nature wins out over the helmet's dominating effect. When it does so, he redirects his reavers away from settled areas before they can do too much damage or pull the residents into their near-mindless violence.

Bands of chaos reavers don't really have a second-in-command, but the doom champions do seek counsel from the oracles who travel with their band. Hespilova Franke, the oldest living chaos reaver in the wastes and the oracle most frequently consulted by Doom Champion Gravis, has ranged with the reavers for close to a decade. In her time, she has provided advice and guidance to six different overlords, as well as the hundreds of reavers who have joined the throng and subsequently fallen prey to violence. Hespilova is a haruspex who prefers to use the entrails of songbirds over those of other creatures when she divines the future. Her talents allow her to exercise her misanthropic and nihilistic desires to make a misery of existence for as many intelligent beings as she can. Under her counsel, Doom Champion Gravis' reavers most often move toward settlements that can post a strong defense against them and the other myriad threats of the wastes.

Through her auguries, Hespilova knows there is no symmetry in the natural world. She knows order is an illusion used by powerful beings to keep the sheep-like masses in line. In her view, chaos is the path to self-determination, and nothing creates chaos faster than mindless violence and destruction.

The barnstormers traveling with the reavers provide the theme for their revels. Chaos reavers are perpetually surrounded by a din of loud music played on magically amplified instruments and accompanied by vocalists ranging in talent and style from throat-shredding shriekers to classically trained concerto singers. The cacophony is further aided by the percussive sounds of the reavers banging on the carts and wagons while stomping along on their path and the wailing and baying of any animals accompanying the group.

Beyond the generally assumed and accepted leadership of the doom champion, there is no appreciable system of rank in place. The remaining reavers are equal, though this mostly amounts to the right of the weaker among them to allow the stronger members to take what they want without fear of reprisal from the overlord or oracles.

While chaos reavers are mostly human, drawn from the residents of the wastes, other races are well represented. Some bands of reavers have completely incorporated longstanding wasteland tribes of gnolls, lizardfolk, goblins, and kobolds. No attempts are made to quell any of the racial antipathy that may exist between different groups, as squabbles, skirmishes, and brawls between members of a band of reavers are commonplace.

CHAOS REAVER

Contact with a band of chaos reavers is enough to shatter even the most steadfast person's sense of self. When that occurs, the resulting new chaos reaver joins the throng, picking fights, destroying property, and resolutely refusing to show respect to anyone other than the doom champion who leads the band.

Chaos Reaver

Medium Humanoid (Any Race), Chaotic Evil

ARMOR CLASS 13 (leather armor)
HIT POINTS 19 (3d8 + 6)
SPEED 30 ft.

STR	DEX	CON	INT	WIS	CHA
13 (+1)	14 (+2)	13 (+1)	11 (+0)	10 (+0)	13 (+1)

SAVING THROWS Con +3
SENSES passive Perception 10
LANGUAGES Common
CHALLENGE 1/4 (50 XP) **PROFICIENCY BONUS** +2

ACTIONS

Club. *Melee Weapon Attack:* +3 to hit, reach 5 ft., one target. *Hit:* 3 (1d4 + 1) bludgeoning damage. If the target is a creature, it must succeed on a DC 11 Wisdom saving throw or use its next action to make an attack or a spell attack against a creature other than the reaver or an object within range. Creatures that are immune to being charmed automatically succeed on the save.

Dagger. *Melee or Ranged Weapon Attack:* +4 to hit, reach 5 ft. or range 20/60 ft., one target. *Hit:* 4 (1d4 + 2) piercing damage.

WASTELAND BARNSTORMER

Wasteland barnstormers travel with the chaos reavers, urging them to perform ever-escalating acts of violence and depravity. Their presence is heard long before they and their cohort are seen, giving wise creatures in the vicinity ample time to vacate to safer premises. When a barnstormer dies, its allies fall upon the body to collect its instrument, if possible, which is passed on to another member of the band. If the instrument can be adorned with trophies gathered from its former user, such as hair or teeth, so much the better.

Wasteland Barnstormer

Medium Humanoid (Any Race), Any Non-Good or Lawful Alignment

ARMOR CLASS 13 (leather armor)
HIT POINTS 33 (6d8 + 6)
SPEED 30 ft.

STR	DEX	CON	INT	WIS	CHA
9 (−1)	14 (+2)	12 (+1)	10 (+0)	10 (+0)	15 (+2)

SAVING THROWS Con +3, Cha +5
SKILLS Performance +5
CONDITION IMMUNITIES deafened
SENSES passive Perception 10
LANGUAGES Common
CHALLENGE 1 (200 XP)   **PROFICIENCY BONUS** +2

Amplified. Deafened creatures are affected by the wasteland barnstormer's Bloody Concert and Chaos Herald features.

ACTIONS

Multiattack. The wasteland barnstormer uses Bloody Concert and makes a Raucous Yawp attack.

Raucous Yawp. *Melee or Ranged Spell Attack:* +4 to hit, reach 10 ft. or range 60 ft., one target. *Hit:* 11 (2d8 + 2) thunder damage.

Bloody Concert. The wasteland barnstormer performs aggressively. All creatures that are within 30 feet of the barnstormer and are friendly toward it deal an extra 3 (1d6) damage when they hit a creature or object with a weapon attack.

Chaos Herald (1/Day). The barnstormer performs in a belligerent display. Each creature within 20 feet of the barnstormer must succeed on a DC 12 Wisdom saving throw or become charmed for 1 hour. A creature charmed in this way must use its action on each of its turns to make a weapon attack or a spell attack against a creature other than the barnstormer or an object within range. Whenever an affected creature takes damage, it can make a new Wisdom saving throw, ending the effect on itself on a success.

ORACLE OF THE WASTES

An oracle of the wastes deprives itself of food, water, and sleep and has been granted gifts of foresight and truth-seeing in exchange. When it receives its gift, an oracle decides what method it uses to perform its auguries. Methods range from aeromancy, the divining of atmospheric phenomena, to haruspicy, the reading of entrails, to cleromancy, the use of dice or knucklebones. Many oracles of the wastes burn a hallucinatory narcotic in a stone bowl while divining the future. The chaos reavers always have at least one oracle traveling with them.

Oracle of the Wastes

Medium Humanoid (Any Race), Any Non-Good Alignment

ARMOR CLASS 14 (Gift of Foresight)
HIT POINTS 58 (13d8)
SPEED 30 ft.

STR	DEX	CON	INT	WIS	CHA
7 (−2)	10 (+0)	10 (+0)	17 (+3)	19 (+4)	13 (+1)

SAVING THROWS Int +5, Wis +5
SKILLS Insight +5, Perception +5
CONDITION IMMUNITIES exhaustion
SENSES passive Perception 13
LANGUAGES Common, Goblin, Umbral
CHALLENGE 4 (1,100 XP)   **PROFICIENCY BONUS** +2

Gift of Foresight. The oracle adds its Wisdom modifier to its Armor Class, its attack rolls, and the damage rolls of its weapon attacks (included in the attack).

ACTIONS

Stone Knife. *Melee Weapon Attack:* +6 to hit, reach 5 ft., one target. *Hit:* 6 (1d4 + 4) slashing damage.

Uttered Doom. *Melee or Ranged Spell Attack:* +6 to hit, reach 5 ft. or range 60 ft., one creature. *Hit:* 14 (2d10 + 3) psychic damage, and the target must succeed on a DC 14 Charisma saving throw or be incapacitated for 1 minute. An incapacitated creature can make a new saving throw at the end of each of its turns, ending the effect on itself on a success.

Crushing Futility (Recharge 6). The oracle grants each humanoid of its choice within 30 feet of it a momentary vision of the creature's inevitable death. On a failed save, a creature takes 17 (5d6) psychic damage and is paralyzed until the end of the oracle's next turn. On a successful save, the creature takes half as much damage and is frightened of the oracle until the end of the oracle's next turn. A creature that dies within 1 minute of failing its saving throw can't be resurrected by anything short of a *wish* spell or the intercession of a deity.

REACTIONS

Twist of Misfortune. If the oracle takes damage from a weapon attack or a spell attack, it can use its reaction to scramble its attacker's fate. The creature that damaged the oracle has disadvantage on attack rolls for 1 minute or until that creature hits a different target.

REAVER ACTIVITIES

Whether you are running an extended campaign, a short run of a few sessions, or a one-shot, the chaos reavers are easy to introduce to your players. Bands of chaos reavers exist to wander the landscape, threatening to pillage and destroy everything their path crosses. Heroic-minded characters will want to stop them vandalizing settlements and abducting the townsfolk, while more larceny-minded characters may appreciate the distraction the reavers cause, making their illicit activities easier to hide. Some ideas for using the chaos reavers, organized by tier of play, follow:

TIER 1

Adventurers have arrived at a hamlet on the border of the wastes that has obviously fallen prey to raiders of some sort. Most of the residents are nowhere to be found, though some fly-covered corpses remain. The few survivors tell them that bandits led by a giant of a man occupied the settlement and spent two days eating, drinking, fighting, and smashing everything that would break. They took most of the surviving residents into the wastes when they left. One of the survivors asks the characters to find their husband and return him to the village.

After traveling the wasteland in pursuit of the bandits, the characters come across a cart with a broken wheel. Several ragged humanoids surround the cart. From a distance, it seems they are trying to repair it, but as the characters draw closer, it becomes evident the opposite is true. The humanoids attack the characters in a chaotic rush. In the aftermath, it is discovered that one of the bandits was a recent resident of the hamlet the characters visited. They tell the characters that the presence of the bandits made them lose their mind and that the band was heading to another settlement to continue the party.

The characters arrive at the next reaver encampment as they are preparing to leave. The doom champion has already left to lead the procession onward. The characters can stop the chaos reavers from taking the village residents with them but may lose the opportunity to follow them immediately as they deal with injured and confused townsfolk. The trail of the reavers leads further into the wastes.

TIER 2

The characters catch up to the reavers as they encamp away from a settlement. They can learn a great deal about the band, their leader, and that a trio of future-seeing oracles counsels the hulking figure they call Doom Champion Tevitz.

Doom Champion Tevitz gives the characters an opportunity to confront him while he is attended by only a few of his followers. The din of the reavers' camp masks any conflict that occurs. When the doom champion falls, the reavers can be more easily scattered. Some of them, free of the doom champion's influence, might ask the characters to help them return to their homes. Older reavers may not have homes to return to. If one of the characters doesn't put the doom champion's helmet on within a few days, it disappears.

The characters hear a rumor that a hulking helmeted figure is leading a chaotic band of reavers in raids against wasteland settlements. Upon investigating, they find this is true. If they have encountered a doom champion before, and they confront him, he speaks to them as though he has met them previously. If they stop the doom champion, his helmet stays with them, even if they try to rid themselves of it.

TIER 3

As long as the characters have a doom champion's helmet in their possession, villagers and other intelligent creatures greet them with violence. Furthermore, the helmet draws an increasing number of chaos reavers to the characters, all of whom seek to take the artifact, preferably by violence. The characters learn that many bands of chaos reavers are being drawn to a location in the wasteland.

The characters travel to the reaver gathering and discover there are several doom champions. One in particular, Doom Champion Rux, appears to be able to control the other doom champions. A different doom champion overcomes the dominating effect of his helmet for a short period of time and tells the characters what Rux's weakness is. An encounter with Rux opens a rift to a location deep beneath the wastes.

TIER 4

Judethel's Crown emits a siren song that reaches for miles. In order to end the danger to the people of the wastes, the characters seek a means to destroy the artifact and enter the rift.

CULT OF THE BLACK GOAT

The Black Flock gathers in many forms, and her speakers preach the truth of the Mother Whose Loins Bring Forth Multitudes in all her grand and terrible manifestations. Her followers devote themselves to themselves, the embodiment of their goddess's children. They feel entitled to lay claim to as much power as they can acquire, as it is their divine right. The Black Flock's influence lies hidden, expansively spread throughout the wastes. It crops up wherever it finds footing and worms its way into the consciousness of individuals hungry for the omnipotent secrets of the Black Goat of the Woods. Lone Speakers and small cults crop up in lost temples and forgotten decaying groves. Scriptures are near non-existent, and her tenets lie founded in a convergence of scattered beliefs, sometimes contradictory, and with little written down.

Nevertheless, nearly all cults devoted to the Black Goat of the Woods uphold unique interpretations of the faith. The diverse ideals allow them to maintain an intimate connection to their mother. Worshipers maintain the uncanny ability to identify each other. Despite contradictions (or perhaps because of them), the flock remains driven to pursue ancient mysteries and fuse to the conscience of the Black Goat of the Woods by assimilation into the flock.

The Cult of the Black Goat stands as one of the most insidious and dominant of the Black Flock. Masquerading behind the assumed roles of existing gods, they offer aid to the ignorant and unwary, luring them into subjugation. Establishing absolute dominance, cultists lead their followers down the Black Goat of the Woods' depraved path of enlightenment. Through shepherding, cultists undergo rebirth for themselves and the mindless, unknowing, and ignorant masses.

INDOCTRINATION

The Cult of the Black Goat deliberately seeks out small and isolated settlements struggling to survive on subsistence farming. When they encounter such a place, they introduce themselves to the locals as wandering priests on a journey of enlightenment. Then slowly, over time, they insinuate themselves into the community until the place is dedicated to her worship.

This process typically plays out as follows. An initial follower, known as a speaker, arrives in a community and stays a few nights, offering his assistance, claiming it is part of his path to aid those in need. He offers gifts, which he travels with, in the form of blessed wheat seed and a pregnant black goat. He then tells the villagers he must continue his journey, but if they desire, he can send another, an herbalist and midwife, to help the community place blessings and aid with childbirth. The speaker then departs, leaving the gifts and marking the village with a wheat field and several black goats.

Several weeks after the speaker leaves, the wheat has started to grow, and the goat has given birth to several kids; the cult sends a shepherd to live in the village. Shepherds enter villages acting as healers and midwives and use magic to ensure the wheat and goats grow strong and healthy. Her work appears miraculous, allowing her to offer services to the villagers, particularly those about to bear children and those tending the wheat and the goats. She blesses the pregnant women, marking their bellies with strange symbols painted in red ochre— wards to protect and strengthen the growing infants. She teaches the farmers to paint similar markings on the goats and

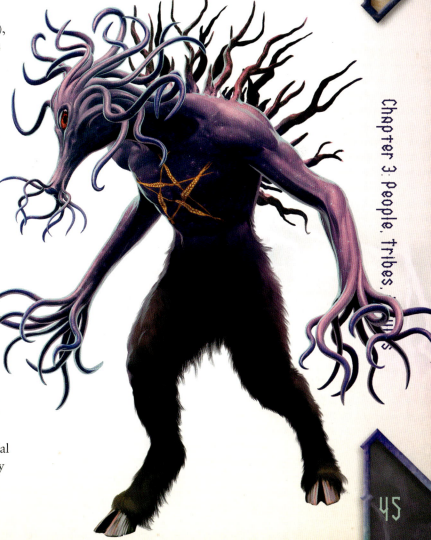

on large broad stones hidden within the wheat fields where she can perform ritual offerings and focus her protective wards.

The shepherd then waits for a strange shift in the weather or other natural phenomena, such as an oddly colored moon or the migration of carrion birds. The shepherd then calls attention to the unusual condition, declaring it an ill-omen. Covertly she allows or induces the wheat to droop, and several villagers become sick. Once the villagers become significantly alarmed, she informs them that they can lift the omen by offering a goat as a sacrifice. The shepherd then leads one of the goats and some of the most influential villagers to the stone within the field, where they perform a ritualized slaughter of the goat. Its blood is placed upon the fields and the sick villagers, and miraculously, they are cured. The stone becomes a consecrated altar of the Black Goat of the Woods.

The shepherd continues this practice for years, disguising tenets and providing certain townsfolk with mysteries and rites that they believe protect the others. She indoctrinates the villagers in the practices and rituals of the Black Goat of the Woods. Slowly these individuals become accustomed to the idea that sacrifice leads to power. The shepherd trains some villagers in the blessings of healing and midwifery, teaching them to paint the magic symbols upon the bellies of pregnant women. She holds secret rituals in the fields with village officials and elders. She teaches farmers the secrets and blessings of growing and cultivating wheat. Still, her true focus remains on the indoctrination of village leaders and influencers, disguising the Goat of the Wood's tenets while slowly increasing offerings and tributes.

As a result, the village becomes more self-empowered, its food supplies prosper, and its people become strong. Once she sufficiently brainwashes the people, she asks for greater blood sacrifices; the villagers view the greater sacrifices as necessary for the common good. At this point, she also introduces the concept of blaming others for the cause of misfortunes. She proposes damnation and curses for disobedience and more powerful blessings for those who strengthen their commitment to the Mother Whose Loins Bring Forth Multitudes. Ultimately, she continues until she becomes the village's dominant influence and can convince at least some of the followers to make human sacrifices within the fields. Sacrifices may be travelers and outsiders or villagers who jeopardize the village's safety and are condemned to exile. Secretly, the exile is later tracked down and ritually murdered in the wheat fields.

In an indoctrinated village, the common folk support worship of the Black Goat of the Woods, though they do not fully recognize her ideals and tenets or the evil she embodies. If outsiders confront villagers with the truth, they argue their ideals. They believe the mother goddess is incapable of destruction or manipulation. They further accuse such speculations of a blasphemous perversion of her religion instigated by non-believers.

Once a village becomes indoctrinated, the Cult of the Black Goat works to increase its strength and success, encouraging outside trade to grow the village into a larger settlement and grooming targeted individuals for their clandestine congregation. The cult doesn't allow those who lack a clear understanding of their intentions to become aware of the growing flock. Instead, they collect sacrifices and offerings from outsiders. They lure the impoverished with hope, offering them land to farm wheat and independence for those who work hard.

Shepherds work to create a facsimile of normality, compassion, strength, and support when dealing with outsiders or potential inductees. Those within the community share a bond as a family. At first, the Cult of the Black Goat appears to provide all those elements, though ultimately, the means by which those qualities are provided slowly reveals the truth of the cult's intentions. Those slipping deeper into indoctrination begin to lose their connection to humanity as they spiral into bestial depravity.

INFIDELS

Some villages resist indoctrination. When this occurs, Black Goat cultists incite tensions with indoctrinated villages to the point where they can target infidels and the village as sacrifices. The cult spares no one, slaughtering every villager and burning the remains of the village to the ground so their foul practices remain secret. They leave the wheat fields wild and untended to hide their blessed stone altar in the center.

DOGMA

The Cult of the Black Goat believes their purpose is to grow the Black Flock and help the mother goddess awaken her influence. First, the cult ruthlessly worms into the myths and needs of ordinary folk until they become utterly indoctrinated. Next, shepherds convert these individuals with promises of freedom and empowerment, growing the flock and ascending consciousness as they transform into an aspect of The Black Goat of the Woods, just as the goddess shed the old masks of her previous incarnations.

The cult insidiously imposes its dogma on outsiders. An insane drive possesses them to convert heathens and appoint themselves shepherds of the sleeping masses, the flock that is yet to come. They prey upon the uninitiated, the ignorant, and the fearful.

The following tenets dominate the dogma of the Cult of the Black Goat: from life comes death, and from death comes life—cyclical and necessary. There exists inherent violence in creation and the faithful must make sacrifices for change to blossom. The Black Goat cult's members take their philosophy to the extreme. The greater the sacrifice, the greater the transformation. Extreme pain unleashes explosions of creativity, the ability to reform and transform the self, revealing the true expression of power.

Hidden power is released with the manipulation of mortal vessels. Speakers of the Cult of the Black Goat lure other believers, others seeking to gain power in the Goat Mother's name, to submit to their physical manipulations. They seek to increase their power, and the power of their goddess, by unlocking the power of the faithful through radical transformation and rebirth. As with the rituals they undergo themselves, the rituals they inflict upon others are extremely dangerous, horrifically painful, and frequently result in death. However, the Cult of the Black Goat does not fear death but understands it to be one of many transformations. They preach that those who die during a transformation ritual merge into the Black Goat of the Woods to become somehow reincarnated within the goddess and attain divinity. Those surviving the ordeals attain radical growth, gaining insight into the will of the Queen of Decadence, undergoing a divine convergence with others within the cult, and transforming into more powerful entities whose purpose is to undergo their next change.

Mortal consciousness binds one to The Mother Whose Loins Bring Forth Multitudes. The cult's prophets preach that all beings possess a subconscious instinct that drives them to merge with the Black Flock. Creatures possessing consciousness yet unaware of the truth falsely conceive their identities as independent or distinct from the mother goddess. Speakers espouse that followers must break all conscious existence beyond the flock. They must reteach those unable to accept the Black Goat of the Woods and cultivate them with the desire to reveal her truths from subconsciousness. The faithful must awaken the exigency for rebirth and transformation and slay the fear of death. Death exists as the true desire of all life and humanity—it cannot be feared; it must be accepted, for in death lies all power. Death reveals the passage to immortality by exposing the clandestine entrance to the realm of the gods.

PLACES OF WORSHIP

The Cult of the Black Goat holds wheat fields as sacrosanct, as the wheat provides sustenance for the masses and has a clear cycle of death and rebirth from seed, all of which requires sacrifice and the feeding of the soil. Therefore, the cult places large stones at the center of wheat fields and consecrates them in the name of the Black Goat of the Woods with blood sacrifices. Cultists hold rites and rituals within these sanctified wheat groves by luring converts and providing tribute. The consecrated stones serve as sacrificial altars.

TEMPLES

Black Goat prophets, driven by their mother's will, recall mystic visions that guide them to fallen temples built by the ancients. Prophets claim the ancients possessed a divine consciousness linked to the old gods, which instilled them with sentience, will, and a profound understanding of the nature of the multiverse. All of this knowledge has been lost by the young races of modern times. The prophets believe themselves reincarnations of the ancients, their souls bound to the Black Goat. Driven by visions, they quest to reclaim these fabled elder temples. While many deny their existence, prophets of the Black Goat uncovered the abandoned ruins of several ancient temples. They claim these temples in the name of the Black Goat of the Woods using foul consecration rituals involving brutal, gory sacrifices, both of their captives and their devotees.

Cultists use temples to host lengthy ceremonies, drawing their congregations from surrounding villages to come and worship, pay tributes, and offer sacrifices to the Black Goat. Worshipers consume a potent liquor distilled from blood-soaked wheat. The rites unfold like a summoning as villagers drawn to the rituals arrive in a stupor of insatiable curiosity, lust, and malevolent violence. Anointed temple priests display their devotion by sloughing their outer layer of skin through ritualized arcane surgeries, exposing pale flesh as deathly as the color of the bark of the goddess's sacred white ash groves. They mask their skin by painting themselves with a mixture of mud taken from the earth of her sacred groves and prepared with potent herbs, blood, and other fluids.

Congregations contain respectable townsfolk who use their covert association to aid their people and maintain their position of power. The cultists

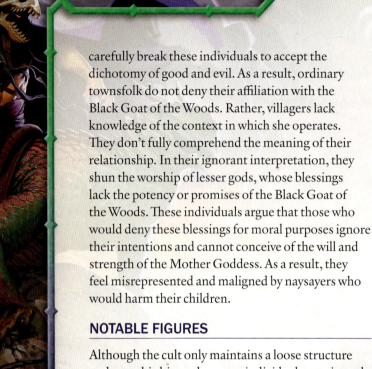

carefully break these individuals to accept the dichotomy of good and evil. As a result, ordinary townsfolk do not deny their affiliation with the Black Goat of the Woods. Rather, villagers lack knowledge of the context in which she operates. They don't fully comprehend the meaning of their relationship. In their ignorant interpretation, they shun the worship of lesser gods, whose blessings lack the potency or promises of the Black Goat of the Woods. These individuals argue that those who would deny these blessings for moral purposes ignore their intentions and cannot conceive of the will and strength of the Mother Goddess. As a result, they feel misrepresented and maligned by naysayers who would harm their children.

NOTABLE FIGURES

Although the cult only maintains a loose structure and anarchic hierarchy, some individuals consistently perform specific roles.

Speakers. These individuals serve as the cult's priests. They hold congregations to disperse the word of the prophets. Their role is to collect prophecy and disseminate it.

Shepherds. These cultists serve as recruiters responsible for the indoctrination of new members and growing and tending the herd. Assuming the mask of followers of a fertility goddess, shepherds offer the people strength and protection while secretly cultivating a connection to the Black Goat of the Woods.

Prophets. These cultists serve as conduits, wild bestial elements who believe their subconscious has entirely merged with the Black Goat of the Woods and is driven solely by its will. They possess the gift of clarity and bestow it upon speakers who interpret the prophecies for the congregation. Prophets undergo painful transformative rituals to express their devotion and commitment. These include scarification that leaves thick keloidal scars along the cheekbones carved into the shape of curving goat's horns and a bloody rite called the ritual of the mother's sight, which narrows their pupils into rectangular slits, clearly identifying them as members of the Black Flock.

Prophet of the Black Goat

Medium Humanoid, Chaotic Evil

ARMOR CLASS 14 (hide)
HIT POINTS 135 (18d8 + 54)
SPEED 30 ft.

STR	DEX	CON	INT	WIS	CHA
17 (+3)	13 (+1)	16 (+3)	12 (+1)	16 (+3)	13 (+1)

SAVING THROWS Con +6, Wis +6
SKILLS Arcana +4, History +4, Insight +6, Religion +4
CONDITION IMMUNITIES frightened
DAMAGE RESISTANCES bludgeoning, piercing, and slashing from nonmagical attacks
SENSES darkvision 60 ft., passive Perception 13
LANGUAGES Common, Void Speech
CHALLENGE 5 (1,800 XP)   **PROFICIENCY BONUS** +3

Burn the Crops. The smoke of burning wheat can be used to silence the prophet's words. If the Prophet of the Black Goat is within 5 feet of burning wheat, it must make a successful DC 13 Wisdom save or be unable to speak until the end of its next turn.

Reckless. At the start of its turn, the prophet of the Black Goat can gain advantage on all melee weapon attack rolls it makes during that turn, but attack rolls against it have advantage until the start of its next turn.

ACTIONS

Multiattack. The prophet of the Black Goat makes two Scythe attacks.

Scythe. *Melee Weapon Attack:* +5 to hit, reach 5 ft., one target. *Hit:* 7 (1d10 + 2) slashing damage.

Spellcasting. The prophet of the Black Goat casts one of the following spells, using Wisdom as the spellcasting ability (spell save DC 14):

At will: *guidance, poison spray*

3/day each: *bane, bestow curse, blindness/deafness, entangle**

1/day each: *augury, fear, spike growth*

*Entangling plants summoned by the Prophet of the Black Goat always manifest as wheat.

BONUS ACTIONS

Word of Prophecy (Recharge 6). The prophet of the Black Goat can utter accursed prophetic words to influence future events. The prophet targets one creature within 30 feet that can hear it. The target must make a DC 14 Wisdom saving throw. On a failed save, it becomes marked by the prophet, and the prophet can cause the creature to suffer one of the effects described below. The mark on a creature dissipates after 24 hours, or it can be removed earlier by a *lesser restoration* spell. The prophet can have as many as three creatures marked at one time.

- **Black Goat's Bite.** Whenever a worshiper of the Black Goat hits the marked creature, it takes an extra 1d6 psychic damage.
- **Black Goat's Hide.** The marked creature has disadvantage on any attack that targets a worshiper of the Black Goat.
- **Black Goat's Voice.** Whenever a marked creature tries to cast a spell, the prophet can use its reaction to cause the energy of the spell to release in the marked creature's throat dealing 1d6 damage per spell level as determined by the spell cast (or psychic damage, if the spell's damage doesn't have a type). The marked creature can make a DC 14 Wisdom saving throw and takes half as much damage on a successful save.

ADVENTURE HOOK

Characters arrive at a small wheat farming village to speak with an individual, perhaps one of the character's siblings or relatives, or perhaps some other contact. Curiously, they cannot seem to locate him anywhere. The locals offer no help but express no concern, even when the man fails to appear after sundown. Eventually, the characters encounter the man's young daughter. The little girl claims she knows the location of her missing father. When asked, she leads the characters into the center of the village's wheat field. In the center lies a large stone covered with strange runes and dripping with human viscera. The girl points to the stone and says, "There's daddy. Daddy saved me. He gave himself to the Black Goat of the Woods."

RED MOON BANDIT GANG

The storytellers who weave tales describing pixies, fairies, and sprites as giggling, harmless joy-makers clearly never encountered the Red Moon Bandit gang. This band of outlawed and exiled fey prowls the wastelands, preying upon travelers, caravans, or, most recently, raiding the surrounding communities. The gang is made up of fey creatures, primarily sprites and corrupted pixies, but a scattering of "big folk" like halflings and gnomes, and a few "bigger folk" like humans and orcs round out the company. Their methods are extreme and as chaotic as they are bloody. The Red Moon seemingly strikes where their cruel whimsy directs, but a malevolent force guides their maliciousness toward a dark goal.

The Red Moon Bandits began one dank night when a magical portal opened and expelled two sprites into the wasteland. Mimsy, a spiky-haired woman with a wide grin, and Cretch, her cruelly sullen companion. The two fugitives fled to the Material plane after one too many transgressions against the lords, ladies and other entities of their home, a distant fey plane distinguished by its dark cruelty and viciousness. Though the wastes was a new environment for the fey, it was an untouched playground of targets for their particular brand of inventive malevolence. They gleefully spent a week convincing a mendicant priest that he was haunted by the spirit of an old lover before stealing the shoes of everyone in a passing caravan. For three months, they plagued anyone and anything to cross their path and might have continued thusly forever, but then Mimsy found the *horn of the crimson moon*. This dark relic, a goat's horn engraved with time-lost glyphs, lay in an ancient shrine, half buried beneath a crumbling fortress built above it. Mimsy believed it to be an artifact of the Horned God, deity of the hunt, and after seizing it, declared herself the leader of the Havoc Hunt. Let humans have their "wild hunt;" the fey would fly on gossamer wings, using tricks and torments as their hunting techniques.

Their prey would fall before their bloody pranks and the hunters would be rewarded. While Mimsy believes she serves a hunting god, the truth is much darker. The *horn of the crimson moon* is a powerful relic of Dark Pan, capricious spirit of chaos, also called Echidna, Shub-Niggurath, and the Black Goat of the Woods. The horn corrupted Mimsy into an avatar of Dark Pan and amplified the sprite's already cruel nature into new depths of violence and viciousness.

Driven by the horn, Mimsy gathered other fey and similar creatures, inducting them into her murderous cult. Her followers are fanatical, her goals are horrid, and death is the preferred outcome of encountering the Red Moon Bandits.

NOTABLE FIGURES

The Red Moon is organized in a twisted parody of one of the Fey Courts, with Mimsy sitting in the role of "queen." She rules her band from the Hall of Teeth and Toes, a hideout built around the shrine housing the *horn of the crimson moon*. The overall goal of the Red Moon Bandits is to honor Dark Pan by causing suffering and pain to their victims, including feasting on the flesh of living creatures. More specifically, the bandits work to build fleshgates in key locations across the wasteland. These eldritch devices, strange occult creations of corrupted magical items and still-living humanoid bodies, will one day allow Dark Pan to manifest physically in the mortal world. However, they require a regular supply of new magical devices and living beings. So, while some bandits seek out items and artifacts among the ruins of the wasteland, others hunt down any magic-users they encounter.

MIMSY BITEFLOWER

Mimsy Biteflower is the undisputed leader of the Red Moon Bandits. Hers is the will behind every plan and every raid, and she is the final arbiter of any dispute among the chaotic members of the band. As an avatar of Dark Pan, Mimsy no longer plays tricks and torments just for the fun of it; now she feasts on the pain and suffering and flesh of the victims of her pranks, all to honor her new god. Mimsy

HORN OF THE CRIMSON MOON

Wondrous item, artifact (requires attunement)

This finger length of carved goat horn was broken off the ever-changing form of the Black Goat of the Woods, a mask of Dark Pan, and imbued with that fell entity's chaotic power.

While it is held by you, the horn projects an aura of randomness around you. Once per round, any creature of the your choice that starts its turn within 30 feet of you must succeed on a Wisdom saving throw (DC is 8 + your proficiency bonus + your primary attribute modifier). On a failed save, the creature must use its reaction to do one of the following (your choice):

- **Comic Dance.** The target moves at half speed with a funny, capering dance until the beginning of its next turn.
- **Blood Offering.** The target injures itself with a weapon (or its teeth if necessary), taking 7 (2d6) damage of the appropriate type.
- **Trip.** The target trips over its own feet, falling prone.

Dark Pan's Touch. While you are attuned to the horn, you gradually become more violent, chaotic, and blood-thirsty.

Destroying the Horn. A creature attuned to the horn must bring it to a location or plane aligned with Law or Order. There it must be bathed in positive energy while mathematical theorems are chanted at it. This will cause the horn to crumble to dust.

takes a childlike delight in her tricks and pranks, so long as they cause pain and blood. She views the core members of the band as her family but isn't as protective of the rank-and-file members. Despite this, Mimsy rules her followers with her powerful force of personality and the corrupting influence of the horn of the crimson moon. The bandits adore her and willingly throw themselves into any bloody act she orders.

Mimsy believes once her followers activate all the fleshgates, Dark Pan will usher in a new age of chaos and blood. Fortunately for the world, this is proving to be difficult. She has begun to exhaust the resources of her territory in the wastes and travelers are sporadic at best. So Mimsy looks beyond the borders of the wastes, spreading the Red Moon into more fertile areas.

Mimsy Biteflower

Lady of the Wasted Court, Mistress of the Hall of Teeth and Toes, and Huntmaster of Havoc

Tiny Fey, Neutral Evil

ARMOR CLASS 15
HIT POINTS 122 (35d4 + 35)
SPEED 10 ft., fly 40 ft.

STR	DEX	CON	INT	WIS	CHA
3 (–4)	18 (+4)	12 (+1)	14 (+2)	14 (+2)	18 (+4)

SAVING THROWS Wis +6
SKILLS Insight +6, Perception +6, Stealth +8
DAMAGE RESISTANCES necrotic
DAMAGE IMMUNITIES psychic
CONDITION IMMUNITIES charmed
SENSES darkvision 60 ft., passive Perception 16
LANGUAGES Common, Elvish, Primordial, Sylvan
CHALLENGE 7 (2,900 XP)   **PROFICIENCY BONUS** +3

Aura of Chaos. While she holds the *horn of the crimson moon*, Mimsy projects an aura of randomness. Once per round, when a creature of her choice starts its turn within 30 feet of her, that creature must make a DC 14 Wisdom saving throw. On a failed save, it must immediately use its reaction to perform one of the following activities, as Mimsy chooses:

- **Slow Motion.** The target moves at half speed until the start of its next turn.
- **Blood Offering.** The target allows her to use her Cursed Bite against it if Mimsy is within 5 feet of it. If not, the target injures itself with a weapon (or its teeth if necessary), taking 7 (2d6) damage of the appropriate type.
- **Trip.** The target trips over its own feet, falling prone.

Magic Resistance. Mimsy has advantage on saving throws against spells and other magical effects.

ACTIONS

Multiattack. Mimsy makes two Bloody Blade attacks and one Cursed Bite attack.

Bloody Blade. *Melee Weapon Attack:* +7 to hit, reach 5 ft., one creature. *Hit:* 6 (1d4 + 4) piercing damage plus 11 (2d10) necrotic damage.

Cursed Bite. *Melee Weapon Attack:* +7 to hit, reach 5 ft., one creature. *Hit:* 13 (2d8 + 4) piercing damage. Mimsy regains a number of hit points equal to the damage dealt by this attack.

Superior Invisibility. Mimsy magically turns invisible until her concentration ends (as if concentrating on a spell). Any equipment she wears or carries is invisible with her.

BONUS ACTIONS

Crimson Grin (Recharge 5–6). After dealing damage with her Bloody Blade, Mimsy can lick the blood from the weapon, briefly staining her sharp teeth red. Until the end of her next turn, other creatures, except those that are immune to being frightened, have disadvantage on attacks against her.

CRETCHSKULL

Cretchskull, **Floating Lord of Burnings and Cracklings,** is Mimsy's constant companion and the unfortunate first victim of her new power as avatar. He objected to his friend's changed nature, so she murdered him and used the power of the horn to return him to life as a glowing, enchanted skull (use statistics for a will-o'-wisp). Bound to her service, Cretchskull does not remember his death and is exceedingly loyal to his mistress. In the gang, Cretchskull acts as Mimsy's eyes and ears, spying on the bandits, punishing transgressions, and enforcing Mimsy's orders as needed. The bandits by and large loathe the floating skull, but they fear his power too much to stand against him directly.

LAPIS BEGONIA BLIGHTSHADE

Lapis Begonia Blightshade is Mimsy's second-in-command and the genius crafter behind the fleshgates. A corrupted being from an unseelie court, Lapis was exiled for forbidden experimentation on living creatures and an unfortunate incident involving reanimating the fur blankets on the bed of the Queen of Night and Magic. She is an eccentric sociopath, fiercely intelligent, passionately focused, and absolutely obsessed with her ongoing experimentation. Lapis' friendship with Mimsy is her only emotional connection, and she values it greatly.

Lapis Begonia Nightshade

Marcher-Countess of Rending and Mending

Tiny Fey, Lawful Neutral

ARMOR CLASS 15 (natural armor)

HIT POINTS 90 (36d4)

SPEED 10 ft., fly 30 ft.

STR	DEX	CON	INT	WIS	CHA
2 (–4)	16 (+3)	10 (+0)	20 (+5)	16 (+3)	15 (+2)

SKILLS Arcana +8, Investigation +8, Nature +8, Perception +6

SENSES darkvision 60 ft., passive Perception 16

LANGUAGES Abyssal, Common, Draconic, Sylvan

CHALLENGE 5 (1,800 XP) **PROFICIENCY BONUS** +3

Magic Resistance. Lapis has advantage on saving throws against spells and other magical effects.

ACTIONS

Multiattack. Lapis makes two Poisonous Blast attacks.

Poisonous Blast. *Melee or Ranged Spell Attack:* +6 to hit, reach 5 ft. or range 120 ft., one target. *Hit:* 14 (2d10 + 3) poison damage.

Flesh Shaping. Lapis can mold living flesh as if it were clay. She can touch a living creature and shape 5 inches of its flesh into any shape that suits her purpose. For instance, she could close over a mouth, bind an appendage to a torso, or even remove the chunk of flesh entirely. Flesh that is removed continues to live and function normally if Lapis uses this feature to remove it. The effects of Flesh Shaping can be reversed by a *lesser restoration* or *greater restoration* spell.

Spellcasting. Lapis casts one of the following spells, requiring no material components and using Intelligence as the spellcasting ability (spell save DC 16):

At will: *alter self, mending, minor illusion, prestidigitation, vicious mockery*

3/day each: *blink, enhance ability, enlarge/reduce*

2/day each: *gaseous form, haste, invisibility*

1/day: *polymorph*

BONUS ACTIONS

Body Enhancement (Recharge 4–6). Lapis has performed extensive experiments on herself. She can activate one of her enhancements, gaining one of the following abilities until the start of her next turn:

Acute Vision. The range of her darkvision doubles and she has advantage on Perception checks, but she gains vulnerability to thunder damage.

Armored Epidermis. Her AC improves by 4, but her speed is halved.

Increased Celerity. Her speed increases by 20 feet, but she has disadvantage on Constitution saving throws.

Lubricious Skin. She has advantage on rolls to escape from a grapple and on saving throws against gaining the restrained condition, but she has disadvantage on Strength checks.

Regenerative Admixture. She regains 10 (2d6 + 3) hit points, but she has disadvantage on Dexterity saving throws.

TOLF TOADLASHES

Tolf Toadlashes, Skirl Master of Wailing and Lord of the Battle Syrinx, is the Red Moon's official minstrel and musician. He is a carillon fey from a sidereal realm of music and melody. Tolf left his home to pursue his obsession with something he calls "discordant arrangements," though most others would refer to it as torture and murder. He uses his magic and music to support his fellow bandits and to cause as much misery among his foes as possible. Tolf is the unofficial quartermaster of the Red Moon gang and social director. He is hopelessly in love with Mimsy, but she doesn't return his feelings and his adoration is beginning to turn to hatred. When not in combat, Tolf plays elaborate practical jokes, some of which are survivable by the targets of his mirth.

Tolf Toadlashes

Skirl Master of Wailing and Lord of the Battle Syrinx

Tiny Fey, Chaotic Neutral

ARMOR CLASS 14

HIT POINTS 76 (17d4 + 34)

SPEED 20 ft., fly 40 ft.

STR	DEX	CON	INT	WIS	CHA
10 (+0)	16 (+3)	14 (+2)	10 (+0)	16 (+3)	18 (+4)

SKILLS Performance +6, Stealth +5

DAMAGE IMMUNITIES thunder

SENSES passive Perception 13

LANGUAGES Common, Umbral

CHALLENGE 4 (1,100 XP) **PROFICIENCY BONUS** +2

Magic Resistance. Tolf has advantage on saving throws against spells and other magical effects.

Ventriloquism. Whenever Tolf speaks, he can choose a point in space within 60 feet of himself that he can see, and his voice emanates from that point.

ACTIONS

Multiattack. Tolf makes two Screaming Rapier or Shortbow attacks and uses Confusing Whispers.

Screaming Rapier. *Melee Weapon Attack:* +5 to hit, range 5 ft., one target. *Hit:* 1 piercing damage plus 9 (2d8) thunder damage.

Shortbow. *Ranged Weapon Attack:* +5 to hit, range 40/160 ft., one creature. *Hit:* 1 piercing damage, and the target must succeed on a DC 13 Constitution saving throw or become poisoned for 1 minute. If the result of its saving throw is 5 or lower, the target falls unconscious for 1 minute, or until it takes damage, or until another creature uses an action to shake it awake.

Confusing Whispers. Tolf can use his Ventriloquism to whisper disturbing truths into the ears of a foe within 60 feet that he can see. The creature must succeed on a DC 13 Wisdom saving throw or use its reaction to make one attack or cast a cantrip that deals damage against one of its allies. If no ally is within range of an attack or an appropriate spell, the creature attacks itself.

Tormenting Fluting (Recharge 5–6). Tolf uses his pan flute to play music drawn from the heart of chaos. Each creature within 20 feet of a point in space that Tolf specifies must make a DC 13 Constitution saving throw. On a failed save, a creature takes 13 (3d8) necrotic damage and falls prone. On a successful save, a creature takes half as much damage and does not fall prone.

BONUS ACTIONS

Emboldening Cry. Tolf shouts encouraging words to an ally within 30 feet that he can see. If the chosen ally can hear Tolf, that creature can use its reaction to make one melee attack or to take the Disengage action.

GANG ACTIVITIES

The Red Moon Bandits can be used in your campaign as enemies in a single encounter, foes for an extended adventure, or as the heart of an extended campaign centered around thwarting Mimsy's goal of bringing the Dark Pan into the mortal world.

TIER 1

Mimsy directs her bandits to hunt travelers and caravans moving through the wasteland with violent tricks and pranks. Each "hunt" must bring back the bodies of any who perish to turn over to Lapis. At the same time, Tolf is dispatched with a small band to search the wastes around their hideout, looking for magical items to power the primary fleshgate. More dark fey flock to Mimsy's banner, along with a scattering of humanoids eager to serve Dark Pan or capitalize on the band's growing wealth.

TIER 2

Once the primary gate becomes active, Mimsy increases the number and frequency of her raids. She breaks the bandits up into smaller bands, sending them to establish new hideouts across the wastelands. The goal shifts to taking captives who are delivered to Mimsy's stronghold, the Hall of Teeth and Toes. Those who are not captured or forced to join the Red Moon are slaughtered to feed the fey's growing bloodlust. The methods of each band's hunt are left up to each group, leading to a wide variety of attacks, tricks, and pranks. Mostly formed fleshgates are transported to each hideout. The growing power of Dark Pan begins to physically affect the wastes, causing chaos storms, planar portals, and seeping corruption.

TIER 3

With the resources of the wasteland waning, Mimsy turns her attention to the surrounding lands. The Red Moon, now the size of a small army, spreads out in individual bands to ransack farms, abduct travelers, and even assault villages and small towns. Nothing is as simple as a straightforward attack. The "assaults" of the Red Moon take the form of complicated tricks, cons, and pranks, with blood and death resulting instead of laughter. The network of fleshgates disgorge chaos creatures who rampage across the countryside.

TIER 4

Mimsy and Tolf set forth with their most elite bandits to begin gathering the arcane items needed for the final ritual to summon Dark Pan. These include holy relics, items of great historical value, and powerful artifacts. The trail of thefts leaves a wake of ruin behind. At the same time, Lapis travels with a heavy guard to each smaller hideout, activating each fleshgate one by one. Once they have the items, Mimsy gathers all the Red Moon in the Hall of Teeth and Toes. In secret, Mimsy, Lapis, and Tolf know the ritual to bring Dark Pan to the mortal world requires sacrificing every member of the Red Moon as raw material to form a corporal body for their chaotic god.

SPIDER FACE GOBLIN TRIBE

Goblins are one of the wastelands' most pervasive creatures. Tribal hordes sweep across the wastes like malignant insects, filling every crevice. While all tribes suffer a lack of morality and instill hatred and fear, there are some whose very existence breeds sorrow and nightmares.

While malicious opportunists and pestilent sneaks infest most goblin tribes, the Spider Face goblins embody pure madness. Driven by the guidance of insane, chaos goblin priests that channel the will of the elder spider god Atlach-Nacha, they have risen from a clan of scavengers to a tribe of monstrous, near demon-like cannibals. Spider Face goblins do not communicate with other creatures or goblins outside their tribe. Instead, they view all other beings as prey or blood sacrifices for their god Atlach-Nacha. Proclaiming worshipers of the Spider God superior to all other creatures, they consider themselves an elder race. They see themselves as mortal receptacles for divine power and fully embrace the timeless chaos that spawned them at the beginning of creation. Consequently, they disdain younger races such as elves, orcs, dwarves, and humans and believe them hideously marked with the scars of their devotion to pitiful laws and misbegotten efforts to tame chaos through organization and manipulation.

The tribe does not refer to themselves as Spider Face goblins. They bear a name given to them by outsiders who identify them by their discolored skin splotches and self-inflicted scars through which they express their devotion to the spider god. Their chaos goblin priests preach that they are the chosen children of Altach-Nacha, The Great Spider, and all bear the marks of their creator. Malformation and ugliness are inherent to their kind, perceived as beauty and celebrated as the divine work of unfettered chaos. Some outsiders claim the tribe took the name Spider Face because their blemishes resemble spiders, but such claims are ignorant.

The origin of the Spider Face goblins remains obscure. Because the tribe's telepathic priests can access their collective memories and history, they have little need for writing except for use in performing rituals or spellcasting.

Tribe members speak little. Instead, they use a unique sign language punctuated with grunts and clicks. Those who speak too much have their tongues ritually cut out to help keep the silence. As a result, outsiders attempting to research their culture or history struggle to acquire accurate information. Below are several commonly held beliefs about Spider Face goblins.

1. Spider-Face goblins are anarchic. They look for meaning in entropy and believe that laws obscure reality.
2. Reality exists in multiple states and connects to all time and space. Certain states of existence open the doors to reality. The goblins believe in eight realities: pain, change, dream, birth, suffocation, sleep deprivation, starvation, and death.

Spider Face goblins survive by scavenging and raiding. They mark the perimeters of their territories with vile effigies and traps or baits to lure prey. Like most goblins, the Spider Face tribe members are ambush fighters and lay elaborate traps targeting caravans and other travelers.

The wastelands hold sparse resources. Supplies in the tent sprawl frequently run short, and the chaos goblin priests and warlords demand their constant replenishing. The Spider Face goblins organize frequent raids on neighboring goblin tribes or anything that enters their territory. Spider Face goblins have little need for material wealth and don't use money except when forced to bargain with outsiders, baiting traps, paying bribes, or as spell components. Instead, they seek prisoners, which they either eat or sacrifice. When warring with neighboring clans, they take the fallen bodies as spoils for food and blood sacrifices. Spider Face goblins prefer to capture enemies alive. Captives are bound and then shunted so the goblins can tap their blood as a food source. This horrific practice eventually kills the captive as the goblins slowly feed off the blood, exsanguinating the victim as a spider drains its prey. All remain silent around prisoners, listening for the reaction and attempting to hear the universe's secrets, which they believe victims utter in death.

RELIGION

The Spider Face goblin tribe worships Atlach-Nacha, an elder god that lives in the outer reaches of the Void. Chaos goblin priests describe Atlach-Nacha as a colossal greenish-black spider with a hideously deformed face and bulging pale eyes resembling a goblin. They believe the spider god spins webs that connect the Void to various points through time and space. These webs form bridges that span the gaps between worlds, the goblins believe life is only a trial in which a mortal prepares itself to cross one of the bridges. All bridges lead to Atlach-Nacha within the black void pit at the end of the multiverse. The worthy become her emissaries to whom she reveals the eight realities and whose purpose is to guide blood sacrifices to the Spider Gods' realm.

Priests seek to connect all members of the tribe to Atlach-Nacha. Her webs stretch through the loom of time and space. Those able to free themselves from the veil of reality understand all creation gleams within her gossamer woven web. Atlach-Nacha reveals the web to the chaos priests. In turn, priests teach that altered states hold value, and all threads connect to power or open them to the whispered entities that live beyond the material realm and reveal secrets of the universe. To attain these altered states, all tribe members imbue potent arcane drugs and practice sleep deprivation, starvation, and deliberate acts of pain. They also believe dreams hold as much significance as waking moments, and during rest periods, priests telepathically feed on the dreams of the clan.

Chaos goblin priests host anarchic ceremonies and offerings to Atlach-Nacha. Worship appears spontaneous. They may demand violent duels, eating contests, chewing fire toads, ritual torture, or blinding. Pain-inducing violence is a crucial element, for the goblins exalt pain as a sacred gift, a connection to the spirit world that strips reality and reveals cosmic truth.

Upon reaching the age of the calling, children transitioning into adulthood must undergo a sacred trial to petition Atlach-Nacha for acceptance into the tribe. First, chaos goblin priests bind the candidate with ropes, then lower them into a spider-filled pit to face the Spider God's judgment. For the next 24 hours, the candidate is sealed within the pit and is feasted upon by swarms of spiders. If the individual survives, the goblins believe Atlach-Nacha has blessed them, and they become full-fledged members of the tribe. The spider bites prominently scar the devotees. Priests read the patterns of the scars, allowing them insights into the fate that Atlach-Nacha bestows upon each candidate. The scars determine the individual's purpose and position within the tribe, including the path to priesthood. After that, tribe members endure the pit multiple times throughout their lives to gain guidance and reconnect their fate with Atlach-Nacha. Each new pattern of scars reveals new meaning and purpose, even if the purpose is to die in sacrifice to Atlach-Nacha.

THE TENT SPRAWL

The Spider Face goblins live within a sprawling tent city deep within the scorched wasteland plains. Crudely crafted tents of skin and hide stretch across struts of bone and wood threaded with dried entrails and encircle towering effigies erected from stone and fallen branches and skinned with the hides of beasts. The tent structures are temporary, and the sprawl shifts slowly, changing its shape and position as it traces the patterns of Atlach-Nacha's webs through constellations in the night sky. The goblins dig tunnels beneath the tent sprawl, creating a maze of warrens that simulate their god's web and its connection to all things. The small, cramped passages make travel difficult for any except goblins. The waste's tough, rocky clay makes tunneling difficult. The warrens are shallow, and the arid, unstable sediments make them prone to collapse or flood during rainy seasons. The goblins mark the perimeter of the sprawl with gruesome effigies resembling skull-headed spiders fashioned from bone, dried gut, and broken weapons. They lay traps around the effigies, such as pits filled with poisoned spikes, and bait the effigies with jewels or gold to lure greedy travelers to their deaths.

Within the sprawls, tribe members congregate in massive swarms clumped together in close quarters, in unsanitary living conditions that often spread diseases. As a result, the goblins suffer high infant mortality rates and short lives. The sprawl is partitioned into smaller districts or villages under the autonomous authority of different priests and warlords. They do not appear to make familial distinctions. Individual goblins perform actions either deemed tribe or not tribe. Villages aren't always on good terms and sometimes raid or steal from other villages in the sprawl.

The goblins waste nothing, though frugality doesn't drive their actions. Instead, the chaos goblin priests' obsessions spur them to interact with everything that might have meaning, including objects and deeds. In chaos, everything has significance and offers some meaning or clue, no matter how morbid or seemingly unimportant.

Some outsiders speculate Spider Face goblins eat their dead. Additionally, they are known to use the bones and skin of their kind as resources, though it remains unknown whether the goblins do this out of reverence or practicality, or perhaps both.

The tribe doesn't domesticate animals and allows captured animals to turn feral. Strays of all sorts wander the sprawl, skittish and aggressive. Any non-goblin creature wandering the sprawl is considered part of the tribe's communal property, with first spoils claimed by residents of the district or village where the creature was collected. This practice includes any intelligent creatures, as the tribe doesn't recognize the autonomy of non-Spider Face goblins.

The chaos goblins are highly xenophobic and don't accept any outsiders except other servants of Atlach-Nacha. Only a chaos goblin priest can determine whether one is a true worshiper, and priests frequently disagree with each other. A true worshipper is willing to take the trial of the spider pit, ritually mutilate themselves, or sacrifice themselves as a blood offering to prove their devotion. Historically, the Spider Face goblins have only accepted a handful of outsiders into the tribe, all before founding the tent sprawl.

While some tales of individuals visiting the tent sprawl circulate the wastes, they are highly suspect. Nearly all such rumors describe a hero bringing the goblins an offering or chaos goblin priests viewing the individual's arrival as a sign. However, Spider Face goblins infamously attack non-Spider Face goblins on sight. Experience dictates that traveling anywhere near the sprawl is extremely dangerous. Even the most ruthless bandits and wasteland reavers give the sprawl a wide berth when crossing through their territory.

NOTABLE FIGURES

Aside from the words of chaos goblin priests, no formal government exists, and the goblins uphold no consistent code of law. Judgment of their priests falls within the moment. Their will is that of the Spider God, fickle and capricious, and their demands shift without notice, depending on current needs or whims. Those below the priest must rely on strength and intimidation when bargaining or claiming spoils. When not following direct orders from the priests, warlords seize power when they feel ambitious or confident enough to take it.

WARLORDS

Priests enforce their absolute authority by the ritual ascension of specially culled tribe members given the title "warlord." Priests control warlords, choosing them from the hordes and then altering them with drugs and magic to serve as their emissaries to the rest of the tribe.

Under the undying oath of Atlach-Nacha, these brutish butchers drive their clans to raid and pilfer the surrounding lands. Theirs is the task of spreading her web and catching "flies" to appease her bestial hunger.

Warlords infrequently speak the phrase "Graz Ak Ng'wa." Its meaning is unknown, but possibly how they refer to themselves, or it may be a title used to describe their priests. On the other hand, it may be an older name from when the priest was more connected to the material realm.

Spider Face Goblin Warlord

Small Humanoid (Goblinoid), Chaotic Evil

ARMOR CLASS 15 (leather armor)
HIT POINTS 99 (18d6+36)
SPEED 30 ft.

STR	DEX	CON	INT	WIS	CHA
12 (+1)	16 (+3)	15 (+2)	10 (+0)	13 (+1)	10 (+0)

SKILLS Athletics +4, Intimidation +3, Perception +4, Stealth +6

SENSES darkvision 60 ft., passive Perception 14
LANGUAGES Common, Goblin
CHALLENGE 5 (1,800 XP)   **PROFICIENCY BONUS** +3

Repugnant. Spider Face goblins are repulsive in appearance to those outside their race. Whenever a non-goblin makes a Charisma-based ability check to attempt a social interaction with a Spider Face goblin, the creature has disadvantage on the check.

ACTIONS

Multiattack. The goblin warlord makes two Flail attacks.

Flail. *Melee Weapon Attack:* +4 to hit, reach 5 ft., one target. *Hit:* 5 (1d8 + 1) bludgeoning damage.

Elixir of Battle Rage. The goblin warlord carries a supply of a foul elixir that it uses to trigger a battle rage. If the goblin warlord consumes one draught of the substance, it gains advantage on Strength checks and Strength saving throws, and its Strength-based melee weapon attacks gain a +2 bonus to damage. The warlord also gains resistance to bludgeoning, piercing, and slashing damage from nonmagical attacks. The warlord's battle rage lasts for 5 rounds or until the warlord is knocked unconscious. At the end of the battle rage, the warlord is poisoned until it finishes a long rest. After consuming a dose of the elixir, the warlord cannot benefit from another dose for 24 hours.

CHAOS GOBLIN PRIESTS

The Spider Face tribe's priests maintain only partial existence within the material world; their minds and consciousnesses exist almost entirely in the Void and outer realms, leaving only their withered and sickly bodies. Their blank faces bear no expression and unnervingly stare outward through their pupilless eyes. Few speak, their lips stitched shut. Instead, they communicate telepathically. Chaos goblin priests sustain themselves with potions and nameless fluids, force-fed by tubes or injected with shunts. Some say the chaos goblin priests do not even bleed and are no longer living creatures. Others contest that the chaos-spawn are no longer goblins but spirits possessing the goblins' mortal flesh.

Chaos goblin priests seek to become reborn—transforming themselves and their followers through arcane surgeries, imbibing foul solutions, and vile orgiastic rituals. Priests and tribe members willingly undergo ritual mutilations to access divine insight or draw power to themselves from the Void. Mutilations include the sacrifice of eyes, the stitching shut of the mouth or removal of the tongue, scarification, or the lopping off of fingers, ears, or even a hand.

Priests appear entirely withered, as if all blood was drawn from them. They frequently partake in ritual bloodletting, feeding upon each other's blood, or perform offerings in which they draw blood and feed it to the Spider God. The deep lines crisscrossing the priests' withered faces resemble a spider's webbing. Some of these appear to be self-afflicted scars, highlighting the mystic patterns.

If chaos goblin priests spoke, perhaps one might expect to gain more clarity of their connections to the outer realms, their rites, and philosophies. Unfortunately, their history and secrets are their own, incomprehensible. Outsiders can only judge the goblin's behaviors and actions.

Chaos Goblin Priest

Small Humanoid (Goblinoid), Chaotic Evil

ARMOR CLASS 15 (natural armor)
HIT POINTS 108 (24d6 + 24)
SPEED 30 ft.

STR	DEX	CON	INT	WIS	CHA
8(–1)	14 (+2)	13 (+1)	10 (+0)	17 (+3)	12 (+1)

SKILLS Arcana +3, History +3, Insight +6, Religion +3, Stealth +5
DAMAGE RESISTANCES psychic
CONDITION IMMUNITIES frightened
SENSES darkvision 60 ft., passive Perception 13
LANGUAGES Common, Goblin, telepathy 120 ft.
CHALLENGE 7 (2,900 XP)   **PROFICIENCY BONUS** +3

Alien Mind. Any creature trying to use magical means to read the goblin priest's thoughts must make a successful DC 14 Wisdom save or take 7 (2d6) psychic damage from exposure to the horrors of the priest's alien mind. This damage doesn't prevent the creature from accessing the priest's mind.

ACTIONS

Spear. *Melee Weapon Attack:* +4 to hit, reach 5 ft., one target. *Hit:* 5 (1d6 + 2) piercing damage.

Psychic Stab (Recharge 6). The goblin priest targets one creature that it can sense within 30 feet. The target must make a DC 12 Intelligence saving throw, taking 7 (2d6) psychic damage on a failed save or half as much damage on a successful one.

Spellcasting. The goblin priest casts one of the following spells, using Wisdom as the spellcasting ability (spell save DC 14):

At will: *guidance, poison spray, resistance, thaumaturgy*

3/day each: *command, inflict wounds, magic circle, spirit guardians**

1/day each: *bestow curse, divination, geas, giant insect*

*The spirit guardians look like hideous goblin-faced spiders.

BONUS ACTIONS

Nimble Escape. The goblin priest takes the Disengage or Hide action.

Swarm Host (Recharge 6). The goblin priest targets a willing ally to serve as a birthing vessel for a swarm of spiders. The priest must be able to contact the ally telepathically. The targeted creature's stomach suddenly begins to bloat. The ally falls to the ground and expels a **swarm of insects** (spiders) from its mouth. The swarm attacks the nearest creature that is not a worshipper of Atlach-Nacha. The swarm dissipates after 10 minutes or when it is destroyed.

WASTELAND WANDERERS

All manner of communities exists in the wastes, but for some, the desolate stretches represent the perfect place to eke out a solitary existence far from the prying eyes of civilization.

DJER HUSKEL'S ABOMINATION

Dull steel plates and clockwork mechanisms have been fused with the stitched flesh of an uncountable number of creatures to create an unsettling figure of meat and metal. When spoken to, the mortal-machine construct responds in a voice that is both delicate and resonant. Its gears tick rhythmically as they turn.

Before she died and was rebuilt by her obsessed husband, the creature now known as Djer Huskel's abomination was a beloved singer and performer. When she was killed in the collapse of the performance hall that destroyed much of her body, he called upon his mastery of necromancy and engineering to preserve what he could of her and construct her a new,

MAD WIZARD'S EXPERIMENTS TABLE

When the brave adventurers venture into the mad wizard's current residence, they discover a bevy of strange experiments, ongoing horrors, and other ephemera of her craft.

d10	Experiments and other Horrors
1	An exquisite sword rests on a pedestal beneath glass. A sign on the glass reads, "No! Too Dangerous"
2	Magical items are set into a device that drains their power and directs it into a fossilized dragon egg.
3	On a slab is a powerful-looking metal construct with working, flesh-and-blood organs pulsing away in its open chest compartment.
4	An unremarkable-looking felt doll sits in the center of several protective rings of runes and symbols.
5	The severed heads of powerful monsters are attached to an eldritch machine and give prophetic advice when levers are pulled.
6	Dangerous monsters and poisonous substances are connected to an alchemical apparatus seemingly designed to distill the perfect dram of whiskey.
7	Inside a soundproof crystal sphere, a human screams silently as he is slowly being transformed into a different type of humanoid.
8	A strange device made of bone, gemstones, and large insectoid bodies is aimed at a scale model of an important capital city. When the device is activated, a miniature earthquake destroys the city.
9	A very helpful and friendly mimic lab assistant named "Weldon" dusts racks of ingredients and reagents.
10	Visibly decaying protections surround a floating rift that opens into a realm of swirling madness and chaos.

more durable body of corpses and clockworks. When he completed his project and animated the result, he was horrified by the unrecognizable creature that spoke in his dead wife's voice.

Always Alone. Unable to bring himself to destroy the abomination, its creator teleported it to a distant, sparsely populated wasteland and left it to wander. Since its banishment, the construct has roved, ever searching, but not cognizant of what it is looking for. Often, it sings softly and sweetly to itself, not really understanding the words but comforted by them all the same. If it becomes confused, it chants the words "Djer Huskel" in a steady, repetitive stream. If asked what the words mean, the construct can't provide an answer. When confronted by other creatures, the abomination is as likely to behave aggressively as benignly. If it happens across a source of music, it stops all activities and listens in place until the music ceases, wherein it becomes active again.

Djer Huskel's Abomination

Medium Construct, Chaotic Neutral

ARMOR CLASS 15
HIT POINTS 114 (12d8 + 60)
SPEED 30 ft.

STR	DEX	CON	INT	WIS	CHA
20 (+5)	12 (+1)	20 (+5)	8 (−1)	10 (+0)	8 (−1)

DAMAGE RESISTANCES acid, fire, lightning
DAMAGE IMMUNITIES poison; bludgeoning, piercing, and slashing from nonmagical attacks that aren't adamantine
CONDITION IMMUNITIES charmed, exhaustion, frightened, paralyzed, petrified, poisoned
SENSES darkvision 60 ft., passive Perception 10
LANGUAGES Common, can sing in Elvish but doesn't understand the language
CHALLENGE 8 (3,900 XP)   **PROFICIENCY BONUS** +3

Aberrant Construction. Djer Huskel's abomination reacts as noted below when it is subjected to certain effects or stimuli.

- When the abomination hears music, such as when a creature makes a Charisma (Performance) check, it becomes incapacitated while it listens.
- When the abomination is hit with an attack that deals cold damage, it takes no damage and instead recovers a number of hit points equal to half the damage rolled.
- When the abomination takes lightning damage, as a reaction, it can immediately move up to half its speed and make a Slam attack.
- When the abomination takes psychic damage, it must make a successful DC 16 Charisma saving throw or be stunned until the end of its next turn.

Unusual Nature. Djer Huskel's abomination doesn't require air, food, drink, or sleep.

ACTIONS

Multiattack. Djer Huskel's abomination makes two Slam attacks or two Static Discharge attacks, or one Slam attack and one Static Discharge attack.

Slam. *Melee Weapon Attack:* +8 to hit, reach 5 ft., one target. *Hit:* 16 (2d10 + 5) bludgeoning damage plus 13 (3d8) lightning damage.

Static Discharge. *Ranged Weapon Attack:* +4 to hit, range 90 ft., one creature. *Hit:* 13 (3d8) lightning damage.

Electrical Overload (Recharge 6). Djer Huskel's abomination releases stored-up electricity in a 30-foot radius around itself. Each creature in the area must make a DC 16 Dexterity saving throw, taking 27 (6d8) lightning damage on a failed save, or half as much damage on a successful one.

MAD WIZARD

The wastelands hold enough forbidden secrets, fell monsters, and corrupted arcana to break the mind of those who simply wish to cross its ruin-strewn environs. The risk is even greater for those who set out to plumb the depths of the wastes' wonders and horrors. Occasionally, some succumb to the ever-changing torments of chaos and reappear as shattered shells of their former selves. The mad wizard is one such sorrowful figure.

This mad wizard was once a powerful archmage, wielding powers and spells few could match. She walked the halls of power, advised kings and emperors, and the fate of the world, or even the planes, hinged on her actions. Not so anymore. Today, she wears torn and tattered magical robes, decorated with odd symbols that make sense only she can decipher. Her belt holds wands and potions alongside random objects that happened to catch her eye. The mad wizard maintains a constant dialogue with herself, posing questions and answering them in the same voice. Though she is unkempt and has the air of unpredictable wildness in her eye, her powerful arcane skills are by no means diminished.

It is difficult, perhaps impossible, to fully understand the plans and goals of someone touched by chaos, especially because these goals tend to change frequently. It is important to understand, however, that to the mad wizard, it makes perfect sense. She is often found guarding a particular ruin, dungeon, or well of magical power that acts as the focus of her latest obsession. Occasionally, she will seek out travelers or adventurers if she believes they need certain items or information or out of an unconscious need for "human" interaction.

Mad Wizard

Small Humanoid (Gnome), Neutral

ARMOR CLASS 17 (torn *robe of the archmagi*)
HIT POINTS 172 (32d8 + 32)
SPEED 30 ft.

STR	DEX	CON	INT	WIS	CHA
10 (+0)	14 (+2)	12 (+1)	20 (+5)	12 (+1)	16 (+3)

SAVING THROWS Int +9, Wis +5
SKILLS Arcana +13, Intimidation +7
DAMAGE RESISTANCES damage from spells
SENSES passive Perception 11
LANGUAGES Abyssal, Common, Celestial, Draconic, Infernal
CHALLENGE 12 (8,400 XP)   **PROFICIENCY BONUS** +4

- ***Legendary Resistance (2/Day).*** If the mad wizard fails a saving throw, she can choose to succeed instead.
- ***Magic Resistance.*** The mad wizard has advantage on saving throws against spells and other magical effects.
- ***Special Equipment.*** The mad wizard wears a torn *robe of the archmagi*, which provides only the benefit to Armor Class.
- ***Unintended Side-Effects.*** Whenever the mad wizard casts a spell, a random creature within 120 feet experiences one of the following magical effects until the start of the mad wizard's next turn:
  - Creature's skin turns a different color.
  - Strange music plays whenever the creature moves or uses an action.
  - Creature's race changes to a random race, though its statistics do not change.
  - Bees or other insects love the creature.
  - Illusory animals caper and frolic around the creature.
  - Creature forgets everyone's names or can speak only in a strange language.
  - Creature gains a new appendage like a tail or arm, but it can't be used to hold or use items.
  - A random Small object falls into an unoccupied space within 5 feet of the creature.
  - The GM creates a similar effect.

ACTIONS

Multiattack. The mad wizard makes two Arcane Burst attacks.

Arcane Burst. *Melee or Ranged Spell Attack:* +8 to hit, reach 5 ft. or range 120 ft., one target. *Hit:* 21 (3d10 + 5) force damage.

Channel Raw Magic. A creature of the mad wizard's choice within 60 feet that she can see must make a DC 17 Charisma saving throw. On a failed save, the target takes 22 (4d10) psychic damage, and one of the following secondary effects is triggered. On a successful save, the target takes half as much damage, and a secondary effect does not occur.

- **Chain.** Three additional foes of the mad wizard within 30 feet of the target must make the Charisma saving throw, taking 18 (4d8) lightning damage on a failed save.
- **Blast.** All creatures within 30 feet of the target must make the Charisma saving throw, taking 18 (4d8) fire damage on a failed save.
- **Healing.** The target instantly regains hit points equal to twice the amount of the psychic damage it took.
- **Teleport.** The target is teleported to an unoccupied space within 120 feet.

Laugh with Me (Recharge 5–6). The mad wizard sees the humor in existence, and her laughter is infectious. Each creature within 120 feet of the mad wizard must make a DC 17 Wisdom saving throw. On a failed save, a creature is overcome with laughing, falls prone, and

becomes incapacitated. At the end of each of its turns, and each time it takes damage, the target can make another Wisdom saving throw, ending the effect on itself on a success.

Spellcasting. The mad wizard casts one of the following spells, requiring no material components and using Intelligence as the spellcasting ability (spell save DC 17):

At will: *mage hand, message, prestidigitation*

3/day each: *confusion, counterspell, dispel magic, mage armor*

1/day each: *globe of invulnerability, teleport*

REACTIONS

Shield of Delusion. When the mad wizard is hit by an attack or targeted by a spell, her loose grip on reality protects her. She reduces the damage to 0, and an ally of her choice within 30 feet of her regains a number of hit points equal to the damage that was negated.

LEGENDARY ACTIONS

The mad wizard can take 3 legendary actions, choosing from the options below. Only one legendary action can be used at a time and only at the end of another creature's turn. The mad wizard regains spent legendary actions at the start of her turn.

- **Cast a Spell.** The mad wizard uses Spellcasting.
- **Chaos Magic.** The mad wizard uses Channel Raw Magic.
- **Arcane Regeneration (Costs 2 Actions).** The mad wizard regains an expended spell slot.

MAD WIZARD STORY HOOKS

Adventures involving the mad wizard might include one of the following:

- A caravan master hires the PCs to recover a valuable relic stolen from his wagon during a trek across the wastes. The heroes must track down the mad wizard, who stole the item, before the cult searching for it finds her.
- The mad wizard contacts the PCs, offering important information or a powerful magical item, if they agree to aid her in exploring a particularly dangerous dungeon she discovered beneath the preserved carcass of a titanic monster.
- An important NPC or ally of the PCs is stricken with a magical malady that no spell or curative can remove. The only hope is the mad wizard, who has secured herself inside a mobile fortress trundling through the wastes.

VOID LORD

The tall, enigmatic figure striding through the wasteland seems at odds with the environment. Wearing dark, expensive robes with wide sleeves, the hooded figure looks more suited as an archmage lecturing in an arcane school or advising the powerful in the halls of a royal palace. As the viewer grows closer, disturbing elements begin to stand out. Its limbs do not match. One arm is large, muscled, and ends in a three-clawed hand; the other is too long for the body it is attached to, and the hand has four overly long fingers with far too many joints. When the face of the figure comes into view, it presents a dichotomy. Inexplicable beautiful, it has no discernable gender and parts of it appear to be a mismatch of many kinds of creatures. Most disturbingly, small tentacles reach out from between the folds of its buttoned-up robes. The figure says nothing as it gestures, then six rips in space open around itself and chaos follows.

The Void Lord is a stalking predator, feeding living creatures to the portals it opens. Those who are pulled, screaming, into its gateways do not return. It was once a dark god worshipped as a divine representation of the Void, the nothingness between planes. But that was long ago. Today, it has only a few scattered followers, mostly half-crazed cultists and apocalyptic nihilists, and has but a fragment of its divine power. It will feed on any living creature but seems to favor spellcasters or those of magical linages.

Encounters with the Void Lord can occur in any area of the wastes or where magical corruption is strong, but it can be attracted to more civilized areas by especially strong magic events.

Void Lord

Medium Aberration, Typically Chaotic Evil

ARMOR CLASS 16

HIT POINTS 153 (18d8 + 72)

SPEED 30 ft.

STR	DEX	CON	INT	WIS	CHA
14 (+2)	15 (+2)	18 (+4)	12 (+1)	14 (+2)	18 (+4)

SAVING THROWS Con +8, Wis +6

SKILLS Arcana +5, Insight +6

DAMAGE RESISTANCES cold; bludgeoning, piercing, and slashing from nonmagical attacks

DAMAGE IMMUNITIES psychic

CONDITION IMMUNITIES charmed, frightened, prone

SENSES blindsight 60 ft., darkvision 60 ft., passive Perception 20

LANGUAGES Common, Void Speech, telepathy 60 ft.

CHALLENGE 10 (5,900 XP)   **PROFICIENCY BONUS** +4

Amorphous. The Void Lord can move through a space as narrow as 1 inch wide without squeezing.

Immutable Form. The Void Lord is immune to any spell or effect that would alter its form.

Legendary Resistance (1/Day). If the Void Lord fails a saving throw, it can choose to succeed instead.

Magic Resistance. The Void Lord has advantage on saving throws against spells and other magical effects.

Spatially Reactive. In addition to its normal reaction, the Void Lord can take one extra reaction every round in a combat, but it can only use this bonus reaction to use its Escape Jaunt feature.

ACTIONS

Multiattack. The Void Lord makes one Void Strike attack and uses its Grasping Portal.

Voidstrike. *Melee or Ranged Spell Attack:* +6 to hit, reach 5 ft. or range 120 ft., one target. *Hit:* 7 (2d6) cold damage plus 7 (2d6) force damage.

Grasping Portal. A rubbery tentacle emerges from a portal that opens in the air near a creature that the Void Lord can see within 60 feet of it. The creature must make a DC 16 Dexterity saving throw or be restrained for 1 minute. A restrained target can repeat the Dexterity

VOID LORD IN MIDGARD

In outward appearance, the Void Lord bears striking similarities to another enigmatic wanderer, Hune the Doorlord. This is not a coincidence. More than ten thousand years ago, in the world before, Karakhune, the God of Portals, stood in eternal conflict with his dark reflection, Khaalga Olsgol, the Hungering Void. When the old gods fell and Midgard was fashioned from the bones of the first giant, the twin deities became pale shadows of their former selves. The Doorlord was reduced to his core function: the creation of portals. Similarly, the Void Lord became a near mindless entity seeking to fulfill his intended purpose. However, the magical gateways he creates exist to consume living creatures. The fringe religious scholars of Zobeck's Society of Speculative Divinity theorize the Void Lord lacks enough worshippers to sustain its divine spark and thus makes up for the lack by sacrificing souls or life force to the Void. While exceedingly rare, some historical evidence suggests that when the Doorlord and the Void Lord cross paths, a so-called "Duel of Portals" occurs. The last such meeting occurred two hundred years ago in the south of Beldestan, on the site of Albathra, the pock-marked mountain. The Void Lord is most likely encountered in the Red Wastes, the Eastern Wilderness, the Goblin Wastes, Black Lotus Mesa, the Aggesal Plains of the Southlands, and other wastelands or areas of magical corruption.

saving throw at the end of each of its turns, ending the effect on itself on a success. The Void Lord can have only one Grasping Portal active at a time.

Gaze into the Void (Recharge 5–6). The Void Lord opens a portal filled with swirling chaos. Each creature within 60 feet that can see the portal must make a DC 16 Wisdom saving throw. On a failed save, a creature is charmed. A creature charmed in this way is incapacitated and has a speed of 0. A charmed target can repeat the saving throw at the end of each of its turns, ending the effect on itself on a success. Otherwise, the effect ends if the target takes damage or if someone uses an action to shake the target out of its stupor.

BONUS ACTIONS

Dimensional Step. The Void Lord can teleport up to 30 feet to an unoccupied space that it can see.

REACTIONS

Escape Jaunt. When a creature the Void Lord can see attacks it with a melee weapon, it opens a portal in its space. The Void Lord immediately enters the portal and reappears in an unoccupied space up to 10 feet away.

LEGENDARY ACTIONS

The Void Lord can take 3 legendary actions, choosing from the options below. Only one legendary action can be used at a time and only at the end of another creature's turn. The Void Lord regains spent legendary actions at the start of its turn.

Clawed Portal. A portal appears within 60 feet of the Void Lord and a clawed hand emerges, swiping at a creature within 10 feet. The target must succeed on a DC 16 Constitution saving throw or take 14 (4d6) slashing damage.

Eye Portal. A portal appears within 60 feet of the Void Lord and a glowing eye emerges, shooting a beam of energy at a creature within 60 feet. The target must succeed on a DC 16 Intelligence saving throw or take 13 (2d12) psychic damage.

Fanged Portal. A portal ringed with sharp teeth appears within 60 feet of the Void Lord, and the teeth bite a creature within 5 feet. The target must succeed on a DC 16 Dexterity saving throw or take 13 (3d8) piercing damage.

Void Portal. A portal appears in an unoccupied space within 60 feet of the Void Lord, and intense gravitational energy emitting from it pulls at all creatures within 30 feet of the portal. Each creature in range must succeed on a DC 16 Strength saving throw or be pulled 15 feet in a straight line toward the portal, stopping in an unoccupied space as close to the portal as possible.

VOID LORD STORY HOOKS

Adventures involving the Void Lord might include one of the following:

- Transported by the Doorlord, the PCs find themselves outside a village under attack by the Void Lord.
- Hurrying to reach an important location, the PCs need to cross a narrow bridge over a high gorge, but the Void Lord blocks the center of the span.
- A mage's critical experiment in the wastes attracts the interest of the Void Lord, and the PCs must protect their employer long enough for her to finish her work.

CHAPTER 4
PLACES OF CHAOS

This chapter presents 11 unique locations found in the wastes for exploration and adventure. Each locale has a map and description to make it immediately ready for the Game Master's use when adventuring.

BLEAKSPIRE, TOWER OF THE LICH KING

Bleakspire, foreboding tower of the Lich King, stands in a remote valley deep in the flinty hills of the wastes. Four hundred years ago, the valley was the site of a fiercely fought battle between warring magocracies, and the rocky ground around the tower is still littered with half-buried ancient bones and rusting weapons. Bleakspire is a slim, 100-foot-tall tower of bone-white marble; its uppermost story is shaped like a grinning skull wearing an iron crown.

The Lich King was once known as Svatobor the Dauntless, one of the greatest archmages who ever lived. During the Mage War, Svatobor defeated the sorcerer Aurufina Stormsoul with the aid of his infamous warlord Gralvrak Magebane (now the Lord of Ruin) and banished her general Karvos Deathstealer to the Eleven Hells. When Gralvrak was killed, Svatobor used long-forgotten magic to reincarnate his loyal commander as an oni and put the dread colossus Nygethuaac into a dreamlike trance.

Once the Mage War was over, Svatobor withdrew from public life to concentrate on arcane research. As he grew older, the archmage's studies took a dark turn as he focused his attention on the means of prolonging his own life. After making a sinister pact with Charun, God of the Dead, Svatobor achieved lichdom and proclaimed himself the Lich King. He traveled to a hidden valley and raised the tower of Bleakspire in a single night with a powerful ritual that turned the bones of the dead into marble.

The Lich King spends his days deep in study and only leaves his tower when absolutely necessary. The last time he emerged was to battle a pair of angry wasteland dragons that attacked his tower nearly a century ago. Their giant skulls and broken bones lie among the remains of the war dead from 300 years earlier on the floor of the valley.

LICH KING

Since he retired from public life and achieved lichdom, the Lich King has immersed himself in his studies. Although he still wears a tall iron crown as befits his self-proclaimed status, his overall appearance is best described as scholarly and preoccupied, rather than evil and terrifying. Long periods of solitude have led him to mutter absent-mindedly to himself as he conducts his esoteric experiments or flicks through the pages of his dusty tomes with his long bony fingers. The Lich King is usually quite amiable with visitors who have proved themselves capable of meeting Bleakspire's challenges.

Increasingly, the Lich King has focused his energies on an ambitious plan to turn back time and undo the magical apocalypse that devastated the wastes, restoring the lands to their green and pleasant former state. He would then rule over this paradise as its wizard king, a benevolent dictator for a magnificent new age. The Lich King is still a long way off from achieving this vision, but he may seek to employ the PCs and other naive fools to gather some of the components he needs or to fetch him a fresh vial of blood from the dread colossus.

The Lich King uses the standard **lich** stat block but often prepares chaos and other spells from Chapter 6 in place of the usual selection.

ADVENTURE HOOKS

The PCs' wealthy patron has offered them a huge sum for an obscure tome entitled *Orlaxis' Collected Esoteries*. The only extant copy is in the Lich King's library, but the adventurers have heard that the undead wizard sometimes has need of the services of folk like them. If they travel to Bleakspire, the Lich King is willing to give them the book if they obtain the thaumaturgic flow capacitor he needs from the ruins of Whisperhaven so he can complete his machine.

EXPLORING THE TOWER

Bleakspire's location is known only to the Lord of Ruin and a handful of noted explorers and sages of the wastes, so the Lich King has few visitors. Only gray, scrubby bushes and stunted trees grow here, and no birds or animals live in the valley. The tower's ominous appearance encourages those who stumble across it while wandering the hills to give it a wide berth.

REGIONAL EFFECTS

The hidden valley containing the Lich King's Tower is warped by the lich's unnatural presence, which creates one or more of the following effects:

- Scrying and all other divination and detection spells within 1 mile of the tower fail unless the caster succeeds on a DC 18 Intelligence (Arcana) check. A failed check means the spell is still expended but without any positive result.
- Undead creatures have advantage on saving throws against effects that turn undead when within 1 mile of the tower.
- Bones rise from the ground to form 2d6 skeletons when anyone approaches within 500 feet of the tower. The Lich King can see through the eye sockets of any of these skeletons, hear through their ear holes, and can speak through their mouths while doing so. The skeletons do not attack unless attacked first.

GETTING AN INVITATION

The Lich King is often too absorbed in his experiments to pay attention to travelers in the valley but will sometimes speak to them through one of the giant dragon skulls or his skeletons. The PCs can earn an invitation to the tower with a story that piques the Lich King's interest and/or a successful DC 19 Charisma (Deception or Persuasion) check. However, the Lich King will warn them he has placed a few "small challenges" in their path to ensure they are worthy of his time.

TOWER EXTERIOR

Constructed from bone-white marble, Bleakspire stands 100 feet tall and is 50 feet in diameter at the base. The top section of the tower is shaped like a giant skull wearing a pointed crown of black iron. A single wooden door at ground level serves as the obvious entrance.

There are tall, narrow windows halfway up the tower at the level of the antechamber (see below). These windows are opaque from the outside and are AC 21 with 27 hp and a damage threshold of 15. The tower's smooth marble surface makes it hard to climb (DC 25).

PCs who ascend the tower or fly up can land on the top of the skull where the points of the crown form black metal crenellations. There are no access points to the tower interior from the top of the skull or through its eye sockets, nasal cavity, or grinning mouth.

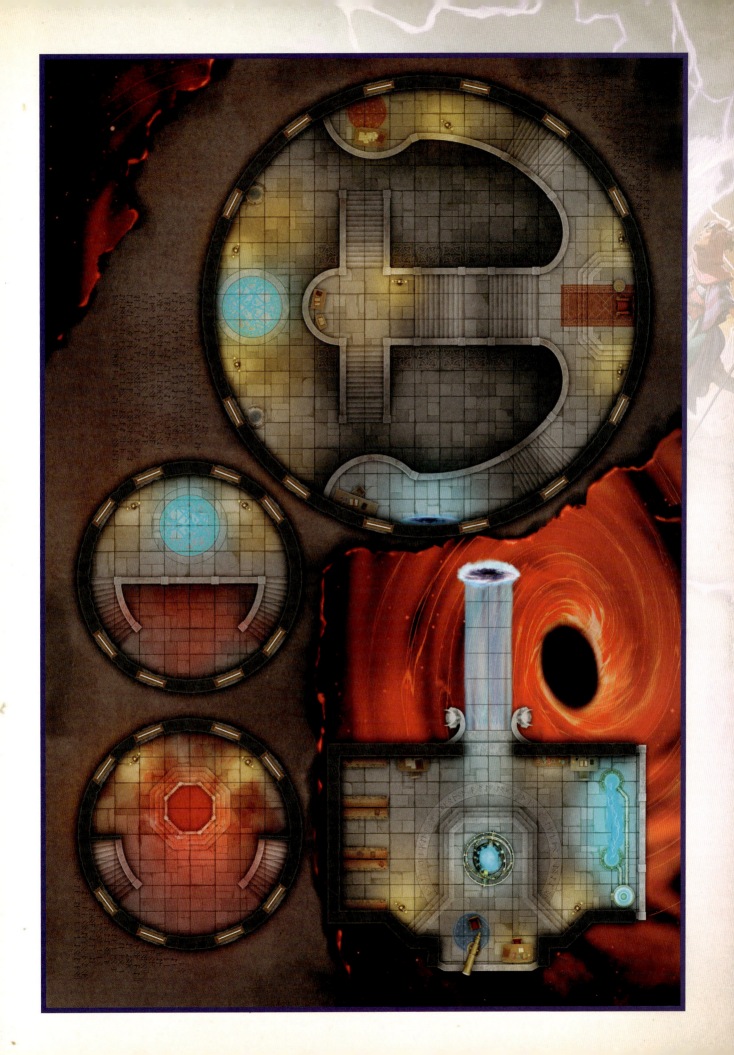

ENTRANCE

The door into the tower is marked with the sigil of Svatobor the Dauntless, recognizable with a successful DC 16 Intelligence (Arcana or History) check. It is locked with *arcane lock* (DC 25) and protected with a *glyph of warding* (7d8 thunder damage, save DC 18).

LOWER FLOORS

PCs wishing to speak with the Lich King—or fight him—must overcome obstacles on each of Bleakspire's lower floors to reach his throne room. There is no map for the bottom three floors.

General Features. Each floor is a single 50-foot-diameter round chamber with a 15-foot ceiling and a flight of steps leading up to the next floor. The walls, floor, and stairs are made from the same yellowish-white marble—the color of old bones. Magical lights illuminate each room dimly, casting odd shadows on the walls. Everything is covered in a faint patina of dust.

GROUND FLOOR

A bronze statue of Svatobor the Dauntless stands in the center of the room, depicting the bald and bearded archmage while alive. Sculpted to appear resolute, Svatobor's statue is holding a staff and wearing an amulet shaped like a spherical cage. The real amulet serves as the Lich King's phylactery which he keeps safe in his extradimensional laboratory.

Creature. An **eye golem** (*Tome of Beasts* or use **stone golem**) guards this chamber. It uses its Primal Voice of Doom ability as soon as a PC approaches the statue or the stairs.

SECOND FLOOR

A roiling vortex of multicolored chaos fills this chamber from floor to ceiling. The vortex counts as difficult terrain. A PC entering the vortex or starting their turn inside it is subject to a random effect from a *prismatic spray* spell (save DC 18). The vortex can be suppressed for 1 minute by casting *dispel magic* and succeeding on a spellcasting ability check against an 8th-level spell. Dispelling the vortex reveals a series of arcane symbols of chaos magic inlaid in bronze on the marble floor.

THIRD FLOOR

Although the Lich King doesn't need to sleep, he finds his concentration improves if he spends an hour or so away from his studies. This floor serves as a lounge of sorts—there are a couple of dusty armchairs and couches, low tables, a large black-and-red embroidered rug on the floor, and tapestries on the walls depicting the region now occupied by the wastes in happier times.

Creature. Green mist wells up from the rug as soon as the PCs set foot in the chamber, forming an **eldritch horror** (see **Chapter 5**).

Scribbled Notes. A torn piece of parchment containing a few random jottings in the Lich King's spidery handwriting lies on a table. The notes provide an insight into the lich's research. As well as names and sketches of obscure components to add to his "reversal engine," he has written "*How far back to go? What was the catalyst?*"

ANTECHAMBER

Occupying the fourth floor of the tower, this chamber has a 30-foot-high ceiling and a dozen tall, narrow windows. Stairs lead up to a balcony. A strong coppery smell fills the air.

Blood Fountain. In the center of the chamber is a magical fountain, filled with bubbling blood harvested from Nygethuaac, the dread colossus. A stone statue of a ghoul reaches out over the fountain with its clawed hand upturned. A dozen candles burn on the steps of the fountain.

The Lich King uses the blood of the fountain to recharge his phylactery by placing it in the ghoul's hand. When he does so the blood bubbles up, drenching the phylactery. To keep its potency, the fountain must be replenished each year with a fresh vial of blood from the dread colossus.

Teleportation Circle. A 15-foot-diameter bronze circle has been inlaid on the floor of the balcony. A creature that steps onto the circle is teleported to the throne room.

THRONE ROOM

This cold and elegant throne room is where the Lich King greets his infrequent visitors. Located inside the giant skull at the top of the tower, the room is larger on the inside than it appears from the outside. A dozen one-way windows look out over the valley below.

PCs arriving via the teleportation circle inlaid into the porphyry floor find themselves looking up at the Lich King's ornate throne on the balcony 30 feet above them. A glowing archway leads off from the balcony to the right.

If the Lich King invited the PCs inside the tower, he is waiting for them on his throne.

FORCE BRIDGE

The glowing archway is a portal to the Void. The air is breathable but thin and has a peculiar scent. It is also bitterly cold. Creatures without cold resistance or suitable protection must succeed on a DC 12 Constitution saving throw each minute or gain a level of exhaustion.

A 10-foot-wide transparent turquoise bridge of magical force crosses the void of space to the Lich King's laboratory. Far below is a crimson, black hole. PCs who fall off the bridge risk becoming lost forever.

LABORATORY

For nearly 400 years, the Lich King has spent most of his time in his laboratory floating in the Void. This chamber is filled with strange mechanical devices, glowing thaumaturgical circles, and the lich's extensive occult library. Steps lead down to a balcony overlooking the vastness of space, complete with an orrery and telescope.

Eldritch Machines. The center of the room is dominated by a large machine with dozens of wires, levers, and switches, topped with a huge glowing crystal. This is the Lich King's "cataclysmic reversal engine" that he has been tinkering with for decades without achieving a breakthrough. Green lightning flashes between two spheres on another machine near the wall opposite the bookcases. Tampering with either machine results in a PC receiving an electric shock as *shocking grasp* (+12 to hit, with advantage if target is wearing metal armor, 4d8 lightning damage).

Bookshelves. As well as a magnificent collection of books on a wide variety of mundane subjects, the lich's library includes spellbooks holding all the wizard spells in the core rules and in Chapter 6.

Secret Compartment. A small panel in the reversal engine, hidden in plain sight among its many controls, can be found with a successful DC 25 Intelligence (Investigation) check. Inside the compartment are the lich's phylactery—a small bronze spherical cage holding a tiny scroll—and 9 diamonds worth 1,000 gp each in small black velvet pouch.

RUSTSPIKE, CASTLE OF THE LORD OF RUIN

Looming above the blasted landscape from atop a bleak tor stands Rustspike, the mighty fortress of the Lord of Ruin. Its imposing walls and high towers are sheathed in rusting metal and studded with cruel iron spikes and jagged blades taken from those who fell before the warlord's fearsome army.

A ferocious oni tyrant, the Lord of Ruin commands a legion of hobgoblins, ogres, and other humanoids, leading them in battle against all comers for control of the wastes. For over four centuries, he has ruled a vast swathe of sparsely populated territory, home to a handful of human and dust-goblin communities that pay him tribute. These pitiful villagers just about manage to eke out a living from the poor soil and game of the magic-ravaged wastes but are forced to hand over most of what little food they can gather to feed the Lord of Ruin's soldiers.

The Lord of Ruin wasn't born an oni. In the distant past, he was a hobgoblin warlord named Gralvrak Magebane, commander of the feared Spineripper Legion of hobgoblin mercenaries. During the Mage War that ravaged the land and led to the creation of the wastes, Gralvrak and his legion were hired by the infamous wizard Svatobor the Dauntless to attack the tower of his biggest rival, the sorcerer Aurufina Stormsoul. The hobgoblin army sacked and then toppled the tower, but Gralvrak was killed by a demon summoned by Stormsoul in the final confrontation. Unwilling to lose his general, Svatobor used a long-forgotten chaos spell to bring Gralvrak back from the dead in a new, more powerful incarnation as a wicked oni. Declaring himself as the Lord of Ruin, the reincarnated warlord embarked on a brutal campaign of conquest, defeating Svatobor's surviving rivals and laying claim to their lands.

Inevitably, the Lord of Ruin and Svatobor's partnership came to an end. With the Mage War ending and most of his enemies eliminated, Svatobor became reclusive. When he withdrew to his tower to conduct his increasingly esoteric arcane experiments and became the Lich King, Svatobor bequeathed much of the land captured in his name to his general. Now a ruler of a large part of the wastes, the Lord of Ruin needed a stronghold befitting his status. Construction began soon afterward on the fortress of Rustspike at the top of a steep hill in the center of the territory he had conquered.

LORD OF RUIN

In his true form, the Lord of Ruin is a 10-foot-tall, well-muscled humanoid with demonic features: bright yellow eyes, tusks, and a pair of short ivory horns growing from his forehead. He has rust-red skin, long white hair tied back in a warrior's ponytail, and long black claws and wears plate armor made from red iron. When receiving visitors, he typically assumes human form, appearing as a cruelly handsome white-haired and bearded warrior, dressed in plate armor of burnished copper and wearing a copper crown. In either form, his fiery glaive (has the powers of a *flame tongue* sword) is never out of reach.

The Lord of Ruin is an **oni** with 169 hp and AC 18. He can cast charm person, cone of cold, gaseous form and sleep 3 times per day each.

Like many tyrants, the Lord of Ruin enjoys being flattered and can be won over by a well-chosen gift—ornate weapons and armor and magic rods are particular favorites. He is always attended to by his champions and personal bodyguards, Sir Gherlach and Sir Lantgrim, the **knights ab-errant** (*Tome of Beasts 2* or use **gladiator,** increasing size to Large). Once ordinary warriors in the Spineripper Legion, these two knights were warped by the magic of the wastes into giant supernatural fighters with a hulking physique.

With centuries of war and conquest behind him, the Lord of Ruin is a sadistic tyrant who indulges in petty acts of cruelty to alleviate the boredom he feels after he reduced the lands as far as the eye can see to a state of desolation. Every so often, he will send out his troops to punish one of the villages under his control for holding back on their tribute or other supposed acts of rebellion. His soldiers will raid the village, round up the "ringleaders," and bring them back to Rustspike where they will end up swinging from the gibbets or, at best, locked in the dungeon.

The Lord of Ruin despises the other rulers and power groups in the wastes and is constantly looking for opportunities to pick a fight with one or more of them so he can enjoy the thrill of battle again. This needs to be a fight he can win, though. As the decades have passed, the Spineripper Legion has become a shadow of its former self, and the Lord of Ruin only has two hundred or so soldiers to call upon. Although the warlord still enjoys leading his army, he delegates command on a day-to-day basis to his general, Brorrzag the Unmerciful, a **one-horned ogre** (*Tome of Beasts 2* or use **troll**). Brorrzag has a black horn in the center of his forehead, a gift from the demon lord Hriggala, and bears a tattoo of the crawling wyrm on his back. For now, the ogre is content to serve the Lord of Ruin but is biding his time until he can seize control of the Spineripper Legion and Rustspike for himself.

ADVENTURE HOOKS

Rion, an **astri** (*Tome of Beasts* or use an awakened raccoon), beseeches the PCs to protect the marsh village of Reedwald it has been watching over from the hobgoblins, worgs, and ogres of the Spineripper Legion. The villagers have already handed over nearly all their meager food stores to the Lord of Ruin's soldiers, but they will soon return for more. Can the PCs train the villagers to defend themselves and drive off the raiders?

The arcane archeologist Soave Dirtscrabbler wants to excavate the caverns beneath the Splintered Megalith of Trox, which lie inside the Lord of Ruin's territory. To avoid earning the warlord's wrath, she hires the PCs to deliver a gift—a magnificent worg saddle—to him at Rustspike in the hope that he will give the excavation his blessing.

EXPLORING THE CASTLE

A narrow path zigzags its way up the 400-foot-tall hill to Rustspike's gatehouse. Large plates of rusty iron cover the outer walls, towers, and battlements of the fortress, and two-foot-long metal spikes and serrated blades jut out from the walls. Five round towers are spaced at semi-regular intervals around the outer walls. The northeast tower is twice as tall as the others and serves as the Lord of Ruin's personal watchtower, offering him unparalleled views over his domain.

Built from red stone, the central keep has four square towers, one on each corner, and a large, imposing demonic visage carved above the entrance.

Walls. The outer walls are 30 feet high and 12 feet thick and are topped with battlements that provide half cover to the castle's defenders. Arrow slits in the walls at ground level provide three-quarters cover. Climbing the walls requires a successful DC 15 Strength (Athletics) check; PCs who fail the check must succeed on a DC 11 Dexterity saving throw or suffer 5 (1d10) piercing damage from the spikes and blades sticking out from between the iron plates.

1. OUTER TOWERS

These round towers are 60 feet tall and topped with crenellated flat roofs. Each tower is staffed by five **hobgoblins** and a hobgoblin **knight** (with the Martial Advantage ability). There is a ballista on each roof operated by an **ogre**.

2. GATEHOUSE

A pair of ironbound double doors and a portcullis of rusted iron serve to prevent uninvited guests from entering the castle. The doors are barred from the inside and require a successful DC 25 Strength (Athletics) check to force open. The portcullis is controlled by a winch inside the gatehouse but can be lifted manually with a successful DC 20 Strength (Athletics) check. The gatehouse is staffed by six **hobgoblins** led by a hobgoblin **knight** (with the Martial Advantage ability). These guards can pull a lever to suppress the magical fear effect of the bone arch (see area 5) for 1 minute but often "forget" to do this when the castle has visitors.

3. LORD OF RUIN'S WATCHTOWER

This 120-foot-tall tower gives anyone climbing to its summit an excellent vantage point for miles around. In addition to a ballista, the tower roof has a large spyglass mounted on a revolving pedestal, allowing the Lord of Ruin to see three times the normal distance when looking through it. The brass spyglass is worth 1,500 gp and weighs 10 lbs. Two huge iron chains run from the tower to 10-foot-square stone blocks in the bailey. They do nothing to support the tower, but the Lord of Ruin thought they looked impressive and insisted they were added.

4. INNER GUARD TOWERS

Connected to the walls by iron-plated stone bridges, these flat-roofed towers allow the four **hobgoblins** stationed on each platform to watch over the bailey.

5. BONE ARCH

After leaving the gatehouse, visitors must pass beneath this archway fashioned from the intertwined bones of a great beast slain by the Lord of Ruin. The arch is enchanted with a fear effect that affects anyone passing through it who fails a DC 13 Wisdom saving throw unless the magic has been suppressed by the guards in the gatehouse. Creatures that fail the save drop whatever they are holding and become frightened of the arch for 1 minute. While frightened in this way, a creature must take the Dash action and move away from the arch by the safest available route on each of its turns, unless there is nowhere to move. Once the creature has fled far enough that it can no longer see the arch, it can attempt another saving throw. On a successful save, the effect ends for that creature.

6. FOUNTAIN

A magical fountain stands in the courtyard between the gatehouse and the keep, surrounded by a ring of 10-foot-tall bone spikes protruding up from the ground. The bones are part of the same creature as the arch. The water in the fountain is an unnaturally bright turquoise and glows slightly.

An ally of the Lord of Ruin drinking from the fountain has their hit-point maximum and current hit points increased by 5 for 1 hour; creatures can only benefit from the fountain once in a 24-hour period. Anyone else drinking from the fountain must succeed on a DC 13 Constitution saving throw or become cursed for 1 minute. Whenever a cursed creature makes an attack roll or a saving throw, the creature must roll a d4 and subtract the number rolled from the attack roll or saving throw.

7. GIBBETS

The Lord of Ruin uses these gibbets to punish those who have angered him. Two dead villagers, one human and one dust goblin, hang from the posts. A white raven perches on top of the gibbet, pecking at the eyes of the corpses.

8. TENTS

While the Lord of Ruin's hobgoblin troops are barracked in the towers or the keep, tents are used for any overspill. Typically, it's the auxiliary troops who end up without a proper bed. There are 1d6+1 **dust goblins** or human **bandits** squeezed into each tent.

9. KEEP

This sturdy two-story structure built from red stone stands in the center of the bailey. The Lord of Ruin's banner—a black tower struck by lightning on a rust-red field—flies from the square towers at each corner. A set of stairs, flanked by the large skulls of gruesome monsters, leads up to a raised patio beneath the keep's imposing facade. A huge sculpted demonic face looms over the patio; those who wish to enter the keep must walk into the fiend's mouth.

Inside the keep are the throne room and private chambers of the Lord of Ruin, as well as the barracks, mess hall, kitchens, and armory. The throne room is located at the front of the second floor, allowing the Lord of Ruin to look down through the eyes of the demon onto the courtyard below. There are normally 3d10 **hobgoblins** and 1d6 **ogres** throughout the keep.

Dungeon. A single unlit chamber beneath the keep serves as the Lord of Ruin's dungeon. In this dank, foul-smelling room are 2d6 human **commoners** or **dust goblins** awaiting the oni's judgement.

Vault. Accessible via a spiral staircase behind a secret door in the Lord of Ruin's bedchamber, this small room under the keep holds the oni's treasure hoard. Finding the secret door requires a successful DC 20 Wisdom (Perception) check, while opening the ironbound door to the vault requires obtaining the key from the Lord of Ruin or a successful DC 20 Dexterity check with thieves' tools.

The hoard consists of 828 cp, 7,952 sp, 2,283 gp, 72 pp, 12 red-brown spinels (worth 100 gp each), a tapestry depicting a pair of blue dragons devastating an orc army with their lightning breath (worth 1,500 gp), a gold plate of fine dwarven workmanship (worth 250 gp), a *potion of stone giant strength*, and *boots of striding and springing*.

10. STABLES

Located behind the keep, the stables house the worgs used by hobgoblin cavalry units. There are usually 1d6 + 6 **worgs** here, along with a **dust goblin** stable hand.

CATHEDRAL OF THE BLACK GOAT

The Cathedral of the Black Goat is hidden in a crater deep in the Blasted Forest, a large tract of woodland burned by the armies of the Lord of Ruin during the Mage War. When the hobgoblins of the Spineripper Legion destroyed the forest, they also burned the sacred grove and secret temple of Bacchana, goddess of night and fertility. Although some trees and other foliage have grown back in recent years, nothing has replaced the mighty oaks felled by the hobgoblins. What was once a verdant forest is now a tangled thicket of thorny bushes, slender saplings, and scorched tree stumps on the border of the Lord of Ruin's domain, inhabited by **warped treants** (see **Chapter 5**) and **flame-scourged scions** (*Creature Codex* or use **awakened trees**).

As the forest slowly recovers, the descendants of Bacchana's followers have returned to the woods. But the atrocities of the Mage War have tainted both the goddess and her worshippers, transforming Bacchana into the Goat of the Woods—a dark deity of chaos and catastrophe—and her adherents into the Black Goat's Flock.

Under the charismatic leadership of Mother Speaker Bonabella, the cult of the Black Goat's Flock has occupied the ruined cathedral that sits on the crater floor at the heart of what was once the sacred grove. The priestess has recruited new members of the cult from the villagers living on the edge of the Lord of Ruin's lands, luring them into taking part in its debauched, hedonistic rituals and then setting them to work on restoring the cathedral until it is worthy of the Goat of the Woods.

With work on the temple almost complete, Mother Speaker Bonabella is urging her followers to rebel against the Lord of Ruin by undermining his directives and lacing the food the villages must give over as tribute with mother's milk (see below). Several villages near the Blasted Forest have been brutally punished for their insolence by the Spineripper Legion, but the Cathedral of the Black Goat continues to stir up trouble for the Lord of Ruin and will not rest until the tyrant has fallen.

MOTHER SPEAKER BONABELLA

Mother Speaker Bonabella presides over the Cathedral of the Black Goat. She is a charismatic but erratic leader, sometimes maternal, at others disturbingly alluring and lascivious, who is driven by both her ambition to restore the Black Goat's Flock to its former glory, and by her desire to satisfy her depraved appetites. PCs who are enemies of the Lord of Ruin may be able to convince Bonabella that they share a common cause, but the Mother Speaker values chaos above all else, so any alliance will likely be short-lived.

ADVENTURE HOOKS

Strange mutations and erratic behavior are rife in the village of Thornscrub on the outskirts of the Blasted Forest as the influence of the cult takes hold. When several of the inhabitants disappear, the village elder asks the PCs to investigate. Can the adventurers rescue the villagers from the cult's influence?

The PCs are traveling through the wastes when they encounter a group of hobgoblins bearing the emblems of the Spineripper Legion and their wagon, filled with food given as tribute by the nearest village and laced with mother's milk. A fight seems to have broken out among the hobgoblins, leaving all but three of them dead. One survivor is unconscious; the other two are suffering from amnesia and cannot remember who they are or what happened to them. They beg the PCs for help.

EXPLORING THE CATHEDRAL

The Cathedral of the Black Goat is a large stone structure built at the bottom of a meteorite crater in the center of the Blasted Forest. Surrounded by tangled brambles, scrubby bushes, and dead trees, the cathedral is hard for intruders to find on foot until they reach the crater and look down into it.

A **warped treant** (see **Chapter 5**) lurks in the vicinity, hiding among the scorched trees. This chaos-

tainted creature will attack anyone approaching the crater who is unaccompanied by a member of the Black Goat's Flock.

The crater is 150 feet across at its widest point and 70 feet deep. The two-story cathedral is built against the north wall, reaching a height of 50 feet, 20 feet below the edge of the crater. The upper level is a partly ruined colonnade; only fragments of its roof remain. Water tumbles from the lower tier, over the facade and into a pool on the crater floor.

1. SOUTH LEDGES

Situated 20 feet below the rim of the crater, these two ledges are joined by a sturdy wooden bridge built above the stream on the cavern floor 50 feet below. Scorched trees, each taller than the level of the crater, stand on each ledge; their branches extend over the rim, allowing the cultists to climb into the trees and descend to the ledge without too much difficulty (DC 8). A set of steep steps cut into the side of the cliff descend from the ledge to the crater floor.

Creatures. A pair of **goat-men** (*Tome of Beasts* or use **minotaur,** decreasing size to Medium) guard the steps and attempt to shove intruders off the ledge.

2. EASTERN LEDGE

This ledge is 15 feet below the rim of the crater. Two large boulders rest on the ledge. The northernmost boulder is 10 feet tall, so its top is just 5 feet below the rim. The southernmost boulder is 5 feet tall. Steep steps lead down from this rock to the crater floor 55 feet below.

Creatures. A **selang** (*Tome of Beasts* or use **satyr**) stands on watch, hiding between the boulders, and will play alien music on its pipes if strangers approach. If the selang sees PCs in combat with the goat-men in area 2, it shoots at them with its shortbow.

3. POOL

Water cascading over the facade of the cathedral has formed an 8-foot-deep pool here. Freshwater eels swimming in the water provide a food source for the cultists and there are often 1d4 **commoners** here with fishing poles during the day. A stream flows south from the pool and enters a cave in the crater wall that connects with area 4.

4. CULTIST CAVES

Four entrances lead into a network of half a dozen small caves and narrow tunnels inside the crater walls. Each cave is 15 to 20 feet in diameter and is home to 1d6 male and female **commoners**. These individuals are a mixture of humans, goblins, and other races who recently abandoned their villages to join the cult. A few of them have small goat-like horns or cloven hooves—if asked, they claim to have been blessed by the Goat of the Woods.

5. FACADE & OUTER HALL

The top of the cathedral's lower tier is 15 feet above the crater floor. Here, three shallow 5-foot-wide channels run north to south across the flat roof, draining the water collected in front of the entrance (area 6) into the pool below.

At ground level, doors at the west and east ends of the facade lead inside to the Outer Hall. This 75-foot-long hallway runs west to east and is painted with murals dating back to the cathedral's original construction, depicting the bawdy rites of Bacchana. Recent additions to the paintings (mostly tentacles) by the Black Goat's Flock have changed their nature from mildly erotic to downright disturbing.

Creatures. Four **black goat cultists** (see **Chapter 5**) are stationed here. Each is supposed to guard one of the four doors leading further into the cathedral, although they often pay more attention to the murals than their guard duties.

6. FLOODED ENTRANCE & INNER HALL

Water pools in front of the stairs leading to the upper tier of the cathedral. Flanking the steps are black stone statues of the Goat of the Woods as a hermaphroditic satyr with large curving horns, dressed in a sheer tunic patterned with stars. One is holding a bundle of wheat; the other is holding the source of the flood—a cursed decanter of water that has no stopper and pours continuously.

At ground level, the doors from area 5 lead to the Inner Hall which runs beneath the west and east towers and the flooded entrance. The walls are carved with spiral patterns. Stairs ascend each tower.

Creatures. Three **gibbering mouthers** roam this hallway; they attack anyone unaccompanied by a member of the Black Goat's Flock.

7. WEST TOWERS

These three-story towers, one round and one oval, rise 50 feet above the crater floor and are topped with flat roofs accessed via trapdoors. The walkway that once ran between the upper stories of the two towers has collapsed. The towers are used as living quarters–the PCs will encounter 2d4 **Black Goat cultists** in each.

8. EAST TOWERS

These towers are identical to the west towers, but the walkway between the upper stories remains intact.

9. COLONNADE

The top floor of the cathedral is largely open to the sky, although parts of its slanted roof remain intact, held up by 15-foot-tall pillars carved with intertwined branches and tentacles. Two worn stone statues of the Goat of the Woods in satyr guise flank the stairs leading down to the inner sanctum below (area 10). During the day, 2d4 **commoners** carry out repairs to the roof, overseen by a **selang** (or use **satyr**). At night, debauched celebrations honoring the Goat of the Woods take place under the stars.

10. INNER SANCTUM

A pair of black oak double doors, carved with a giant goat's face within a pentagram, open into the cathedral's inner sanctum where the deity's most blasphemous rites take place. Situated beneath the colonnade and extending under the wall of the crater, this high-ceilinged chamber measures 75 feet by 50 feet.

Statues. Three 12-foot-tall statues depicting the loathsome Goat of the Woods stand on plinths to the north, west, and east. The goddess is depicted in her true form, that of a writhing, galloping crab thing, covered with strange growths and tentacles. The statues are carved from a mottled green-and-black stone that glistens with a nauseating, unnatural sheen—this stone comes from the meteorite that originated in the Void and created the crater the cathedral sits in. More disturbing still, each statue has udders like that of a goat beneath its crab-like carapace that continually drip with white fluid. Wooden bowls are positioned under each statue to catch the liquid, known as mother's milk.

Creatures. Mother Speaker Bonabella, a **Black Goat priestess** (see **Chapter 5**), can usually be encountered here, accompanied by two **cult fanatics** and two **Black Goat cultists.** The Mother Speaker is a full-figured human woman, dressed in black and green robes and a black and white goat mask topped with a pair of impressive horns. Her bare shoulders and arms are covered in magical tattoos of entwined branches and tendrils that twist and writhe disconcertingly. A pentagram made from five stalks of golden wheat hangs around her neck—the holy symbol of the Goat of the Woods—and she wields a tall staff of gnarled, knotted wood—a *Zoantharian staff* (see **Chapter 7**).

The Mother Speaker can command the three statues to bleat tunelessly as a bonus action. A creature who is not a member of the Black Goat's Flock that starts its turn with 20 feet of a statue and can hear the bleating must succeed on a DC 13 Wisdom saving throw or suffer the same effects as the Gibbering ability of a gibbering mouther.

Secret Door. A well-hidden secret door in the inner sanctum's north wall behind one of the statues can be found with a successful DC 17 Intelligence (Investigation) check. This leads to the Mother's Speaker's bedchamber.

11. SECRET BEDCHAMBER

Beyond the secret door is the luxuriously furnished bedchamber of the Mother Speaker, complete with a large four-poster bed with green silk sheets, where she entertains her favorite followers. A jade statuette of a priapic satyr (worth 250 gp) stands on a bedside table.

Hanging on the wall, framed and behind a sheet of glass, is Mother Speaker's most treasured possession—a tattered piece of blue-green metal foil, acid-etched with words in a forgotten language. This fragment of the *Viridian Codex*, the unholy text of the Black Goat's Flock, contains the spell *doom of the tentacle* (see **Chapter 6**) hidden within it.

A chest beneath the bed holds the rest of the cult's treasure: 2,457 gp and 11 jet gemstones (100 gp each).

> ### MOTHER'S MILK
>
> The cultists of the Cathedral of the Black Goat put drops of this alien fluid into their drinking water and food to receive the goddess's blessing. Sometimes, they also add mother's milk to the food they hand over as tribute to the Lord of Ruin to sow madness and confusion among their enemies.
>
> A creature consuming mother's milk must make a DC 10 Constitution saving throw. Repeat consumers of mother's milk make this saving throw with advantage. On a failed save, the creature is poisoned for 1 hour during which time it experiences a series of terrifying hallucinations. The creature must succeed on a DC 10 Wisdom saving throw or experience a bout of long-term madness lasting 1d10 hours. On a successful save, the creature isn't poisoned and instead experiences a series of pleasant hallucinations for one hour, often lewd in nature.
>
> A creature that consumes mother's milk more than seven times in a month manifests a physical sign of the Goat of the Woods' blessing: their feet transform into cloven hooves, they grow small horns, or an extra tentacular appendage sprouts from somewhere on their body.

GHOST LIGHT MARSHES

The Ghost Light Marshes are a large area of wetlands, around 50 miles across, that formed four centuries ago following a magical apocalypse and have been slowly expanding ever since. Craters filled with swamp water dot the landscape; these hollows were created by arcane explosions during the Mage War. Marshy islands and the occasional stretch of higher ground provide patches of semi-dry land for travelers without boats to get around.

Motes of pale blue light bob and float throughout the wetlands. These are the "ghost lights" that give the marsh its name. Some people believe the ghost lights mark the location of the sunken ruins of an ancient magocracy destroyed during the war, and that anyone brave enough to dive down beneath the water's surface might discover its lost riches. Others say the ghost lights are evil spirits that attempt to lure greedy adventurers to their dooms.

Both tales are inaccurate, but neither is entirely false. There are sunken ruins below the surface of the swamp and **will-o'-wisps** lurk in the marshes, often hiding in plain sight among the ghost lights. But the true story of the ghost lights is even more unusual: the lights are the residual magical energy left behind by the dread colossus Vh'al Zhubbuth after it was defeated by another alien monstrosity, the toad-like Nygethuaac, at the height of the Mage War.

Vh'al Zhubbuth was one of the gargantuan entities summoned from the Void by powerful but foolish wizards during the Mage War. Resembling a colossal mound of rotting vegetation piled up in a vaguely humanoid shape, Vh'al Zhubbuth was called forth by a cabal of sorcerers and charged with protecting the great city of Aubergne from its enemies. Unfortunately, the wizards of Aubergne's biggest rival, the Palatinate of Granchevel, were as skilled and as rash as their counterparts. Granchevel's mages summoned their own alien monstrosity, Nygethuaac the dread colossus, and unleashed both the being and their mightiest spells on Aubergne. The city and its surrounding farms and villages were devastated in the ensuing cataclysm, and Vh'al Zhubbuth was torn apart in the confrontation—huge clumps of its plant-like body were scattered across the landscape.

In the aftermath, torrential rains fell and the waters rose, covering the ruins of Aubergne. The physical remains and magical essence of Vh'al Zhubbuth were absorbed into the newly created marsh, causing the ghost lights to manifest. Anyone encountering the ghost lights is, to all intents and purposes, coming into contact with an alien entity from the Void.

AMABEL MERRYWEATHER

Known to the otterfolk and others as the "wise woman" of the Ghost Light Marshes, Amabel Merryweather is a **green hag** who lives deep in the swamp in a wooden shack. Weird fetishes woven from reeds, dead snakes, lizards, and other small animals hang from the porch. Steps lead down into the water where a rowboat is moored to a post.

Amabel uses her Illusory Appearance ability to appear as a smiling, rosy-cheeked middle-aged woman in a bright yellow dress, with her greying hair tied up in a bun. She has five cats of various colors that meow constantly. An estranged daughter of Aunty Gremblewick (see **Chapter 1**), Amabel is not as black-hearted as most hags and is polite to her visitors, offering them a nice cup of tea, a biscuit, and a friendly chat. She has lived in the Ghost Light Marshes since they were formed and knows their history and the true nature of the ghost lights. Amabel quite likes the otterfolk, as they bring her gifts and interesting people like the PCs to talk to, and she tolerates the lizardfolk. She regards the Marsh Queen as an upstart and would be happy to see the swamp naga dead or driven out of the swamp for good. She knows that the biggest threat to the marshes is Vh'al Zhubbuth and keeps a careful eye on its children, the shambling mounds.

Amabel makes a sickly-smelling salve by crushing swamp irises, shambling mound moss and other marsh plants with her mortar and pestle. When rubbed onto the skin, the wearer glows with a pale blue luminescence and can move freely around the ghost lights without triggering their effects for 1 hour. If she takes a shine to the PCs, Amabel may give them a jar of the substance, enough for each party member.

ADVENTURE HOOKS

Recently, the shambling mound population has grown rapidly and now the plant creatures are starting to congregate around an aged cypress in the middle of the marsh. If the PCs travel to see Amabel Merryweather, they can learn that if enough mounds gather together, they can merge, creating a new body for Vh'al Zhubbuth's alien intelligence to occupy. To put a stop to this, the PCs must retrieve Amabel's *Stygian crook* (*Vault of Magic* or use a *staff of withering*)—a powerful magic item they can use to destroy the plant creatures—from the clutches of the Marsh Queen who stole it.

EXPLORING THE MARSHES

Traveling through the Ghost Light Marshes is an eerie experience. A thin mist pervades the marsh most of the time, obscuring vision, and constant dark clouds overhead serve to block out the sun and moon, making the flickering ghost lights the only source of illumination. As the PCs journey through the wetlands, they may come across the tops of ruined buildings protruding from the water or stumble upon a wooden shack built on stilts or other occasional signs of humanoid habitation.

In most places, the water is only 2 to 3 feet deep, but in areas where there are lots of craters, the depth can be as much as 30 feet. In the center of the marshes is a large lake, half a mile across. Fifty feet beneath its surface lie the ruins of Aubergne. Since the city was razed to the ground by battling monstrosities and arcane bombardment, little remains, but there is still treasure to be found hidden among the rubble and giant reeds. **Befouled weirds** (*Tome of Beasts* 2 or use **water elemental**) lurk among the ruined buildings.

Intelligent creatures found elsewhere in the Ghost Light Marshes include a tribe of **lizardfolk** and their enemies, a bevy of **otterfolk** (*Tome of Beasts* 2 or use **goblin**). The territorial lizardfolk dwell in a small hut village built on stilts. They are hostile to strangers, hunting them for food or as tribute to be offered to the Marsh Queen, a **swamp naga** (*Tome of Beasts* 2 or use **spirit naga**) who lairs in a half-submerged ruin on the edge of the lake above Aubergne.

The martial-minded otterfolk live in a hole beneath a huge cypress tree on a large island. They are sometimes willing to act as guides for adventurers wanting to navigate the marshes or visit the "wise woman," Amabel Merryweather (see below). They charge a higher price if the PCs don't look like they can handle themselves in a fight with lizardfolk or other swamp creatures.

The fallen dread colossus Vh'al Zhubbuth's influence over the marsh is not confined to the ghost lights. Its "children," **shambling mounds** and **will-o'-wisps**, are found throughout the Ghost Light Marshes, preying on travelers. Crocodiles, snakes, swarms of mosquitoes and leeches are also common. Victims of the marsh's denizens are often transformed into **putrid haunts** (*Tome of Beasts* or use **ghasts**) after death.

MARSH BATTLE MAP

This battle map shows a typical area in the Ghost Light Marshes. Crater pools brimming with swamp water are separated by ridges of boggy land where clumps of tall reeds and swamp irises grow. Pale blue ghost lights float above the pools. A small hill rises to the northeast.

GHOST LIGHTS

The ghost lights shed bright light in a 10-foot radius, and dim light for a further 10 feet. The lights bob up and down and can move slowly (speed 10 ft.) but cannot stray more than 20 feet from their initial location or beyond the boundary of their crater. Ghost lights are not creatures and cannot be attacked. A *dispel magic* spell causes a ghost light to wink out for 12 hours.

When a creature approaches within 5 feet of a ghost light, roll on the table below.

1. CRATER POOLS

Each of these pools is 1d6 + 2 feet deep and is filled with stagnant swamp water with algae growing on the surface. One or more ghost lights float a few feet above the water.

2. TREACHEROUS MUCK

This pool is 5 feet deep and has a single ghost light floating above it. A PC who succeeds on a DC 13

d10	Effect
1–3	No effect
4–5	The ghost light makes a melee spell attack: +4 to hit, reach 5 ft., one creature. Hit: 9 (2d8) lightning damage.
6–7	The creature must succeed on a DC 13 Wisdom saving throw or take 7 (2d6) psychic damage and experience an alien revelation as Vh'al Zhubbuth grants a glimpse into the Void. This revelation can be the location of the nearest treasure, a useful clue, or simply the knowledge that the ghost lights are a manifestation of the dread colossus.
8	The creature must succeed on a DC 13 Wisdom saving throw or fall under the effects of a *suggestion* spell, carrying out the instructions of Vh'al Zhubbuth to the best of its ability.
9	The ghost light transforms into a **will-o'-wisp** and is now a creature. Roll its initiative.
10	A **shambling mound** rises from the swamp and attacks. Roll its initiative.

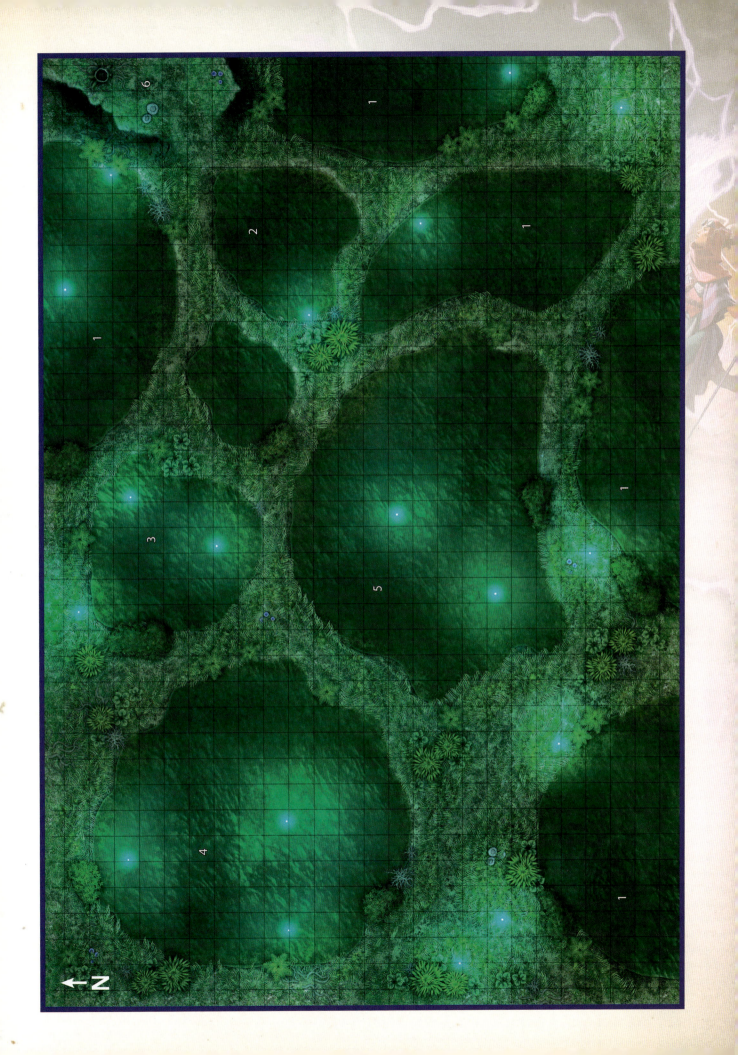

Wisdom (Perception) check spots something glinting in the muck at the bottom of the crater: an orichalcum bangle decorated with unsettling geometric patterns, worth 150 gp.

If a PC steps onto the bottom of the pool, they sink 1d4 feet into the muck and become restrained. At the start of each of their turns, they sink another 1d4 feet and start to suffocate if they become submerged. A PC who becomes stuck must make a successful Strength check as an action to get free with a DC of 10 plus the number of feet they have sunk into the mud.

3. SKELETAL REMAINS

Two ghost lights float above this 12-foot-deep pool. A lizardfolk skeleton can be seen lying on the bottom inside the smaller crater in the southwest corner. The skeleton has a cracked tortoiseshell shield strapped to one arm and a gold kraken-shaped pendant—a *necklace of adaptation*—hanging around its bony neck.

4. SUBMERGED RUINS

This large crater pool is 60 feet across and 20 feet deep, with three ghost lights floating above its surface. There is a second shallow crater in the bottom of the pool near the northern edge, measuring 15 feet across. Anyone peering into the water can see large chunks of broken masonry on the bottom. These stone blocks were once part of a wizard's stronghold that was destroyed in the Mage War.

A greenish copper scroll tube, sealed with wax, pokes out beneath the rubble and can be found with a successful DC 13 Intelligence (Investigation) check. The scroll inside is intact and describes the complex incantations, multiple participants, and rare arcane components needed to summon the entity called Vh'al Zhubbuth from the Void.

5. MIRE FIEND DEN

Two ghost flights float above the western end of this large 15-foot-deep crater pool. On the bottom a **mire fiend** (see **Chapter 5**) has built a den of sticks and woven grasses around a second, smaller crater and several broken stone blocks. The creature has succumbed to the suggestions of Vh'al Zhubbuth and lurks here, ready to attack intruders with its spear.

Treasure. The mire fiend has a small stash of loot inside a clay jar in its den. The hoard consists of 118 sp, 35 ep, 85 gp, and 9 moss agates (worth 50 gp each).

6. WRECKED MACHINE

The twisted wreckage of an ancient machine lies at the top of this small hill. Ferns and other plants grow in and around the rusted contraption's gears and springs.

GOBLIN TOWN OF NICHENEVIN

When the smoldering fires of the Mage War were finally extinguished, tribes of goblins slowly emerged from their tunnels beneath the mountains and ventured out into the blasted landscape of the wastes. Forced from their underground caverns by aggressive dwarven expansion, these goblins learned to adapt to life on the surface and made new homes in the badlands. The most widespread group are the **dust goblins** (see **Chapter 5**) who live in small settlements throughout the wastes, burrowing beneath ancient, ruined cities or dwelling in the shattered towers of the magocracies. Many of their communities lie within the domain of the Lord of Ruin and pay him tribute, but not all. Just beyond the borders of the tyrant's territory stands the proudly independent Free Town of Nichenevin, a walled tent village that's home to a dust goblin tribe dubbed the Scrap Gleaners by human explorers travelling in the wastes. In their own language, the dust goblins call themselves the Bacha Divvod, or "Brave Pioneers" in Common.

The dust goblins of Nichenevin have an affinity for technological items of all kinds, so the free town is the ideal location for PCs to visit if they need to have a mysterious item restored to working order or are interested in purchasing a refurbished piece of gear. It's also a good spot to hire a guide for archaeological expeditions in the wastes.

FEEGLE RUSTSPANNER

Feegle is Nichenevin's artificer-in-chief and its second oldest dust-goblin resident, after fellow village elder Crox Ruszta. He's scrawny and stooped, with a wrinkled green face, and wears a leather apron filled with his impressive tool collection and an ornate orichalcum bracelet shaped like a mechanical scorpion (functions as *bracers of defense*).

Feegle is happy and excitable when his mechanical projects are going well and prone to bad-tempered ranting when they aren't. Currently, Feegle is attempting to construct a deadly war machine to strike fear into the hearts of Nichenevin's enemies, but things are not going to plan. He will bark instructions at any PCs who stick their heads inside his tent, calling for his left-handed sprocket wrench or ordering them to tighten the valves on the flamethrower fuel tanks. Once it becomes apparent that the PCs aren't his apprentices, he'll climb down from his machine and explain animatedly how it's meant to work to anyone who cares to listen.

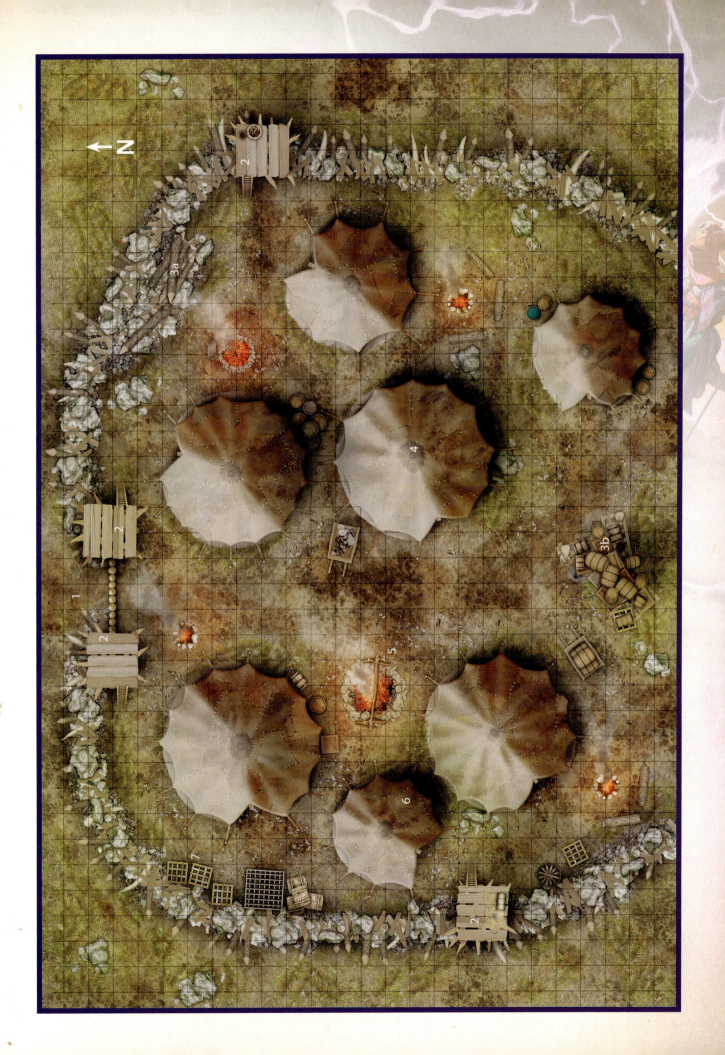

Feegle has Nichenevin's best interests at heart and is determined to keep the town safe from the Lord of Ruin and the Spider Face goblins, but he has fallen out with Crox over how to achieve this. Crox is opposed to Feegle meddling in ancient and corrupt technology he doesn't fully understand. She may have a point.

ADVENTURE HOOKS

The whispers of Vh'al Zhubbuth drive Crox to sabotage Feegle's war machine. Unfortunately, her interference activates the construct, which rampages through the town breathing fire on the tents and snapping at goblins with its vicious jaws. Can the PCs help Feegle put a stop to the rampage?

EXPLORING NICHENEVIN

The somewhat grandly named Free Town of Nichenevin is home to around 100 dust goblins who make a living by salvaging useful—and sometimes not so useful—items and materials from the many ruins and ancient battlefields dotting the desolate landscape of the wastes. Occasionally the Scrap Gleaners "salvage" unattended items that have owners, leading to trouble when they come looking for them. The usual goblin response is feigned innocence and an offer to sell the item back at a discount.

Because Nichenevin is less than a day's march from the borders of the Lord of Ruin's domain in one direction, and a day's travel from the territory of the infamous Spider Face goblins in another, the residents of the Free Town take their security seriously. The village is surrounded by a 15-foot-high wooden palisade with several 25-foot-high guard towers, but these are not Nicheneven's only defenses.

Guardian. Feegle Rustspanner, Artificer-in-Chief (see below), has reassembled and reprogrammed a **warden robot** (see **Chapter 5**) to patrol the town. There is a 75% chance that the construct is present when the PCs first visit Nichenevin. Otherwise, it is out accompanying a goblin scavenging expedition. After scanning visitors, the robot ignores them until they behave violently, at which point it deploys deadly force to neutralize the threat.

Note. The map shows the northern part of the town. There is another junk pile, a few more tents, and another two guard towers in the southern section.

1. MAIN GATE

Situated at the north end of town, the main gates are always barred from the inside and are only opened when the guards on the western tower give the signal. Forcing the gates open requires a successful DC 20 Strength (Athletics) check. There are usually 1d4 **dust goblins** on duty here.

2. GUARD TOWERS

Long wooden ladders are used to climb up to the guard platforms at the top of these 25-foot-tall wooden towers. Two **dust goblins** are stationed on each platform to keep watch over the wastes and raise the alarm if enemies are spotted. Each platform has several metal pots and pans hanging from a wooden post that the goblins can bang loudly to alert the village.

The goblins on the tower to the west of the main gate play a tune on a row of tin bells to signal their comrades below that they should open the gates. The correct sequence of notes is changed each day or so.

3. JUNK PILES

Not everything the dust goblins collect is useful right now, but they don't like to throw anything out in case it might prove handy later. The junk pile against the northeast wall (3a) is 10 feet high and 25 feet long, while the southern pile (3b) is an 18-foot-tall pyramid of rusty metal, wood, and other debris. An even bigger scrap heap lies off the edge of the map to the south (3c); this pile is 30 feet long and 20 feet high.

There are usually 1d6 **dust goblins** hanging around each junk pile and occasionally rearranging things. They can be persuaded to let the PCs poke around in the piles with a DC 11 Charisma check.

Climbing the piles requires a successful DC 12 Strength (Athletics) check, while searching through the junk to discover something interesting requires 1 minute of searching and a successful DC 15 Intelligence (Investigation) check. PCs who search the junk piles must also succeed on a DC 10 Dexterity saving throw for each minute they search or take 3 (1d6) slashing or piercing damage from sharp edges and protruding nails. If the PC fails the saving throw by 5 or more, part of the junk pile collapses, and the PC takes 10 (3d6) damage.

Roll on the table located on the next page when a PC discovers something in the junk pile. If they want to keep the item, they will have to agree to a price with the dust goblins or conceal it on their person without the goblins noticing.

4. ARCANE WORKSHOP

Sounds of banging, hammering, and frequent cursing can be heard from inside this large tent. This is the workshop and home of Feegle Rustspanner.

Dominating the center of the tent is a 20-foot-long, two-headed mechanical dog made from assorted mismatched metal components. The stooped figure of

d20	Junk Pile Find
1	Hunting trap—succeed on a DC 13 Dexterity saving throw or trigger the trap, taking 1d4 piercing damage. Roll a d6: on an even number, an arm is trapped; on an odd number, a leg.
2	Annoyed **giant rat**
3	Set of manacles without a key
4	Bullseye lantern with the glass missing
5	Cracked magnifying glass
6	Set of merchant's scales
7	Brass hunting horn
8	3-foot-diameter bronze cog
9	Greatsword sized for a giant
10	Copper chamber pot with handles in the shape of snakes
11	Mine cart with one missing wheel
12	Dented head of a robot
13	Bronze puzzle box
14	Thick brass-topped glass canister containing a human-sized brain floating in fluid
15	25 feet of coiled hosepipe of waxed leather
16	Six 1-foot-long orichalcum rods
17	Mechanical spider leg
18	Dead vril battery
19	Goblin war chariot
20	Ancient artifact or tech item

Feegle is standing on top of the construct, adjusting the controls inside the pilot's compartment behind the two heads and swearing profusely in Goblin.

Several workbenches covered in metal plates, cogs, rods, and schematics stand around the circumference of the tent; Feegle's camp bed is in one corner.

5. COOKING PIT

A large cauldron of unappetizing-looking brown stew bubbles over the fire pit here, night and day. Any food the goblins scavenge—including rats, cockroaches, mutated pumpkins, and tentacles—is stirred into the pot by the near-toothless **dust goblin** cook, Gnelux Stankpit, who cackles gleefully as he hands out billycans of stew to anyone who wants one.

Although edible and nutritious, the stew smells like old, sweaty socks and has a peculiar blend of flavors, likely to upset the delicate stomachs of adventurers. Non-goblins who eat a bowl of stew for the first time must succeed on a DC 10 Constitution saving throw or vomit profusely, becoming poisoned for 1 minute.

There are usually 2d4 **dust goblins** at the cooking pit getting food, so it's a great place for the PCs to hang out and meet useful NPCs:

- Khalsa Freggish is a scruffy dust goblin **scout** who hires herself out as a guide to the wastes for 5 gp per day. Khalsa claims to have discovered a series of caverns beneath the Splintered Megalith of Trox filled with weird machines built by the ancients. Unwashed and unrepentant, she is a competent guide but is likely to pocket one or two choice finds if not closely watched.
- Wirlem Vurt is a wily **dust goblin** merchant dealing in ancient artifacts and chaos items who usually has one or two interesting items for purchase. Irritatingly cheerful and overly familiar with potential buyers, Wirlem constantly licks his lips when making a sale.

6. DRUID'S TENT

The outside of this tent is painted with pictographs telling the story of the dust goblins' flight from the mountains and how they came to the wastes. This is the home of Crox Ruszta, village elder and Nichenevin's spiritual leader. Crox is a tiny, old, yellow-skinned dust goblin, dressed in a shabby black dress; she leans heavily on her gnarled staff of black wood.

Crox is a **druid** and champions nature over technology, bringing her into constant conflict with Feegle. She keeps a fern that she found in the Ghost Light Marshes in her tent. Crox claims it whispers the secrets of protecting nature to her. In fact, the voice she is hearing belongs to the dread colossus known as Vh'al Zhubbuth, which is manipulating her into doing its foul bidding.

7. CAGES

The goblins keep **death dogs** in these cages as pets and hunting hounds. The ugly creatures bark loudly when strangers approach.

TANGLESIDE, CHAOS WASTES VILLAGE

The peaceful town of Whisperhaven was devastated during the Mage War, its grand buildings and splendid plazas reduced to ruins. Today, a small village called Tangleside has sprung up in its former location, made up of makeshift shacks and other tumbledown structures that have been built on top of the foundations and surviving stone walls of the town. Homes are piled one on top of the other and connected by a confusing network of

ladders, catwalks, bridges, and ropes. The village is surrounded on three sides by abandoned ruined buildings—the remains of Whisperhaven.

Tangleside is ruled by its fearsome overlord, Karvos Deathstealer, the infamous doom champion who served as the general of Aurufina Stormsoul's army in the Mage War. Karvos disappeared from the battlefield in the middle of one of the greatest confrontations of the war when Svatobor the Dauntless opened a portal and banished him to the Eleven Hells.

Trapped and tormented in the infernal realms for four centuries, Karvos transformed into something even greater than he was before, a **doom champion overlord** (see **Chapter 5**). He eventually escaped, slaughtering dozens of demons and devils as he battled his way back to the Material Plane. By the time he returned, the Mage War was long over and Aurufina Stormsoul had been defeated. After wandering the wastes for several months, Karvos arrived in the small settlement of Tangleside, triumphed over its headman in the arena, and declared himself overlord. No one was brave enough to stand in his way, and he has ruled over Tangleside ever since.

KARVOS DEATHSTEALER

The overlord of Tangleside is a brutal, muscular warrior of indeterminate race, clad in black plate armor and a demonic-looking helm that covers his entire face with the sole exception of his eyes. He enjoys terrifying his enemies with a baleful stare before bashing their skulls in with his great maul or running them through with his lance.

Karvos's formidable appearance strikes fear in both his foes and the inhabitants of Tangleside, who believe him to be an immortal half-demon. But he is actually human and beginning to feel the effects of his 64 years in this world—not to mention the four centuries he spent in the Eleven Hells—in his aching joints. He is careful to ensure no one notices his discomfort when he gets up from his throne.

Despite his aches and pains, Karvos is not ready to hang up his helm. He still takes great pleasure in sheer, bloody violence—hence his monster-hunting expeditions into the ruins—and sees himself as Tangleside's savior and protector, rather than its oppressor. The village is close to the edge of the Lord of Ruin's domain and the doom champion overlord has taken up arms several times to deal with trespassing squads of Spineripper Legionaries.

ADVENTURE HOOKS

Karvos harbors feelings of deep hatred toward Svatobor the Dauntless for the centuries of torment he suffered in the Eleven Hells but knows he is not powerful enough to take on a lich. Recently, rumors have surfaced of a magical amulet recovered from an ancient tower somewhere in the wastes that can turn spells back on their caster. Unwilling to leave Tangleside undefended while the Lord of Ruin's soldiers are at large, the doom champion overlord hires the PCs to steal the amulet from the scavengers who found it.

EXPLORING THE VILLAGE

Tangleside is a rough-and-tumble place with a population of around 500 individuals from a mixture of different races, including humans, dust goblins, dragonborn, wasteland orcs, and tieflings. The population is concentrated in about 30 buildings in the southern section of the original town. They tend to be suspicious of strangers and start with an attitude of Indifferent to player characters. The Terror Dome, a large gladiatorial arena, sits in the center of the village, providing bloody entertainment for the inhabitants.

Houses. Tangleside's inhabitants live in stacked, terraced houses, built from mud, wood, and stones salvaged from the ruins. The stacks are typically two to three stories high and are connected to each other by ladders and narrow catwalks, allowing the inhabitants to move around above ground level. Poor construction or bad weather can make the stacks unstable. Recently, several homes collapsed, killing two villagers and injuring six more.

Statues. Several ancient, weathered stone statues are arrayed around the village; some are missing limbs or even heads. Most depict important citizens of Whisperhaven dating back to before the Mage War, but a few have been built since and resemble twisted monstrosities (see area 3).

Ruins. To the north, west, and east of the village are the ruined parts of the former town, destroyed during the Mage War. Fell creatures such as **bulettes, chimeras, manticores** and **slitherjacks** (see **Chapter 5**) lair in the buildings and sometimes threaten Tangleside. When these incursions get out of hand, the doom champion overlord leads hunting parties into the ruins, offering a bounty to anyone willing to accompany him and slay these monsters. The Terror Dome also pays handsomely for exotic beasts for its gladiators to fight in the arena.

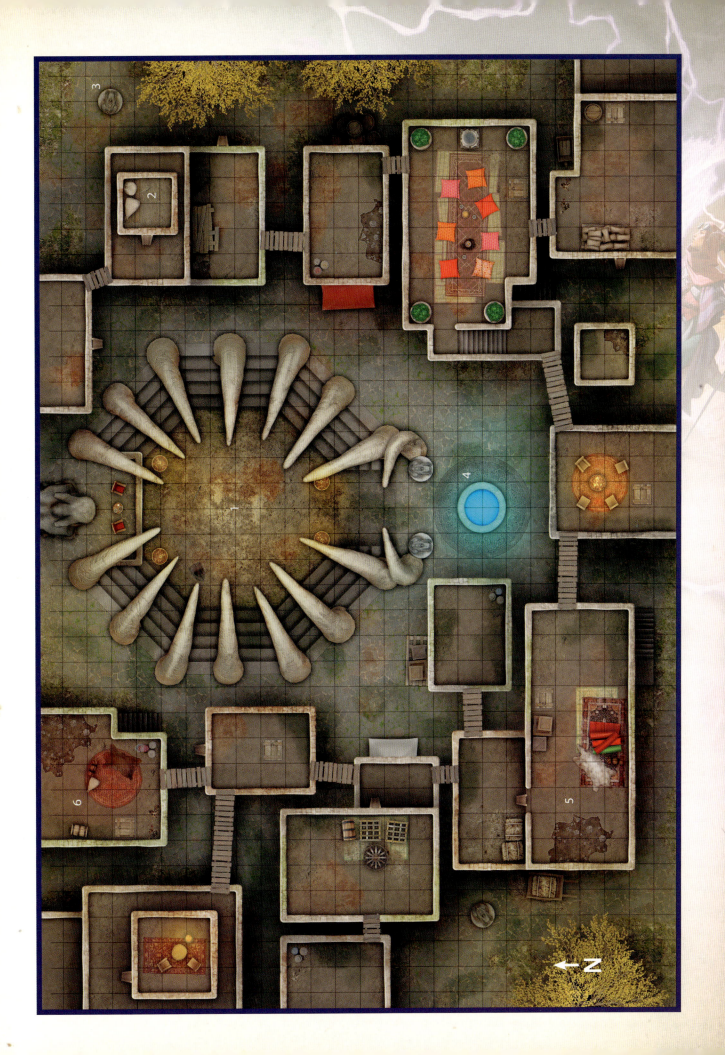

1. TERROR DOME

At the center of the village, the enormous rib cage of an ancient beast surrounds a sunken, sandy-floored arena stained with blood. Banks of tiered seats allow spectators to watch the brutal action that takes place at least once a week between Terror Dome regulars and challengers, as well as enemies of the doom champion overlord fighting for their freedom. Newcomers to Tangleside who wish to gain an audience with the doom champion overlord must first prove themselves worthy in the Terror Dome.

Fighters pass beneath two huge arching ribs to enter the arena floor; stone statues of tentacled felines crouch on either side of the entrance, as if ready to pounce. Opposite the entrance is a raised dais from which the doom champion overlord can enjoy the fighting and determine who lives or dies with a thumb signal. The skull of a giant monstrosity serves as his gruesome throne.

Tonja Throatcrusher (CN female wasteland orc **gladiator**) is the longest-surviving fighter in the Terror Dome. Originally sent to the arena for disobeying the doom champion overlord, Tonja has won her freedom dozens of times over but chooses to stay on the sands and fight all challengers.

Tall, muscular, and wiry, with battle-scarred tan skin, cropped spiky black hair, and two prominent tusk-like lower teeth, Tonja wears an eyepatch over her missing right eye. She wields a double-headed axe in one hand and a mace in the other and fights in mismatched armor cobbled together from pieces taken from her defeated opponents. Each time she wins a fight, Tonja adds a small, raised branding scar to her arm. She has sworn an oath to kill Karvos Deathstealer and liberate Tangleside when she reaches a total of 99 scars. She has less than half a dozen to go.

2. JATRU'S ROOFTOP CANTINA

Precariously perched on top of a stack of homes overlooking the Terror Dome, this wooden shack is Tangleside's most popular—and only—drinking establishment. Jatru (CG female human **commoner**), a middle-aged woman with dark skin and long gray locks, serves a pungent rotgut made from local cactus and a flat, slightly soapy-tasting ale. Spicy deep-fried cockroaches are the only food items available. Jatru loathes the doom champion overlord, blaming him for the death of her son on a monster-hunting expedition into the ruins, and doesn't suffer complaints about her cantina—or any other nonsense for that matter—gladly. She employs a heavily tattooed former gladiator named Rannik (N male dwarf **veteran**) as a bouncer who delights in shoving the most irksome troublemakers off the roof.

3. SINISTER STATUE

Situated behind Jatru's, this weathered stone statue depicts a three-legged humanoid monstrosity with two arms ending in long claws and a long, coiling tentacle for a head and radiates an unsettling supernatural aura. A living creature that approaches within 10 feet of the statue must succeed on a DC 10 Wisdom saving throw or become frightened of the statue for 1 minute. A creature that succeeds on its saving throw is permanently immune to the aura. Most of the villagers find the reaction of strangers to the statue rather amusing, but kinder souls may offer a warning to newcomers.

4. GLOWING WELL

To the south of the arena, an ancient stone well stands in the middle of a cracked and faded mosaic. Before the Mage War, this well provided the inhabitants with fresh water. Today, it is filled with glowing green sludge that inflicts 7 (2d6) acid damage on anyone coming into contact with it. Gurtri (area 6) uses this substance to make her glow bombs.

5. OVERLORD'S HOME

More sturdily constructed than the rest of the village, this stack of three buildings to the southwest of the Terror Dome is home to Karvos Deathstealer, Overlord of Tangleside. The doom champion overlord holds court in his audience chamber seated on a demonhide throne on the second floor surrounded by tridents, barbed whips, glaives and other weapons taken from his defeated foes.

Four **doom champions** (see **Chapter 5**) serve as the doom champion overlord's lieutenants and personal bodyguards; at least two accompany him at all times. The doom champions wear helms that cover their faces and do not speak in public. A dozen or so **guards** and servants (**commoners**) also live here, and Karvos' beloved **nightmare** steed, Hellsflare, is stabled in the adjoining building.

6. HIDDEN GEMS BAZAAR

A lopsided, badly painted wooden sign advertises the motley collection of stalls located within this building and on its rooftop. In addition to stalls selling surprisingly tasty street food such as jerk rock lizard kabobs and prickly pear wraps, there are traders selling mundane and adventuring gear and a few offering weird items salvaged in the ruins of Whisperhaven.

Tarim Sunwalker (NG male tiefling **mage**) is a bespectacled scholar and explorer who has been attempting to map what's left of the former town. Softly spoken and mild-mannered, Tarim often has interesting items for sale, including some of the magic items in Chapter 6.

Gurtri (CN female **kobold alchemist** [*Tome of Beasts* or use **druid**]) has a stall on the roof—perhaps a bit too close to the jerk lizard kabob grill for comfort—selling alchemist's fire, acid, antitoxins, and glow bombs (see **Chapter 7**). Gurtri reeks of strange chemicals and her hands are often wrapped in bandages after frequent mishaps, but she is an enthusiastic salesperson and pays well for rare ingredients such as skitterhaunt stingers.

MAZE CAVERNS OF THE WASTELAND DRAKE

Deep in the desolate, sun-scorched badlands of the wastes lies the Forsaken Canyon, a great rift in the surface of the earth that holds the entrance to the Maze Caverns of the Wasteland Drake. This labyrinthine network of tunnels and caves dug into the canyon walls is home to an ill-tempered young **wasteland dragon** (see **Chapter 5**) named Everstrife and his devoted band of scaly humanoid followers. Everstrife—or Valampalinax to use his draconian name—is feared throughout the region for preying on travelers and raiding local villages for their livestock.

Centuries ago, long before the Mage War, an ancient dragonborn civilization laid claim to the area and built an extensive underground complex into the walls of Forsaken Canyon to serve as an academy for their mightiest sorcerers and wizards, the Conclave of Spellscales. The dragonborn carved a magnificent facade from the rock to serve as the academy's grand entrance and excavated a series of subterranean passages and chambers. Throughout the complex, talented sculptors produced wondrous statues of the conclave's dynamic arcanists and its twin patrons—a mated pair of adult brass dragons.

Through the decades, the members of the Conclave of Spellscales devoted themselves to the study and creation of magical portals, filling the tunnels and chambers of their underground complex with dozens of teleportation circles and interdimensional gateways. Ultimately, it was these portals that were to prove their undoing.

As the Mage War began, the dragonborn of the Conclave were loath to become involved, continuing to immerse themselves in their research as they had always done. But the warped magical energies brought about by the clashes between warring mages had unpredictable effects on the Conclave's portals. Strange and hostile creatures appeared in the dragonborn's midst, newly arrived from other worlds through the portals, and overran the Maze Caverns. At the same time, the Conclave's two mighty dragon patrons began to change. Their shining brass scales became rust-colored and dull, and their gleaming horns turned grey and withered as they transformed into wasteland dragons. Although the dragonborn of the Conclave valiantly tried to hold back the chaos, their efforts were in vain. Abandoned by their corrupted dragon patrons, the Conclave of Spellscales fell into ruins, and the dragonborn civilization collapsed.

ADVENTURE HOOKS

The **Void Lord** (see **Chapter 3**) stalks the wastes, and Gerd Fogbottle (female gnome **mad wizard** [see **Chapter 3**]) believes an ancient dragonborn device capable of banishing him to the Void through one of his own portals is to be found in the Maze Caverns. Are the PCs brave enough to retrieve it from Everstrife's hoard?

EXPLORING THE CAVERNS

A narrow gorge known as the Dragon's Gullet leads to the Forsaken Canyon and the entrance to the Maze Caverns. This dark, twisting passageway through the sandstone is half a mile long and between 10 and 15 feet wide. The enclosing walls are 300 feet high; ancient representations of dragons and dragon-headed humanoids have been carved into the sandstone along the route.

PCs with aerial mounts or magical means of flight can avoid passing through the Dragon's Gullet but risk encountering the **chaos drakes** (see **Chapter 5**) that lair atop the sandstone walls as they fly overhead, or worse still, Everstrife himself.

At the end of the Dragon's Gullet, the gorge enters the Forsaken Canyon, a deep rift around 300 feet wide, and 12 miles long. Its striated sandstone walls, layered in different shades of yellow, pink, and reddish brown, ascend 300 feet from the canyon floor.

The main entrance to the Maze Caverns lies directly opposite the Gullet in the north wall, with the intention that travelers rounding the last turn in the passage would be awed by the sight of the academy's wondrous facade. Today, most of this stonework lies in rubble on the ground; only the lower legs and clawed feet of the great twin dragons that once flanked the 50-foot-high doorway remain.

Half a dozen smaller cave openings, also leading inside the Maze Caverns, can be found along the north wall.

INSIDE THE CAVERNS

Beyond the main entrance lies the impressive audience chamber where the conclave's dragonborn would meet with their two patrons to discuss the latest magical discoveries. Huge columns with stone dragons coiling around them still support the vaulted ceiling 75 feet above. The ceiling is carved to resemble dragon scales and cracked in places. The vast chamber's floor is littered with debris, while wide stone arches in the curved walls lead to passageways going deeper into the Maze Caverns.

Past the audience chamber lies a bewildering complex of twisting passageways and rubble-strewn chambers and caverns. Crumbling stone arches lead from one room to the next, and thick pillars adorned with draconic motifs support—or used to support— the high ceilings. These chambers have long since been looted by Everstrife's followers, so there is little treasure to be found, but weird monsters such as **slitherjacks** (see **Chapter 5**) and **dorreqi** (*Tome of Beasts* or use **cloakers** and **darkmantles**) still wander the tunnels.

Portals. Throughout the complex, the PCs come across the ancient portals of the dragonborn. Appearing as shimmering zones of a single color floating just above the ground, each portal is 10 feet across and can be spotted with a successful DC 11 Wisdom (Perception) check.

Once used by the dragonborn to visit fascinating destinations throughout the world and the planes, the portals no longer function as intended. Instead, all bar one (in area 8) teleport a creature stepping into them to another portal of the same color elsewhere in the Maze Caverns. You can use the portals to send the PCs to different chambers of your own devising within the complex or simply have the first portal they step into transport them to the corresponding portal at the entrance to Everstrife's lair. If you're feeling mischievous, you can teleport any PCs that follow their comrade to the portal at area 8 in the heart of the lair instead.

The portals are two-way, so the occupants and PCs can use them to move around the caverns. A creature needs to visualize the destination portal as they step into it to arrive at the right one; otherwise, their destination will be random.

Chaos Surges. There is a greater chance of a chaos surge inside the Maze Caverns due to the presence of so many portals. Roll a d20 whenever anyone casts a spell of 1st level or above. A chaos magic surge (see **Chapter 6**) takes place on a roll of 1 or 2.

EVERSTRIFE'S LAIR

Located several hundred feet inside the Maze Caverns is a large chamber that serves as the lair of the wasteland dragon and his followers. The average ceiling height is 50 feet.

1. NORTHEAST ENTRANCE

A shimmering purple portal floats a foot or so above the cavern floor. A creature stepping into this portal is teleported to the purple portal in area 8.

2. SOUTHEAST ENTRANCE

A shimmering red portal floats above the cavern floor, close to a stone column. A creature stepping into the portal is teleported to the red portal in area 8. The column stretches 50 feet to the ceiling and carved with bas-reliefs telling the story of the Conclave of Spellscales and their experiments with portal magic.

Creature. A half-wasteland dragon troll lurks in this area and ferociously attacks intruders. It keeps its collection of victims' bones at the base of the column.

- The half-dragon uses the **troll** stat block with the following changes:
- It gains blindsight with a radius of 10 ft., resistance to force damage, and the ability to speak Draconic.
- It gains the breath weapon of a wyrmling wasteland dragon:

    Warped Energy Breath (Recharge 6). The half-dragon blasts warped arcane energy in a 20-foot line that is 5 feet wide. Each creature in that line must make a DC 11 Dexterity saving throw, taking 22 (5d8) force damage on a failed save, or half as much damage on a successful one.

3. SOUTHERN ENTRANCE

A shimmering green portal floats above the cavern floor. A creature stepping into this portal is teleported to the green portal in area 8. Lying on the floor close by is a fallen column capital. The damaged column it came from, carved with bas-reliefs depicting life in the Conclave of Spellscales, stands to the northeast.

4. SOUTHWESTERN ENTRANCE

A shimmering blue portal floats above the cavern floor. A creature stepping into this portal is teleported to the blue portal in area 8.

5. DRAGONBORN STATUE

A worn and chipped statue of a robed dragonborn stands on a plinth in front of a wall of stone. Its clawed

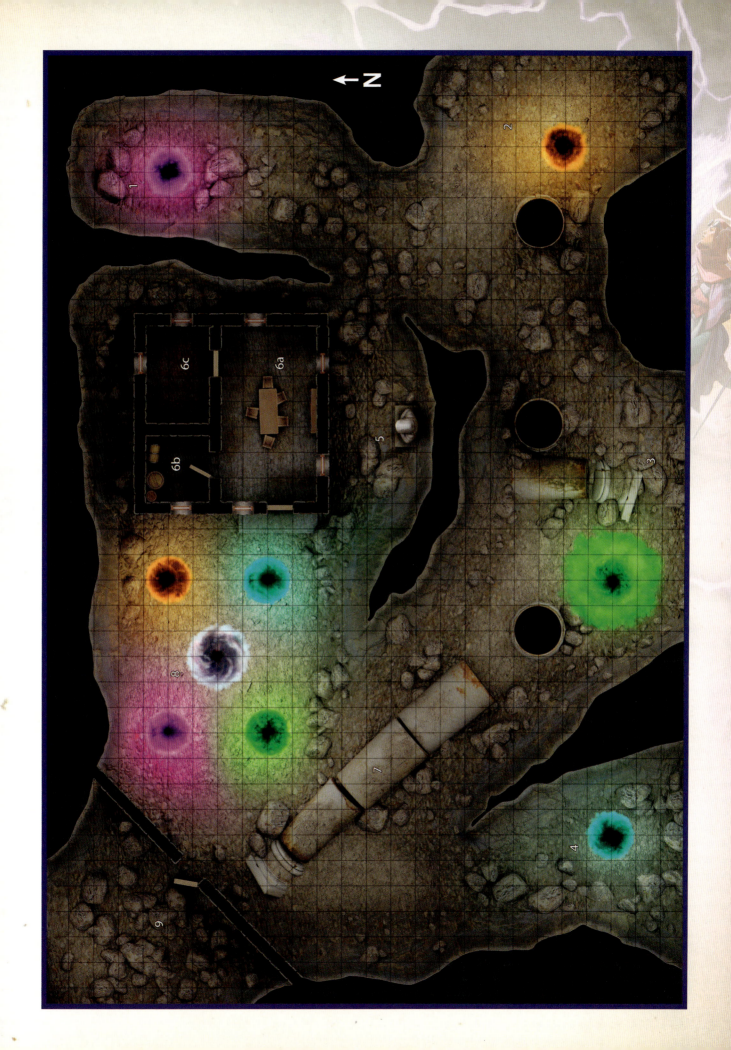

hands hold a broken scepter and a winged diadem rests upon its head. The name "Azirath Boldstaff" is inscribed in Draconic on the plinth. With a successful DC 17 Intelligence (History) check, a PC can recall that Azirath was a famous dragonborn wizard, renowned for his prowess in the conjuration tradition.

6. FOLLOWERS' QUARTERS

Before the Mage War, this single-story stone building was the home of an influential member of the conclave. Now, it serves as the living quarters of Everstrife's scaly humanoid followers. The roof is gone but its three rooms are mostly intact.

Creatures. A dozen kobold **scouts** (equipped with shortbows) inhabit rooms 6a and 6b. There are typically 2d4 here eating, sleeping, or bickering. The rest will be elsewhere in the cavern or out in the wastes on a raid.

The kobolds' leader is Ilphix (N male wasteland dragonborn **bandit lord**; *Tome of Beasts* or use **bandit captain** with 91 hp) who serves as the dragon's loyal steward. Ilphix has rust-colored scales and dull gray horns and wears plain brown robes and a gold medallion with a stylized maze pattern—the symbol of the Maze Caverns. He wields a magical rod of ancient dragonborn origin topped with a large crystal that either functions as a *wand of lightning bolts* or a *wand of wonder* when used (50% chance of each). The rod has 7 charges, regaining 1d6 + 1 expended charges daily at dawn, and requires attunement by a spellcaster. Ilphix's Spellscale blood allows him to attune to the rod.

Ilphix lives in room 6c, which is furnished with an ornate rug (worth 750 gp) and a few other items scavenged from the ruins. The steward has been studying several badly burned tomes recovered from the library (area 9) without success to see if there is a way to transform his master into a metallic dragon. A spell scroll *of earth swim* (see **Chapter 6**) can be found among the books.

7. DRAGON'S PERCH

One of the ancient stone columns has toppled over, leaving just the bottom 10 feet standing. Everstrife (CN male **young wasteland dragon**) likes to perch on top of the fallen column and make arrogant proclamations to Ilphix and the kobolds in which he threatens to obliterate all mages from the face of the earth. Everstrife reserves particular hatred for the Lich King (see **Bleakspire,** above), whom he blames for both the Mage War and the death of his parents—the former patrons of the Conclave of Spellscales. The dragon is angered by intruders, particularly spellcasters, but can be parlayed with by canny PCs bearing gifts who succeed on a DC 20 Charisma (Persuasion) check.

8. PORTALS

Shimmering purple, red, blue, and green portals surround a larger yellow portal. The smaller portals operate in the same way as those in areas 1 through 4, teleporting a creature to another portal of the same color elsewhere in the caverns. Everstrife and his allies will use these portals to move around the lair or to escape from the PCs if combat goes badly.

The large yellow portal teleports a creature to a random destination in the wastes. Roll a d12 and consult the table below.

d12	Destination
1	Cathedral of the Black Goat
2	Ghost Light Marshes
3	Lich King's Tower
4	Nichenevin
5	Nygethuaac, the Dread Colossus
6	Raw Chaos Portal
7	River of Alchemy
8	Rustspike
9	Shattered Towers of the Mage War
10	Shrine of Ancient Light
11	Tangleside
12	Vault of the God-King

9. RUINED LIBRARY

This building was once the library of the Conclave of Spellscales. Worn bas-reliefs carved into its facade depict a pair of brass dragons looking on benevolently as dragonborn mages appear and disappear through portals. The 20-foot-tall wooden door stands ajar. Inside, the structure is partly filled with rubble and other debris.

Everstrife has buried his hoard beneath the rubble and usually sleeps on top of the heap. The PCs can find the cache with a successful DC 20 Intelligence (Investigation) check. Clearing enough space to crawl through and access the hoard takes 4 hours of digging.

Treasure. Everstrife's hoard includes 13,715 sp, 5,111 gp and 304 pp in ancient coins of the dragonborn and fallen magocracies; 22 greenish-blue bloodstones (50 gp each), a gold circlet studded with rubies (1,000 gp), a mysterious 3-inch cube of lightweight metal that is warm to the touch, a fist-sized glass prism containing a moving image of a fiery dragon, an *amber skull of*

Nogg (see **Chapter 7**), a *headband of intellect*, a *portal loupe* (see **Chapter 7**), and a *+1 wand of the war mage*.

NYGETHUAAC, THE DREAD COLOSSUS

Plodding blindly through the wastes at a snail's pace, the dread colossus Nygethuaac is a gargantuan, toad-like monstrosity that was summoned from beyond time and space during the Mage War. Standing 100 feet tall at the shoulder, the alien creature is huge enough to host a ramshackle village built on its head, shoulders, and back. Nygethuaac's skin is furry like a bat's and is dotted here and there with poisonous pustules and small clumps of psychotropic mushrooms.

Inhabited by chaos goblins (see **Chapter 5**), the village is made up of simple wooden huts and platforms connected by ladders and walkways and is secured to the colossus by chains and struts. There are ballistae mounted on some of the platforms, iron cages dangling from its shoulders, and rope ladders leading down to the ground, allowing the goblins to get on and off the monstrosity as it meanders slowly through the wastelands.

Summoning Nygethuaac and other gargantuan monstrosities from the Void was one of the most misguided strategies of the rival magocracies that waged the Mage War. After the first wizard ripped a hole in the fabric of reality to call forth one of these alien beings to destroy his enemies, other mages followed suit. Cities were laid waste and entire kingdoms collapsed as the so-called dread colossuses ravaged the landscape. In the end, a few surviving wizards realized their terrible mistake and banded together to stop the titanic creatures from destroying the world. After a circle of arcanists failed to dismiss Nygethuaac with a ritual of banishment, Svatobor the Dauntless cast a powerful spell that put the giant monstrosity into a dreamlike trance. Bound to wander across the wastes for all eternity, the dread colossus still follows a complex route today that appears completely random to anyone trying to predict where it will go next.

PHYSIOLOGY OF THE DREAD COLOSSUS

Nygethuaac is so huge that it dwarfs even the legendary tarrasque in size. The dread colossus measures 300 feet from head to tail, with a pair of rear legs almost as long as its body. Since it cannot be harmed by any known magical or physical means, no monster stat block is provided.

Movement. Each day, Nygethuaac travels 1d6 – 1 miles in a seemingly random direction, although it is actually following the route it was given by Svatobor the Dauntless when he cast his original spell around 400 years ago.

The colossus moves by making a series of toad-like leaps of 600 feet at irregular intervals throughout the day. The Toad Whisperer (see below) is aware when Nygethuaac is about to leap and shouts a warning through his megaphone. On hearing the warning, the goblins secure themselves to the rope loops hanging throughout the village and hold on tight. When Nygethuaac leaps, unsecured creatures inside the village must succeed on a DC 15 Dexterity saving throw or suffer 3 (1d6) bludgeoning damage and fall prone. On a roll of 5 or less, the creature falls off the colossus to the ground below, suffering 35 (10d6) bludgeoning damage.

Senses. Nygethuaac's large bulbous eyes are milky white and blind. The colossus has Blindsight 120 feet.

Croaking. Every so often, Nygethuaac croaks loudly. These bouts of croaking can last a few minutes or several hours and are extremely disturbing to anyone who is unused to the sound. Creatures who hear the croaking must succeed on a DC 13 Wisdom saving throw or become afflicted with short-term madness for 1d10 minutes. On a successful save or after the madness effects wear off, a creature is immune to the croaking for 24 hours.

The goblins are immune to the effects of the croaking thanks to regularly consuming the mushrooms growing on Nygethuaac's body (see below) and regard the sound as attempts at communication by their host. The Toad Whisperer claims to be able to interpret the colossus' croaks.

Tongue. The dread colossus has a long, sticky tongue that whips out to grab creatures or objects before swallowing them and transporting them to the pocket dimension inside its stomach.

The dread colossus targets one Huge or smaller creature or object that it can see within 120 feet of it. The target must make a DC 20 Strength saving throw. On a failed save, the target is pulled into the colossus's mouth and swallowed. Creatures that are swallowed by Nygethuaac are unharmed but find themselves inside a strange pocket dimension (See the adventure "Down the Gullet" in *Tales from the Wastes* for details). Alternatively, swallowed creatures are teleported to a random location in the wastes.

Poisonous Pustules. Nygethuaac's furry skin is peppered with disgusting yellow pustules around 5 to 10 feet in diameter. A creature coming into contact with the pustules must succeed on a DC 13 Constitution saving throw or be poisoned for 1 minute. The poisoned creature is paralyzed. The creature can repeat the saving throw at the end of each of its turns, ending the effect on itself on a success.

The goblins climb down to these pustules on ropes and smear the poison on their ballista bolts (area 1). The poison lasts for 48 hours when used to coat weapons and ammunition.

Psychotropic Mushrooms. Patches of 2-foot-high, white-spotted purple mushrooms grow at irregular intervals on Nygethuaac's body. These patches are between 3 and 5 feet across and often sprout up near the poisonous pustules. The mushrooms are edible—they can be eaten raw or made into tea.

A creature eating these mushrooms must succeed on a DC 13 Wisdom saving throw or experience surreal hallucinations for 1d10 minutes, becoming charmed and incapacitated with a speed of 0.

Roll a d6; on a roll of 1–5, the hallucinations are bright and beautiful, but on a 6, they are dark and frightening. A creature can choose to voluntarily fail the saving throw to experience these effects. Eating the mushrooms for three consecutive days confers immunity to the effects of Nygethuaac's croaking.

THE TOAD WHISPERER

Becoming the Toad Whisperer has undoubtedly changed the chaos goblin formerly known as Hunvreek. Months of consuming the mushrooms growing on Nygethuaac's back and communicating telepathically with the colossus have transformed him into a squat, bow-legged chaos goblin with toad-like features and brownish green, warty skin covered in pustules. The Toad Whisperer is almost bald with bulging eyes, a wide grin, and a very long, thin tongue which he can elongate to 10 feet and use to pick up objects weighing less than 5 pounds. He wears a shabby, knee-length green robe and carries a brass megaphone for warning the goblins in the village when Nygethuaac is about to leap.

Although Nygethuaac has spent the past four centuries in the magical trance created by Svatobor the Dauntless' spell, the dread colossus is aware of the Toad Whisperer and the two are able to communicate with each other telepathically. Nygethuaac has shared some of the secrets of the Void with his seer and lets the goblin know when he is about to move. In turn, the Toad Whisperer's soothing words of homage calm the colossus, and several times he has successfully guided the huge creature away from trampling through a wasteland village.

EXPLORING THE GOBLIN VILLAGE

About fifty chaos goblins live in the rickety wooden shacks that make up the village. They came to live on the dread colossus a few years ago after their leader Hunvreek—who now calls himself the Toad Whisperer—climbed up the monstrosity's body and ate a patch of the mushrooms he found growing there.

Hunvreek experienced a wondrous vision of the future and persuaded the other goblins to sample the mushrooms. After everyone had done so, the tribe decided they would be safe from their many enemies if they built homes on top of the creature. Since that day, the goblins have lived on Nygethuaac and have gone wherever the colossus has.

Reaching the Village. The chaos goblins use 100-foot-long rope ladders to come and go from the village on hunting and trading expeditions. These ladders can be pulled up if the village is threatened, but most of the time, the goblins leave them in place.

The goblins don't get many visitors, because most travelers in the wastes have heard tales of the dangers of getting too close to the dread colossus. Unless the Toad Whisperer declares them to be enemies, the goblins receive guests in the assembly hall (area 2) and offer them mushroom tea.

Houses. The goblins live in simple one- or two-story wooden shacks that are secured to the colossus and each other with a bewildering tangle of chains, ropes, and wooden supports. Each is home to 2d4 chaos goblins and has a series of rope loops secured to the walls which the goblins strap themselves into if Nygethuaac is about to leap.

1. BALLISTA PLATFORMS

Three chaos goblins are stationed on each of these platforms, acting as crew for a ballista on a swivel mount that allows it to fire in a 180-degree arc on the colossus' left or right side. The crew have two dozen bolts as ammunition; half are coated with poison (see Poisonous Pustules, above).

2. ASSEMBLY HALL

This is the largest building in the village, used at mealtimes and for gatherings of the entire tribe. It has a 20-foot-high ceiling and a 10-foot-high balcony overlooking the rows of long tables below. Every few days, the Toad Whisperer calls the tribe together and stands on the balcony to pronounce what the dread colossus has told him in his dreams and visions. There are usually 2d6 chaos goblins in the hall drinking mugs of steaming-hot mushroom tea. If player characters visit the village, they are each offered a mug (see Psychotropic Mushrooms, above).

3. TOAD WHISPERER'S TOWER

A rickety wooden staircase ascends 20 feet from the large platform fixed to the colossus's head. Although well secured, it sways alarmingly on windy days and whenever more than four Small or two Medium creatures climb the stairs. The Toad Whisperer stands at the top of this tower each day to communicate telepathically with Nygethuaac.

4. TOAD WHISPERER'S SHACK

The Toad Whisperer lives in this single-story wooden hut. Inside, every inch of the walls and ceiling are covered with his charcoal scribbles written in an incomprehensible mixture of Goblin and Void Speech. These are his attempts to capture everything he has learned from Nygethuaac on the nature of the Void.

Treasure. The Toad Whisperer keeps a small lightweight metal box of ancient alien origin under his bed. The box has a sliding lid and contains his precious collection of a dozen or so assorted frog and toad statuettes. Although most of these are only of interest to another collector, one is orichalcum with small emeralds for eyes (worth 800 gp) and another is a *figurine of wondrous power* (jade frog). This uncommon wondrous item functions like other magical figurines and can become a giant frog for up to 6 hours. Once it has been used, it can't be used again until 2 days have passed.

5. PRISON CAGES

Several iron cages hang on chains from the sides of the buildings and are used to hold prisoners. Only one (5a) is currently occupied—the prisoner is Gerhorn Marrak, a wandering human barbarian (**berserker**) whom the Toad Whisperer had locked up for insulting the dread colossus. Gerhorn has just 6 hp remaining and has four levels of exhaustion.

ADVENTURE HOOKS

Saxger Dustblood, sagacious hermit and noted expert of the wastes, has spent the past few years monitoring the route traveled by the dread colossus to fathom its meaning, if any. Recently, he has determined that Nygethuaac is speeding up. Could this be a sign that Svatobor's spell is starting to lose its potency? As the huge monstrosity heads directly for the goblin town of Nichenevin, Saxger urges the PCs to speak to the Toad Whisperer and find out what he knows.

RAW CHAOS PORTAL

Though it is currently the heart of a grand, twisting temple in the desolation of the wastes, the raw chaos portal existed long before the cultists arrived. Once a tiny, marble-sized rift in the fabric of existence, the portal called out to those who had the heart and mind to hear it. Individuals of all walks of life, from lands both near and far, felt an unexplainable draw to this location and, following the strange whispers in their dreams, arrived at an unremarkable span of earth in the blasted wastelands. Bit by bit and stone by stone, the cultists built a massive temple around the rift. Using their strange gifts and dark powers gained by their constant proximity to the rift, they encouraged it to grow until it became a dark pool in the foundation of the temple.

The swirling portal is a doorway to another realm entirely, spitting pure, unfettered chaos into the world. The portal twists and alters the space around it, causing constant, unexpected, and unpredictable fluctuations in the terrain and summoning—or creating—eldritch creatures and wild anomalies. The cultists, who now call themselves the Order of the Black Horizon, revel in the chaos and offer periodic sacrifices to the portal. Their bodies and minds have been warped and twisted by their time in the temple, but they regard the changes as a blessing from the power beyond and tailor their garb to show off their marked skin or their altered limbs. They are strangely welcoming, believing visitors will see the truth of existence given enough time. After all—any who become disruptive can simply be fed to the portal.

REGIONAL EFFECTS

The portal and its chaotic energies have wreaked havoc on the surrounding landscape, and strange entities have leaked, crawled, or been summoned from the portal to wander the wastes and establish new homes. In addition to the dangers of the land and creatures, the portal and its energies pose a threat to any who spend too long within its proximity.

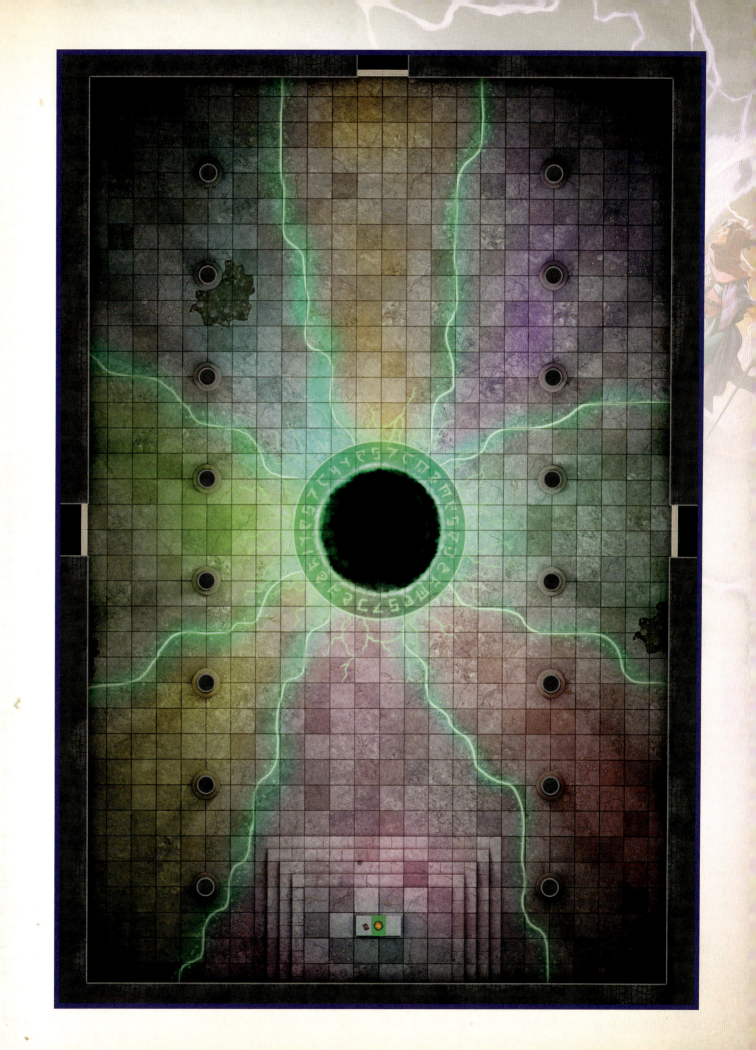

WITHIN FIVE MILES

The area within five miles of the chaos portal looks normal, but magic used within this area is volatile and unpredictable. Whenever a spell is cast or a magic item is activated or used within this area, roll on the Regional Chaos Magic Effects table. Reroll any irrelevant results.

WITHIN THREE MILES

The area within three miles of the portal is under more extreme effects. In addition to the effects above, creatures within this region become twisted and changed. Animals found here may have extra heads or feet or may exhibit unexpected magical abilities. The GM may roll on the Regional Chaos Mutations table to provide one or more changes to any creatures encountered in this area. Reroll any irrelevant results.

EXPLORING THE AREA

The area surrounding the temple and the raw chaos portal is made of dry, scrubby, badland-like wastes. Boulders lie scattered about, as if strewn by some giant hand. Ravines split the landscape, some as shallow as five feet, while others cut swaths hundreds of feet deep and wide. The landscape is constantly changing, some ravines sealing up without warning and others opening with only a rumble heralding their arrival. Occasionally, a river or lake springs into existence, and may remain for a few hours or a few years before vanishing again.

The temple containing the raw chaos portal sits on a wedge of land a mile long and half a mile wide between two surprisingly stable ravines. Each of these ravines is 40 feet wide and 150 feet deep.

UNSTABLE RAVINES

The ravines in this area are not formed by natural erosion but are a result of the chaos energy seeping from the portal in the temple. As such, they may exist for years or may seal up after a matter of hours. For those ravines that have been around for more than a few days, local wildlife takes up residence within its cracks and crevices. Birds nest in the walls, lizards bask on the ledges, and bats lair in caves. Other, stranger creatures may also live within the ravines, such as **dust mephits, giant wasps, ankhegs, manticores,** and perhaps even a **roc**.

REGIONAL CHAOS MAGIC EFFECTS

d20	Effect
1	A massive, lidless, Medium-sized eye appears in an unoccupied space within five feet of the target and remains for 1 minute. During this time, it never takes its gaze off the caster and moves when the caster moves, maintaining its proximity. If it takes any damage, it disappears in a puff of smoke.
2	The GM randomly determines the target. Include the caster in these calculations.
3	A sprinkle of glitter appears over the caster's head, coating them in a fine layer of sparkling green dust. They are under the effects of the *faerie fire* spell for the next minute.
4	If a creature would take damage from the spell or effect, it is healed instead; convert the damage to hit points regained.
5	A chime sounds, deep and mournful.
6	The caster feels their eyeballs flip upside-down in their sockets. This has no noticeable mechanical effect.
7	The spell or item has no effect. Instead, pink feathers float down onto the battlefield.
8–15	No effect.
16	The caster becomes flat and one-dimensional until the beginning of their next turn. This has no noticeable mechanical effect, but it's incredibly off-putting for everyone involved.
17	The sound of babbling and shrieking voices fills the space within a 15-foot-radius sphere centered on the caster and lasts for 1 minute. Any creature that starts its turn within this area must succeed on a DC 16 Wisdom saving throw or become stunned until the beginning of their next turn.
18	A rabbit appears beside the caster. It is solid black, with solid white eyes with no pupils. It has 2 hp, an AC of 20, and a fly speed of 40 ft. It is otherwise a completely normal rabbit.
19	If a creature would be healed by the spell or effect, it is damaged instead; convert the hit points regained to psychic damage.
20	The spell or effect doubles in potency. Double the damage or healing done to the target. For an area-of-effect spell with no damage (such as *faerie fire*), double the area effected.

REGIONAL CHAOS MUTATIONS

d10	Mutation
1	The creature can cast *blink* once per day.
2	The creature has twice as many appendages as normal. Their movement speed is doubled.
3	Instead of bludgeoning, piercing, or slashing damage, the creature's attacks instead deal cold, fire, or lightning damage.
4	The creature's skin, fur, or feathers have been replaced with inky-black, shimmering scales. Its AC is increased by +2.
5	It has extra eyes. So many eyes. Too many eyes. The creature gains +5 to its Wisdom (Perception) and cannot be surprised.
6	Human-like mouths have sprouted across the creature's body, and they babble incessantly. Any creature within five feet must succeed on a DC 14 Wisdom saving throw or become frightened of the creature for 1 minute.
7	The creature appears normal, but it speaks Common in the voice of one of the PC's parents.
8	Any creature that succeeds on a melee attack against the creature must make a DC 14 Constitution saving throw as black ichor spurts from the wound. On a failure, the attacker takes 1d6 acid damage.
9	The creature can cast *dispel magic* three times per day.
10	The creature gains a climb speed equal to its walking speed, and can move up, down, and across vertical surfaces, even upside-down on the ceiling.

RIVERS AND LAKES

While there is little in the way of water in the wastes surrounding the chaos portal, occasionally a river or lake may spontaneously appear (or disappear). Water drawn from these sources carries the sharp taste of ozone. There is a 10% chance the water hides a subterranean cavern that houses an **aboleth**. Such a creature appears and disappears with the water.

THE TEMPLE

The temple consists of a ring of outer rooms surrounding a central chamber that houses the raw chaos portal. In contrast to the rest of the landscape (and even the appearances and personalities of the cultists that reside within), the temple is a simple, symmetrical rectangle, with thick pillars supporting the ceiling 60 feet above. Double doors open into the temple, centered on each of the building's four sides. These double doors open into a 10-foot-wide hallway that encircles the interior perimeter of the building, with a single door set into the interior wall every 30 feet. These doors lead to the outer rooms.

THE OUTER ROOMS

Each of the doors in the outer perimeter hallway leads into the outer rooms. These rooms serve as the bedrooms, research libraries, labs, and other personal chambers for the cultists of the Order of the Black Horizon. There is no set layout for these rooms, however—walking through one door does not necessarily lead where it's expected to lead, and walking back through a door you just came through may lead to a completely new location altogether. Each room in the outer rooms is 30 feet square, has a 15-foot-tall ceiling, is brightly lit by ambient lighting, and has a single door on all four walls. None of these doors are locked, nor are they trapped.

Navigating the Outer Rooms

Moving through the outer rooms is not as simple as it seems. Opening any door from one outer room into another leads to the north door in a randomly determined room. Attempting to map the outer rooms quickly leads the characters to the realization that the layout makes no sense and that there seems to be more rooms in one place than could be physically possible. To get through the outer rooms and into the inner perimeter hallway, the characters must enter each type of room (library, alchemy lab, bedroom, kitchen, dining room) and exit each room via the east door. If they ask any cultist how to get out of the maze of rooms, the cultist simply points to the east door of the room.

When a character first enters the outer rooms from the outer perimeter hallway, they find themselves in a library. After that, roll on the table below whenever a character opens a new door to determine the room they find behind it.

THE OUTER ROOMS

d8	Room
1	Library (uninhabited)
2	Library (inhabited)
3	Alchemy Lab
4	Bedroom (uninhabited)
5	Bedroom (inhabited)
6	Kitchen (dirty)
7	Kitchen (clean)
8	Dining Room

Library

Bookshelves line the walls of this room, filled with books and dotted with trinkets. Two heavy leather chairs sit on either side of a circular end table. If the characters attempt to read any of the books, they discover it is written in a language they do not understand. If they attempt to use magic to decipher the script (such as with *comprehend languages*), incomprehensible screaming fills their mind and they are blinded for the next hour.

The first time they enter the library, it is inhabited by Gideon (CN elf **cultist**) sitting in one of the two chairs. His hood hides his face until he raises his head, when he looks up at the characters with three eyes. He introduces himself and welcomes them to his space. He only becomes hostile if he or his library is attacked. If the library is inhabited when randomly determined, they meet Gideon again, and he has no memory of meeting them any previous time.

Alchemy Lab

This lab holds a table with an array of tubes and glass bottles. A crucible sits on the end of the table. A heavy tome is open on a rotating book reader and is subject to the same effects as the books in the library (above). A successful DC 14 Intelligence (Investigation) check reveals a *potion of many forms* (see **Chapter 7**) amidst the bottles. They can only find this potion here once.

Bedroom

This bedroom holds a chest of drawers, a wash basin, a chamber pot, and a single bed with rumpled blankets. If it is inhabited, Gemini (CN human **cultist**) is asleep in the bed. If awakened, she introduces herself and welcomes the characters. When she speaks, her voice is layered with many different voices, some speaking different languages entirely. She is friendly and only becomes hostile if attacked. If the characters meet her more than once, she has no memory of meeting them.

Kitchen

The kitchen holds a stove, pots and pans hanging above a butcher's block island, a pantry filled with nonperishable foodstuffs, and an empty washbasin. If the kitchen is dirty, a few of the pots and pans are missing from the hanging rack and are instead on the stove, crusted with food, and one of the pans is soaking in the cold, dirty water in the washbasin.

Dining Room

The dining room has a long, rough-hewn table, with stools enough for eight people. It is set with mismatched plates and flatware. A **cultist** (CN human) sits at the table, her four hands laid in her lap as if she's waiting patiently for something. When the characters enter, she watches them quietly. She does not speak but if is treated kindly, she smiles broadly, and if she laughs, her mouth splits both vertically and horizontally, and she has two tongues. If they ask any of the other cultists about her, they inform them her name is Marcella.

The Inner Perimeter Hallway

This hallway leads off to the left and right and runs the perimeter between the outer rooms and the inner temple. A single door stands every 30 feet on the outer wall of the hallway. The inner walls have a double door directly in the center that leads into the inner temple.

THE INNER TEMPLE

This room is surprisingly large, 115 feet wide, 155 feet long, and 80 feet tall. Two columns of 5-foot-wide pillars split the room into thirds. At the east end stands a raised dais with a heavy stone altar. The floor is made of polished marble, and everything seems well made and well-tended. At the altar stands High Priestess Ciara (CN human **mage** under the effects of *spider climb*) and two of her **cult fanatics,** Llora (CN human) and Tomman (CN dwarf). High Priestess Ciara welcomes the characters and only becomes hostile if the characters harm her, her cultists, the temple, or the portal. Glowing runes cover High Priestess Ciara's arms. Llora has a second, smaller head at the meeting of her neck and shoulder, and Tomman's eyes each have three pupils.

In the center of the room is the raw chaos portal itself. Set in the floor, it almost looks like a round, inky pool, but periodic flashes of energy or light bely the truth. Glowing runes five feet tall are carved into the floor around the portal, glowing with an eerie light. The tile is cracked around the portal, releasing strange vapors.

Portal Effects

Radiating out from the portal are seven beams of wavering light, and the beams divide the room into eight nearly identically sized slices. Each of these slices is subject to a different effect, as listed in the chart below. At the top of every round, roll a d20; on a result of 1–5, there is a flash of light, and the entire "pie" of effects rotates one spot clockwise.

RIVER OF ALCHEMY

The River of Alchemy was an accidental creation, created after an explosion ripped through a gnomish alchemical laboratory set in the base of a mountain. The location was chosen specifically in an attempt to harness the powerful wild magics that ravage the wastes in the lowlands, but, perhaps unsurprisingly, things did not go entirely to plan. The explosion created a crater in the mountainside a mile deep and tainted the source of the spring-fed river the gnomes once used as a base for their potion-crafting. The result is a river of fluids of various colors and viscosities that mix and mingle in unpredictable ways. The River of Alchemy is a treasure trove of rare or unique potions and poisons—and a powder keg of unstable magic.

CHAOS PORTAL EFFECTS

Zone	Effects
1	**Frost.** Ice coats the floor in this zone. It is considered difficult terrain, and creatures who attempt to use the Dash action must make a DC 14 Dexterity saving throw. On a failure, they fall prone. When the zones shift, the ice remains for 1 round.
2	**Fire.** Flames erupt from the ground here without warning. When a character starts their turn in this zone, they must make a DC 14 Dexterity saving throw, taking 1d6 fire damage on a failure or half as much on a success.
3	**Eyes.** 1d4 globules of floating eyeballs (Medium size) pop into existence in this zone. Whatever they see, High Priestess Ciara sees. Creatures in this zone have disadvantage on Dexterity (Stealth) checks. If the globules of eyes take damage, they explode, dealing 2d4 force damage to any creature within 5 feet. When the zones rotate, any remaining globules stay in their current spot, and 1d4 new globules pop into existence in the new zone.
4	**Gas.** Cracks in the tile open and seep strange gasses. Any creatures who start their turn in this zone must make a DC 14 Constitution saving throw. On a failure, they take 1d4 poison damage and are subject to the effects of the *confusion* spell until the beginning of their next turn.
5	**Electricity Orb.** A 5-foot-wide orb of electricity floats around the confines of this zone. It has a movement speed of 15 feet and heads toward the nearest creature at the top of the round. At the end of its movement, it pulses with electricity; every creature within 10 feet of the orb must succeed on a DC 14 Dexterity saving throw or take 2d4 lightning damage. The orb moves with the zone when it rotates.
6	**Tentacles.** A 10-foot-diameter circle filled with tentacles and eyes opens in the floor in a random location in this zone. The tentacles have a reach of 10 ft. Whenever a character comes within range, one of the tentacles lashes out and grapples the character (escape DC 13). A character grappled in this way is considered restrained. If a tentacle takes damage, it disappears in a splash of sludge, and another takes its place. There can be no more than eight tentacles at a time.
7	**Void Pool.** A 15-foot-wide puddle of inky blackness appears at a random location within this zone and remains for as long as the zone is in place. A character who enters the puddle falls into icy darkness and takes 1d4 force damage. At the beginning of their next turn, they may roll a d20. On a roll of 11 or higher, they reappear 30 feet above a random unoccupied space and fall prone, taking 3d6 bludgeoning damage; on a failure, they take another 1d4 force damage and remain in darkness.
8	**Peace.** This zone is calm and refreshing. A warm wind blows. Any creature that starts its turn in this zone regains 1d4 hit points.

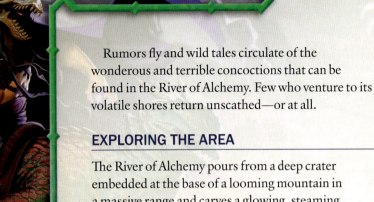

Rumors fly and wild tales circulate of the wonderous and terrible concoctions that can be found in the River of Alchemy. Few who venture to its volatile shores return unscathed—or at all.

EXPLORING THE AREA

The River of Alchemy pours from a deep crater embedded at the base of a looming mountain in a massive range and carves a glowing, steaming, bubbling path across the wilderness. Traveling near the river is dangerous—the winds can shift at any moment, bringing toxic gasses, the constantly churning mix can explode with unpredictable effects at any moment, and terrible creatures born in the boiling brew climb onto the land without warning.

THE RIVER PROPER

The main branch of the river runs from the cavernous crater in the mountains, winds across fields and grasslands, then empties into a sinkhole. The river averages between 50 and 100 feet wide and is typically around 30 feet deep at its deepest points and 2 feet deep at its shallowest. Any creature who gets within 20 feet of the riverbank or starts its turn there must make a DC 14 Constitution saving throw from the toxic gasses, taking 1d4 poison damage on a failed save and half as much on a success.

Entering the river is extremely ill-advised, and the results of such an action vary wildly. If a creature enters the river, roll on the River of Alchemy Effects table below to determine the effects. The creature can only be under one effect at a time.

RIVER CREATURES

Numerous strange creatures are spawned from the alchemical mélange, crawling forth to attack and devour everything in their path. These creatures include **gray oozes, gelatinous cubes, ochre jellies, black puddings,** and other oozes, and aberrations such as **gibbering mouthers** and **dread mouthers** and **slitherjacks** (see **Chapter 5**). All of these creatures are hostile and attack other creatures on sight.

RIVER OF ALCHEMY EFFECTS

d12	Effect
1	The creature is subject to the effects of the *polymorph* spell for the next hour. Roll a d6 to determine if its transforms into a goat (1), raven (2), weasel (3), flying snake (4), giant toad (5), or ankylosaurus (6).
2	The creature grows bright green feathers across its entire body. This effect can only be removed with a *greater restoration* or similar spell.
3	The creature becomes ethereal for the next hour, as per the *etherealness* spell.
4	The creature grows gills. It can only breathe water or other liquid (like that found in the river). When on dry land, the creature immediately begins to suffocate. This effect lasts for 1 hour and can only be removed with *alter self* or a similar spell.
5	The creature takes 2d4 acid damage, repeated each round it remains in the river.
6	The creature's hair, if it has any, falls out and is replaced by gently rustling oak leaves. This effect can only be removed with *greater restoration* or a similar spell.
7	The creature takes 2d6 poison damage, repeated each round it remains in the river, and gains the poisoned condition.
8	The creature takes 1d10 fire damage, repeated each round it remains in the river.
9	The creature's skin oozes a green slime from its pores. It has disadvantage on Charisma checks and advantage on Dexterity checks to escape a grapple or slip through tight spaces. This effect can only be removed with *greater restoration* or a similar spell.
10	Any non-magical items made of metal or wood being worn or carried by the creature immediately begin to corrode. Weapons take a permanent and cumulative –1 penalty to damage rolls each round it's exposed to the river. If its penalty drops to –5, the weapon is destroyed. Armor takes a permanent and cumulative –1 penalty to the provided AC. If its penalty drops to –5, the armor is destroyed. Non-magical fabric immediately dissolves.
11–12	No effect.

THE CRATER

The crater that vomits forth the River of Alchemy delves nearly a mile into the mountain. Here, the creatures created by the river itself can be found in greater proliferation and include cave-dwelling creatures such as **cloakers,** along with **anthema locusts** and **insatiable broods** (see **Chapter 7**) and the gasses here are more concentrated, dealing 1d6 damage instead of 1d4. Here, pieces of the former alchemical laboratory can be found, scattered amid the piles of stone and rock or half-submerged in the river itself.

THE SOURCE

Adventurers who are bold or foolish enough to delve to the very back of the crater can discover the source of the river: a massive metal sphere, 40 feet in diameter, wedged beneath a pile of boulders. The sphere has 15 nozzles (each nearly 5 feet long) with circular handles dotting the surface; eight of these snapped off in the disaster, and liquids of all types and colors spew forth from the broken nozzles in violent sprays. The liquids all flow down the walls and drip from the ceiling to the crater floor, where they gather and form the River of Alchemy. Casting *dispel magic* on one of the broken nozzles halts the flow of liquid for 1 minute, after which it begins flowing again.

Reaching the source is tricky indeed, as most of the nearby surfaces are coated in one liquid or another, and several drip from the ceiling like rain in a 30-foot radius centered on the source sphere; touching any of these liquids or being within this radius requires a roll on the River of Alchemy Effects table above.

Deactivating the source requires multiple, extensive skill checks. For each of the eight broken nozzles, a character must succeed on three DC 25 Strength checks or three DC 20 Dexterity checks with tinker's tools or smith's tools to bend the nozzle back into place. If the character fails on three checks before they succeed on three, the DC increases by 5, and each successive failure increases the difficulty by 5. Once they have succeeded on three checks, the flow of liquid from that nozzle stops, and remains repaired for 24 hours, after which the force of the liquid from within bursts through the repairs.

FONT OF LIFE

Deep within the crater, a large eddy hidden behind a massive boulder holds a mysterious power and is what alchemists and other magic users call the Font of Life. Only known as a rumor and conjecture, the Font of Life is what breathes life into the river's strange creatures. The potent and specific mix of liquids here somehow can gift the spark of life and is a treasure beyond comprehension.

A dead creature placed in the Font of Life returns to life as per the *true resurrection* spell. Liquid drawn from the Font of Life can be applied to a dead creature, which is then restored to life as per the *resurrection* spell. Liquid taken from the Font of Life in this way maintains its efficacy for 5 days, after which it becomes inert. The effects of the Font of Life can even restore constructed humanoids to life.

Locating the Font of Life requires 24 hours of searching, three successful DC 25 Intelligence (Investigation) checks, and two successful DC 20 Intelligence (Arcana) checks.

POTENTIAL POTIONS

Liquid drawn from the River of Alchemy has the potential for creating a potent poison or marvelous potion. If a character drinks or draws liquid from the river, roll on the River Alchemy table below to see what, if any, potion or poison is created.

RIVER ALCHEMY

1dx	Alchemical Result
1	*philter of love*
2	*poison (basic)*
3	*potion of animal friendship*
4	*potion of diminution*
5	*potion of etherealness*
6	*potion of flying*
7	*potion of gaseous form*
8	*potion of giant strength*
9	*potion of growth*
10	*potion of healing*
11	*potion of heroism*
12	*potion of invisibility*
13	*potion of many forms* (see **Chapter 7**)
14	*potion of poison*
15	*potion of resistance*
16	*potion of supreme healing*
17	*potion of vitality*
18	*potion of water breathing*
19	*philter of love*
20–100	foul-tasting, inert liquid

VAULT OF THE GOD-KING

It is said the desolation of the badlands hides many secrets. Recently, whispered rumors tell of the discovery of the twisted wreckage of a metal meteor driven by a godlike antihuman sorcerer whose terrifying powers transported him between the worlds. His disciples call him god-king and claim him a blood descendant of the dread colossuses who speaks to otherworldly beings that reveal the secrets of divine ascension.

The god-king is a myth of sorts. The metal meteor is a crashed alien spacecraft that encountered another race known only as **children of the silver sphere** (see **Chapter 5**) during its travels. The children of the silver sphere overran the ship, forcing it to crash. Now living within the ruins, the children have established themselves as agents of divinity. Using their considerable psychic magic and the ship's unique bio-tech artificial intelligence, they lure humanoids into the vault of the god-king by offering to teach the secrets of divine ascension to mortals seeking to attain divinity. Those foolish enough to submit to the desire become unknowing guinea pigs for their manipulative experiments. Each month, the children of the silver sphere choose a new god-king from their fold of disciples. The current god-king is a sorcerer named Aroth whom the aliens implanted with the belief that he bears the bloodline of a dread colossus.

EXPLORING THE CRAFT

The crashed craft is fabricated from an unidentifiable alloy with a scintillating blue hue. The metal is noticeably cold to the touch, slightly reflective, and eerily glistens when light strikes it. The incredibly durable metal's physical properties closely resemble adamantine.

Sliding Doors. Unless otherwise noted, metal sliding airlock doors seal off all inner corridors and chambers. Without power, they must be pried open with a successful DC 14 Strength ability check using a crowbar or similar object. Individuals lacking such a tool can spend 1 minute scavenging scrap metal.

The doors are hollow and filled with a pressurized insulating fluid. If damaged, a clear, semi-viscous fluid bursts out, filling the corridor and sealing it fast. Breaking a door with a successful DC 12 Strength check releases the pressurized fluid in a 20-foot cone. Creatures caught in the blast take 3d6 acid damage, after which the fluid rapidly hardens, trapping them. Characters making a successful DC 14 Dexterity save take half damage and avoid becoming stuck. In the first round, the blast area becomes difficult terrain. In the next round, anyone in the area must also make a DC 13 Strength check to avoid becoming grappled. In the third round, grappled individuals must escape or become restrained. In the fourth round, the liquid hardens to the strength of wood.

Option. If a character rolls a natural 20 while attempting to pry open the doors, they accidentally damage the seal, triggering the release of the pressurized fluid.

Manipulatives. Several locations within the ship have switches, knobs, and other manipulatives. Long drained of their primary power supplies, some of the ship's auxiliary instruments run off stored power sources. Characters that haphazardly manipulate the equipment risk triggering random surge effects.

d6	Surge Effects
1	A low hum vibrates along the walls.
2	Lights power up for a second, flickering wildly before shutting off again.
3	A jolt of electrical energy shoots from the panel. The character manipulating the panel must make a successful DC 13 Dexterity save or take 2d6 electrical damage.
4	A communications system unleashes a jarring howl of static blended with a high-pitched squeal of alien gibberish.
5	Lights flash in sync with an ominous beeping.
6	A blast of icy cold gas bursts from the panel. The character manipulating the panel must make a successful DC 13 Dexterity save or take 2d6 cold damage.

ACCESSING THE CRAFT

While Location 1 provides characters with the easiest and safest way to enter the craft, they may attempt to access it from another point.

Option 2. There are two exterior doors located at the aft, in area 11. One is entirely sealed but can be excavated as described in the entry. The other is readily accessible.

Option 3. Characters can attempt to climb on top of the craft and locate another access point. If they discover the courtyard (area 10), they can enter through the break in the adjoining corridor.

GM note. As written, this places the characters adjacent to the adventure's main antagonists. If characters take this approach, the GM should consider moving antagonists elsewhere within the ship.

1. ENTRANCE

An opening in the weathered metal wall exposes an unlit corridor strewn with rubble and twisted metal debris.

Anyone inspecting the walls just inside the opening notices a passage of graffiti coarsely scratched into the metal. In Void Speech, it reads, "*Bow low in humility all who enter the Vault of the God-King!*"

About halfway down the corridor, a bent metal door torn from an arch in the north wall rests upon the grated metal floor. At the end of the hall, a set of sliding double doors blocks the western exit. The doors rest in a slightly open position, allowing characters to peep through the crack into area 4.

Creatures. A lone sentry hides behind the broken door in the north arch.

As soon as he spots intruders, he attempts to sneak into area 2 and activate the hologram. Afterward, he dashes to area 3 and rouses the other disciples. If the characters prevent him from getting to area 3, he instead shouts a warning that there are intruders.

As soon as the sentinel is successfully targeted with a spell or takes physical damage, the ship's biotech AI alerts the Children of the Sphere in area 9.

2. BRIDGE

The door to this room lies on the floor of the adjacent hall, battered from its frame. The threshold opens into a broad chamber cramped with twisted metal objects and jagged rock covered in shards of broken glass. Scorch marks scar the panels, and serpentine coils of torn wiring hang from the ceiling, walls, and other objects. A section of the metal wall is bent inward, ruptured by the rocky side of a hill.

This is the bridge of the ship. Characters can readily identify some of the wreckage as furniture. Other objects such as navigation equipment, sensors, and tracking systems are beyond understanding.

The hologram. A curious chalk circle marks one of the panel buttons. If pressed, it triggers a holographic message prepared by the children of the shining sphere. A translucent rainbow-colored image appears of a blindfolded man wearing long robes accompanied on either side by two beautiful children. The man speaks in Common, "*Welcome, blessed ones, for you have entered the Vault of the God-King. Here all truths are revealed to those willing to accept their awakening.*"

3. PODS

Everything in this chamber is corroded and coated with several layers of fine grayish crystalline dust. The north wall has collapsed inward, and boulders and other debris have tumbled into the room. Beneath one of the larger boulders lies a dented oblong metal canister fitted with ridged pipes. A row of three c-shaped alcoves faces the room. A badly cracked sheet of glass covers one of the alcoves. At the bottom of the alcove rests a large pile of resinous brown and red glop.

Creatures. Three disciples (**bandit captains**) occupy the room. They gather the crystalline dust, scraping it from the walls and floor and placing it into a glass tube. If they spot outsiders, they throw their hands in surrender and proselytize about the great blessing of how fate led them to the vault. They offer to lead the characters to see the god-king, but only if they leave behind their weapons. They claim the king doesn't accept violence within the vault. The statement is accurate; however, the disciples resort to violence if necessary.

4. PULSE DRIVE CORE

This chamber sustained considerable damage. Its metal panels ripple, and cracks breach the resin-coated floor. Solidified rivers of an unknown fluorescent green substance trail through the chamber. They emanate from a series of cracked glass cylinders vertically mounted to the east wall. The south ceiling has compressed and collapsed inward.

Anyone touching the fluorescent substance discovers it has a thick, rubbery skin, while the inside feels like a viscous liquid.

The fluid connects the biotech artificial intelligence that operates the ship. Unfortunately, the Material Plane cannot provide the specific environmental conditions required for the fluid to function efficiently. At present, it only has minimal sentience.

Any physical contact with the liquid puts individuals in contact with the ship itself. They begin hearing sporadic bursts of strange alien voices in an unknown language, accompanied by pangs of trauma and a foreboding sense of danger. Beyond that, the meaning is indecipherable. The voice persists until the character spends an entire day outside of the ship and takes a long rest. Every 1d20 minutes, the voices escalate, forcing the character to make a DC 12 Wisdom save or take 1d6 psychic damage. If the character rolls a 1 on the save, the AI fluids report their presence to the aliens, who can then contact the characters each time they fail the Wisdom save to avoid damage from the contact.

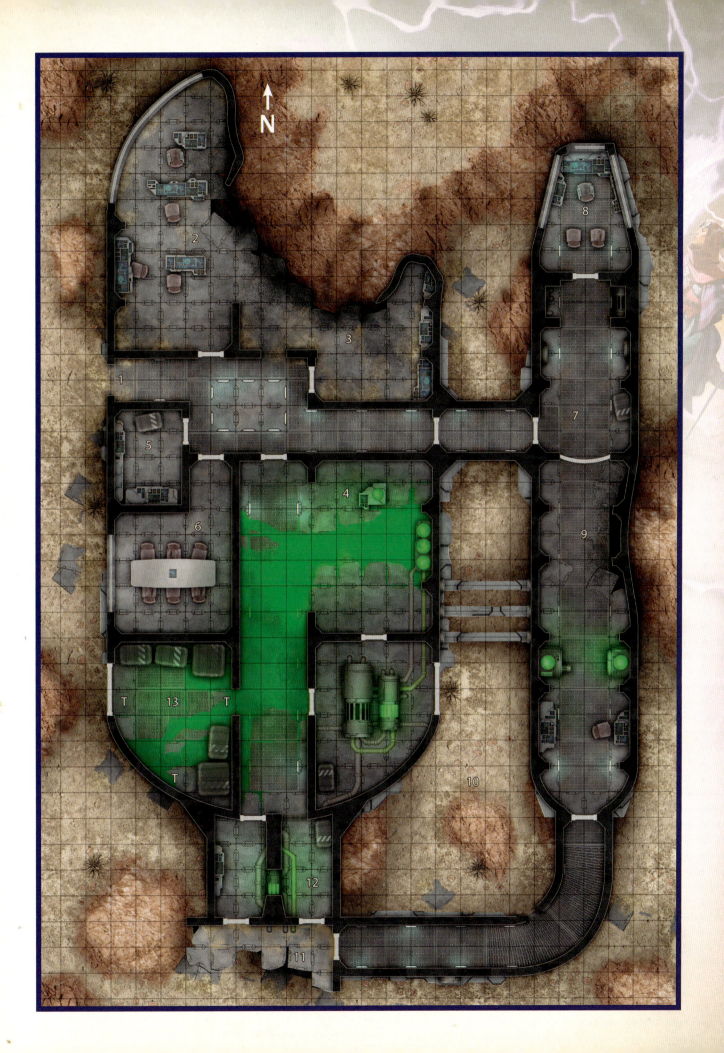

Creatures. A single **acolyte** wanders into this room. She is blindfolded and led by what appears to be a small child with long auburn hair and otherworldly silver eyes (**child of the silver sphere**, see **Chapter 5**). If approached, the woman pleasantly welcomes the characters to the Vault of the God-King. The beautiful child then releases her hand from the disciple and extends it to the characters, offering to lead them to the place where they will truly see and understand reality.

Tactics. The child of the silver sphere attempts to contact outsiders to activate its metasoma ability. Once it accesses a character's desires, it manipulates them toward seeking the path to divinity. It is connected to others of its kind and alerts the other two children in area 9 that there are newcomers to the vault who may be challenging to recruit. The child attempts to lead individuals off and separate the group. If attacked, she uses spells and attempts to flee but if cornered reverts to her true hideous form and counter-attacks while telepathically calling for aid from her kin and other disciples.

5. STASIS CENTER

A large metal and ceramic box features an array of polymer ducts exiting in every possible direction. On the face of the box swirl fluid-filled crystalline globes. Beneath the globes runs a series of dials labeled with unknown symbols.

All the machinery here remains intact. There are six globes, three filled with florescent green fluid of identical color to the fluorescent green fluid found elsewhere in the ship. Chartreuse, orange, and yellow fluids fill the remaining globes. The chartreuse knob is set at 10 o'clock, the orange at 11 o'clock, and the yellow at 5 o'clock. If characters decipher the writing, the chartreuse reads "Purge," the orange reads "Siphon," and the yellow reads "Regulate."

The dials control the speed and direction of the swirling liquids. Rotating the dial left causes the liquid to swirl counter-clockwise, increasing speed as the knob turns toward 6 o'clock. Rotating the dial right causes the liquid to swirl clockwise with increasing speed. If set to 12 o'clock, the speed and flow of the liquid stops, and its color slowly changes to fluorescent green. Characters manipulating the knobs can change the effect of how all creatures connected to the biotech AI communicate.

Purge (chartreuse) fills or removes liquid from the vats in area 9. If increased, the liquid drains off in several hours; if decreased, the vats overflow, spilling more of the AI fluid into the ship.

Siphon (orange) drains or restores psychic energy from every creature connected to the AI. If increased, all connected creatures gain resistance to psychic damage. If decreased, all connected creatures gain vulnerability to psychic damage. If set to 12 o'clock, divide psychic damage between all creatures connected to the biotech AI.

Regulate (yellow) controls the flow of communication between creatures connected by the AI. If decreased, all creatures can hear and respond equally; if increased, only creatures of equal CR or lower can communicate freely. If set to 12 o'clock, all communications cease.

6. SPECIMEN ROOM

A massive tank filled with green fluid pins the door to this location shut. A successful DC 20 Strength (athletics) check allows a character to slide the tank enough to gain access to the chamber.

Inside the room, several panels along the west wall collapse inward, exposing the damaged framework beneath.

Parasites. A door to the north opens on a storage closet filled with several dozen sealed cylindrical ceramic cases. Characters with a prybar or tinker's tools can attempt to break the seal and open the case with a DC 12 Strength check. Inside each is a glass tube preserving a sample of organs collected from alien creatures. If a character rolls a natural 20 when opening the case, they accidentally rupture the glass, exposing everyone in the room to an alien parasite (treat the parasite like the sewer plague aspect of the *contagion* spell).

7. COILS

The door to the south bulges inward as if struck by a tremendous force. To the north extends a circular corridor with translucent gray walls. Visibly sealed behind the walls lie coils of thick tubes filled with a slow-moving viscous fluid. There are bubbles in the fluid. Halfway up the corridor, the coils empty into a sealed vat with several layers. The frothy fluid only fills the bottom third of the vat.

The door to the north is sealed and requires a security clearance. Without clearance, any attempt to force open the doors triggers the release of its pressurized fluid, as described in the sliding doors feature section. Once opened, the door provides access to area 9.

8. NAVIGATION

A tapering chamber with a low, arching ceiling consists of a metal-and-glass framework. The glass is yellowed with age and covered with crystalline dust. Thick ceramic and metal panels flank the entrance, floor to ceiling. Each face bears an elaborate array of knobs, switches, and colored crystalline beads.

Near the center of the chamber, a blindfolded man dressed in a gossamer robe sits upon a polished white throne before a broad, curved table covered with switches, dials, gauges, and meters.

The auxiliary helm was used for navigation and monitoring various ship functions and provided a failsafe that could override the main controls and pilot the craft. The white throne is a swivel chair cast from an alien polymer. The table houses the control unit.

Anyone scraping away the dust on the glass can see the landscape outside the ship.

Creature. The man (**mage**) on the chair is seemingly in a trance. If characters attempt to communicate with him, he identifies himself as God-King Aroth, the first of his line. He then expresses his joy that others have come to bear witness to his ascension. The children have driven him mad, believing he is to become a god. If characters question his beliefs, he offers to take them to speak with the children. If physically threatened, he warns them of his tremendous power and near omnipotence and arrogantly demands they bow before him. If characters persist, he bellows gibberish and the phrase, "In the name of Aroth, First of his line of divinity! I banish thee!" and launches spell attacks. The children are content to observe what happens and do not come to his aid or otherwise intervene.

If, instead, the characters cure Aroth, the children gather outside the door in their true forms and ambush the characters as they attempt to leave.

9. AUXILIARY CORE

Battered machinery clutters much of the chamber, and the northern area appears badly damaged, with large cracks angrily zigzagging across the floor. Long, resinous pipes run the length of the inner walls and across the low, curved ceiling. Two massive metal vats occupy the chamber's center, sealed with bulbous, crystalline lids that emanate an otherworldly fluorescent green glow. Of the more identifiable debris, two chairs face a blackened sheet of cracked glass. Two humans sit in the chairs, facing the screens, each connected to a tangle of fine flexible hollow tubes that protrude from a resinous console. A pair of stunningly beautiful children with silvery eyes hold each of their hands.

The Vats. Both sealed vats hold the florescent green fluid described in area 4.

Creatures. The two human **adepts** have blank expressions and remain entirely motionless unless characters attempt to interact with them. The humans connected to the biotech AI have gone mad. They believe they are talking to the god-king and do not want to be disconnected. Unless cured of their madness, they cannot be reasoned with and violently attack anyone attempting to break the connection. The children (**child of the silver sphere**, see **Chapter 5**) notice anyone entering the room; however, they are slow to react if the characters do not display immediate threatening actions. They instead welcome the characters and attempt to get them to see the truth. If the characters turn violent, they assume their true forms and attack. If either alien becomes badly injured, they exit combat and attempt to flee.

10. COURTYARD

Sand and rubble spill into this curved corridor from a gaping hole in the north wall.

The hole opens into a makeshift courtyard. Near a pile of boulders, a ruptured ceramic and metal tank spills hundreds of fine translucent cables and tiny scintillating rubbery orbs. Along the edges of the wall lie small piles of cracked bones.

The bones are the humanoid remains of the courtyard's occupant, a towering **hill giant** whose amputated right hand is replaced with an unwieldy chunk of scrap metal that he uses to smash opponents. When first approached, Stumpy asks the characters if they have seen the children. He claims he is hungry, and they have promised him food. He knows nothing about the god-king. The dim-witted, brutish creature lacks patience and restraint. If the characters cannot tell him where the children have gone or where his food is, he decides the characters shall be his next meal and attacks.

11. RIFT

Jagged strips of bent metal protrude from the walls, marking where this section ripped free from the main hull during the original crash. The walls of the main structure intersect, forming a corner that indicates it was once part of the starship's interior. Hunks of scrap and debris lie piled against two doors, one leading north and the other leading west (area 10). A hard, transparent glass-like substance (emergency insulation fluid triggered by the initial crash) seals the western door. Breaking through requires significant effort and takes several hours.

12. CORE DRIVE

This cramped, arched chamber centers around a massive semi-hollow cylindrical metal device. Several other machines line the walls that hold glass-plated gauges. Sloppily scribbled messages in dried blood cover the walls, and a trail of dried bloody footprints runs out the north door.

The messages written in Void Speech consist of rambling diatribes decrying the lies of the silver oracle, the rise of false gods, and the apocalyptic death of divine ascension. The handwriting is like that found on the door in area 1.

13. BATTERED HULL

This section of the ship suffered extensive damage. These chambers are cramped and filled with jagged metal debris and broken glass. Where the ceiling collapsed, rain has caused extensive rust damage, and fungus and moss growth have penetrated the hull. Treat movement in this area as difficult terrain. Anyone attempting the Dash action must make a successful DC 14 Dexterity (Acrobatics) check to avoid taking 1d8 slashing damage from rubbing against jagged metal.

More of the sentient florescent fluid pools in the western corner of the room. If characters interact with the fluid, they risk connecting with the ship's AI, as described in area 4.

Creatures. A madman **berserker** hides within this section of the ruins. He fled here after the children's experiments drove him insane. He believes the children are hunting him and has rigged three collapsing ceiling traps that each inflict 3d6 bludgeoning damage in order to protect himself. If anyone enters, he assumes the children have sent them, or they are children, and cannot be convinced otherwise. He first attempts to stalk opponents and, using stealth, tries to lure them into his traps. If confronted, he goes berserk and attacks with a makeshift scrap-metal handaxe. If cured of his madness, he offers the characters 250 gp and a useful uncommon magic item for his safe return.

ADVENTURE HOOKS

- An individual of interest to the characters made a pilgrimage to the Vault of the God-King and has yet to return.
- Characters require rare metals or other materials possibly found in the strange metal meteor.
- Reavers attack characters traveling through the wastes. The reavers then flee into the hills and attempt to hide in the vault.

Chapter 5
Monsters of the Wastes

This chapter describes creatures found in the wastes of varying challenge ratings, ranging from its nomadic goblin inhabitants to the dread colossuses that might have been the cause of the cataclysm that created the wastes.

ANATHEMA LOCUST

Patterns of black splotches decorate the crimson carapace of this tiny locust.

An anathema locust is about 3 inches in length. Its bite secretes an acidic spittle that melts organic material. Even a single anathema locust would be more than a nuisance, but these insects never show up singly. In enormous groups of hundreds or thousands, these creatures hibernate beneath the dust or the ruins of a wasteland, awaiting the arrival of the rainy season. Then, the locust swarms become active and make their way to the surface to feed on the plant life that was nourished by the rain. Most inhabitants of these areas dread the locusts, which can strip the crops from a field faster than they can be harvested.

Dangerous Pest. Countries that border the areas where the locusts hibernate keep a close watch for the vermin during the growing season. As long as the locusts remain distant from civilized areas, they are tolerated. But if a swarm approaches one of the bordering realms, defenders are quick to destroy them.

Hunters and Hunted. Although swarms of anathema locusts feed mainly on defenseless plant life, they also try to attack and devour creatures that disturb their feeding or happen to be in a potential feeding ground when they descend. Some of the denizens of the wastes where the locusts hibernate hunt the swarms for food, since the insects provide a rich source of protein. These hunters use finely woven nets to ensnare a swarm, which is then quickly drowned, smothered, or killed by some other means.

Swarm of Anathema Locusts

Medium Swarm of Tiny Beasts, Unaligned

ARMOR CLASS 12 (natural armor)
HIT POINTS 36 (8d8)
SPEED 20 ft., climb 20 ft., fly 40 ft.

STR	DEX	CON	INT	WIS	CHA
3 (−4)	12 (+1)	10 (+0)	1 (−5)	8 (−1)	1 (−5)

DAMAGE RESISTANCES bludgeoning, piercing, and slashing from nonmagical attacks
CONDITION IMMUNITIES charmed, frightened, grappled, paralyzed, petrified, prone, restrained, stunned
SENSES blindsight 10 ft., passive Perception 9
LANGUAGES —
CHALLENGE 1 (200 XP)   **PROFICIENCY BONUS** +2

Swarm. The swarm can occupy another creature's space and vice versa, and the swarm can move through any opening large enough for a Tiny insect. The swarm can't regain hp or gain temporary hp.

ACTIONS

Bite. *Melee Weapon Attack:* +3 to hit, reach 0 ft., one creature in the swarm's space. *Hit:* 5 (2d4) piercing damage plus 7 (2d6) acid damage, or 2 (1d4) piercing damage plus 3 (1d6) acid damage if the swarm has half its hp or fewer.

REACTIONS

Defensive Retreat. When a creature the swarm can see attacks it while within 5 feet of it, the swarm can move up to half its speed away from the attacker without provoking opportunity attacks, spraying a cloud of acid at the attacker as it retreats. The cloud lasts until the start of the swarm's next turn. While it persists, the area in a 5-foot radius around the attacker is heavily obscured. Each creature that enters the cloud for the first time on a turn or starts its turn in the cloud takes 7 (2d6) acid damage, or 3 (1d6) acid damage if the swarm has half its hp or fewer.

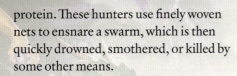

BAT, SABER-TOOTHED

This large bat bares two exceptionally long fangs.

Despite its relatively small size, the saber-toothed bat fulfills the promise of its threatening name. The body of this bat is about the size of a small dog's, but its 5-foot wingspan makes it appear much larger to most of the creatures it preys on. It's a vicious carnivore that hunts and kills just about anything of its size or smaller, including other bats.

Saber-Toothed Bat

Small Beast, Unaligned

ARMOR CLASS 13
HIT POINTS 31 (9d6)
SPEED 10 ft., fly 40 ft.

STR	DEX	CON	INT	WIS	CHA
8 (−1)	17 (+3)	10 (+0)	3 (−4)	11 (+0)	10 (+0)

SAVING THROWS Dex +5
SKILLS Perception +2, Stealth +5
SENSES blindsight 60 ft., passive Perception 12
LANGUAGES —
CHALLENGE 1 (200 XP)   **PROFICIENCY BONUS** +2

Diving Pounce. If the saber-toothed bat is flying and moves at least 20 feet straight toward a creature and then hits it with a Claw attack on the same turn, that creature must succeed on a DC 13 Strength saving throw or be knocked prone. If the target is already prone, the bat can make one Bite attack against it as a bonus action.

Echolocation. The saber-toothed bat can't use its blindsight while deafened.

Flyby. The saber-toothed bat doesn't provoke opportunity attacks when it flies out of an enemy's reach.

Keen Hearing. The saber-toothed bat has advantage on Wisdom (Perception) checks that rely on hearing.

Stone Camouflage. The saber-toothed bat has advantage on Dexterity (Stealth) checks made to hide in rocky terrain.

ACTIONS

Bite. *Melee Weapon Attack:* +5 to hit, reach 5 ft., one creature. *Hit:* 10 (2d6 + 3) piercing damage.

Claws. *Melee Weapon Attack:* +5 to hit, reach 5 ft., one creature. *Hit:* 5 (1d4 + 3) slashing damage.

BLACK GOAT CULTISTS

Of all the myriad masks the Goat of the Woods adopts, her most terrifying manifestation is the Black Goat of One Thousand Young. This aspect demands nothing from mortals but instead seizes what she wants without relying on mortals to give her offerings. She consumes all life, devouring it, and replaces it with her wretched spawn's foul and deformed transformations. She becomes the apocalypse, the harbinger of change that foretells the end of all things and the creator of all that exists. Those who worship the goddess in this aspect know she has no use for them other than as vessels for transformation. They exist only as mortal protoplasm to be devoured and reborn according to her whim.

Only the truly devout enter into the cult of the Black Goat. Through intense and lengthy indoctrination, they achieve a mental state that they describe as the Kiss of Oblivion. They choose to accept the inevitable and hail the coming apocalypse without fear, regret, love, or longing. They fully accept the will of the Black Goat with One Thousand Young because they wish to bear witness to the inevitable, to experience the transformation and not just contemplate it. They hold great respect for those who challenge their efforts but consider their resistance futile.

Missionaries of the Flock. Black goat priestesses work to spread the coming of their goddess by targeting the naive, the hopeless, and the destitute for recruitment into the Black Flock. They offer aid and assistance but preach that gain comes only with sacrifice. In the harsh wastes where each day threatens an individual's existence, this lesson rarely goes unheard. The priestess remains open in her intent but can convince others that submission provides the most significant benefit until the arrival of the inevitable. One must respect the apocalypse, celebrate its onset, and reap the benefits of each moment.

VARIANT: BLACK GOAT'S SPAWN

Some insane Black Goat cultists try to fuse themselves to the Goat of the Woods by undergoing ritual surgery to transform themselves into warped, demonic creatures. As a result, these cultists gain one or more of the following traits.

Hirsute. The cultist grows a thick, hairy, goatlike hide, giving it a natural Armor Class of 13.

Mother's Eyes. The cultist's eyes become narrow with slitted pupils. The first time it locks its gaze with an opponent, the opponent must make a successful DC 13 Wisdom saving throw or become frightened of the cultist for 1 round.

Mother's Horns. A pair of asymmetrical, curving, goatlike horns sprout from the cultist's head. The cultist gains an additional melee attack that deals bludgeoning damage of 1d6 plus its Strength modifier.

Black Goat Cultist

Medium Humanoid, Chaotic Evil

ARMOR CLASS 13 (hide)
HIT POINTS 52 (8d8 + 16)
SPEED 30 ft.

STR	DEX	CON	INT	WIS	CHA
14 (+2)	13 (+1)	14 (+2)	10 (+0)	13 (+1)	11 (+0)

SAVING THROWS Wis +3, Con +4

SKILLS Deception +2, Religion +2, Survival +3

SENSES darkvision 60 ft., passive Perception 11

LANGUAGES Common, Void Speech

CHALLENGE 1 (200 XP)   **PROFICIENCY BONUS** +2

Black Goat's Blessing. The black goat cultist has advantage on saving throws against being poisoned or frightened.

Black Goat Priestess

Medium Humanoid, Chaotic Evil

ARMOR CLASS 14 (hide armor)

HIT POINTS 110 (20d8 + 20)

SPEED 30 ft.

STR	DEX	CON	INT	WIS	CHA
11 (+0)	14 (+2)	13 (+1)	12 (+1)	17 (+3)	14 (+2)

SAVING THROWS Con +3, Wis +5

SKILLS Arcana +3, Deception +4, History +3, Insight +5, Intimidation +4, Persuasion +4, Religion +3

SENSES darkvision 60 ft., passive Perception 13

LANGUAGES Common, Void Speech

CHALLENGE 3 (700 XP)   **PROFICIENCY BONUS** +2

Black Goat's Blessing. The priestess has advantage on saving throws against being poisoned or frightened.

Spellcasting. The black goat priestess is an 8th-level spellcaster. The priestess casts the following spells, using Wisdom as the spellcasting ability (spell save DC 13).

  At will: *guidance, poison spray, thaumaturgy*

  3/day each: *bane, command, shield of faith*

  1/day each: *bestow curse, blight, blindness/deafness, confusion, enthrall, fear, spirit guardians*

ACTIONS

Multiattack. The black goat cultist makes two Sickle attacks or one Javelin attack.

Sickle. *Melee Weapon Attack:* +4 to hit, reach 5 ft., one creature. *Hit:* 5 (1d6 +2) slashing damage plus 3 (1d6) poison damage.

Javelin. *Melee or Ranged Weapon Attack:* +3 to hit, reach 5 ft. or range 30/120 ft., one creature. *Hit:* 5 (1d6 + 2) piercing damage.

Spellcasting. The black goat cultist casts the following spell, using Wisdom as its spellcasting ability (spell save DC 11).

  1/day: *hunter's mark*

ACTIONS

Multiattack. The black goat priestess makes two Morningstar attacks or three Throwing Dagger attacks.

Morningstar. *Melee Weapon Attack:* +2 to hit, reach 5 ft., one creature. *Hit:* 3 (1d6) piercing damage.

Throwing Dagger. *Ranged Weapon Attack:* +4 to hit, range 20/60 ft., one creature. *Hit:* 4 (1d4 + 2) piercing damage plus 3 (1d6) poison damage.

CHAOS ORB

An eyeball swollen to the size of a large melon hovers in the air, only observable to those that see invisible creatures. Others might feel the hair on their neck rise with a creeping sense of anxiety, as if they're being watched by an unpredictable, malevolent presence.

A chaos orb forms when a wizard's connection to an arcane eye is severed by a catastrophe that ruptures the ordinary flow of magic. The eye takes on a life of its own as a magical construct, mimicking a fragment of the panicked thoughts of its former master as they lost control of the spell. They draw their sustenance from the magical energy of the world and can rapidly rebuild their physical form when injured. A chaos orb maintains the particular qualities of an arcane eye, being invisible and able to squeeze through tight openings. They aimlessly wander the ruins of the wastes, desperate to reconnect with their former masters. Unable to do so by any means short of a *wish* spell, they become paranoid and lash out at the creatures they encounter.

Chaos orbs keenly observe their targets and then attack with psychic blasts, a vestige of the spellcasting that created them. When badly injured, they lash out wildly against anything near them, projecting their fear and confusion onto others. Experienced delvers in the wastes know to avoid them as they neither carry nor hoard treasure, but once an adventurer is aware of an invisible chaos orb, it is usually too late to avoid it. Captured chaos orbs can be very valuable to the right party, for they are rumored to remember everything they see.

Chaos Orb

Small Construct, Chaotic Evil

ARMOR CLASS 12
HIT POINTS 78 (12d8 + 24)
SPEED 0 ft., fly 30 ft. (hover)

STR	DEX	CON	INT	WIS	CHA
1 (–5)	14 (+2)	15 (+2)	16 (+3)	10 (+0)	11 (+0)

SKILLS Insight +3, Perception +3
DAMAGE RESISTANCES acid, cold, fire, lightning, thunder; bludgeoning, piercing, and slashing from nonmagical attacks
DAMAGE IMMUNITIES poison, psychic
CONDITION IMMUNITIES charmed, exhaustion, frightened, paralyzed, petrified, poisoned, prone
SENSES darkvision 30 ft., passive Perception 13
LANGUAGES understands the languages of its creator but can't speak
CHALLENGE 6 (2,300XP)   **PROFICIENCY BONUS** +3

Amorphous. The chaos orb can move through a space as narrow as 1 inch wide without squeezing.

Antimagic Susceptibility. The chaos orb is incapacitated while in the area of an antimagic field. If targeted by *dispel magic*, the chaos orb must succeed on a Constitution saving throw against the caster's spell save DC or fall unconscious for 1 minute.

Construct Nature. The chaos orb doesn't require air, food, drink, or sleep.

Invisible. The chaos orb is invisible.

Regeneration. The chaos orb regains 10 hit points at the start of its turn if it has at least 1 hit point.

ACTIONS

Multiattack. The chaos orb makes two Psychic Bolt attacks.

Psychic Bolt. *Melee or Ranged Spell Attack:* +6 to hit, reach 30 ft., one creature. *Hit:* 16 (3d8 + 3) psychic damage.

REACTIONS

Panic Aura. When the chaos orb is reduced to half its hp maximum, each creature within a 10-foot-radius sphere must succeed on a DC 14 Wisdom saving throw or take 34 (7d8 + 3) psychic damage and be frightened. While frightened by the chaos orb, the target suffers the effects of the *confusion* spell. A creature can repeat the saving throw at the end of each of its turns, ending the effect on itself on a success. A target that successfully saves is immune to this chaos orb's aura for the next 24 hours.

CHILD OF THE SILVER SPHERE

A beautiful human child wearing gossamer robes playfully twirls a lock of her long auburn hair. The child wears a broad smile, and her silvery eyes glow faintly.

Children of the silver sphere are aliens that can travel at will throughout the cosmos. Some who know of them say they have visited a thousand worlds and might even have the ability to shift between planes, dimensions, and time. Their motives and intents lie beyond mortal understanding. When they appear on the Material Plane, they always do so in the guise of a small child with gleaming silver eyes. Why they choose this form is unknown, though some speculate it is because the image is not intimidating. Although not outwardly predatory, they are highly manipulative, suggesting they are interested in experimenting with and learning more about creatures from other worlds.

Stratified. Children of the silver sphere create highly structured systems for interacting with each other. Each creature has a specific role and adheres to a certain behavior identifiable by other group members. These mannerisms include speech patterns and gestures, though most are too subtle for those outside their group to detect.

Influence Wielders. Children of the silver sphere use their considerable intelligence and psychic powers to influence less intelligent mortals to treat them as deities. They frequently demand that followers bring sacrifices and tributes or perform certain quests or rituals. Sometimes these demands align with the belief systems of existing gods; other times, they fabricate the demands entirely.

Grotesque. A child of the silver sphere's true form resembles a pair of bloated lungs from which droop six long, slender, mucus-covered tentacles surrounding a dangling, articulated hook-shaped spike like the leg of a giant crab. Within the center of the creature's body floats a pulsing silvery orb.

Child of the Silver Sphere

Medium Monstrosity, Lawful Evil

ARMOR CLASS 14 (natural)
HIT POINTS 88 (16d8 + 16)
SPEED 30 ft., fly 60 ft. (hover)

STR	DEX	CON	INT	WIS	CHA
13 (+1)	15 (+2)	12 (+1)	18 (+4)	13 (+1)	15 (+2)

SAVING THROWS Cha +5, Int +7
SKILLS Arcana +7, Deception +5, Insight +4, Perception +4
DAMAGE RESISTANCES poison; bludgeoning, piercing, and slashing from nonmagical attacks
DAMAGE IMMUNITIES psychic
SENSES darkvision 60 ft., passive Perception 14
LANGUAGES Common
CHALLENGE 5 (1,800 XP) **PROFICIENCY BONUS** +3

Shapechanger. The child of the silver sphere can use its action to polymorph into a Medium humanoid form that resembles a beautiful human child, with pale silver eyes and dressed in fine robes, or back into its true form. Its statistics remain the same in each form. Any equipment it is wearing or carrying isn't transformed. It reverts to its true form if it dies.

ACTIONS

Multiattack. The child of the silver sphere makes two Tentacle attacks and one Metastoma attack. If it is grappling creatures with all six of its tentacles, it can still attack with its metastoma. In addition, while grappling an opponent, the child can use a bonus action to activate its Psychic Link on that creature.

Tentacles. *Melee Weapon Attack:* +6 to hit, reach 10 ft., one target. *Hit:* 11 (1d8 + 4) bludgeoning damage. The target is grappled (escape DC 13) if it is a Medium or smaller creature. Until the grapple ends, the target is restrained and has disadvantage on Strength checks and Strength saving throws.

Metastoma. *Melee Weapon Attack:* +6 to hit, reach 5 ft., one creature. *Hit:* (1d8 + 4) piercing damage. The target must make a DC 13 Constitution saving throw, taking 14 (4d6) psychic damage on a failed save, or half as much damage on a successful one.

Spellcasting. The child of the silver sphere casts one of the following spells, using Intelligence as the spellcasting ability (spell save DC 15):

At will: *comprehend languages, dancing lights, detect magic, detect thoughts, invisibility, message, minor illusion*

3/day each: *clairvoyance, dispel magic, faerie fire, hypnotic pattern, sleep*

BONUS ACTIONS

Psychic Link. One creature grappled by the child must succeed on a DC 14 Intelligence saving throw, or the target becomes stunned and psychically linked to it. The child can read the target's thoughts and communicate with the target telepathically. If the child takes damage while linked to the target, it transfers half of the damage to the target as psychic damage. The target can repeat the saving throw at the end of each of its turns, ending the effect on itself on a success.

DEMON, MIRE FIEND

A fiendish, translucent praying mantis with a segmented tail tipped by a stinger rises from the muck, wielding a bamboo spear.

Mire fiends were once normal insects that became mutated by exposure to magical runoff that drained into their swampy wasteland home. Over time, the creatures grew in size and intelligence, and they developed their own rudimentary society. They live in hives, building networks of dens out of sticks and grasses that are accessed only from beneath the water line.

Intelligent Hunters. Mire fiends are omnivorous, indiscriminate hunters, attacking any prey they find that is large enough or plentiful enough to feed the hive. A mire fiend is just as likely to kill a

wayward traveler as to barter with it, but it will attack horses or other beasts of burden before going after humanoids. Mire fiends have learned to craft basic tools, such as spears, and they set up rudimentary traps in their territory to catch prey and dissuade predators. A mire fiend might venture out on its own to hunt, but often, the creatures are encountered in hunting parties of three to five.

Mire Fiend

Medium Fiend (Demon), Neutral Evil

ARMOR CLASS 16 (natural armor)
HIT POINTS 64 (12d8 + 10)
SPEED 40 ft., swim 40 ft.

STR	DEX	CON	INT	WIS	CHA
14 (+2)	16 (+3)	12 (+1)	11 (+0)	14 (+2)	6 (–2)

SAVING THROWS Dex +6, Con + 4
SKILLS Perception +5, Stealth +6, Survival +5
DAMAGE IMMUNITIES poison
CONDITION IMMUNITIES poisoned
SENSES blindsight 10 ft., darkvision 60 ft., passive Perception 15
LANGUAGES Abyssal
CHALLENGE 5 (1,800 XP)   **PROFICIENCY BONUS** +3

Amphibious. The mire fiend can breathe air and water.

Pack Tactics. The mire fiend has advantage on an attack roll against a creature if at least one of the mire fiend's allies is within 5 feet of the creature and the ally isn't incapacitated.

Swamp Camouflage. The mire fiend has advantage on Dexterity (Stealth) checks made to hide in swampy terrain.

Final Strike. When the mire fiend is reduced to 0 hp, it expels acid in a 30-foot cone. Each creature in the area must make a DC 16 Dexterity saving throw. A creature takes 14 (4d6) acid damage on a failed save, or half as much damage on a successful one.

ACTIONS

Multiattack. The mire fiend makes one Claw attack, one Spear attack, and one Stinger attack. When its Stunning Snap is available, it can use that action in place of its Claw attack or its Stinger attack.

Claw. *Melee Weapon Attack:* +5 to hit, reach 5 ft., one creature. *Hit:* 8 (1d8 + 3) slashing damage, and the creature is grappled (escape DC 13). A creature grappled in this way is also restrained.

Spear. *Melee Weapon Attack:* +5 to hit, reach 10 ft., one creature. *Hit:* 5 (1d6 + 2) piercing damage.

Stinger. *Melee Weapon Attack:* +5 to hit, reach 10 ft., one creature. *Hit:* 7 (2d6) poison damage, and the target must make a DC 15 Constitution saving throw. On a failed save, the creature is poisoned.

Stunning Snap (Recharge 5–6). If the mire fiend has no creature grappled, it snaps its front claws together with great force, creating a miniature sonic boom. Each creature within 20 feet of the mire fiend must make a DC 15 Constitution saving throw. On a failed save, a creature takes 7 (3d4) thunder damage and is stunned until the end of the mire fiend's next turn.

DOOM CHAMPION

It is hard to tell which is most arresting about the seven-foot-tall creature, the baleful yellow eyes glaring out from beneath the horned greathelm or the hulking musculature. It is when the doom champion hefts an axe, its haft almost as long as it is tall, that its most prominent feature becomes evident.

The doom champion has always walked the wastes. No one can remember a time before. Its adherents whisper that it is immortal, the offspring of a god of ruin sent to lead them through the pain of this world into a perfect next life, free of the constraints of law and morality. Even on the rare occasions its followers have seen it fall, it returns to them within a day or two, ready to lead them on their careening path once again.

Cursed Headwear. In truth, the power of the doom champion is in its helmet. Once a creature puts it on, the helmet alters its personality and appearance within a few days. Creatures wearing the helmet become greedy and erratic, unable to focus for long on tasks beyond urging the chaos reavers to kill and despoil. It isn't known whether any victim of the helmet has survived its removal.

Doom Champion

Medium Humanoid (Human), Chaotic Evil

ARMOR CLASS 16 (breastplate)
HIT POINTS 110 (13d8 + 52)
SPEED 30 ft.

STR	DEX	CON	INT	WIS	CHA
18 (+4)	14 (+2)	19 (+4)	12 (+1)	14 (+2)	18 (+4)

SAVING THROWS Str +7, Con +7
SKILLS Animal Handling +6, Athletics +7, Intimidation +6, Perception +5
DAMAGE RESISTANCES bludgeoning, piercing, and slashing from nonmagical attacks
CONDITION IMMUNITIES blinded, deafened
SENSES truesight 30 ft., passive Perception 15
LANGUAGES Common, Gnoll
CHALLENGE 6 (2,300 XP)   **PROFICIENCY BONUS** +3

Helm of Truth. While wearing its helmet, the doom champion has truesight out to a range of 30 feet and can't be blinded or deafened. It also has advantage on saving throws against spells cast on it by attackers it can see. If the doom champion is charmed, a creature can use its action to remove its helmet by succeeding on a DC 15 Strength check.

Hulking Mein. The doom champion can wield its greataxe in one hand, though it doesn't add its Strength modifier to its damage when it does so. While the overlord is grappled, it can still move half its speed.

Waste Walker. The doom champion has advantage on saving throws against traps and any environmental effect that could harm it, such as a cave-in or avalanche.

ACTIONS

Multiattack. The doom champion makes two Greataxe attacks, or it tries to grapple a creature and makes one Greataxe attack.

Greataxe. *Melee Weapon Attack:* +7 to hit, reach 10 ft., one target. *Hit:* 16 (2d12 + 4) slashing damage. If the target is a creature, it must succeed on a DC 15 Strength saving throw or be pushed 5 feet away from the overlord.

LEGENDARY ACTIONS

The doom champion can take 3 legendary actions, choosing from the options below. Only one legendary action option can be used at a time and only at the end of another creature's turn. The overlord regains spent legendary actions at the start of its turn.

Greataxe. The doom champion makes a Greataxe attack.

Thundering Charge (Costs 2 Actions). The doom champion moves up to its speed and makes a Greataxe attack at the end of its movement.

Sweeping Staredown (Costs 2 Actions). Each creature the doom champion can see within 30 feet of it must succeed on a DC 15 Wisdom saving throw or be frightened of it until the beginning of the overlord's next turn.

Doom Champion Overlord

Medium humanoid (human), chaotic neutral

ARMOR CLASS 18 (plate)
HIT POINTS 117 (18d8 + 36)
SPEED 35 ft.

STR	DEX	CON	INT	WIS	CHA
18 (+4)	10 (+0)	14 (+2)	12 (+1)	13 (+1)	18 (+4)

SAVING THROWS Str +7, Wis +4, Cha +7
SKILLS Animal Handling +4, Athletics +7, Intimidation +7
SENSES passive Perception 11
LANGUAGES Common, Infernal
CHALLENGE 7 (2,900 XP)   **PROFICIENCY BONUS** +3

Charge. If the doom champion overlord is mounted and moves at least 30 feet in a straight line toward a target and then hits it with a melee attack on the same turn, the target takes an extra 10 (3d6) damage.

Fueled By Fear. The doom champion overlord deals an extra 7 (2d6) damage when it hits a creature suffering from the Frightened condition.

Magic Weapons. The doom champion overlord's weapon attacks are made with magical (+1) weapons.

Menacing Advance. Whenever the doom champion overlord moves within 15 feet of a target, it can activate its Terrifying Visage feature as a bonus action.

ACTIONS

Multiattack. The doom champion overlord makes two Maul attacks or two Lance attacks. If it is riding a nightmare, its mount can then make a Hooves attack.

Maul. *Melee Weapon Attack:* +8 to hit, reach 5 ft, one target. *Hit:* 12 (2d6 + 5) bludgeoning damage.

Lance. *Melee Weapon Attack:* +8 to hit, reach 10 ft., one target. *Hit:* 11 (1d12 + 5) piercing damage.

Terrifying Visage (3/day). The doom champion overlord can glare at a target within 30 feet. If the target can see the doom champion overlord, it must succeed on a DC 15 Wisdom saving throw or become frightened of the doom champion overlord for 1 minute. If the doom champion overlord has already damaged the target in combat, it has disadvantage on its saving throw. A creature can repeat the saving throw at the end of each of its turns. If a creature's saving throw is successful, the effect ends on it. A target that successfully saves is immune to the doom champion overlord's gaze for the next 24 hours.

REACTIONS

Victor's Roar. When the doom champion overlord scores a critical hit or reduces an enemy to 0 hp, it can use its reaction to unleash a bloodcurdling screech, targeting all enemies within 15 feet with Terrifying Visage.

DRAKE, CHAOS

This draconic creature is covered in thick, uneven scales in various exotic shades. Kaleidoscopic drool drips from the creature's maw as it regards you with hungry anticipation.

Few creatures of the wastes exemplify the nature of chaos better than the chaos drake. Its every action is an exercise in unpredictability. Chaos drakes have been known to rescue or protect other creatures in one moment and then turn on them a short time later. The only thing that a chaos drake can be counted on to do is to behave irrationally.

Painful Existence. Chaos drakes are one of the few kinds of drakes that have no immunity to their own breath weapons. In fact, their breath weapon causes them excruciating pain, so they rarely use it unless they are cornered or desperate. Mating between chaos drakes is a tense affair, and few pairings produce offspring, making them one of the rarest of the varieties of drakes.

Uncontrollable. Taming a chaos drake is virtually impossible for other creatures to accomplish, and most chaos drakes would fight to the death rather than succumb to the will of another creature. Nonetheless, some figures have learned to coexist with chaos drakes after a fashion, and tales are sometimes heard of barbarian warlords and other rulers of the wasteland riding chaos drakes into battle.

Drake, Chaos

Medium Dragon, Chaotic Neutral

ARMOR CLASS 14 (natural armor)
HIT POINTS 45 (7d8 + 14)
SPEED 30 ft., fly 60 ft.

STR	DEX	CON	INT	WIS	CHA
16 (+3)	13 (+1)	14 (+2)	7 (–2)	13 (+1)	10 (+0)

SAVING THROWS Con +4

SKILLS Perception +3, Survival +3
SENSES darkvision 60 ft., passive Perception 13
LANGUAGES Draconic
CHALLENGE 2 (450 XP)   PROFICIENCY BONUS +2

Warping Aura. A field of chaos surrounds the drake in a 15-foot radius. Each creature that starts its turn in the aura must make a DC 14 Wisdom saving throw. On a failed save, all the creature's dice rolls are reduced by 1d4 for 1 minute. The creature can make a new saving throw at the end of each of its turns to end the effect on itself. Once a creature succeeds on its saving throw against the aura, it is immune to that chaos drake's aura for 24 hours.

ACTIONS

Multiattack. The chaos drake makes one Bite attack and two Claw attacks.

Bite. *Melee Weapon Attack:* +5 to hit, reach 5 ft., one target. *Hit:* 10 (2d6 + 3) piercing damage.

Claw. *Melee Weapon Attack:* +5 to hit, reach 5 ft., one creature. *Hit:* 6 (1d6 + 3) slashing damage.

Chaos Breath (Recharge 5–6). The drake exhales a 15-foot cone of multicolored chaotic energy. Each time the chaos drake uses its Chaos Breath, roll on the following table to determine the type of damage it deals.

d8	Damage Type	d8	Damage Type
1	acid	5	lightning
2	cold	6	necrotic
3	fire	7	poison
4	force	8	radiant

Each creature struck by the drake's breath weapon must make a DC 14 Constitution saving throw, taking 14 (4d6) damage on a failed save, or half as much damage on a successful one.

DRAKE, RUINS

This small dragon has smooth, dark brown scales and tiny wings. Its eyes gleam with barely suppressed malevolence as it rubs its minuscule humanlike hands together in glee.

Ruins drakes are one the smallest species of drakes, their bodies barely reaching 2 feet in length, with a slender tail and tiny front claws unsuitable for combat. Their small size makes them expert sneaks, however, and they are adept at hiding amid crumbling buildings and in dank subterranean vaults. Ruins drakes have something of an inferiority complex regarding their size, and any mention of it is likely to set them off. Perhaps due to this complex, ruins drakes make up for their size in sheer malice, and they like nothing better than to waylay and kill those bigger than they are.

Devious Trapsters. Ruins drakes are adept at constructing simple yet effective traps involving tripwires, spikes, knives, and the like. They take great pride in their traps and are outraged when a rogue or some similar individual disables or bypasses one of them. In such instances, the drakes do everything in their power to kill the upstart.

Deadlier in Numbers. Though they are generally solitary creatures by nature, ruins drakes gather into small bands from time to time for mutual protection and to produce bigger and more complex traps. Gangs of ruins drakes are sometimes employed by assassins' guilds or bandits, but only if the reward is worthwhile and they are allowed to wreak maximum mayhem. Ruins drakes have been known to ally with clans of evil kobolds, though they always strive to be the dominant partners in such a relationship.

Ruins Drake

Small Dragon, Neutral Evil

ARMOR CLASS 15 (natural armor)
HIT POINTS 33 (6d6 + 12)
SPEED 30 ft., fly 60 ft.

STR	DEX	CON	INT	WIS	CHA
14 (+2)	16 (+3)	14 (+2)	13 (+1)	13 (+1)	10 (+0)

SAVING THROWS Dex +5, Con +4
SKILLS Arcana +3, Perception +3, Stealth +7
DAMAGE RESISTANCES poison
CONDITION IMMUNITIES charmed, poisoned
SENSES darkvision 90 ft., passive Perception 13
LANGUAGES Common, Draconic
CHALLENGE 1 (200 XP)   **PROFICIENCY BONUS** +2

ACTIONS

Bite. *Melee Weapon Attack:* +4 to hit, reach 5 ft., one target. *Hit:* 5 (1d6 + 2) piercing damage plus 3 (1d6) poison damage.

Poison Breath (Recharge 5–6). The drake exhales a 10-foot cone of poisonous violet mist. Each creature in the cone must make a DC 14 Constitution saving throw, taking 10 (3d6) poison damage on a failed save, or half as much damage on a successful one.

Trap-Setting. A ruins drake is adept at setting up rudimentary traps. As an action, the ruins drake can create a basic trap that has the following statistics.

Simple Trap. *Melee Weapon Attack:* +4 to hit, reach 5 ft., one target. *Hit:* 5 (1d10) piercing or slashing damage.

A creature can detect a ruins drake's trap with a successful DC 15 Wisdom (Perception) check and can disable it by making a successful DC 15 Dexterity check using thieves' tools. A ruins drake's trap lasts 1 hour before falling apart and becoming unusable.

Ruins drakes are immune to the effects of any traps they create.

DREAD MOUTHER

A massive flood of thick putrescent slime bubbles with a chaotic jumble of mouths and eyeballs. The glop quickly spreads across the ground, roiling and splashing like waves striking angrily against a seawall during a hurricane.

The wake of death and destruction that followed the mage wars left thousands of bodies tainted with unknown eldritch energies. The littered wastelands drew the voracious appetites of foul and monstrous scavengers that fed upon the dead, stoking their gluttony and mutating them to immense sizes. The plagues of gibbering mouthers that stalked the wastes were no exception. Dread mouthers amplify every horror of their smaller kin. They even eat other gibbering mouthers as they fuse more and more entities into their deranged consciousness.

Children of an Elder God. Many wasteland cults devoted to old gods believe dread mouthers are the holy spawn of an elder god. As part of their ceremonies, cultists bring the creatures living sacrifices and proclaim that absorption into the creature's consciousness is a supreme blessing.

Corpse Feeders. Dread mouthers feed constantly and are drawn to locations such as battlefields and graveyards where they can acquire massive amounts of food with little effort. However, the sounds of war and death draw them out, especially when food supplies are scarce. Dark hordes have attempted to lure the creatures into battle but must remain vigilant as they cannot control who or what the dread mouther targets.

Dread Mouther

Large Aberration, Neutral

ARMOR CLASS 12
HIT POINTS 120 (16d8 + 48)
SPEED 15 ft., swim 20 ft.

STR	DEX	CON	INT	WIS	CHA
14 (+2)	8 (−1)	16 (+3)	6 (−2)	12 (+1)	6 (−2)

DAMAGE RESISTANCES bludgeoning, piercing, and slashing from nonmagical attacks
CONDITION IMMUNITIES prone
SENSES darkvision 60 ft., passive Perception 11
LANGUAGES —
CHALLENGE 7 (2,900 XP)   **PROFICIENCY BONUS** +3

Aberrant Terrain. The ground in a 15-foot radius around the dread mouther is dough-like difficult terrain. Each creature that starts its turn in that area must succeed on a DC 14 Strength saving throw or have its speed reduced to 0 until the start of its next turn.

Babbling. The dread mouther unleashes a constant barrage of incoherent babble while it can see any creature and isn't incapacitated. Each creature that starts its turn within 20 feet of the mouther and can hear the babbling must make a DC 13 Wisdom saving throw. On a failed save, the creature cannot take reactions until the start of its next turn, and it rolls a d8 to determine what happens on its current turn.

d8	Effect
1–4	The creature becomes frightened of the mouther.
5–6	The creature takes no actions or bonus actions and uses all its movement to move toward the dread mouther in a blank-faced daze.
7–8	The creature falls prone and takes 4d6 psychic damage.

ACTIONS

Multiattack. The dread mouther makes three Bite attacks and, if it can, uses its Blinding Spittle.

Bite. *Melee Weapon Attack:* +6 to hit, reach 5 ft., one creature. *Hit:* 17 (5d6) piercing damage. If the target is Medium or smaller, it must succeed on a DC 15 Strength saving throw or be knocked prone. If this damage kills the target, the dread mouther consumes it.

Radiant Spittle (Recharge 5–6). The mouther spits a chemical glob at a point it can see within 20 feet of it. The glob explodes in a blinding flash of light on impact. Each creature within 5 feet of the flash must succeed on a DC 15 Dexterity saving throw or take 10 (3d6) radiant damage and be blinded until the end of the mouther's next turn. On a successful save, a creature takes half damage and is not blinded.

DREAD COLOSSUS FLESH GOLEM

Hunched over before you is a horrid monstrosity fashioned from lumps of gray-green flesh, sculpted into the form of a toadlike humanoid. It raises its oversized head, displaying a mouth filled with rows of teeth. Eerily, the vile thing appears to have no eyes.

At the height of the Mage Wars, several of the most powerful arcanists began experimenting with dread colossus flesh as a raw material for enhancing undead creations and crafting golems.

Varied Forms. Only two factors limit the creation of a dread colossus flesh golem: the ability of the crafter and the availability of dread colossus flesh in some form or another. Most golems are vaguely humanoid in shape and Medium in size, but some tales circulate of larger and formidable dread colossus flesh golems fashioned into inhuman shapes, sometimes resembling the colossus from which the golem's body was salvaged.

Dread Colossus Flesh Golem

Medium Construct, Neutral

ARMOR CLASS 14 (natural)
HIT POINTS 82 (11d8 + 33)
SPEED 30 ft.

STR	DEX	CON	INT	WIS	CHA
17 (+3)	12 (+1)	16 (+3)	6 (–2)	10 (+0)	5 (–3)

SKILLS Athletics +6
DAMAGE IMMUNITIES poison; bludgeoning, piercing, and slashing from nonmagical attacks that aren't adamantine
CONDITION IMMUNITIES charmed, exhaustion, frightened, paralyzed, petrified, poisoned
SENSES darkvision 60 ft., passive Perception 10
LANGUAGES understands Void Speech but can't speak
CHALLENGE 5 (1,800 XP)   **PROFICIENCY BONUS** +3

Death Curse. When the dread colossus flesh golem dies, it unleashes a burst of the dread colossus's consciousness. Each creature within 20 feet of it must make a successful DC 13 Wisdom saving throw, or unknowable horrors flood its mind, dealing it 4 (1d8) psychic damage.

Immutable Form. The dread colossus flesh golem is immune to any spell or effect that would alter its form.

Lacerating Grappler. The dread colossus flesh golem has advantage on attack rolls against any creature it has grappled. In addition, when it maintains a grapple, its bony protrusions deal 10 (3d6) piercing damage per round. Conversely, it deals 10 (3d6) slashing damage at the start of its turn.

Magic Resistance. The dread colossus flesh golem has advantage on saving throws against spells and other magical effects.

Magic Weapons. The dread colossus flesh golem's weapon attacks are magical.

Standing Leap. The dread colossus flesh golem's long jump is up to 30 feet and its high jump is up to 15 feet, with or without a running start.

ACTIONS

Multiattack. The dread colossus flesh golem makes one Bite attack and two Claw attacks.

Bite. *Melee Weapon Attack:* +6 to hit, reach 5 ft., one target. *Hit:* 8 (2d4 + 3) piercing damage.

Claw. *Melee Weapon Attack:* +6 to hit, reach 5 ft., one target. *Hit:* 7 (1d8 + 3) slashing damage.

ELDRITCH HORROR

A low-lying expanse of thick green mist flows across the landscape. As it gets closer, images of shrieking faces become apparent within the fog, and then their screaming can be heard.

A native of an unknown universe, an eldritch horror crosses into the mortal world when a sentient creature comes face to face with its own death. Each individual occurrence of such an instance draws forth an eldritch horror too small and weak to do much harm (though the mortal in question typically doesn't survive the experience), but when loss of life occurs on a large scale, such as during a war, famine, or plague, the result is a huge eldritch horror that billows out across the landscape, searching for more life to snuff out.

Tools of Destruction. Cultists who revere the Void and other dark entities might know how to summon eldritch horrors for their own purposes (whatever those may be). Often, the success of such an attempt involves the mass slaughter of many people, and a large group of cultists could subject an entire town or a small farming community to this fate. In more cases than not, the cultists become the horror's first victims after it appears, though whispers persist that some groups have learned how to protect themselves from the creature's deadly presence.

Eldritch Horror

Huge Aberration, Chaotic Evil

ARMOR CLASS 11
HIT POINTS 95 (10d12 + 30)
SPEED fly 40 ft. (hover)

STR	DEX	CON	INT	WIS	CHA
10 (+0)	12 (+1)	16 (+3)	18 (+4)	10 (+0)	6 (−2)

DAMAGE IMMUNITIES acid, necrotic, poison, psychic; bludgeoning, piercing, and slashing from nonmagical attacks
CONDITION IMMUNITIES charmed, frightened, exhaustion, grappled, paralyzed, petrified, poisoned, prone, restrained
SENSES blindsight 60 ft.
LANGUAGES Abyssal
CHALLENGE 5 (1,800 XP)   **PROFICIENCY BONUS** +3

Eldritch Screams. Images of faces move and contort within the body of the eldritch horror, their mouths stretched in harrowing screams. Each creature that starts its turn within 30 feet of the eldritch horror and can hear the screams must succeed on a DC 15 Constitution saving throw or take 10 (3d6) psychic damage.

Misty Form. The eldritch horror can move through a space occupied by a creature or an object, flowing around and over it. It can pass through small holes, narrow openings, and even mere cracks, though it treats liquids as though they were solid surfaces.

Life Sense. The eldritch horror can sense the location of any living creature within 120 feet of it.

ACTIONS

Multiattack. The eldritch horror makes two Void Touch attacks.

Void Touch. *Melee Weapon Attack:* +3 to hit, reach 5 ft., one creature. *Hit:* 7 (2d6) psychic damage plus 5 (1d10) necrotic damage.

EONIC LONER

The scent of ozone permeates the space around a lone figure's mummified-seeming visage. It is garbed in scraps of metal and leather fused with crystals, some of which flicker with wan blue light. Its expression as it scans the landscape is one of hopeless resignation.

When an eonic drifter (see *Tome of Beasts*) gives up any hope of returning to its home time or of saving its civilization, it isolates itself from others and becomes a reclusive wayfarer. These eonic loners continue to wander, collecting scraps of metal and leather which they use to transform their time-distorting belts into crystal-studded patchwork armor. Loners no longer see the point in hopping through time or building or maintaining relationships and are either indifferent or, occasionally, outright hostile to others.

Fonts of Knowledge. Despite their reclusive natures, eonic loners know a great deal about history, much of which would be considered the future to humanoids they encounter. If they can be roused from their ennui, they may be enticed to share some of their knowledge with others.

Eonic Loner

Medium Humanoid (Human), Chaotic Neutral

ARMOR CLASS 16 (piecemeal armor)
HIT POINTS 75 (10d8 + 30)
SPEED 30 ft.

STR	DEX	CON	INT	WIS	CHA
12 (+1)	14 (+2)	17 (+3)	18 (+4)	13 (+1)	13 (+1)

SAVING THROWS Con +6
SKILLS Arcana +7, History +7, Insight +4, Survival +4
SENSES passive Perception 11
LANGUAGES Common, Eonic, Goblin
CHALLENGE 5 (1,800 XP) **PROFICIENCY BONUS** +3

Future State. When an eonic loner dies, its self from an alternate future is summoned to the location and time of its death. The future self has the original loner's statistics and a full complement of hit points. Immediately after appearing, it takes a turn, assuming the original loner's place in the initiative order. If the loner's future self dies, another future self is not summoned.

Temporal Nudge. The eonic loner swaps a spell scroll or wand with an exhausted future version of the item for a split second. When the loner is targeted by a spell that is cast from a scroll or a wand by an attacker that it can see, and if that spell allows its target to make a saving throw for reduced damage, the loner instead takes no damage on a successful save.

ACTIONS

Multiattack. The eonic loner makes two Time Warping Staff attacks.

Time Warping Staff. *Melee Weapon Attack:* +5 to hit, reach 5 ft., one target. *Hit:* 7 (1d10 + 2) plus 10 (3d6) necrotic damage.

Spring Forward (Recharge 6). Each living creature within 30 feet of the eonic loner must make a successful DC 15 Charisma saving throw or be thrust forward in time along with the loner, effectively ceasing to exist in the present time. All affected creatures reappear in their previous locations 1d4 rounds later at initiative count 20. Creatures occupying those spaces at that moment are pushed 5 feet in a direction of their choosing. Each of the affected creatures must then make a successful DC 14 Constitution saving throw or be stunned for 1 minute. A creature that is stunned in this way can make a new saving throw at the end of each of its turns, ending the condition on itself on a success.

REACTIONS

Spacetime Slip. When the eonic loner takes damage for the first time in a round, it can slip through time and move up to half its speed away from its attacker to an unoccupied space. If the creature targeting the loner can attack more than once with its action, such as with Multiattack or Extra Attack, this reaction takes effect after the first instance of damage is dealt.

GELLIMITE

A glint of light catches your eye, reflecting off a tiny transparent cube as it quivers slightly.

Gellimites are minuscule, magically altered gelatinous cubes. Extremely aggressive, a gellimite actively seeks living prey, which it feasts on by burrowing into its target's flesh.

Arcane Assassins. A cult of sorcerer-assassins created the first gellimites as a way to make sacrifices to their deity. The tiny oozes fetch a high price on the black market and are sold enclosed in specially crafted vessels designed to be worn as amulets. Some owners have made failed attempts to turn gellimites into familiars, since the creatures lack tangible intelligence.

Gelatinous Clones. Even though they are driven to consume flesh, gellimites are magical creatures that do not grow or propagate. The cult that developed the secret ritual used to create them has never shared this knowledge with anyone outside the group. The process entails magically dividing a gelatinous cube into dozens of smaller cubes.

Gellimite

Tiny Ooze, Unaligned

ARMOR CLASS 6
HIT POINTS 3 (1d4 + 1)
SPEED 15 ft.

STR	DEX	CON	INT	WIS	CHA
6 (–2)	3 (–4)	12 (+1)	1 (–5)	6 (–2)	1 (–5)

DAMAGE VULNERABILITIES fire
CONDITION IMMUNITIES blinded, charmed, deafened, exhaustion, frightened, prone
SENSES blindsight 60 ft. (blind beyond this radius), passive Perception 8
LANGUAGES —
CHALLENGE 0 (10 XP)   **PROFICIENCY BONUS** +2

Ooze Cube. The gellimite takes up its entire space. Other creatures can enter the space, but a creature that does so is subjected to the gellimite's Caustic Burrow and has disadvantage on the saving throw. A creature within 5 feet of the gellimite can use an action to burn a burrowing gellimite out of a creature.

Transparent. Even when a gellimite is in plain sight, it takes a successful DC 15 Wisdom (Perception) check to spot a gellimite that has neither moved nor attacked. A creature that tries to enter a gellimite's space while unaware of the gellimite is surprised by the ooze.

Caustic Burrow. If a gellimite strikes a creature with its pseudopod, the target must make a DC 12 Dexterity saving throw. On a failed save, the gellimite burrows into its flesh, dealing 3 (1d6) acid damage per round until the gellimite is removed or destroyed.

Fire Aversion. A gellimite recoils from fire. An individual can use an open flame, such as a torch, to drive a burrowing gellimite from a host with a successful DC 12 Wisdom (Medicine) check. On a failed check, the fire deals additional 1d8 damage to the treated individual. If the host takes any damage from magical or normal fire that targets the gellimite's point of entry, the gellimite also takes fire damage, and if it survives, uses its following move action to leave the host.

ACTIONS

Pseudopod. *Melee Weapon Attack:* +2 to hit, reach 5 ft., one creature. *Hit:* 3 (1d6) acid damage plus Caustic Burrow (see above).

GOBLIN, CHAOS

This goblin's skin ripples and flows like melting cheese, its color shifting from gray to brown to green and back again as you watch. The creature would look almost pitiful except for its deranged expression and the short sword clenched in its fist.

Within the most blighted of wastes lives the chaos goblin, a creature whose very skin writhes under the influence of corrupt magic. The first chaos goblins were produced when many ordinary goblins were subjected to brutal chaotic sorceries, which warped their bodies and unhinged their minds. Since then, the race has bred true and has spread across the desolation. The typical chaos goblin is about 3 feet tall and weighs 80 pounds.

Servants of Chaos. Chaos goblins are instinctively drawn to serve powerful creatures of chaos, including cultists, black dragons, and chaotic aberrations. Most chaos goblins worship the Goat of the Woods, pledging their meager lives to its service, though some also follow demon lords like Hriggala.

Cursed Outcasts. Chaos goblins are treated poorly by the rest of goblin society. When they are not outright shunned or killed, chaos goblins are kept as menial laborers or cannon fodder in the goblins' wars against other creatures. Of course, chaos goblins can quickly turn this situation around with their fearsome abilities, and more than one dust goblin tribe has been routed by a force of angry chaos goblins.

Chaos Goblin

Small Humanoid (Goblinoid), Chaotic Evil

ARMOR CLASS 16 (hide armor)
HIT POINTS 22 (4d6 + 8)
SPEED 30 ft.

STR	DEX	CON	INT	WIS	CHA
10 (+0)	16 (+3)	14 (+2)	10 (+0)	10 (+0)	7 (−2)

DAMAGE RESISTANCES bludgeoning, piercing, and slashing from nonmagical attacks
SENSES darkvision 60 ft., passive Perception 10
LANGUAGES Goblin
CHALLENGE 1 (200 XP)   **PROFICIENCY BONUS** +2

Chaotic Form. A chaos goblin is immune to critical hits.

Shifting Strikes. A chaos goblin has advantage on its attack rolls if it moves at least 10 feet before making an attack on its turn.

ACTIONS

Multiattack. The chaos goblin makes two Shortsword attacks.

Shortsword. *Melee Weapon Attack:* +5 to hit, reach 5 ft., one target. *Hit:* 6 (1d6 + 3) piercing damage.

CHAOS GOBLIN MUTATIONS

Some chaos goblins are born with a mutation that can substantially alter their capabilities. Roll on the table below to determine whether a chaos goblin has a mutation.

Psychic Blast (Recharge 6). The chaos goblin unleashes an explosion of psychic energy in a 15-foot cone. Each creature in the area must make a DC 14 Wisdom saving throw, taking 9 (2d8) psychic damage on a failed save, or half as much damage on a successful one.

GOBLIN, NOMADIC

This goblin looks leaner and meaner than most of its kind, its skin a dark shade of greenish brown and its arms and hands covered in bulging calluses and scar tissue. The goblin rides atop a massive wolf as if it were second nature.

In contrast to the goblins that live in abandoned mines, ruins, or similar locations, nomadic goblins roam the open plains, in large bands, following the herds of bison and similar creatures that live there. They are consummate hunters and trackers, especially formidable when they travel on the backs of their wolf mounts. Nomadic goblins ambush caravans and raid human villages along their path, using hit-and-run tactics to outmaneuver superior forces and whittle them down. They are just as cowardly as their more sedentary kin, however—not above fleeing if the fight turns against them.

Wolf Friends. Nomadic goblins have a deep bond with **wolves, dire wolves,** and **worgs**. In most goblin tribes, only a select few warriors can ride such creatures, but nomadic goblins are virtually born in the saddle, and only the very young do not have their own mounts. Most adult nomadic goblins ride wolves, while the more powerful or important tribe members ride dire wolves or worgs.

d8	Mutation
1–3	No mutation.
4	The skin of the goblin is translucent, revealing the creature's musculature, blood vessels, and skeletal structure. Its hideous appearance gives it advantage on Charisma (Intimidation) checks.
5	The goblin can change the color of its skin at will, giving it advantage on Dexterity (Stealth) checks.
6	The goblin's body is covered in acidic pustules. The goblin has resistance to acid damage, and whenever it is hit with a slashing or piercing weapon, the pustules rupture, dealing 1d4 (2) acid damage to the attacker if it is within 5 feet of the goblin.
7	The goblin has an extra arm or leg. If it has an extra arm, it can wield an additional weapon and makes three attacks instead of two when it uses the Multiattack action. If it has an extra leg, its speed increases to 40 feet.
8	The goblin's brain is larger than normal, making its forehead bulge out noticeably. Its intelligence score is 18, it has telepathy out to a range of 60 feet, and it has resistance to psychic damage. In addition, the goblin gains the Attack action described below. This mutation increases the goblin's challenge rating to 2 (450 XP).

Pressed into Service. Nomadic goblins rarely associate with other kinds of goblins, since they typically steer clear of where other tribes live. On occasion, powerful goblin warlords have been known to take over or hire a tribe of nomadic goblins to serve as elite cavalry units, and for that reason, nomadic goblins can sometimes be found in the front line of a goblin army.

Goblin, Nomadic

Small Humanoid (Goblinoid), Neutral Evil

ARMOR CLASS 14 (leather armor)
HIT POINTS 9 (2d6 + 2)
SPEED 30 ft.

STR	DEX	CON	INT	WIS	CHA
8 (−1)	14 (+2)	12 (+1)	10 (+0)	12 (+1)	8 (−1)

SKILLS Animal Handling +3, Stealth +4, Survival +5
SENSES darkvision 60 ft., passive Perception 11
LANGUAGES Common, Goblin, Worg
CHALLENGE 1/4 (50 XP)　　**PROFICIENCY BONUS** +2

Lupine Affinity. Nomadic goblins have a special rapport with wolves, worgs, and other wolflike creatures. They add double their proficiency bonus to Wisdom (Animal Handling) checks when dealing with such creatures, and wolves, dire wolves, and worgs will not attack a nomadic goblin unless magically compelled to do so.

Mounted Slash. When a nomadic goblin mounted on a wolf, worg, or dire wolf hits a target with its scimitar, the attack deals an extra 1d4 slashing damage.

ACTIONS

Scimitar. *Melee Weapon Attack:* +4 to hit, reach 5 ft., one target. *Hit:* 5 (1d6 + 2) slashing damage.

Shortbow. *Ranged Weapon Attack:* +4 to hit, range 80/320 ft., one target. *Hit:* 5 (1d6 + 2) piercing damage.

GOBLIN, DUST

A ragged creature emerges from the sand. Its spindly frame is encased in a hodge-podge of armor scraps and rusted weapons. A long, hooked nose protrudes over a wide mouth filled with sharp teeth.

Dust goblins vary greatly in size and appearance, although they are universally scrawny, bony, and lanky. They seem to suffer from malnutrition even when in perfect health, a perception reinforced by the way their bellies distend after they've gorged themselves on flesh. Their skin is always dry and cracked, ranging from dusky gray to dark green in color.

Rule the Wastelands. Dust goblins are twisted creatures, tainted by many generations of life in a blasted wasteland. After a magical war devastated the dust goblins' homeland, they rose to become the most dominant inhabitants. They inhabit ancient ruins and ambush travelers who stray too close to their borders.

Twisted Minds. The lingering magical energy saturating the wastes of their home, coupled with the harsh conditions in which they scratch out a living, have tainted the minds of all dust goblins. Their thinking is alien and unfathomable to most creatures. Whereas most goblins are cowardly, dust goblins don't seem to experience fear. To the contrary, they enjoy wearing skull helmets and using ghostly whistles to frighten foes. Owing to this alien mindset, dust goblins get along disturbingly well with Aberrations. The creatures often forge alliances and work together for mutual benefit, while making their unnerving mark on communal lairs.

Dust Goblin

Small Humanoid (Goblinoid), Neutral Evil

ARMOR CLASS 14 (leather armor)
HIT POINTS 16 (3d6 + 6)
SPEED 30 ft.

STR	DEX	CON	INT	WIS	CHA
8 (−1)	16 (+3)	14 (+2)	10 (+0)	8 (−1)	8 (−1)

SKILLS Stealth +7

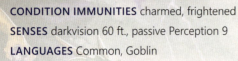

CONDITION IMMUNITIES charmed, frightened
SENSES darkvision 60 ft., passive Perception 9
LANGUAGES Common, Goblin
CHALLENGE 1/4 (50 XP)   **PROFICIENCY BONUS** +2

Twisted. When the dust goblin attacks a creature from hiding, the target must succeed on a DC 10 Wisdom saving throw or be frightened until the end of its next turn.

ACTIONS

Shortsword. *Melee Weapon Attack:* +5 to hit, reach 5 ft., one target. *Hit:* 6 (1d6 + 3) piercing damage.

Light Crossbow. *Ranged Weapon Attack:* +5 to hit, range 80/320 ft., one target. *Hit:* 7 (1d8 + 3) piercing damage.

Dust Goblin Archmage

Small Humanoid (goblinoid), Neutral Evil

ARMOR CLASS 12 (15 with *mage armor*)
HIT POINTS 143 (22d8 + 44)
SPEED 40 ft.

STR	DEX	CON	INT	WIS	CHA
8 (−1)	14 (+2)	14 (+2)	17 (+3)	13 (+1)	8 (−1)

SAVING THROWS Int +7, Wis +5
SKILLS Arcana +7, Stealth +7, Survival +5
SENSES darkvision 60 ft., passive Perception 11
LANGUAGES Common, Goblin, and two ancient languages
CHALLENGE 10 (5,900 XP)   **PROFICIENCY BONUS** +4

Erratic Casting. Whenever the dust goblin archmage casts a spell of level 1 or higher, roll a d20. On a result of 19 or 20, a chaos magic surge occurs.

Twisted. When the dust goblin archmage attacks a creature from hiding, the target must succeed on a DC 15 Wisdom saving throw or be frightened until the end of its next turn.

ACTIONS

Multiattack. The dust goblin archmage makes three Chaos Burst attacks.

Chaos Burst. *Melee or Ranged Spell Attack:* +7 to hit, reach 5 ft. or range 120 ft., one target. *Hit:* 36 (6d10 + 3) acid, cold, fire, force, lightning, or necrotic damage. Determine the damage type by rolling a d6: 1 = Acid, 2 = Cold, 3 = Fire, 4 = Force, 5 = Lightning, 6 = Necrotic. If the dust goblin archmage scores a critical hit, the burst explodes. The target and each creature within 10 feet of it must succeed on a DC 15 Dexterity saving throw or take 36 (6d10) damage. Determine the damage type by rolling a d6, as above.

Spellcasting. The dust goblin archmage casts one of the following spells, using Intelligence as the spellcasting ability (spell save DC 15):

At will: *mage hand, message, thaumaturgy*
2/day each: *confusion, divination, mage armor*
1/day: *twist of fate* (see **Chapter 6**)

REACTIONS

Counterspell Chaos Surge (2/Day). When the dust goblin archmage can see a creature within 60 feet casting a spell, it can attempt to interrupt it. If the target is casting a spell of 3rd level or lower, its spell fails and has no effect. If it is casting a spell of 4th level or higher, the dust goblin archmage makes an Intelligence check. The DC equals 10 + the spell's level. On a success, the target's spell fails and has no effect. Whether the spell is successfully cast or fails, the dust goblin archmage can force the target to roll on the Chaos Magic Surge table (see **Chapter 6**).

INSATIABLE BROOD

The closely packed mass of tiny, winged heads dives down, the jagged teeth of each head gnashing hungrily.

These ravenous beasts are always found in great, gnawing swarms. Each individual in an insatiable brood is a head, slightly larger than a human fist, with bulging black eyes and a large mouth lined with teeth. Wasp-like wings protrude from where the ears would be on a humanoid head. The sound of gnashing teeth precedes the brood as it travels.

Unceasing Appetite. True to its name, an insatiable brood tries to devour everything it can reach, leaving a trail of devastation in its wake. Where the material a brood consumes actually goes is a mystery. Some sages speculate that the maws of these creatures are gateways to the Void. Others say the Void-stuff of which they are composed simply disintegrates what they ingest.

Killers of Life, Destroyers of Beauty. Although an insatiable brood is satisfied with devouring everything in its path, it will target any living creatures first, with special attention to those trying to flee. When it senses no living targets nearby, an insatiable brood usually devours examples of natural or artificial beauty—artwork or other finely crafted objects—in preference over less attractive targets.

Insatiable Brood

Medium Swarm of Tiny Aberrations, Neutral Evil

ARMOR CLASS 13
HIT POINTS 66 (12d8 + 12)
SPEED 0 ft., fly 50 ft.

STR	DEX	CON	INT	WIS	CHA
10 (+0)	17 (+3)	13 (+1)	3 (−4)	12 (+1)	7 (−2)

DAMAGE RESISTANCES cold; bludgeoning, piercing, and slashing from nonmagical attacks
CONDITION IMMUNITIES charmed, frightened, grappled, paralyzed, petrified, prone, restrained, stunned
SENSES darkvision 60 ft., passive Perception 11
LANGUAGES understands Void Speech but can't speak
CHALLENGE 3 (700 XP)   **PROFICIENCY BONUS** +2

Siege Monster. The insatiable brood deals double damage to objects and structures.

Swarm. The insatiable brood can occupy another creature's space and vice versa, and the brood can move through any opening large enough for a Tiny creature. The brood can't regain hp or gain temporary hp.

Void Traveler. The insatiable brood requires no air, warmth, ambient pressure, food, or water, enabling it to travel safely through interstellar space and similar environments.

ACTIONS

Bites. *Melee Weapon Attack:* +5 to hit, reach 0 ft., one creature in the swarm's space. *Hit:* 14 (4d6) piercing damage plus 9 (2d8) force damage, or 7 (2d6) piercing damage plus 4 (1d8) force damage if the insatiable brood has half its hp or fewer. This attack is magical, and a creature that has resistance to piercing damage does not benefit from that resistance if it is hit by this attack.

ROBOT, DRONE

This metallic construct resembles a beetle with three legs spaced equidistantly around an oval body. A jet of blue flame shoots from its underside, keeping the creature aloft as it zips across the terrain. The creature smells strongly of burning oil.

Robot drones were created by an advanced civilization to spy on enemy forces, their miniature size and ability to fly enabling them to keep tabs on foes without being detected. This invention did not save the civilization from eventual destruction, leaving most of the surviving drones without a master. The typical drone is smaller than 1 foot in diameter and weighs roughly 20 pounds, though smaller and bigger versions have been found.

Wasteland Rarities. Only a few robot drones still roam the wasteland. Most of the original drones have succumbed either to the ravages of time or the attacks of various beasts. Adventurers and explorers are much more likely to find an odd leg, a stray piece of machinery, or a ruined eye than a complete specimen.

Drone Robot

Tiny Construct, Unaligned

ARMOR CLASS 16
HIT POINTS 21 (6d4 + 6)
SPEED 20 ft., fly 40 ft. (hover)

STR	DEX	CON	INT	WIS	CHA
7 (−2)	18 (+4)	12 (+1)	8 (−1)	12 (+1)	6 (−2)

SKILLS Perception +5, Stealth +6
DAMAGE VULNERABILITIES lightning
DAMAGE RESISTANCES cold, fire
DAMAGE IMMUNITIES poison, psychic
CONDITION IMMUNITIES charmed, exhaustion, frightened, paralyzed, petrified, poisoned
SENSES darkvision 60 ft., passive Perception 15
LANGUAGES understands the language of its creators but cannot speak
CHALLENGE 1/2 (100 XP)   **PROFICIENCY BONUS** +2

Electrical Malfunction. If the robot drone takes lightning damage, it must make a successful DC 10 Wisdom saving throw or become confused until the end of its next turn.

Unusual Nature. The robot drone doesn't require air, food, drink, or sleep.

Nimble Attacker. The robot drone doesn't have disadvantage on its attack rolls when using its Flame Jet attack within 5 feet of an enemy.

ACTIONS

Slam. *Melee Weapon Attack:* +0 to hit, reach 5 ft., one target. *Hit:* 1 (1d6 − 2) bludgeoning damage.

Flame Jet. *Ranged Weapon Attack:* +6 to hit, range 5/15 ft., one target. *Hit:* 8 (1d8 + 4) fire damage.

ROBOT DRONE FAMILIARS

Though such occurrences are exceedingly rare, some robot drones have been turned into familiars under the control of spellcasters interested in artifice and lost technology. A robot drone that becomes a familiar shares a telepathic bond with its master just as any other familiar does, enabling the master to sense what the drone senses as long as it is within 1 mile of its master. In addition, while its master is within 10 feet of the familiar, the master gains the drone's Nimble Attacker trait when making ranged attacks using weapons or spells.

ROBOT, WARDEN

Resembling a member of the city guard made of steel and a glass-like material, this construct seems suited for combat. It holds a baton that gives off blazing blue light, and a similarly colored light is visible on its chest plate.

Constructed to be guardians and warriors, robot wardens are humanoid-shaped devices similar to clockwork constructs but powered by science rather than magic. The only real weakness robot wardens have is to lightning damage, which interferes with their circuitry and causes them to go haywire. A typical robot warden is over 6 feet tall and weighs more than 500 pounds.

Trapped in Ruins. Most of these constructs are scattered throughout the wastes in hidden bunkers, fallen citadels, and even crashed spaceships. Most robot wardens have gone dormant during the years they have been trapped to conserve power, but a warden can activate itself at a moment's notice when intruders enter its area. Some wardens might not be immediately hostile, depending on their original orders, but will not hesitate to take aggressive action if threatened.

Warden Robot

Medium Construct, Unaligned

ARMOR CLASS 15 (natural armor)
HIT POINTS 52 (8d8 + 16)
SPEED 30 ft.

STR	DEX	CON	INT	WIS	CHA
17 (+3)	10 (+0)	15 (+2)	12 (+1)	12 (+1)	8 (−1)

SKILLS Perception +4
DAMAGE VULNERABILITIES lightning
DAMAGE RESISTANCES cold, fire
DAMAGE IMMUNITIES poison, psychic

NO ROBOTS IN MY FANTASY, PLEASE!

Many players and GMs don't like to mix fantasy and science fiction, preferring to keep the two genres separate, and might be turned off by a campaign setting or adventure that incorporates both. The elegant solution to this problem, rather than simply getting rid of the sci-fi elements, is to modify them to make them more palatable to a fantasy audience. A death ray gun might become an archaic wand from a fallen civilization that fires beams of energy, and a robot is simply a golem in a different shell. Even a spaceship can be redefined. Perhaps it is a sky barge of one of the gods of the campaign world or a wondrous gnomish invention powered by elemental forces or tamed dragons.

CONDITION IMMUNITIES charmed, exhaustion, frightened, paralyzed, petrified, poisoned

SENSES darkvision 60 ft., passive Perception 14

LANGUAGES understands and speaks the language of its creator

CHALLENGE 3 (700 XP) **PROFICIENCY BONUS** +2

Electrical Malfunction. Whenever the warden robot takes lightning damage, it must make a successful DC 10 Wisdom saving throw or become confused until the end of its next turn.

Unusual Nature. The robot warden doesn't require air, food, drink, or sleep.

Vigilant Patroller. A robot warden has advantage on Wisdom (Perception) checks involving creatures within 30 feet of it.

ACTIONS

Multiattack. The robot warden makes two Force Baton attacks.

Force Baton. *Melee Weapon Attack:* +5 to hit, reach 5 ft. *Hit:* 10 (2d6 + 3) force damage.

Disrupter Beam (Recharge 5–6). The robot warden fires a beam of blue force from its chest plate. The beam is a line 30 feet long and 5 feet wide. Any creature caught in the beam must make a DC 14 Dexterity saving throw, taking 14 (4d6) force damage on a failed save or half as much damage on a successful one. A creature that fails its saving throw is also stunned until the end of its next turn.

SATARRE INFILTRATOR

This slim, unassuming reptile bows low, speaking in a reasonable tone with a silvered tongue.

Shorter and slighter than most other satarre (see *Tome of Beasts 2*), infiltrators are natural saboteurs that slip unnoticed into places that are targets of their sabotage. An infiltrator can beguile the unwary into inviting it into their camp, believing it to be harmless or even friendly, only to have it unravel their defenses and bring the dark of the Void crashing down on them.

Means to an End. Nihilistic and apparently suicidal, the satarre think nothing of sacrificing themselves or anyone else to bring the world closer to the brink of destruction. Yet they are not simply bloodthirsty murderers. Their leaders espouse the dissolution of the ephemeral structure that keeps the world together.

Master Saboteurs. Satarre infiltrators that ingratiate themselves into a group or a society of other creatures work to weaken the creatures' faith, erode their trust in their leaders and belief systems, and

VARIANT: PARALYZING RAY

A few robot wardens have been manufactured to capture targets for interrogation rather than kill them outright. These wardens have the following attack in place of the Disrupter Beam attack:

Paralyzing Ray (Recharge 5–6). The robot warden fires a beam of emerald energy from its chest plate. The beam is a line 30 feet long and 5 feet wide. Any creature caught in the beam must make a DC 14 Constitution saving throw. On a successful save, a creature is restrained until the end of its next turn. On a failed save, it is paralyzed for 1 hour. A paralyzed creature can make a new saving throw at the end of each of its turns, ending the effect on itself with a success. If a creature fails three consecutive saving throws, however, it remains paralyzed for the entire duration.

encourage them to believe that honor is pointless. In this way, they slowly fray the cords that bind the universe together, an act considered just as

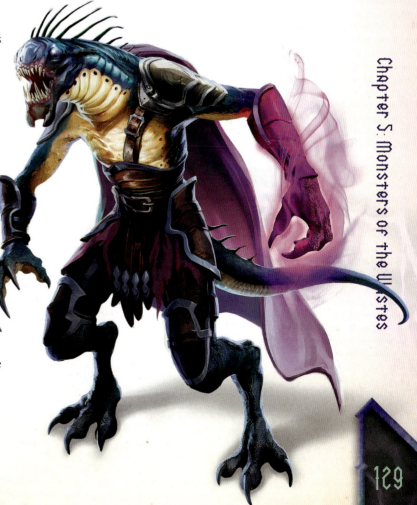

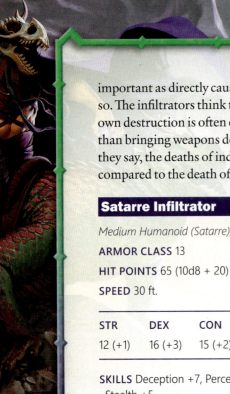

important as directly causing death—perhaps more so. The infiltrators think that guiding others to their own destruction is often easier and more effective than bringing weapons down upon them. After all, they say, the deaths of individuals are insignificant compared to the death of hope itself.

Satarre Infiltrator

Medium Humanoid (Satarre), Neutral Evil

ARMOR CLASS 13
HIT POINTS 65 (10d8 + 20)
SPEED 30 ft.

STR	DEX	CON	INT	WIS	CHA
12 (+1)	16 (+3)	15 (+2)	12 (+1)	13 (+1)	17 (+3)

SKILLS Deception +7, Perception +3, Persuasion +7, Stealth +5
DAMAGE RESISTANCES necrotic
SENSES darkvision 60 ft., passive Perception 13
LANGUAGES Common, Void Speech
CHALLENGE 3 (700 XP) **PROFICIENCY BONUS** +2

Void Strength. The infiltrator has advantage on Wisdom (Perception) checks and on saving throws against being blinded, charmed, deafened, frightened, stunned, or knocked unconscious.

Magic Weapons. The infiltrator's weapon attacks are magical.

ACTIONS

Multiattack. The infiltrator makes two Void Claw attacks.

Void Claw. *Melee Weapon Attack:* +5 to hit, reach 5 ft., one target. *Hit:* 8 (2d4 + 3) slashing damage plus 4 (1d8) necrotic damage.

BONUS ACTIONS

Dark Step. While in dim light or darkness, the infiltrator magically teleports, along with any equipment it is wearing or carrying, up to 30 feet to an unoccupied space it can see that is also in dim light or darkness, and then takes the Hide action.

SLITHERJACK

At first glance, this levitating creature looks like an opalescent moray eel. As it moves, however, it extends tentacles that pulse and ripple, propelling it through the air as an octopus moves through the water.

Slitherjacks haunt fey forests, eldritch swamps, mages' towers, ruins, dungeons, and other places where magic is likely to be present. Acting as the leeches of the arcane world, slitherjacks feed off the ambient magic that surrounds arcane practitioners and imbues natural fonts of arcane energy, and they can also drain magic items of their power if given the chance.

Arcane Scavengers. Slitherjacks consume only magic, and they are not interested in fighting or killing unless a creature stands between them and their next meal. One slitherjack confronted by a group of adventurers might flee, but rarely is just one slitherjack encountered—the presence of magical energy draws them like a flame attracts moths.

Slitherjack

Small Aberration, Chaotic Neutral

ARMOR CLASS 14
HIT POINTS 35 (10d6)
SPEED fly 40 ft. (hover)

STR	DEX	CON	INT	WIS	CHA
11 (+0)	16 (+3)	10 (+0)	14 (+2)	11 (+0)	6 (−2)

SAVING THROWS Dex +5
SKILLS Perception +4, Stealth +5
DAMAGE VULNERABILITIES psychic
DAMAGE RESISTANCES bludgeoning, piercing, and slashing from nonmagical attacks
DAMAGE IMMUNITIES acid, cold, fire, force, lightning, necrotic, thunder, or radiant damage from magical attacks
CONDITION IMMUNITIES prone
SENSES blindsight 300 ft.
LANGUAGES understands Abyssal, Deep Speech, Draconic, and Infernal but cannot speak
CHALLENGE 3 (700 XP) **PROFICIENCY BONUS** +2

Absorb Energy. If the slitherjack is hit with a magical attack that deals acid, cold, fire, force, lightning, necrotic, thunder, or radiant damage, it regains 1d6 hp. Additionally, it can store some of that energy, and the next time the slitherjack hits with a Tentacle attack, the target takes an extra 1d6 damage of the stored type.

Arcane Sensitivity. The slitherjack can innately sense the presence of magic with 300 feet of it and can pinpoint its location.

Consume Magic. If the slitherjack has possession of a magic item for more than 10 minutes, it siphons energy from the item, suppressing its magical properties, and the item becomes nonmagical for the next 24 hours. An item that remains in the slitherjack's possession for 24 continuous hours becomes permanently nonmagical.

Limited Telepathy. The slitherjack can magically communicate simple ideas, emotions, and images telepathically with any creature within 60 feet of it that can understand a language.

Magic Resistance. The slitherjack has advantage on saving throws against spells and other magical effects.

Scintillating Appearance. The slitherjack's skin is a constant swirl of disorienting color and light. Any creature that attacks the slitherjack and can see it has disadvantage on its attack roll.

ACTIONS

Multiattack. The slitherjack makes two Tentacle attacks.

Tentacle. *Melee Weapon Attack:* +5 to hit, reach 10 ft., one target. *Hit:* 7 (2d4 + 3) slashing damage, and if the target is a creature, it must make a DC 13 Dexterity saving throw. On a failed save, the slitherjack takes possession of one magic item the creature is wearing or holding onto. If the slitherjack has four items in its possession, it can no longer make Tentacle attacks.

Strobe. The slitherjack flares its tentacles, creating a burst of light and color. Any creature within 30 feet of the slitherjack that can see it must make a successful DC 13 Wisdom saving throw or become stunned until the end of the slitherjack's next turn.

REACTIONS

Death Burst. When the slitherjack dies, the arcane energy within it explodes. Each creature within 15 feet of the slitherjack must make a DC 13 Constitution saving throw, taking 14 (4d6) force damage on a failed save, or half as much damage on a successful one.

SPIDER, SONG

A tiny, green spider is barely visible at the edge of a leaf, the only obvious hints of its presence the eerie song that echoes around it and the sleeping animals dotting the forest floor.

Song spiders are minuscule creatures, smaller than a coin and easy to overlook. Thanks to their iridescent green coloration that enables them to blend in easily with the plants and other greenery of the forest, song spiders spend most of their lives out of sight—if not out of mind.

Enchanting Song. Song spiders can produce an enchanting melody by rubbing their pedipalps together in a particular way. The resulting song has a soporific effect on all nearby creatures that can hear it, lulling most of them into a deep slumber. The spider then creeps onto its slumbering victims and lays its eggs beneath their skin or in their hair.

Trained Pets. Song spiders can be captured and trained to use their song only at certain times, or when given certain cues. An innkeeper might have a song spider in a jar hidden in the rafters of the establishment and trained to sing only at bedtime; the guests awaken amazed at the wonderful night's rest they just got. Others might use trained spiders for malicious purposes, such as sending one into a mark's room and then sneaking in after the target has been put to sleep.

Song Spider

Tiny Beast, Unaligned

ARMOR CLASS 14
HIT POINTS 6 (4d4 − 4)
SPEED 10 ft., climb 10 ft.

STR	DEX	CON	INT	WIS	CHA
1 (−4)	16 (+3)	8 (−1)	8 (−1)	10 (+0)	5 (−2)

SAVING THROWS Dex +5
SKILLS Perception +2, Stealth +5
SENSES darkvision 120 ft.
LANGUAGES —
CHALLENGE 1/8 (25 XP)   **PROFICIENCY BONUS** +2

Forest Camouflage. The song spider has advantage on Dexterity (Stealth) checks made to hide in forest terrain.

Spider Climb. The song spider can climb difficult surfaces, including upside down on ceilings, without needing to make an ability check.

ACTIONS

Bite. *Melee Weapon Attack:* +5 to hit, reach 5 ft., one creature. *Hit:* 1 piercing damage, and the target must succeed on a DC 13 Constitution saving throw or take an extra 2 (1d4) poison damage.

Soporific Song. The song spider emits a soothing but disorienting melody. Each creature within 30 feet that can hear the spider must make a DC 13 Wisdom saving throw. On a failed save, a creature falls unconscious and remains in a slumber until it takes damage or someone else uses an action to shake or slap it awake. If the spider uses its action to make a Bite attack or do anything else, it stops singing. When the spider stops singing, an affected creature can repeat the saving throw at the end of each of its turns, ending the effect on itself on a success. If the spider uses Soporific Song on consecutive turns, creatures that succeeded on the saving throw in the previous round must make the saving throw again.

BONUS ACTIONS

Nimble Escape. The song spider can take the Dash, Disengage, or Hide action.

TENTACLED CRAB

The hulking crabs relentlessly lumber forth across the land. Strange, orange tentacles rise up from their drab topsides and sway gently back and forth, humming a hypnotic alien song. They press on as though seeking something no one else can see.

When an arcane calamity of uncontrolled power tore the veil between planes, the tentacled crabs crossed over into the wastes from another world. They gather in herds and roam the land, feeling the air with their tentacles for eldritch energy. They are particularly drawn to planar portals, where their songs can hypnotize and draw forth their preferred prey, creatures with innate magical qualities. No one has successfully tamed a tentacled crab, but there are tales told of bold individuals who have caught and kept one in order to follow it to magically rich locations.

Tentacled crabs are not normally aggressive unless they sense magic in or on a creature. If they have gone without consuming magical energy for some time, they will eat whatever creatures are stunned by their song, converging in a group to devour them before resuming their endless search.

Experienced explorers of the wastes know that tentacled crabs are more dangerous in large numbers, as the strength of the hypnotic effect of their communal song depends on how many of them are present. The best way to escape or distract a herd of tentacled crabs is to toss a magic item to them, for they will spend days crushing it with their claws to destroy it and consume its energy. Frequent travelers in the wastes with the means to do so often carry some minor magic item that they're willing to sacrifice should they encounter a herd.

Tentacled Crab

Large Monstrosity, Neutral

ARMOR CLASS 15 (natural armor)
HIT POINTS 123 (13d10 + 52)
SPEED 30 ft., swim 30 ft.

STR	DEX	CON	INT	WIS	CHA
18 (+4)	15 (+2)	18 (+4)	2 (-4)	9 (-1)	3 (-4)

SKILLS Stealth +4
SENSES truesight 30 ft., passive Perception 6
LANGUAGES —
CHALLENGE 4 (1,100 XP)   **PROFICIENCY BONUS** +2

Amphibious. The crab can breathe air and water.

Arcane Sense. The crab knows the direction to every creature with innate magical abilities, magic item, planar portal, and spell cast within 1 mile of it.

Magic Resistance. The crab has advantage on saving throws against spells and other magical effects.

ACTIONS

Multiattack. The tentacled crab makes two Claw attacks.

Claw. *Melee Weapon Attack:* +6 to hit, reach 5 ft., one target. *Hit:* 22 (4d8 + 4) force damage, and the target is grappled (escape DC 14). The crab has two claws, each of which can grapple only one target.

BONUS ACTIONS

Tentacle Song. The tentacled crab begins humming with its tentacles. A tentacled crab can continue singing until its concentration is broken (as if concentrating on a spell). Any creature within 120 feet of it who can hear it must make a DC 14 Wisdom saving throw. On a failed save, the creature is charmed by the tentacled crab and incapacitated. While charmed in this way, the target's movement is controlled by the tentacled crab. A charmed target may repeat the saving throw at the end of each of its turns, ending the effect on itself on a success or if it can no longer hear the song. If a creature's saving throw is successful or the effect ends for it, the creature is immune to any tentacled crab's Tentacle Song for 24 hours.

Whenever the tentacled crab deals damage to the charmed creature, the charmed creature can repeat the saving throw, ending the effect on itself on a success.

The DC of the saving throw increases by 1 for each additional tentacled crab that can be heard singing by a creature, but a creature can only be targeted by one crab's Tentacle Song on its turn.

TIEFLING DIABOLIST

The tiefling strides forward resplendently garbed in black robes embroidered in crimson, her curling horns capped in small globes of solid gold. She smirks as she starts to spit foul sounding words. A haze of greasy, brimstone scented vapor begins to swirl as her tone increases in volume.

Many tieflings consider themselves the heirs of the Hells, but a tiefling diabolist knows it as a certainty. Unlike the mewling fools that form pacts with the archdevils of the nether realms, accepting scraps of power in exchange for becoming the playthings and catspaws of their betters, a diabolist commands the fear and respect of lesser fiends.

Paranoid Schemers. A tiefling diabolist patiently works to achieve its far-reaching plans. So long as it is the acknowledged leader, the diabolist is happy to work with a team toward those goals. A diabolist's underlings, on the other hand, may not be so sanguine with the situation. Members of the team are subjected to regular tests of their loyalty, which are often bizarre and sometimes uncomfortable. They are also subtly encouraged to spy on their teammates and report even the slightest infraction or suspicion of wrongdoing to the leader. The most successful tiefling diabolists tend to be loners that work exclusively with devils they've summoned themselves.

Tiefling Diabolist

Medium Humanoid (Tiefling), Lawful Evil

ARMOR CLASS 13 (16 with mage armor)
HIT POINTS 121 (22d8 + 22)
SPEED 30 ft.

STR	DEX	CON	INT	WIS	CHA
8 (−1)	16 (+3)	12 (+1)	20 (+5)	14 (+2)	18 (+4)

SAVING THROWS Int +9, Wis +6
SKILLS Arcana +9, Deception +8, Insight +6, Perception +6
DAMAGE RESISTANCES fire
SENSES darkvision 60 ft., passive Perception 16
LANGUAGES Abyssal, Common, Infernal
CHALLENGE 10 (5,900 XP) **PROFICIENCY BONUS** +4

Heir of Hell. The tiefling diabolist has advantage on Charisma checks it makes to deceive, intimidate, or persuade a devil. If the diabolist is attacked by a devil that has been summoned by another creature, including another devil, it has advantage on saving throws against spells and other magical effects cast by the summoned devil, and the summoned devil has disadvantage on attack rolls against the diabolist.

ACTIONS

Multiattack. The tiefling diabolist makes two Hellfire Burst attacks.

Hellfire Burst. *Melee or Ranged Spell Attack:* +9 to hit, reach 5 ft. or range 120 ft., one target. *Hit:* 16 (2d10 + 5) fire damage plus 11 (2d10) necrotic damage.

Summon Devil (1/Day). The tiefling diabolist summons 2d4 lemures, two bearded devils, or one barbed devil. A summoned devil appears in an unoccupied space within 60 feet of the diabolist, acts as an ally of the diabolist, and can't summon other devils. It remains for 1 minute, until the diabolist dies, or until its summoner dismisses it as an action.

Spellcasting. The tiefling diabolist casts one of the following spells, using Intelligence as the spellcasting ability (spell save DC 17):

At will: *mage hand, message, minor illusion, thaumaturgy*
2/day each: *charm person* (as a 5th-level spell), *darkness, detect thoughts, fly, greater invisibility, mage armor*
1/day each: *banishment, dominate person, true seeing*

BONUS ACTIONS

Summon Imp Familiar (1/Day). The tiefling diabolist summons an imp. The imp appears in an unoccupied space within 5 feet of the diabolist, whom it obeys. It takes its turn immediately after the diabolist. It lasts for 24 hours, until it or the diabolist dies, or until the diabolist dismisses it as a bonus action.

TROLL, CHAOS

This troll stands close to 20 feet tall. Its grotesque form is covered in pustules, veins, spikes, and oddly colored patches of flesh. It lumbers forward, seemingly intent on devouring everything in its path.

A chaos troll is created when an ordinary troll is subjected to an enormous dose of raw, primal chaos. This event causes a troll to increase in size and strength and substantially alters the creature's regenerative ability. Because chaos trolls tower over their lesser kin, they are treated with deference and caution by other trolls they consort with.

Ultimate Omnivores. Chaos trolls are constantly famished and will eat anything they can fit into their mouths, including meat or plant life that is poisonous, rotten, or otherwise damaged or corrupted. In the worst of times, a chaos troll might be forced to eat parts of its own body, such as an arm or a foot, to stave off starvation (in the knowledge that the extremity will soon grow back).

Prone to Mutation. Due to the unpredictable effects of raw chaos infusing their bodies, many chaos trolls have unsightly or bizarre mutations. Most of these mutations improve the troll's fighting ability or change how it interacts with its environment.

Chaos Troll

Huge Giant, Chaotic Evil

ARMOR CLASS 15 (natural armor)
HIT POINTS 115 (10d12 + 50)
SPEED 40 ft.

STR	DEX	CON	INT	WIS	CHA
22 (+6)	10 (+0)	20 (+5)	7 (−2)	9 (−1)	6 (−2)

SKILLS Perception +2
SENSES darkvision 60 ft., passive Perception 11
LANGUAGES Giant
CHALLENGE 7 (2,900 XP) **PROFICIENCY BONUS** +3

Shifting Regeneration. The troll regains 10 hp at the start of its turn. Whenever the troll takes acid, cold, fire, lightning, necrotic, or poison damage, roll on the table below. If the result of the roll matches the attack's damage type, or if the troll takes radiant damage, this trait doesn't function at the start of the troll's next turn. The troll dies only if it starts its turn with 0 hp and doesn't regenerate.

d6	Damage Type	d6	Damage Type
1	acid	4	lightning
2	cold	5	necrotic
3	fire	6	poison

ACTIONS

Multiattack. The chaos troll makes one Bite attack and two Claw attacks.

Bite. *Melee Weapon Attack:* +9 to hit, reach 5 ft., one target. *Hit:* 11 (1d10 + 6) piercing damage. If the troll scores a critical hit with its Bite attack, it can make another Bite attack against the same target as a bonus action.

Claw. *Melee Weapon Attack:* +9 to hit, reach 10 ft., one target. *Hit:* 15 (2d8 + 6) slashing damage.

CHAOS TROLL MUTATIONS

Some chaos trolls have a mutation that can substantially alter their abilities. Roll on the following table to select from the possibilities.

d8	Mutation
1–3	No mutation.
4	The troll has two heads. It gains an additional Bite attack when it uses the Multiattack action.
5	The troll's hide is covered in stony plates. Its AC increases by 2, but its speed decreases to 30 feet.
6	The troll's body is sprinkled with several blinking eyes. These eyes enable the troll to see invisible objects, as the effect of the *see invisibility* spell.
7	The troll has an extra arm or leg. If it has an extra arm, it gains an additional Claw attack when it uses the Multiattack action. If it has an extra leg, its speed increases to 40 feet.
8	The troll has immunity to disease and to the poisoned condition.

TROLL, NECROMANCER

This slender, bone-white troll smells of decaying meat. Black drool drips from its jaws as it peers at you with glowing red eyes. A bag stitched together from pieces of human skin is strapped to its waist, and from it the troll pulls forth a severed, swollen human head.

Necromancer trolls are similar to ordinary trolls in appearance but with bleached white skin, red eyes, and stinking black saliva. A necromancer troll carries a bag made of human, dwarven, or elven skin that holds a variety of decapitated humanoid heads bloated by necrotic energy.

Unknowable Origin. How necromancer trolls came into being is unknown and likely to remain so. Everyone who tries to research the subject abandons the attempt for fear of going insane because of what might be discovered. No matter their genesis, necromancer trolls are a blight on the world—even other trolls are found nowhere near them. The only creatures known to associate with these monsters are undead and fiends related to death and decay.

Troll, Necromancer

Large Giant, Chaotic Evil

ARMOR CLASS 17 (natural armor)
HIT POINTS 161 (14d10 + 84)
SPEED 30 ft.

STR	DEX	CON	INT	WIS	CHA
18 (+4)	14 (+2)	22 (+6)	9 (−1)	13 (+1)	16 (+3)

DAMAGE IMMUNITIES necrotic
CONDITION IMMUNITIES frightened, paralyzed
SENSES darkvision 90 ft., passive Perception 11
LANGUAGES Giant
CHALLENGE 10 (5,900 XP)   **PROFICIENCY BONUS** +4

Deathly Regeneration. The troll regains 5 hp at the start of its turn. If a creature is dying within 20 feet of the troll when the troll starts its turn, the troll regains 20 hp instead. If the troll takes acid or fire damage, this trait doesn't function at the start of the troll's next turn. The troll dies only if it starts its turn with 0 hp and doesn't regenerate.

Decapitation. If the troll reduces a target to 0 hp with a Claw attack, it tries to rip the target's head from its shoulders. The target must make a successful DC 18 Constitution saving throw or be decapitated and instantly killed. Creatures without heads are immune to this ability.

ACTIONS

Multiattack. The troll makes one Bite attack and two Claw attacks.

Bite. *Melee Weapon Attack:* +8 to hit, reach 5 ft., one target. *Hit:* 9 (1d10 + 4) piercing damage plus 9 (2d8) necrotic damage.

Claw. *Melee Weapon Attack:* +8 to hit, reach 5 ft., *Hit:* 11 (2d6 + 4) slashing damage plus 9 (2d8) necrotic damage.

Head Toss. The necromancer troll hurls a decapitated head infused with necrotic energy at a space within 30 feet of it. When the head hits, it erupts in a 10-foot-radius sphere of necrotic energy. Any creature in the area must make a DC 17 Dexterity saving throw, taking 27 (6d8) necrotic damage on a failed save, or half as much damage on a successful one.

BONUS ACTIONS

Infuse Head. A necromancer troll can infuse a decapitated head with necrotic energy. It typically has 1d4 infused heads in its possession at the beginning of combat.

VILE LOOTER

A lithe woman in leather armor and comfortable boots picks her way through the grisly corridor, stopping at each unfortunate dart-studded victim to relieve them of their now unneeded valuables.

Vile looters raid tombs, despoil temples, and smuggle antiquities. They can be found delving for valuables throughout the wasteland and are a common threat to legitimate explorers and heroic adventurers alike. Many vile looters become such familiar fixtures in their areas of operations that they can be identified by one or more notable characteristics.

Stirring Up Trouble. Vile looters prefer to get into a ruin or treasure site, grab as many valuables as they can carry, and get out again without having to deal with irritations such as a site's residents or treasure guardians. This often brings trouble to nearby settlements as those selfsame residents and guardians search for the individuals that despoiled their home or sacred place. Some looters are even more malicious. They delight in setting up ambushes for other explorers to spring as they exit a site, tired from their endeavors. The vile looters then pick up easy loot from the corpses of their victims.

VILE LOOTER NOTABLE CHARACTERISTICS

d10	Notable Characteristic
1	High crowned, wide brimmed sable-skin-hat
2	Pipe with a long stem and a fat bowl
3	Gold front tooth
4	Ragged and torn earlobe from an old injury
5	Livid scar running from brow to chin
6	Cold eyes and a self-satisfied smirk
7	Gold framed monocle edged in tiny diamonds
8	Ostentatious ring set with a large ruby that it fidgets with while speaking
9	Voice that is completely devoid of inflection or emotion
10	Flamboyant pompadour waxed into the shape of a cresting wave

Vile Looter

Medium Humanoid (Any Race), Neutral Evil

ARMOR CLASS 15 (studded leather)
HIT POINTS 97 (15d8 + 30)
SPEED 30 ft.

STR	DEX	CON	INT	WIS	CHA
12 (+1)	17 (+3)	15 (+2)	15 (+2)	16 (+3)	14 (+2)

SAVING THROWS Dex +5, Cha +4
SKILLS Athletics +3, Investigation +4, Perception +5, Sleight of Hand +5
SENSES passive Perception 15
LANGUAGES any three languages
CHALLENGE 4 (1,100 XP)   **PROFICIENCY BONUS** +2

Help Myself (Recharges after a Short or Long Rest). The vile looter has advantage on an ability check that doesn't use one of its skills.

ACTIONS

Multiattack. The vile looter makes two Whip attacks or two Hand Crossbow attacks, or one Whip attack and one Hand Crossbow attack. If it is targeting a creature it has grappled, it makes two Unarmed Strike attacks instead.

Hand Crossbow. *Ranged Weapon Attack:* +5 to hit, range 30/120, one target. *Hit:* 6 (1d6 + 3) piercing damage.

Whip. *Melee Weapon Attack:* +5 to hit, reach 10 ft., one target. *Hit:* 7 (1d8 + 3) slashing damage. If its target is a Medium or Small creature, the vile looter can use its bonus action to grapple it. The creature can avoid being grappled by succeeding on a DC 13 Strength (Athletics) or Dexterity (Acrobatics) check. If the looter is using its whip to grapple a creature, it can't make a Whip attack until the grapple ends.

Unarmed Strike. *Melee Weapon Attack:* +5 to hit, reach 5 ft., one target. *Hit:* 6 (1d6 + 3) bludgeoning damage.

Hasty Retreat (1/Day). The vile looter disappears in a puff of noxious gray smoke and teleports to an unoccupied space it can see that is within 500 feet of it. Creatures within 5 feet of the looter when it disappears must succeed on a DC 13 Constitution saving throw or be poisoned for 1d6 rounds.

VILE RECONSTRUCTOR

A small, lithe humanoid with pale skin and a maw of needle-sharp teeth looks up through a monocular fused to one of its beady eyes. Several curious tools and devices are affixed to a belt around its waist. Three rod-tipped mechanical arms protrude from its back, each whirring and gesticulating in concordance with the creature's erratic motions.

Cousins to the sinister **vile barbers** (see *Tome of Beasts*), these impish unseelie fey are often tasked with resetting the triggers of complex traps and other contraptions. Their ability to traverse shadows, combined with their mechanical acumen and eldritch implants, enable vile reconstructors to infiltrate many places considered dangerous or unreachable.

Bad Science. Upon its enlistment or enslavement, a vile reconstructor is subjected to a series of physical and mental modifications under the supervision of an alchemist, wizard, or other individual who specializes in creating constructs or manipulating bodies. These procedures bestow upon the creature an array of heightened abilities and a macabre complement of skin-grafted tools and weapons, fracturing its mind in the process. A vile reconstructor is most often fitted with leftover mechanical parts from constructs, but unusual varieties of vile reconstructors, such as creatures with tentacles or the arms of a different creature instead of mechanical extremities, have been encountered in the wild.

Inconvenient Saboteurs. Adventurers most often encounter vile reconstructors when they are in the act of repairing or resetting traps or other mechanisms, but they are sometimes spotted in the most awkward and ill-timed of circumstances. The creatures delight in making those moments as deadly as possible in an effort to please themselves and satisfy the whims of their twisted creators.

Vile Reconstructor

Small Fey, Lawful Evil

ARMOR CLASS 14
HIT POINTS 31 (9d6)
SPEED 30 ft.

STR	DEX	CON	INT	WIS	CHA
12 (+1)	18 (+4)	10 (+0)	10 (+0)	14 (+2)	11 (+0)

SKILLS Investigation +2, Perception +4, Sleight of Hand +6, Stealth +6
DAMAGE RESISTANCES bludgeoning, piercing, and slashing from nonmagical attacks not made with cold iron weapons
CONDITION IMMUNITIES frightened
SENSES darkvision 60 ft., passive Perception 14
LANGUAGES Common, Sylvan, Umbral, Undercommon
CHALLENGE 2 (450 XP) **PROFICIENCY BONUS** +2

Inhumanly Quick. The vile reconstructor can take two bonus actions on its turn instead of one. It can't use the same bonus action twice during the same turn.

Monocular Graft. The vile reconstructor has advantage on Intelligence (Investigation) and Wisdom (Perception) checks that rely on sight.

ACTIONS

Multiattack. The vile reconstructor makes one Mechanical Claw attack and one Torch Rod attack, or it makes two Torch Rod attacks.

Mechanical Claw. *Melee Weapon Attack:* +6 to hit, reach 10 ft., one target. *Hit:* 9 (2d4 + 4) slashing damage.

Torch Rod. *Melee or Ranged Weapon Attack:* +6 to hit, reach 5 ft. or range 60 ft., one target. *Hit:* 7 (1d6 + 4) fire damage or lightning damage (the vile reconstructor's choice).

Mending Rod. The vile reconstructor touches an object with one of its rod-tipped arms and repairs the object. This effect works like the *mending* spell, except that the vile reconstructor can repair an object that measures up to 5 feet in any dimension.

BONUS ACTIONS

Mock. The vile reconstructor mocks a creature within 60 feet that can hear it. The target must succeed on a DC 12 Charisma saving throw, or attack rolls against it are made with advantage until the end of its next turn.

Nimble Escape. The vile reconstructor can take the Disengage or Hide action.

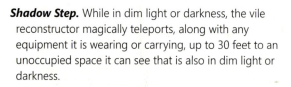

Shadow Step. While in dim light or darkness, the vile reconstructor magically teleports, along with any equipment it is wearing or carrying, up to 30 feet to an unoccupied space it can see that is also in dim light or darkness.

VOID WITNESS

The eyes of this bedraggled and wild human are red-rimmed and weep tears of liquid darkness.

The lowest-ranking members of cults dedicated to the Void are known as witnesses. Unlike **void cultists** (see *Creature Codex*), who have been fully exposed to the corruption of the Void, witnesses have been given only a brief glimpse of the great darkness beyond. As their minds descend into madness, witnesses become inexorably bound to the cult while simultaneously freeing themselves from any other connection to the world. Though witnesses haven't yet fully comprehended the Void, its emptiness can sometimes be seen reflected in their eyes—with devastating effects for those that meet their gaze.

Void Witness

Medium Humanoid, Chaotic Evil

ARMOR CLASS 12 (leather armor)
HIT POINTS 26 (4d8 + 8)
SPEED 30 ft.

STR	DEX	CON	INT	WIS	CHA
14 (+2)	12 (+1)	15 (+2)	9 (−1)	10 (+0)	12 (+1)

SKILLS Athletics +4, Stealth +3
DAMAGE RESISTANCES psychic
SENSES passive Perception 10
LANGUAGES Common, Void Speech
CHALLENGE 1/2 (100 XP)   **PROFICIENCY BONUS** +2

Insane. The void witness has advantage on saving throws against being charmed or frightened.

Reflection of the Void. When a creature that can see the void witness starts its turn within 30 feet of the witness, the creature must make a DC 12 Charisma saving throw if the witness isn't incapacitated and can see the creature. On a failed save, the creature becomes frightened of the witness until the start of its next turn. If the saving throw fails by 5 or more, the creature also suffers a random form of short-term madness. On a successful save, the creature is immune to this witness's Reflection of the Void for 24 hours.

ACTIONS

Morningstar. *Melee Weapon Attack:* +4 to hit, reach 5 ft., one target. *Hit:* 6 (1d8 + 2) piercing damage.

VOID-BOUND WARLOCK

Some warlocks strike bargains with the ancient gods that lie in the black places between the stars. Drawn to the Void by dark dreams, they fuel many of their abilities with its essence, reveling in their role in the unmaking of the world.

Void-Bound Warlock

Medium Humanoid, Chaotic Evil

ARMOR CLASS 13 (studded leather)
HIT POINTS 130 (20d8 + 40)
SPEED 30 ft.

STR	DEX	CON	INT	WIS	CHA
14 (+2)	12 (+1)	15 (+2)	13 (+1)	9 (−1)	17 (+3)

SAVING THROWS Wis +2, Cha +6
SKILLS Arcana +4, Intimidation +6, Perception +2
SENSES passive Perception 12
LANGUAGES Common, Void Speech, plus any one language
CHALLENGE 6 (2,300 XP)   **PROFICIENCY BONUS** +3

Feed the Void. When the void-bound warlock reduces a creature to 0 hp, it gains 10 (3d6) temporary hp.

Insane. The void-bound warlock has advantage on saving throws against being charmed or frightened.

Magic Weapons. The void-bound warlock's weapon attacks are magical.

Tainted Blood. A creature that touches the void-bound warlock's blood or that deals piercing or slashing damage to the warlock while within 5 feet of it takes 3 (1d6) necrotic damage.

ACTIONS

Multiattack. The void-bound warlock makes three Spear attacks or three Void Bolt attacks. It can replace one attack with a use of Spellcasting.

Spear. *Melee or Ranged Weapon Attack:* +5 to hit, reach 5 ft. or range 20/60 ft., one target. *Hit:* 5 (1d6 + 2) piercing damage plus 7 (2d6) necrotic damage, or 6 (1d8 + 2) piercing damage plus 7 (2d6) necrotic damage if used with two hands to make a melee attack.

Void Bolt. *Ranged Spell Attack:* +6 to hit, range 120 ft., one target. *Hit:* 13 (3d6 + 3) necrotic damage.

Channel the Void (Recharge 5–6). If the warlock doesn't have all its hp, it can channel the essence of the Void that seeps from its wounds, briefly manifesting tentacles of darkness that lash out at each creature within 10 feet of it. A creature must make a DC 14 Dexterity saving throw, taking 13 (3d8) cold damage plus 10 (3d6) necrotic damage on a failed save, or half as much damage on a successful one.

Spellcasting. The void-bound warlock casts one of the following spells, using Charisma as the spellcasting ability (spell save DC 14):

At will: *detect magic, disguise self, levitate, mage hand, minor illusion, thaumaturgy*

1/day each: *blight, hold person, ray of enfeeblement*

WARPED BEHEMOTH

This enormous, malformed giant stands nearly half again as tall as others of its kind. Its hairy hide is covered in oozing sores and swollen pustules. One of its arms is longer than the other, knuckles trailing on the ground.

Almost all the creatures caught in magical cataclysms are debilitated or killed by the terrible transformations that wrack their bodies. Rarely, a particularly durable or lucky specimen is warped into an even mightier creature from its exposure to the energy. Greatly enhanced in size and strength and imbued with (mostly) beneficial new abilities, these creatures are known as warped behemoths.

Ruled by Hunger. Most warped behemoths are solitary creatures motivated only by their own needs. The common reaction of a behemoth to other creatures is violence, as it lashes out in rage or in an attempt to consume enemies to sate its hunger. Occasionally, a warped behemoth has or develops the presence of mind to cooperate with other creatures. Most often, a behemoth allies with those of its original type, but any creatures resourceful enough to meet a warped behemoth's needs have a chance to gain a powerful ally so long as they keep the creature fed.

WARPED BEHEMOTH TEMPLATE

Any beast, fey, giant, humanoid, or monstrosity that has been exposed to a surge of chaotic energy can become a warped behemoth. When a creature becomes a warped behemoth, it retains its statistics except as described below.

Type. The behemoth's type changes to Aberration.

Armor Class. The behemoth has natural armor that gives it an AC of 11 + its Dexterity modifier. If the creature already had natural armor, its AC increases by 1 instead.

Size. The behemoth's size increases by two categories if the creature was Tiny or Small, or by one category if the creature was Medium, Large, or Huge.

Ability Scores. The behemoth's Strength score increases by 4, and its Intelligence and Charisma scores are each reduced by 2.

Skill Proficiencies. The behemoth has proficiency in the Athletics and Intimidation skills.

Body Distortions. The behemoth's body is warped by its exposure to magical energy. It has two body distortions, determined by rolling a d10 and consulting the Behemoth Body Distortions table (rerolling any duplicate result). If the warped behemoth already has resistance to a type of damage and gains the same resistance from a result on the table, the behemoth has immunity to that type of damage instead.

Challenge Rating. The behemoth's challenge rating increases by 1, and its proficiency bonus also increases by 1 if necessary.

Virulent Pustules. When the behemoth takes piercing or slashing damage, the pustules on its hide erupt in a noxious spray. Each creature within 5 feet of the behemoth must make a Constitution saving throw (DC 8 + the behemoth's proficiency bonus + its Constitution modifier). On a failed save, a creature takes poison damage equal to the behemoth's Constitution modifier and is poisoned for 1 minute. On a successful save, a creature takes half damage and isn't poisoned. A poisoned creature can repeat the saving throw at the end of each of its turns, ending the effect on itself on a success.

Ogre Warped Behemoth

Huge Aberration, Chaotic Evil

ARMOR CLASS 10 (natural armor)
HIT POINTS 59 (7d10 + 21)
SPEED 40 ft.

STR	DEX	CON	INT	WIS	CHA
23 (+6)	8 (−1)	16 (+3)	3 (−4)	7 (−2)	5 (−3)

SKILLS Athletics +8, Intimidation −1
DAMAGE RESISTANCES bludgeoning from nonmagical attacks

BEHEMOTH BODY DISTORTIONS

d10	Body Distortion
1	The creature's natural armor increases by 1.
2	The creature gains resistance to one of the following damage types (roll a d6): (1) acid, (2) cold, (3) fire, (4) lightning, (5) poison, or (6) thunder.
3	The creature gains resistance to nonmagical damage of one of the following types (roll a d6): (1–2) bludgeoning, (3–4) piercing, or (5–6) slashing. The creature's attacks count as magical for the purpose of overcoming resistance or immunity to nonmagical attacks and damage.
4	The creature gains darkvision out to a range of 60 feet. If the creature already had darkvision, its range increases by 30 feet instead.
5	The creature gains a climbing speed equal to its walking speed. If the creature already had a climbing speed, it is doubled instead.
6	The creature grows fleshy wings and gains a flying speed equal to its walking speed. If the creature already had a flying speed, a burrowing speed, or a swimming speed, treat this result as no effect.
7	The creature grows multiple eyes and gains advantage on Wisdom (Perception) checks that rely on sight.
8	The creature gains advantage on saving throws against spells and other magical effects.
9	The creature grows an oversized limb and gains a Slam attack. This attack has a reach of 10 feet for a Small or smaller creature or 15 feet for a Medium or larger creature. The attack deals bludgeoning damage based on the behemoth's size (1d6 for Medium, 1d8 for Large, 1d10 for Huge, or 1d12 for Gargantuan).
10	Roll one additional time on this table. A creature can't have more than three body warps.

SENSES darkvision 60 ft., passive Perception 8
LANGUAGES Common, Giant
CHALLENGE 3 (700 XP) **PROFICIENCY BONUS** +2

Body Distortions. This ogre warped behemoth has body distortions that grant it a Slam attack and resistance to nonmagical bludgeoning damage.

Virulent Pustules. When the behemoth takes piercing or slashing damage, the pustules on its hide erupt in a noxious spray. Each creature within 5 feet of the behemoth must make a DC 13 Constitution saving throw. On a failed save, a creature takes 3 poison damage and is poisoned for 1 minute. On a successful save, a creature takes half damage and isn't poisoned. A poisoned creature can repeat the saving throw at the end of each of its turns, ending the effect on itself on a success.

ACTIONS

Greatclub. *Melee Weapon Attack:* +8 to hit, reach 5 ft., one target. *Hit:* 15 (2d8 + 6) bludgeoning damage.

Slam. *Melee Weapon Attack:* +8 to hit, reach 15 ft., one target. *Hit:* 11 (1d10 + 6) bludgeoning damage.

Javelin. *Melee or Ranged Weapon Attack:* +8 to hit, reach 5 ft. or range 30/120 ft., one target. *Hit:* 13 (2d6 + 6) piercing damage.

WARPED TREANT

A tree creature shuffles forward. Some of its branches have been transformed into tentacles, others into eyestalks. The face depicted in its gray-green bark is frozen in a never-ending scream.

Once a renowned defender of the forest, a warped treant is a corrupted version of its original self, brought about when dark energy seeps into the earth where a treant is rooted. The creature is twisted into a servant of a vile power. It now guards its domain and anything in it from interlopers.

Attuned to Chaos. Warped treants still have an affinity for the forest, but this extends only to other plants and creatures changed by the same dark influences. Their roots delve deep and far, and they are aware of everything that treads upon their grounds. They feel at home amid other twisted beings and have forgotten their original purpose, listening only to the whispers in their minds that speak of chaos.

Warped Treant

Huge Plant, Chaotic Evil

ARMOR CLASS 15 (natural armor)
HIT POINTS 114 (12d12 + 36)
SPEED 30 ft.

STR	DEX	CON	INT	WIS	CHA
18 (+4)	11 (+0)	17 (+3)	12 (+1)	15 (+2)	5 (−2)

SAVING THROWS Str +7, Con +6
SKILLS Perception +5
DAMAGE VULNERABILITIES fire
DAMAGE RESISTANCES bludgeoning and piercing from nonmagical attacks
DAMAGE IMMUNITIES poison, necrotic
SENSES blindsight 120 ft., darkvision 60 ft., passive Perception 15
LANGUAGES Abyssal, Common, Deep Speech, Elvish, Sylvan
CHALLENGE 7 (2,900 XP) **PROFICIENCY BONUS** +3

Necrotic Sap. Any creature within 5 feet of the treant that hits it with a melee attack takes 5 (2d4) necrotic damage.

Deep Roots. The treant has advantage on ability checks and saving throws to avoid being knocked prone.

Keen Sight. The treant has advantage on Wisdom (Perception) checks that rely on sight.

Regeneration. The treant regains 10 hp at the start of its turn. If the treant takes fire damage, this trait doesn't function at the start of the treant's next turn. The treant dies only if it starts its turn with 0 hp and doesn't regenerate.

ACTIONS

Multiattack. The treant makes three Tentacle attacks.

Tentacle. *Melee Weapon Attack:* +10 to hit, reach 5 ft., one target. *Hit:* 12 (3d6 + 4) bludgeoning damage.

Rock. *Ranged Weapon Attack:* +10 to hit, range 60/180 ft., one target. *Hit:* 22 (4d10 + 4) bludgeoning damage.

Entangle (Recharge 5–6). The warped treant can command nearby vines and roots to attack its foes. Each creature within 30 feet of the treant must succeed on a DC 15 Dexterity saving throw or take 7 (1d6 + 4) piercing damage plus 10 (3d6) necrotic damage and be restrained until the end of the treant's next turn.

BONUS ACTIONS

Unearthly Howl. The warped treant lets out a bone-chilling wail. Each creature within 120 feet of it must succeed on a DC 15 Wisdom saving throw or become frightened of the treant for 1 minute. A creature can repeat the saving throw at the end of each of its turns, ending the effect on itself on a success.

WASTELAND LIZARD

As nimble as they are hardy, these giant horned lizards are prized as mounts by travelers in the wastes. Their scales are dusty green and gold, and their wide-splayed legs are poised to move quickly. Their eyes continuously scan their surroundings, flicking back and forth, always on the lookout for danger.

Wasteland lizards evolved rapidly in unnatural environments, developing the means to persist in a broken landscape full of unusual and often magical threats. Though not particularly fast, they are able to scramble up and over obstacles and can travel for days with minimal sustenance. They possess a sort of sixth sense that drives them to scuttle out of potentially dangerous areas. Exposure to the arcane hazards of the wastes has led the lizards to develop some resistance to otherworldly damage.

Consummate survivors, wasteland lizards prefer to avoid danger rather than face it head on. In a fight, they try to toss their opponents away with their horns to clear a path to flee. If this fails, they have one more escape trick: they can spray an acidic fluid from glands near their eyes to frighten predators. There is some debate about whether the sight of a panicked lizard spraying acid from its eyes shocks attackers into a fearful state, or whether the acid carries some other intrinsic chemical quality, but it can be quite effective.

Wasteland lizards can be tamed and guided in battle by a capable handler, and they confer some of the defensive benefits of their adaptations to their riders. Eggs and hatchlings fetch handsome sums in the markets that serve travelers in the wastes, and some wranglers make good (if dangerous) livings capturing and breaking wild adult lizards. Some alchemists conduct experiments with wasteland lizard acid glands, but the animals are generally worth more alive than for their organs.

Wasteland Lizard

Large Beast, Unaligned

ARMOR CLASS 14 (natural armor)
HIT POINTS 76 (10d10 + 21)
SPEED 30 ft., climb 30 ft.

STR	DEX	CON	INT	WIS	CHA
19 (+4)	9 (–1)	17 (+3)	2 (–4)	10 (+0)	7 (–2)

SAVING THROWS Con +4, Dex +1
SKILLS Perception +2, Survival +2
DAMAGE RESISTANCE force
SENSES darkvision 30 ft., passive Perception 12
LANGUAGES —
CHALLENGE 3 (700 XP)   **PROFICIENCY BONUS** +2

Confer Force Resistance. The wasteland lizard can grant resistance to force damage to anyone riding it.

Spider Climb. The wasteland lizard can climb difficult surfaces, including upside down on ceilings, without needing to make an ability check.

ACTIONS

Multiattack. The wasteland lizard makes one Bite attack and one Gore attack.

Bite. *Melee Weapon Attack:* +6 to hit, reach 5 ft., one target. *Hit:* 13 (2d8 + 4) piercing damage.

Gore. *Melee Weapon Attack:* +6 to hit, reach 5 ft., one target. *Hit:* 13 (2d8 + 4) piercing damage, and if the target is Medium or smaller, it is thrown up to 10 feet in a direction of the lizard's choosing and knocked prone. If a thrown target strikes a solid surface, the target takes 3 (1d6) bludgeoning damage. If the target is thrown at another creature, that creature must succeed on a DC 14 Dexterity saving throw or take the same damage and be knocked prone.

Blood Spray (Recharge 5–6). The wasteland lizard sprays acid in a 15-foot cone. Each creature in the cone must make a DC 13 Dexterity saving throw. On a failed save, the creature takes 22 (4d8) acid damage and is frightened of the wasteland lizard for 1 minute. On a successful save, the creature takes half as much damage and isn't frightened.

REACTIONS

Out of Harm's Way. When the wasteland lizard is in an area that will be subjected to an effect such as a spell or other hazard, it can use its reaction to move up to its speed.

WARPLING

The presumed child's features began to shift with mercurial fluidity. Its skin sprouted patches of fur, feathers, and scales in myriad colors. It slouched, as thought to hide itself, still keenly observing everything around it.

Warplings are true inheritors of the chaotic aspects of the wastes. They warp reality around them, distorting space, time, and material objects and constantly shift their own appearances. They are fascinated by other humanoids and like to disguise themselves as wandering children, hoping to be taken in so that they can observe how others live. However, the unpredictable effects that follow them eventually reveal their true nature, and they are generally shunned for the havoc that they wreak.

Being relatively small of stature, warplings are not often combative. When threatened, they can shape their limbs into animal-like unnatural weapons, such as bone clumps, claws, and horns. However, they are easily frightened, especially by the sight of blood, and often lose control of their reality warping powers when distressed. This has unpredictable effects on battles, and warplings take advantage of the ensuing confusion to flee or hide.

Some folk value the friendship of warplings, for they see many places and meet a variety of people in their travels. They often have insights that few others have into the settlements of a region, and their innate magic resistance helps them access some of the more dangerous sites in the wastes. If a warpling's trust can be won, it can be a valuable source of information in otherwise unknown lands.

Warpling

Small Fey, Chaotic Neutral

ARMOR CLASS 13
HIT POINTS 55 (10d8 + 10)
SPEED 30 ft.

STR	DEX	CON	INT	WIS	CHA
12 (+1)	16 (+3)	12 (+1)	12 (+1)	13 (+2)	16 (+3)

SKILLS Stealth +5, Survival +4
DAMAGE RESISTANCES bludgeoning, piercing, and slashing from nonmagical attacks
CONDITION IMMUNITIES charmed
SENSES darkvision 60 ft., passive Perception 12
LANGUAGES Common, Elvish
CHALLENGE 2 (450 XP)   **PROFICIENCY BONUS** +2

Chaos Form. The warpling's appearance shifts and changes constantly, taking on various colors and textures.

Fey Ancestry. The warpling has advantage on saving throws against being charmed, and magic can't put it to sleep.

Magic Resistance. The warpling has advantage on saving throws against spells and other magical effects.

Shifting Aura. The warpling subtly distorts reality within 15 feet of it. Any creature observing the affected area has disadvantage on Wisdom (Perception or Insight) checks.

2d6	Reality Warp Effect
2	Times shifts erratically. The creature must make a new Dexterity check to determine their place in the initiative order.
3	The creature is subjected to the effects of the *slow* spell.
4	The creature is befuddled and incapacitated.
5	Weapons wilt and wrinkle. The creature's weapon attacks are made at disadvantage and deal half damage.
6	Distance folds and the creature is moved 5 feet horizontally to an unoccupied space in a random direction.
7	The creature is subjected to the effects of the *faerie fire* spell.
8	Armor softens and shields fold. The creature's AC is decreased by 2.
9	The creature loses friction with the ground. They move at half their normal speed and their melee weapon attacks are made at disadvantage.
10	The creature is charmed by the warpling.
11	The creature is subjected to the effects of a *haste* spell.
12	The creature is subjected to the effects of the *polymorph* spell. Roll 1d6 to determine the creature they transform into: 1 = ankheg, 2 = baboon, 3 = death dog, 4 = giant crab, 5 = gibbering mouther, 6 = quasit.

ACTIONS

Multiattack. The warpling makes two Unnatural Weapon attacks.

Unnatural Weapon. *Melee Weapon Attack:* +3 to hit, reach 5 ft., one target. *Hit:* 8 (2d6 + 1) bludgeoning, piercing, or slashing damage. The warpling chooses the type of damage when making the attack and shapes its body appropriately.

Control Chaos Form. The warpling can make itself look like another creature of the same general size and humanoid shape. It reverts to its normal form if its concentration is broken (as if concentrating on a spell). A creature must take an action to visually inspect the warpling and succeed on a DC 13 Intelligence (Investigation) check to discern that the warpling is disguised.

BONUS ACTIONS

Reality Warp. The warpling warps reality for creatures in a 15-foot radius around it until the start of its next turn. As a bonus action on subsequent turns, the warpling can maintain the effect. Roll 2d6 to determine the effect. A creature can resist the effect by making a successful DC 13 Charisma saving throw.

REACTIONS

Easily Frightened. When a warpling sees another creature take damage, it must make a Constitution saving throw to maintain control of its Reality Warp. The DC equals 10 or half the damage taken by the target, whichever number is higher. On a failure, its Reality Warp is activated or the effect may change if it is already active. Roll 2d6 to determine the effect.

WASTELAND DRAGON

Rust-colored wings darken the sky, and a gout of bright energy erupts from the creature's jaws.

Dark-tempered beasts who rule the magic-blasted wastes with a merciless territoriality, wasteland dragons prowl among the ruins of dead cities and dust-blown, haunted and barren lands that once were verdant.

Territorial for a Reason. They consider all other dragons to be enemies, but no creatures are so hated by wasteland dragons as spellcasters and any who employ magic. They blame spellcasters—somewhat correctly—for the state of the lands they roam and, indeed, for their own current form.

Though these dragons breed true, they were once of different breeds altogether before they were warped by an unfettered magical catastrophe and the foul energies brought through to this world from the Void. Their once-brilliant scales have dimmed to the color of rust and soil; their crests and horns have gone grey and withered; the lands they rule now host horrors which even they must fear; and their natural defenses have been warped and supplanted by the very energies which wrought so much destruction. Dragons have long memories, and these atrocities, as far as they are concerned, could have happened yesterday. Thus, they attack, without warning or mercy, any who trespass, showing spellcasters particular cruelty.

Predatory Zeal by Necessity. Dedicated carnivores, wasteland dragons prefer to eat recent arrivals to their land. Beyond the practical consideration that they would likely kill the newcomers in any case, creatures corrupted by the wastes can be hazardous in unpredictable ways; poison, infections, and infestations can occur, and the taste of wastelands creatures is incredibly foul.

When they are unable to find travelers or migratory animals, wasteland dragons hunt the livestock of settlements, confident that few would dare pursue them to their horrifying homelands afterward.

Deadly Hoards. The hoard of a wasteland dragon might contain a good deal of very old coins and treasures in the conventional sense, but they also possess dangers of their own. These dragons often bring home curious devices, arcane tomes, and relics of the dead places in which they live, some likely infused with forbidden magic. Though the dragons have little use for such things other than to add to a collection, a plundered hoard could spell disaster for the world outside.

A WASTELAND DRAGON'S LAIR

Wasteland dragons make their homes among the ruins of dead civilizations, often inside surviving structures vast enough to contain them and protect them from the elements. Old cisterns of sufficient size, auditoriums, or the audience chambers of forgotten nobles all make suitable lairs for a wasteland dragon. They are not above making their home in a cave, but it will likely be near a ruined settlement of some size; wasteland dragons grow bored easily, and rummaging through ruins, either for curiosities or interlopers, takes up a good deal of their time.

A legendary wasteland dragon infuses its surroundings with traces of the magic it seeks to deny the outside world. It might hear the thoughts of trespassers as though they were carried on a breeze. Magic items and spells may behave unpredictably, becoming more powerful, functioning in a new way, or failing to function at all. Prolonged exposure to the environment near a wasteland dragon's lair may lead to mutations and even madness, though the latter often passes once the sufferer is taken from the area.

Clever creatures, wasteland dragons often make some use of the arcane items they find, seeing no hypocrisy in doing so; after all, they are hardly as foolish as humans! The approach to the creature's lair might be protected by strange energy fields, or weakened barriers between this world and another, or by creatures of the wastes who are smart enough to otherwise avoid annoying the dragon. The dragon confronted in its lair might forego its general inclination to attack immediately in favor of luring the intruders into such traps.

LAIR ACTIONS

On initiative count 20 (losing initiative ties), the dragon takes a lair action to cause one of the following effects; the dragon can't use the same effect two rounds in a row:

- A random encounter occurs, as creatures who were given shelter and protection by the dragon in exchange for their services earn their keep and attack the PCs.
- An object the dragon can see within 120 feet of it flashes with arcane energy and bursts. Each creature within 20 feet of the object must succeed on a DC 14 Dexterity check or take 10 (3d6) piercing damage and become blinded for 1 minute. A creature can take an action to rub its eyes and end the blindness at the beginning of its next turn.
- Creatures within 30 feet of the dragon receive a momentary, jumbled telepathic communication from one of the many warped and alien beings of the wastes. Each creature in that area must succeed on a DC 14 Wisdom saving throw or be incapacitated until the end of its next turn.

REGIONAL EFFECTS

The region containing a legendary wasteland dragon's lair is further warped by the dragon's magic, which creates one or more of the following effects:

- Ghostly figures fighting battles from long ago appear within 5 miles of the dragon's lair.
- Dust goblins and other creatures native to the wastes within 3 miles of the dragon's lair report trespassers to it as soon as possible.
- Long-hidden entrances to buried structures open themselves within 1 mile of the dragon's lair.

WASTELAND DRAGON WYRMLING

Medium dragon, chaotic evil

ARMOR CLASS 17 (natural armor)
HIT POINTS 60 (8d8 + 24)
SPEED 30 ft., burrow 15 ft., climb 30 ft., fly 50 ft.

STR	DEX	CON	INT	WIS	CHA
17 (+3)	10 (+0)	17 (+3)	12 (+1)	11 (+0)	13 (+1)

SAVING THROWS Dex +2, Con +5, Wis +2, Cha +3
SKILLS Perception +2, Stealth +2
DAMAGE IMMUNITIES force
SENSES blindsight 10 ft., darkvision 60 ft., passive
PERCEPTION 12
LANGUAGES Draconic

CHALLENGE 3 (700 XP)   **PROFICIENCY BONUS** +2

ACTIONS

Bite. *Melee Weapon Attack:* +5 to hit, reach 5 ft., one target. *Hit:* 14 (2d10 + 3) piercing damage.

Warped Energy Breath (Recharge 6). The dragon blasts warped arcane energy in a 20-foot line that is 5 feet wide. Each creature in that line must make a DC 11 Dexterity saving throw, taking 22 (5d8) force damage on a failed save, or half as much damage on a successful one.

YOUNG WASTELAND DRAGON

Large dragon, chaotic evil

ARMOR CLASS 18 (natural armor)

HIT POINTS 178 (17d10 + 85)

SPEED 40 ft., burrow 20 ft., climb 40 ft., fly 70 ft.

STR	DEX	CON	INT	WIS	CHA
21 (+5)	10 (+0)	21 (+5)	12 (+1)	11 (+0)	12 (+1)

SAVING THROWS Dex +4, Con +9, Wis +4, Cha +5

SKILLS Perception +4, Stealth +4

DAMAGE IMMUNITIES force

SENSES blindsight 30 ft., darkvision 120 ft., passive Perception 14

LANGUAGES Common, Draconic

CHALLENGE 9 (5,000 XP)   **PROFICIENCY BONUS** +4

ACTIONS

Multiattack. The dragon makes two Claw attacks and one Bite attack.

Bite. *Melee Weapon Attack:* +9 to hit, reach 10 ft., one target. *Hit:* 16 (2d10 + 5) piercing damage.

Claw. *Melee Weapon Attack:* +9 to hit, reach 5 ft., one target. *Hit:* 12 (2d6 + 5) slashing damage.

Warped Energy Breath (Recharge 6). The dragon blasts warped arcane energy in a 40-foot line that is 5 feet wide. Each creature in that line must make a DC 15 Dexterity saving throw, taking 49 (11d8) force damage on a failed save, or half as much damage on a successful one.

ADULT WASTELAND DRAGON

Huge dragon, chaotic evil

ARMOR CLASS 18 (natural armor)

HIT POINTS 225 (18d12 + 108)

SPEED 40 ft., burrow 30 ft., climb 40 ft., fly 70 ft.

STR	DEX	CON	INT	WIS	CHA
26 (+8)	10 (+0)	21 (+5)	14 (+2)	13 (+1)	16 (+3)

SAVING THROWS Dex +6, Con +11

SKILLS Perception +6, Stealth +5

DAMAGE IMMUNITIES force

SENSES blindsight 60 ft., darkvision 120 ft., passive Perception 16

LANGUAGES Common, Draconic

CHALLENGE 17 (18,000 XP)   **PROFICIENCY BONUS** +6

Legendary Resistance (3/Day). If the dragon fails a saving throw, it can choose to succeed instead.

ACTIONS

Multiattack. The dragon can use its Frightful Presence. It then makes two Claw attacks and one Bite attack.

Bite. *Melee Weapon Attack:* +12 to hit, reach 10 ft., one target. *Hit:* 19 (2d10 + 8) piercing damage.

Claw. *Melee Weapon Attack:* +12 to hit, reach 5 ft, one target. *Hit:* 15 (2d6 + 8) slashing damage.

Tail. *Melee Weapon Attack:* +12 to hit, reach 15 ft., one target. *Hit:* 17 (2d8 + 8) bludgeoning damage.

Frightful Presence. Each creature of the dragon's choice that is within 120 feet of the dragon and aware of it must succeed on a DC 18 Wisdom saving throw or become frightened for 1 minute. A creature can repeat the saving throw at the end of each of its turns, ending the effect on itself on a success. If a creature's saving throw is successful or the effect ends for it, the creature is immune to the dragon's Frightful Presence for the next 24 hours.

Warped Energy Breath (Recharge 5–6). The dragon blasts warped arcane energy in a 60-foot line that is 5 feet wide. Each creature in that line must make a DC 18 Dexterity saving throw, taking 49 (11d8) force damage on a failed save, or half as much damage on a successful one.

LEGENDARY ACTIONS

The dragon can take 3 legendary actions, choosing from the options below. Only one legendary action option can be used at a time and only at the end of another creature's turn. The dragon regains spent legendary actions at the start of its turn.

Detect. The dragon makes a Wisdom (Perception) check.

Tail Attack. The dragon makes a tail attack.

Wing Attack (Costs 2 Actions). The dragon beats its wings. Each creature within 10 feet of the dragon must succeed on a DC 18 Dexterity saving throw or take 15 (2d6 + 8) bludgeoning damage and be knocked prone. The dragon can then fly up to half its flying speed.

ANCIENT WASTELAND DRAGON

Gargantuan dragon, chaotic evil

ARMOR CLASS 22 (natural armor)

HIT POINTS 333 (18d20 + 144)

SPEED 40 ft., burrow 30 ft., climb 40 ft., fly 80 ft.

STR	DEX	CON	INT	WIS	CHA
28 (+9)	10 (+0)	26 (+8)	16 (+3)	15 (+2)	19 (+4)

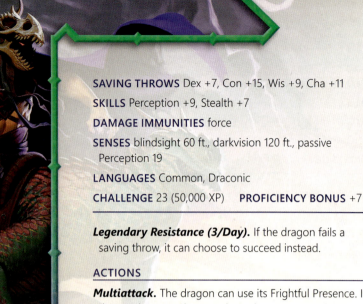

SAVING THROWS Dex +7, Con +15, Wis +9, Cha +11
SKILLS Perception +9, Stealth +7
DAMAGE IMMUNITIES force
SENSES blindsight 60 ft., darkvision 120 ft., passive Perception 19
LANGUAGES Common, Draconic
CHALLENGE 23 (50,000 XP)   **PROFICIENCY BONUS** +7

Legendary Resistance (3/Day). If the dragon fails a saving throw, it can choose to succeed instead.

ACTIONS

Multiattack. The dragon can use its Frightful Presence. It then makes two Claw attacks and one Bite attack.

Bite. *Melee Weapon Attack:* +16 to hit, reach 10 ft., one target. *Hit:* 20 (2d10 + 9) piercing damage.

Claw. *Melee Weapon Attack:* +16 to hit, reach 10 ft., one target. *Hit:* 16 (2d6 + 9) slashing damage.

Tail. *Melee Weapon Attack:* +16 to hit, reach 15 ft., one target. *Hit:* 18 (2d8 + 9) bludgeoning damage.

Frightful Presence. Each creature of the dragon's choice that is within 120 feet of the dragon and aware of it must succeed on a DC 20 Wisdom saving throw or become frightened for 1 minute. A creature can repeat the saving throw at the end of each of its turns, ending the effect on itself on a success. If a creature's saving throw is successful or the effect ends for it, the creature is immune to the dragon's Frightful Presence for the next 24 hours.

Warped Energy Breath (Recharge 5–6). The dragon blasts warped arcane energy in a 90-foot line that is 5 feet wide. Each creature in that line must make a DC 20 Dexterity saving throw, taking 90 (20d8) force damage on a failed save, or half as much damage on a successful one.

LEGENDARY ACTIONS

The dragon can take 3 legendary actions, choosing from the options below. Only one legendary action option can be used at a time and only at the end of another creature's turn. The dragon regains spent legendary actions at the start of its turn.

Detect. The dragon makes a Wisdom (Perception) check.

Tail Attack. The dragon makes a tail attack.

Wing Attack (Costs 2 Actions). The dragon beats its wings. Each creature within 15 feet of the dragon must succeed on a DC 20 Dexterity saving throw or take 16 (2d6 + 9) bludgeoning damage and be knocked prone. The dragon can then fly up to half its flying speed.

WASTELAND MONARCH

This figure is at once majestic and frightful. It wields a morningstar awash with flame and bellows out commands to its underlings.

The wasteland monarch is the self-appointed leader of a band of wasteland bandits, marauders, or tribesmen, using a combination of raw strength and potent charisma to keep its underlings in line. Clad in heavy plate and with a shield typically decorated with skulls or other savage paraphernalia, the wasteland monarch is a force to be reckoned with on the battlefield and is often attended by a wasteland priest in addition to regular troops.

Borderlands Threat. Those captured by a wasteland monarch are usually executed or enslaved, though a monarch might hold an important person for ransom. Not all wasteland monarchs are evil, and some would prefer to trade with others rather than simply kill or capture them.

WASTELAND MONARCH LAIR

Most wasteland monarchs live in heavily fortified encampments above ground, normally on the fringes of the wastes and within easy striking distance of other settlements, though others might live in ruined castles or even in underground settings, depending on the conditions on the surface and the threats in the area.

A wasteland monarch has a challenge rating of 10 (5,900 XP) when encountered in its lair.

LAIR ACTIONS

On initiative count 20 (losing initiative ties), the wasteland monarch takes a lair action to cause one of the following effects; the wasteland monarch can't use the same effect two rounds in a row:

- The wasteland monarch shrugs off the effects of being frightened, paralyzed, or stunned and is immune to all these conditions until it regains the use of its lair action on initiative count 20 of the following round.
- The wasteland monarch calls upon an Aberration, Monstrosity, or Humanoid of CR 3 or lower to aid it in battle. The creature appears within 60 feet of the monarch in an unoccupied space. The called creature acts as an ally of the monarch and obeys its verbal commands. The creature remains for 1 hour, until it is killed, or until the monarch uses this lair action again.
- The wasteland monarch challenges an opponent to personal combat. That creature must succeed

on a DC 17 Charisma saving throw or be unable to attack any creature other than the wasteland monarch until the monarch takes another lair action or dies. A creature that successfully ignores the wasteland monarch's challenge is unaffected by this lair action for 24 hours.

REGIONAL EFFECTS

The wasteland monarch's lair affects the surrounding region in the following ways:

- A sense of lawlessness pervades the region within 10 miles of a wasteland monarch's lair. People are more likely to break minor laws or to defy the orders of their superiors, and animals are more inclined to disobey their owners. This does not affect PCs, but they still feel the urge to take these actions.
- The ground within 1 mile of the wasteland monarch's lair, whatever its composition, is difficult terrain. Wisdom (Survival) checks in that area are made with disadvantage.
- Clerics and paladins of lawful deities feel a sense of unease when they are within 100 feet of a wasteland monarch's lair. Such an individual in that area must make a successful DC 10 Constitution check to maintain concentration on a spell. Once an individual succeeds on this check, they do not have to repeat it for 24 hours.

Wasteland Monarch

Medium Humanoid (Human), Any Non-Lawful Alignment

ARMOR CLASS 20 (plate, shield)
HIT POINTS 127 (17d8 + 51)
SPEED 30 ft.

STR	DEX	CON	INT	WIS	CHA
20 (+5)	14 (+2)	16 (+3)	10 (+0)	12 (+1)	16 (+3)

SAVING THROWS Str +9, Con +7, Cha +7
SKILLS Athletics +8, Perception +5
SENSES passive Perception 15
LANGUAGES Common
CHALLENGE 9 (5,000 XP) **PROFICIENCY BONUS** +4

Legendary Resistance (3/Day). If the wasteland monarch fails a saving throw, it can choose to succeed instead.

Pack Tactics. The wasteland monarch has advantage on an attack roll against a creature if at least one of the monarch's allies is within 5 feet of the creature and the ally isn't incapacitated.

Magic Weapons. The wasteland monarch's weapon attacks are magical.

ACTIONS

Multiattack. The wasteland monarch makes three Flaming Morningstar attacks.

Flaming Morningstar. *Melee Weapon Attack:* +10 to hit, reach 5 ft., one target. *Hit:* 10 (1d8 + 6) piercing damage plus 3 (1d6) fire damage.

Authority of the Wastes (1/Day). The wasteland monarch can compel any creature in a 60-foot radius to submit to its authority. Each creature in the area must succeed on a DC 17 Wisdom saving throw or be charmed by the wasteland monarch for 1 hour. On a successful save, a creature is immune to this effect for 24 hours. Creatures native to the wastes or wasteland-type settings (such as dust goblins and chaos trolls) have disadvantage on their saving throws.

Torrent of Flame (Recharge 5–6). The wasteland monarch spins its morningstar over its head and unleashes a blast of flame that hits each creature or object in a 10-foot radius. A creature in the area can make a DC 19 Dexterity saving throw, taking 17 (5d6) fire damage on a failed save, or half as much damage on a successful one.

LEGENDARY ACTIONS

The wasteland monarch can take 3 legendary actions, choosing from the options below. Only one legendary action option can be used at a time and only at the end of another creature's turn. The wasteland monarch regains spent legendary actions at the start of its turn.

Attack. The wasteland monarch makes a Flaming Morningstar attack.

Move. The wasteland monarch can move up to its speed.

Rallying Cry (Costs 2 Actions). The wasteland monarch shouts encouragement to one of the monarch's allies within 60 feet that can hear the monarch. That ally can make a saving throw to try to end the charmed, frightened, or stunned condition on itself.

WASTELAND PRIEST

Garbed in dingy half-plate with its deity's holy symbol worn prominently around its neck, this priest reeks of pious fervor.

The wasteland priest is a holy warrior that reveres one of the lawless, fickle, and often evil gods of the wastes, using its abilities to aid a group of bandits, scavengers, or other outcasts. Many priests serve wasteland monarchs as advisors and healers while trying to manipulate the monarch into advancing the agenda of their deities.

Inspiring Presence. A wasteland priest is adept at infusing its nearby allies with religious fervor by its mere presence, making them less likely to succumb to the influence of their enemies. These priests seem to be empowered by the very wastes, and most of them exhibit strange behavior, often seen talking to an unseen entity or decorating their bodies with mysterious runes.

Not All Bad. Contrary to the belief of many outsiders' beliefs, not every wasteland priest is a raving lunatic or an evil monster. Some serve the cause of righteousness in their own way, protecting the wastes from the ills that might befall it.

Wasteland Priest

Medium Humanoid (Human), Any Non-Lawful Alignment

ARMOR CLASS 17 (half-plate, shield)
HIT POINTS 84 (13d8 + 26)
SPEED 30 ft.

STR	DEX	CON	INT	WIS	CHA
16 (+3)	10 (+0)	14 (+2)	12 (+1)	18 (+4)	14 (+2)

SAVING THROWS Wis +7, Cha +5
SKILLS Persuasion +5, Religion +5
DAMAGE RESISTANCES cold, fire, psychic
CONDITION IMMUNITIES exhaustion, paralyzed
SENSES passive Perception 14
LANGUAGES Common
CHALLENGE 7 (2,900 XP)   **PROFICIENCY BONUS** +3

Religious Zeal. Allies within 30 feet of a wasteland priest have advantage on saving throws against being charmed or frightened.

ACTIONS

Multiattack. The wasteland priest makes two Mace attacks.

Mace. Melee Weapon Attack: +6 to hit, reach 5 ft., one target. *Hit:* 7 (1d6 + 3) bludgeoning damage.

Whispers of the Wastes (Recharge 5–6). The wasteland priest unleashes a barrage of otherworldly whispers at an enemy it can see within 30 feet of it. The target must make a DC 17 Wisdom saving throw. On a failed save, it takes 27 (6d8) psychic damage and becomes frightened of the priest for 1 minute. On a successful save, the target takes half as much damage and is not frightened. A frightened creature can make a new saving throw at the end of each of its turns to end the effect on itself.

Spellcasting. The wasteland priest casts one of the following spells, requiring no material components and using Wisdom as the spellcasting ability (spell save DC 17):

At will: *sacred flame, thaumaturgy*
3/day each: *bestow curse, cure wounds, dispel magic*
1/day each: *freedom of movement, insect plague*

WASTELAND SWARMS

Despite its ravaged ecosystem, the wastes provide shelter to uncountable numbers of scurrying and slithering vermin. Although these creatures typically scavenge for food, numerous travelers' tales warn of aggressive swarms of grotesque rodents that suddenly burst from their surroundings to violently strike at stragglers and strays.

SWARM OF WARP RATS

Little, hairless rodents spill out from the cracks in a broken wall. These creatures are pale and wrinkled, with thick, serpentine bodies that slither forward rapidly on four pairs of stunted legs.

Warp rats look like a cross between centipedes and rodents. They travel in large swarms, seeking easy prey such as lone travelers or small groups sleeping in the open. When a swarm bites a creature, the rats' corrosive saliva can cause the wound to continue to bleed even after the attack is over.

Swarm of Warp Rats

Large Swarm of Tiny Beasts, Unaligned

ARMOR CLASS 14
HIT POINTS 60 (8d10 + 16)
SPEED 30 ft., burrow 10 ft., climb 30 ft.

STR	DEX	CON	INT	WIS	CHA
8 (−1)	18 (+4)	15 (+2)	1 (−5)	12 (+1)	3 (−4)

DAMAGE RESISTANCES cold; bludgeoning, piercing, and slashing from nonmagical attacks
CONDITION IMMUNITIES charmed, frightened, grappled, paralyzed, petrified, prone, restrained, stunned
SENSES blindsight 10 ft., passive Perception 11
LANGUAGES —
CHALLENGE 4 (1,100 XP) **PROFICIENCY BONUS** +2

Blood Frenzy. The warp rat swarm has advantage on melee attack rolls against any creature that doesn't have all its hp.

Swarm. The warp rat swarm can occupy another creature's space and vice versa, and the swarm can move through any opening large enough for a Tiny creature. The swarm can't regain hp or gain temporary hp.

ACTIONS

Bites. *Melee Weapon Attack:* +6 to hit, reach 0 ft., one creature in the swarm's space. *Hit:* 7 (2d6) piercing damage plus 7 (2d6) necrotic damage, or 3 (1d6) piercing damage plus 3 (1d6) necrotic damage if the swarm has half its hp or fewer. The target must make a successful DC 13 Constitution saving throw, or the wound continues to bleed, causing the target to take 7 (2d6) piercing damage at the end of its next turn.

SWARM OF ZOOGS

A large roiling swarm of sickly rat-like creatures whose snouts erupt with rubbery tendrils tears across a wasted patch of desert.

Though individual zoogs (see *Creature Codex*) are deviant, they become more bestial and act with far less rationality when they gather in swarms. They target specific individuals, evoking madness and insanity as the swarm engulfs its target.

Swarm of Zoogs

Large Swarm of Tiny Beasts, Chaotic Evil

ARMOR CLASS 13
HIT POINTS 65 (10d10 + 10)
SPEED 30 ft., climb 30 ft.

STR	DEX	CON	INT	WIS	CHA
9 (−1)	16 (+3)	12 (+1)	11 (+0)	10 (+0)	8 (−1)

SKILLS Perception +2
DAMAGE RESISTANCES bludgeoning, piercing, and slashing from nonmagical attacks
CONDITION IMMUNITIES charmed, frightened, grappled, paralyzed, petrified, prone, restrained, stunned
SENSES darkvision 60 ft., passive Perception 12
LANGUAGES Deep Speech, Void Speech
CHALLENGE 3 (700 XP) **PROFICIENCY BONUS** +2

Swarm. The swarm can occupy another creature's space and vice versa, and the swarm can move through any opening large enough for a Tiny creature. The swarm can't regain hp or gain temporary hp.

ACTIONS

Bites. *Melee Weapon Attack:* +6 to hit, reach 0 ft., one target in the swarm's space. *Hit:* 14 (4d6) piercing damage, or 7 (2d6) piercing damage if the swarm has half its hp or fewer.

Steal Secrets. Zoog swarms collect secrets for their demon lord patron, Chittr'k'k. In Void Speech, they demand that their victims reveal their secrets. A creature that fails its saving throw against the zoog swarm's Void Chattering risks disclosing secrets to the zoog swarm. Alternatively, a frightened creature can voluntarily end the effect by uttering aloud one personal secret. Swarms disperse after gathering the secret they were sent to collect or (if they weren't explicitly sent to collect secrets) after collecting 1d4 random secrets.

Void Chattering. A creature attacked by a zoog swarm is tormented by a terrifying barrage of chittering Void Speech. The creature must succeed on a DC 15 Wisdom saving throw or be frightened of the swarm for 1 minute. A creature can repeat the saving throw at the end of each of its turns, ending the effect on itself on a success.

WASTELAND TROLLKIN

A deformed humanoid stands before you. The creature's tall frame, wrapped in rope-like cords of muscle, hunches slightly. Its rubbery knuckles clasp a tremendous club.

Wasteland trollkin eat whatever meat they can acquire. They will eat rotten flesh or corpses, and only rarely do they take living hostages for food. Ingesting tainted food does not harm them internally, thanks to their strong immune systems, but as a side effect, all wasteland trolls carry a disease that causes their flesh to break out in boils. The malady is highly infectious, particularly when the pustules rupture, but it has little effect on other trollkin or trolls.

Warped and Worse. Like virtually all other wasteland creatures, the trollkin of the wastes have been warped and mutated by eldritch energies and arcane fallout. Often their heads and limbs are asymmetrical and disproportionate in size. Some have longer limbs, drooping claws, or protruding chins and noses. Such deformities make them appear even more hideous or fearsome than other trollkin to creatures of other races. As a result, wasteland trollkin do not usually get along with other creatures; they generally remain in their own tribes, either living in the hills or traveling the wastes as nomads.

Wasteland Trollkin

Medium Humanoid, Chaotic Neutral

ARMOR CLASS 14 (piecemeal armor)
HIT POINTS 75 (10d8 + 30)
SPEED 30 ft.

STR	DEX	CON	INT	WIS	CHA
17 (+3)	12 (+1)	16 (+3)	9 (−1)	12 (+1)	10 (+0)

SAVING THROWS Con +5, Wis +3
SKILLS Intimidation +2, Performance +2, Survival +3
DAMAGE RESISTANCES necrotic, poison
CONDITION IMMUNITIES frightened
SENSES darkvision 60 ft., passive Perception 11
LANGUAGES Common, Trollkin
CHALLENGE 3 (700 XP)   **PROFICIENCY BONUS** +2

Keen Senses. The trollkin has advantage on Wisdom (Perception) checks.

Noxious Pustules. When the wasteland trollkin takes piercing or slashing damage, some of its infected pustules burst. Each enemy within 10 feet of it must make a DC 14 Constitution saving throw. On a failed save, a creature takes 7 (2d6) necrotic damage and contracts the disease known as wasteland flesh boils, which causes pustules to erupt on its skin. Until it is cured of the disease, the creature has disadvantage on Charisma checks and vulnerability to all damage.

Regeneration. The trollkin regains 10 hp at the start of its turn if it has at least 1 hp. This trait doesn't function if the trollkin took acid or fire damage since the end of its previous turn. The trollkin dies if it starts its turn with 0 hp and doesn't regenerate.

Thick Hide. The trollkin's skin is thick and tough, granting it a +1 bonus to Armor Class. This bonus is already factored into the trollkin's AC.

ACTIONS

Multiattack. The trollkin makes two Greatclub attacks or two Scrap Shard attacks.

Greatclub. *Melee Weapon Attack:* +5 to hit, reach 5 ft., one target. *Hit:* 12 (2d8 + 3) bludgeoning damage.

Scrap Shard. *Ranged Weapon Attack:* +5 to hit, range 30 ft., one target. *Hit:* 10 (2d6 + 3) piercing damage.

BONUS ACTIONS

Aggressive. The trollkin can move up to its speed toward a hostile creature it can see.

WASTELAND WORM

A cluster of three-foot-long, slimy flatworms emerges from small holes in the earth, each one wriggling its way toward you.

Wasteland worms are covered with shimmering slime over translucent flesh that brings their internal organs into view. They move by expanding and contracting in an undulating fashion. When one gets close to its prey, it vomits forth a milky, putrefying liquid that burns through flesh.

Opportunistic Hunters. Wasteland worms hunt and eat any living creatures they encounter. They dig into the soil, perforating the surface of the land with small holes that can be easy to overlook. When they sense prey in the area, the worms rapidly burrow beneath their targets and ambush them by erupting from the ground.

Regenerative Reproducers. Wasteland worms reproduce through regeneration. When sliced in half, each part functions independently, though it takes time for the lower half to regenerate a new head. Even when ripped into pieces, each severed segment regenerates into a new worm. Strangely, electrical current speeds the regeneration process; therefore, they are attracted to electrical currents. As a result, they rush from the ground during thunderstorms and slither across the earth's surface.

Wasteland Worm

Medium Beast, Unaligned

ARMOR CLASS 10 (natural)
HIT POINTS 38 (7d8 + 7)
SPEED 10 ft., burrow 50 ft.

STR	DEX	CON	INT	WIS	CHA
15 (+2)	12 (+1)	13 (+1)	14 (+2)	11 (+0)	13 (+1)

SKILLS Perception +2, Stealth +3
DAMAGE IMMUNITIES acid, poison
CONDITION IMMUNITIES blinded, charmed, poisoned
SENSES blindsight 30 ft., passive Perception 12
LANGUAGES —
CHALLENGE 1 (200 XP)   **PROFICIENCY BONUS** +2

Ambusher. In the first round of combat, the wasteland worm has advantage on attack rolls against any creature it surprised.

Regeneration. The wasteland worm regains 5 hp at the start of its turn if it has at least 1 hp. If the wasteland worm takes lightning damage, it regains 10 hp instead. If the worm takes fire damage, this trait doesn't function until the start of the worm's next turn.

ACTIONS

Caustic Constrict. *Melee Weapon Attack:* +4 to hit, reach 5 ft., one creature. *Hit:* 7 (1d8 + 2) bludgeoning damage plus 2 (1d4) necrotic damage. The target is grappled (escape DC 14). Until this grapple ends, the creature is restrained, and the wasteland worm can't grapple another target. If the worm maintains its grapple, it deals 7 (1d8 + 2) bludgeoning damage plus 2 (1d4) necrotic damage to its victim at the start of its turn.

Caustic Vomit (Recharge 5–6). The wasteland worm regurgitates a 20-foot-long, 5-foot-wide line of necrotic vomit. Each creature in the area must make a DC 11 Constitution saving throw, taking 10 (3d6) necrotic damage on a failed save, or half as much damage on a successful one.

XOTLIAC

The creatures you behold have broad, flat heads with a frill of dangling external gills, two pairs of bulbous white eyes, and wide mouths filled with needle-like teeth. Their upper torsos are vaguely humanoid, with spiny rows running along the neck and back that connect to the webbing along the backs of their arms. Their stunted, vestigial legs are webbed, apparently used only for swimming.

Xotliacs are amphibious humanoids that live in small tribal colonies in the harsh and desolate marshlands of the waste. Primarily hunter-gatherers, they spend most of their time below the surface of the water hunting fish and smaller amphibians or gathering grubs and crustaceans. These highly reclusive creatures rarely allow outsiders to observe them. Still, travelers should be wary of them, because they don't hesitate to attack other humanoids that wander into their territory. When they take on prey larger than they are, they hunt and fight communally, assembling groups from multiple tribes if necessary.

Shifting Roles and Colors. Each tribe of xotliacs is organized in a system where different tribe members have responsibility for performing certain duties. Their society treats all duties as equally important, and during an individual xotliac's life, it might switch duties several times.

Xotliacs display a range of skin coloration, from pale green to greenish brown to deep reddish brown, occasionally embellished with patterns of spots. When a xotliac assumes different responsibilities within its tribe, its color changes to reflect that change in status. These skin tones and markings enable xotliacs to identify each other by communicating an individual's tribe, abilities, and current role in society.

Untouchable. In addition to the creature's prickly dorsal spines, their skin secretes a thick, slimy mucous, making them extremely slippery and difficult to grapple. Furthermore, a xotliac's mucous gives a distinct scent that the creatures can alter to display simple emotions such as affection, anger, sadness, and fear.

Xotliac

Small Humanoid (Xotliac), Neutral

ARMOR CLASS 15 (natural armor)
HIT POINTS 18 (4d6 + 4)
SPEED 10 ft., swim 40 ft.

STR	DEX	CON	INT	WIS	CHA
11 (+0)	15 (+2)	12 (+1)	12 (+1)	13 (+1)	9 (−1)

SKILLS Perception +3, Stealth +4, Survival +3
DAMAGE RESISTANCES cold, poison
SENSES darkvision 90 ft., passive Perception 13
LANGUAGES Xotliac
CHALLENGE 1/4 (50 XP) **PROFICIENCY BONUS** +2

Amphibious. The xotliac can breathe air and water.

Keen Senses. The xotliac has advantage on Wisdom (Perception) checks.

Swamp Camouflage. The xotliac has advantage on Dexterity (Stealth) checks made to hide in swampy terrain.

Regeneration. The xotliac regains 3 hp at the start of its turn if it has at least 1 hp.

ACTIONS

Multiattack. The xotliac makes two melee attacks, one Bite attack and one Spear attack.

Bite. *Melee Weapon Attack:* +3 to hit, one target. *Hit:* 5 (1d8 + 1) piercing damage.

Spear. *Melee or Ranged Weapon Attack:* +3 to hit, reach 5 ft. or range 20/60 ft., one target. *Hit:* 4 (1d6 + 1) piercing damage, or 5 (1d8 + 1) piercing damage if used with two hands to make a melee attack.

Chapter 6
Spells and Magic

This chapter presents some of the magical traditions particular to the wastes, waiting to be unleashed on the wider world. It includes dark spells that can be taught only by the cults of the wasteland, lost ancient spells that can be rediscovered by enterprising adventurers, and the secrets of chaos magic.

Ancient Magic

In the distant past, what is now the wasteland was dominated by a glorious empire ruled by elite wielders of magic. The reason for the sudden extinction of these mages is shrouded in mystery, but the ruins of their great cities remain. Explorers with sufficient fortitude and skill can delve into these buried necropolises to discover potent arcane secrets from an era long past.

BARD SPELLS

7th Level
Draconic essence (Transmutation)

CLERIC SPELLS

7th Level
Draconic essence (Transmutation)

9th Level
Life siphon (Necromancy)

DRUID SPELLS

2nd Level
Rock to mud (Transmutation)

6th Level
Earth swim (Transmutation)

7th Level
Draconic essence (Transmutation)

PALADIN SPELLS

7th Level
Draconic essence (Transmutation)

SORCERER SPELLS

2nd Level
Rock to mud (Transmutation)

7th Level
Draconic essence (Transmutation)

8th Level
Twist of fate (Divination)

9th Level
Life siphon (Necromancy)

WARLOCK SPELLS

2nd Level
Rock to mud (Transmutation)

7th Level
Draconic essence (Transmutation)

8th Level
Twist of fate (Divination)

9th Level
Life siphon (Necromancy)

WIZARD SPELLS

2nd Level
Rock to mud (Transmutation)

6th Level
Earth swim (Transmutation)

7th Level
Draconic essence (Transmutation)

8th Level
Metamorphosis (Transmutation)
Twist of fate (Divination)

9th Level
Life siphon (Necromancy)

SPELL DESCRIPTIONS

This section contains descriptions of each ancient magic spell.

Draconic Essence

7th-level Transmutation | Bard, Cleric, Druid, Paladin, Sorcerer, Warlock, Wizard

Casting Time: 1 action
Range: Self
Components: S, M (250 gp worth of dragon scales)
Duration: 1 hour

You channel the essence of a dragon, assuming some of its traits. Scales coat your body, wings sprout from your back, your nails lengthen into talons, and your mouth extends into the shape of a dragon's muzzle. You gain a +2 bonus to AC and a flying speed of 60 feet. Your unarmed strikes count as magical attacks and deal 1d10 slashing damage on a hit. You also gain a breath weapon according to the color of dragon scales you used for the spell, as listed in the Draconic Essence table, and you have resistance to the type of damage your breath weapon deals.

You can use an action to exhale your breath weapon. When you do so, each creature in the area of the effect must make a saving throw using the appropriate ability score against your spell save DC. A creature takes 8d6 damage on a failed save, and half as much damage on a successful one.

DRACONIC ESSENCE

Scale Color	Damage Type	Breath Weapon
Black	Acid	5 ft.-by-60-ft. line (Dexterity save)
Blue	Lightning	5-ft.-by-60-ft. line (Dexterity save)
Brass	Fire	5-ft.-by-60-ft. line (Dexterity save)
Bronze	Lightning	5-ft.-by-60-ft. line (Dexterity save)
Copper	Acid	5-ft.-by-60-ft. line (Dexterity save)
Gold	Fire	60-ft. cone (Dexterity save)
Green	Poison	60-ft. cone (Constitution save)
Red	Fire	60-ft. cone (Dexterity save)
Silver	Cold	60-ft. cone (Constitution save)
White	Cold	60-ft. cone (Constitution save)

Earth Swim

6th-level Transmutation | Druid, Wizard
Casting Time: 1 minute (ritual)
Range: 60 feet
Components: V, S, M (a handful of dirt)
Duration: 8 hours

You and up to eight willing creatures can move through earth as easily as if it were water. Each of you can sink into an area of stone, soil, mud, clay, or other earth at least 5 feet wide, and move through the material without disturbing it. For this purpose, each affected creature has a swimming speed equal to your walking speed. You and your companions can breathe when submerged in the substance, and each of you also gains tremorsense out to a range of 60 feet while submerged. Any individuals who are submerged when the spell ends rise directly to the surface at a rate of 60 feet per round and appear in an unoccupied space nearest to where each one emerges.

Life Siphon

9th-level Necromancy | Cleric, Sorcerer, Warlock, Wizard
Casting Time: 1 action
Range: Self
Components: V, S
Duration: Instantaneous

Tendrils of necromantic energy spiral off you and leach the life force from nearby creatures. Choose up to six living creatures within a 120-foot-radius sphere centered on you. Each target must succeed on a Constitution saving throw or take 8d6 necrotic damage. For each creature that takes damage, you regain hit points equal to the amount of necrotic damage dealt to that creature.

Metamorphosis

8th-level Transmutation | Wizard
Casting Time: 1 minute
Range: Touch
Components: V, S, M (1,000 gp worth of raw silk, which the spell consumes)
Duration: Instantaneous

You touch a willing creature and transform it in one of the four ways described below, as you choose:

- Its race changes to another race of your choice. It loses the racial traits and abilities associated with its former race and gains the traits and abilities associated with its new race.
- It is no longer proficient in two skills or tools of your choice. Instead, pick two new skills or tools. The creature gains proficiency in those skills or tools.
- You lower one of its ability scores by 2, or two different ability scores by 1 each, and reallocate the points to increase a different ability score by 2 or two different ability scores by 1 each, to a maximum of 20.
- You give the creature wings, either birdlike or batlike. It gains a flying speed of 30 feet. Alternatively, you can remove its wings, which takes away an existing flying speed.

A creature can be affected by this spell only once a year. If the spell is cast on it again before a year has passed, the casting fails and the spell slot is expended.

Rock to Mud

2nd-level Transmutation | Druid, Sorcerer, Warlock, Wizard
Casting Time: 1 action
Range: 60 feet
Components: S
Duration: Instantaneous

You choose an area of rock or mud that fits within a 20-foot cube, centered on a point within range. Nonmagical rock in the area transforms into the same volume of mud. You can choose the size and depth of the area to transform; the area can be as shallow as 1 inch deep, with a maximum depth of 20 feet. The mud is considered difficult terrain.

Additionally, you can use this spell to turn an area of mud into solid rock. A creature in the mud when you cast the spell must make a Dexterity saving throw. On a successful save, the creature leaps free of the mud and lands safely on a nearby solid surface; on a failed save, the creature becomes stuck in the rock and is restrained. A stuck creature, or another creature within reach, can use an action to try to break the rock. The rock has AC 17 and 25 hit points and is immune to psychic and poison damage.

At Higher Levels: When you cast this spell using a spell slot of 3rd level or higher, the size of the affected area increases by 5 feet for each slot level above 2nd.

CHAOS MAGIC

Raw chaos infuses the environment of the wastes, making it an abundant energy source for casters willing to embrace its entropic potential. The spells presented in this section have been crafted by those devoted to mastery over such forces.

BARD SPELLS

2nd Level
Forced chaos surge (Abjuration)

3rd Level
Scintillating chaos (Conjuration)

CLERIC SPELLS

2nd Level
Forced chaos surge (Abjuration)

SORCERER SPELLS

2nd Level
Forced chaos surge (Abjuration)

3rd Level
Scintillating chaos (Conjuration)

WARLOCK SPELLS

2nd Level
Forced chaos surge (Abjuration)

3rd Level
Scintillating chaos (Conjuration)

7th Level
Invoke chaos (Conjuration)

WIZARD SPELLS

2nd Level
Forced chaos surge (Abjuration)

7th Level
Invoke chaos (Conjuration)

3rd Level
Scintillating chaos (Conjuration)

SPELL DESCRIPTIONS

This section contains descriptions of each chaos magic spell.

Twist of Fate

8th-level Divination | Sorcerer, Warlock, Wizard
Casting Time: 1 action
Range: Self
Components: V, S
Duration: Concentration, up to 1 minute

A halo of six red, alien eyes encircle your head, enabling you to peer into the realm of possibilities. Whenever a creature within 60 feet of you that you can see hits or misses with an attack roll, or fails or succeeds on a saving throw, you can expend one of the eyes to add or subtract 1d10 from the creature's roll. Additionally, while this spell is active, you do not have disadvantage on any roll, and no attack roll against you has advantage.

The spell ends when all six eyes have been expended or when the duration expires.

Forced Chaos Surge

2nd-level Abjuration (Chaos) | Bard, Cleric, Sorcerer, Warlock, Wizard
Casting Time: 1 reaction, which you take when you see a creature within 60 feet of you casting a spell
Range: 60 feet
Components: V, S
Duration: Instantaneous

You interrupt a creature in the process of casting a spell and force it to roll a Concentration check against your spell DC. If the creature fails, it must roll on the Chaos Magic Surge table.

CHAOS MAGIC SURGE

d100	Effect
01–02	You fall unconscious. You remain so for 24 hours, or until you take damage, or a creature uses its action to shake or slap you awake.
03–04	You cast *confusion* as a 6th-level spell, centered on yourself. You must also make the saving throw and are affected by the spell on a failed save. The effect lasts for 1 minute and does not require concentration.
05–06	1d100 goodberries (as if produced by the *goodberry* spell) spill from the sky above you. They remain for 1 hour, after which any unconsumed berries disappear.
07–08	Scrawled, graffiti-like tattoos appear across your skin. The tattoos are in Abyssal, Deep Speech, or Celestial (GM's choice) and are all expressions of profanity. A *remove curse* spell ends this effect.
09–10	Your arms become black tentacles for 1 minute. You drop any weapons or items you were holding. In this form, your unarmed strikes are magical, you are proficient with them, they deal 1d6 slashing damage, and you have a reach of 10 feet.
11–12	You cast *barkskin* on yourself.
13–14	An ethereal kitten controlled by the GM appears in an unoccupied space within 5 feet of you. It remains for 1 minute, then disappears in a puff of pink glitter.
15–16	You smell like rotten fish for the next 24 hours.
17–18	You cast *chain lightning*, targeting a creature of your choice within range.
19–20	Oversized, unblinking eyes appear in the air above you and remain for 1 hour. They cannot be harmed. They follow you no matter where you go and stare down at you, watching your every move. You cannot take a short or long rest for the duration.
21–22	The ground splits open and a tree grows in your space, shoving you harmlessly into an unoccupied space within 5 feet. The tree is 3 feet in diameter and stands 40 feet tall, and its branches span a 30-foot radius. If a ceiling or other structure would impede the growth of the tree, it magically grows through the obstacle without breaking it.
23–24	A rat appears in your pack.
25–26	Up to six creatures of your choice within 30 feet of you each regain hit points equal to your spellcasting ability modifier.
27–28	Up to six creatures of your choice within 30 feet of you each take psychic damage equal to your spellcasting ability modifier.
29–30	The ambient temperature within a 1-mile radius of you drops by 15 degrees for 24 hours.
31–32	The smell of ozone fills the space around you, and a bolt of lightning splits the skies. You take 3d10 lightning damage and are stunned until the end of your next turn.
33–34	Every creature within 15 feet of you, including yourself, is under the effect of a *haste* spell until the end of its next turn.
35–36	Every creature within 15 feet of you, including yourself, is under the effect of a *slow* spell until the end of its next turn.
37–38	You cast *black tentacles* on a 20-foot square you can see within range.
39–40	You cast *no reflection*.
41–42	A second head sprouts on your shoulder beside your own head. The head looks exactly like your original, except the eye sockets are empty black voids, and the head screams continuously. You gain advantage on Wisdom (Perception) checks that rely on sight and disadvantage on Dexterity (Stealth) checks. A *remove curse* spell ends this effect.
43–44	Pyrotechnics shoot 80 feet into the air above you and explode in a flash of light and sound that can be seen and heard up to 5 miles away.
45–46	You cast *invisibility* on yourself.
47–48	You gain a minor lactose intolerance if you do not already have one. A *lesser restoration* spell ends this effect.
49–50	You cast *fire shield* on yourself.

51–52	Your tongue becomes forked.
53–54	You become Tiny for 1 minute. Everything you are wearing and carrying reduces in size along with you. Your speed is halved, your weapon attacks do 2d4 less damage (minimum of 1), and you have disadvantage on Strength checks and Strength saving throws until the effect ends.
55–56	A **zoog swarm** (see **Chapter 5**) controlled by the GM appears in your space.
57–58	Clouds fill the sky above you in a 300-foot radius around your location. At the start of your next turn, a heavy rain begins to fall, and it continues for 1 minute.
59–60	You are stunned until the end of your next turn as you spend the next round vomiting up teeth.
61–62	You heal 2d4 hp and gain advantage on your next attack roll, saving throw, or ability check.
63–64	You disappear and instantly reappear in an unoccupied space 30 feet away in a random direction.
65–66	Your tongue elongates and sharpens to a point. You can attack with it as an action, using it as an unarmed strike with a reach of 10 feet. On a hit, you deal 1d4 piercing damage, and you regain the same amount of hit points. This effect lasts for 1 minute.
67–68	A vial of an oil-like potion appears in your inventory and remains for 1 minute. During this time, a creature can consume the vial's contents. To determine the effect on the drinker, roll a d4: (1) it regains 4d6 hp; (2) it takes 5d6 psychic damage; (3) it gains resistance to all damage types for 1 hour; or (4) it gains 1 level of exhaustion.
69–70	You hear voices whispering in your head for the next hour. You can't understand what they're saying, but you feel compelled to listen. You gain disadvantage on attack rolls, ability checks, and saving throws for the duration.
71–72	Fragrant, blood-red flowers sprout beneath your feet. When you walk, they grow up in your wake. A *remove curse* spell ends this effect.
73–74	A silver platter piled with enough food to feed five creatures appears in an unoccupied space within 5 feet of you.
75–76	You cast *polymorph* on yourself. On a failed save, you turn into a frog for 1 hour.
77–78	The ground in a 10-foot radius centered on you turns into 2-foot-deep purple muck. It is considered difficult terrain.
79–80	For the next hour, whenever you speak, laughter fills the air around you.
81–82	You cast *haste* on a creature of your choice that you can see.
83–84	Shimmering black butterflies appear in your space and remain clustered about you for 1 minute. They obscure the space around you, making it hard to see. For the duration, attacks against you are made with disadvantage, and you have disadvantage on your attack rolls.
85–86	You grow an extra finger on each hand.
87–88	A gelatinous cube falls from the sky and lands with a splat in an unoccupied space within 20 feet of you. It is confused and hostile.
89–90	Your skin becomes coated in a fine layer of glitter. It never seems to wash off, no matter how many times you bathe, and prestidigitation has no effect.
91–92	A **chaos drake** (see **Chapter 5**) appears in an unoccupied space you can see within 5 feet of you. It is friendly toward you and your allies. It remains until it is reduced to 0 hp, whereupon it vanishes.
93–94	Your eyes protrude from their sockets on long eyestalks, allowing you to look in more than one direction at a time, including behind yourself. You have advantage on Wisdom (Perception) checks relying on sight, and you cannot be surprised. After 24 hours, your eyeballs return to their sockets with a wet popping sound, and the effect ends.
95–96	A black spot appears on the palm of your hand.
97–98	You can pinpoint the exact location of every dog within a half-mile of you.
99–100	You cast *wish*.

Invoke Chaos

7th-level conjuration (chaos) | Warlock, Wizard
Casting Time: 1 action
Range: 120 feet
Components: V, S, M
Duration: Concentration, up to 1 minute

Chaos erupts from four different points you can see within range. Roll on the Invoke Chaos table to determine the effect that arises from each point, as though you had just cast the spell in question, either centered on that point or originating from it. If any of the effects require concentration, you can maintain concentration on more than one at a time. If the duration of an effect is normally longer than 1 minute, the duration is shortened to 1 minute for this version of the spell.

INVOKE CHAOS

d100	Spell Effect
01	No effect
02–05	*black tentacles*
06–09	*fireball*
10–14	*calm emotions*
15–18	*shatter*
19–24	*darkness*
25	*insect plague*
26–30	*entangle*
31–34	*faerie fire*
35–39	*call lightning*
40–44	*fog cloud*
45–49	*sleet storm*
50	*cloudkill*
51–55	*hypnotic pattern*
56–59	*stinking cloud*
60–65	*plant growth*
66–69	*confusion*
70–74	*silence*
75	*ice storm*
76–79	*spike growth*
80–85	*moonbeam*
86–90	*daylight*
91–94	*grease*
95–99	*zone of truth*
100	*mass cure wounds*

Scintillating Chaos

3rd-level conjuration (chaos) | Bard, Sorcerer, Warlock, Wizard
Casting Time: 1 action
Range: Self
Components: S, M (powdered gemstones worth 25 gp)
Duration: Instantaneous

You blow a handful of gemstone dust into the air, which transforms into swirling, colorful bubbles that float out before you in a 20-foot cone. Each creature in the area must make a successful Dexterity saving throw to avoid the bubbles. On a failed save, a creature must roll on the Scintillating Chaos table below as one of the bubbles hits it and pops, producing a random effect.

SCINTILLATING CHAOS

d8	Effect
1	A **gibbering mouther** appears in an unoccupied space within 5 feet of the target and is hostile toward it. If the target is reduced to 0 hp, it becomes hostile to all other creatures. It remains for 1 minute or until it is reduced to 0 hp, whereupon it dissolves into foul-smelling mist.
2	The bubble bursts in a flash of light and color. The target is blinded until the end of your next turn.
3	Glitter rains down on the target. It is under the effect of the *faerie fire* spell for 1 minute.
4	The target is under the effect of the *blink* spell for 1 minute.
5	A bolt of lightning splits the sky and strikes the target. It takes 3d10 lightning damage and is stunned until the end of its next turn.
6	Glitter rains down upon the target. It heals 1d4 hp.
7	The target is under the effect of the *confusion* spell for 1 minute. If it takes any damage, the effect ends early.
8	Black tentacles, as per the spell, fill the space, centered on the target and remain for 1 minute.

DOOM MAGIC

Doom magic is prevalent in the wastes, practiced by doombringers, members of dark cults, and others willing to risk manipulating this dangerous arcana. Such magic often requires some sort of sacrifice—of others or of the self—and its effects might corrupt those who use its power too often. Doom magic arises from the power of entropy, the slow march toward death and loss, and one of its best and worst attributes is that the targets of such magic are aware that their doom approaches, ever inevitable, and they must live with this anticipation.

BARD SPELLS

3rd Level
Doom of the crawling (Conjuration)

CLERIC SPELLS

1st Level
Doom of the oracle (Enchantment)
Doom of the warped skull (Necromancy)

2nd Level
Doom of deceleration (Transmutation)
Doom of the vulnerable (Transmutation)

3rd Level
Doom of stolen breath (Evocation)
Doom of the crawling (Conjuration)

4th Level
Doom of the void (Evocation)

5th Level
Doom of the dead (Necromancy)
Doom of the oasis (Transmutation)

DRUID SPELLS

1st Level
Doom of the warped skull (Necromancy)

2nd Level
Doom of deceleration (Transmutation)
Doom of the vulnerable (Transmutation)

3rd Level
Doom of the crawling (Conjuration)
Doom of the tentacle (Transmutation)

4th Level
Doom of the void (Evocation)

5th Level
Doom of the oasis (Transmutation)

SORCERER SPELLS

1st Level
Doom of the oracle (Enchantment)
Doom of the warped skull (Necromancy)

2nd Level
Doom of deceleration (Transmutation)
Doom of splintered shards (Evocation)
Doom of the vulnerable (Transmutation)

3rd Level
Doom of false friendship (Enchantment)
Doom of stolen breath (Evocation)
Doom of the crawling (Conjuration)
Doom of the tentacle (Transmutation)

4th Level
Doom of horrid visages (Illusion)
Doom of the void (Evocation)

5th Level
Doom of the baleful rune (Abjuration)
Doom of the intangible touch (Transmutation)
Doom of the oasis (Transmutation)

WARLOCK SPELLS

1st Level
Doom of the oracle (Enchantment)
Doom of the warped skull (Necromancy)

2nd Level
Doom of deceleration (Transmutation)
Doom of splintered shards (Evocation)
Doom of the vulnerable (Transmutation)

3rd Level
Doom of false friendship (Enchantment)
Doom of stolen breath (Evocation)
Doom of the crawling (Conjuration)
Doom of the tentacle (Transmutation)

4th Level
Doom of horrid visages (Illusion)
Doom of the void (Evocation)

5th Level
Doom of the baleful rune (Abjuration)
Doom of the dead (Necromancy)
Doom of the intangible Touch (Transmutation)
Doom of the oasis (Transmutation)

WIZARD SPELLS

1st Level
Doom of the oracle (Enchantment)
Doom of the warped skull (Necromancy)

2nd Level
Doom of deceleration (Transmutation)
Doom of splintered shards (Evocation)
Doom of the vulnerable (Transmutation)

3rd Level
Doom of false friendship (Enchantment)
Doom of stolen breath (Evocation)
Doom of the crawling (Conjuration)
Doom of the tentacle (Transmutation)

4th Level
Doom of horrid visages (Illusion)
Doom of the void (Evocation)

5th Level
Doom of the baleful rune (Abjuration)
Doom of the dead (Necromancy)
Doom of the intangible touch (Transmutation)
Doom of the oasis (Transmutation)

SPELL DESCRIPTIONS

This section contains descriptions of each doom magic spell.

Doom of Deceleration

2nd-level Transmutation | Cleric, Druid, Sorcerer, Warlock, Wizard

Casting Time: 1 action
Range: 30 feet
Components: V, S, M (a small knife)
Duration: Instantaneous

You stab yourself in the leg while you cast this spell, dealing 1d4 damage to yourself. Each creature within range, including you, must make a Wisdom saving throw. On a successful save, the creature's speed is reduced by 10 feet until the start of your next turn. On a failed save, the creature becomes restrained for 1 minute. At the end of each of its turns, the target can make another Wisdom saving throw. On a success, the target is no longer restrained.

Doom of False Friendship

3rd-level Enchantment | Sorcerer, Warlock, Wizard

Casting Time: 1 action
Range: 30 feet
Components: V, S
Duration: 1 hour

You try to convince a creature you can see within range that you are its ally. The target must make a Wisdom saving throw. On a failed save, it will try to avoid treating you as an enemy for the duration. If combat occurs while the target is affected, the creature does not attack you unless no other targets are available to it, and it does not choose you as the target of a harmful spell. If the target casts a spell or otherwise produces an effect that specifically targets enemies, you are not affected. If the target does attack you, it tries to render you unconscious rather than kill you. Creatures that are immune to being charmed are not affected by this spell.

At Higher Levels. When you cast this spell using a spell slot of 6th level or higher, you can choose an additional target for each slot level above 5th.

Doom of Horrid Visages

4th-level Illusion | Sorcerer, Warlock, Wizard
Casting Time: 1 action
Range: 30 feet
Components: V, S, M (a crumpled paper)
Duration: 1 minute

You reach into the mind of a creature within range and alter its perception to make it see terrible images surrounding it. The target must make a Wisdom saving throw. Creatures that are immune to being frightened automatically succeed on this saving throw. On a failed save, the target begins to see images of angry, twisted faces on any surface it perceives, causing it to become frightened of those images. The target will flee in a random direction, away from the faces.

Any creature that begins its turn within 10 feet of the target, including you, must succeed on an Intelligence saving throw or be subject to the effects of this spell, with the same duration and limitation as if it had just been cast on the creature.

At Higher Levels. When you cast this spell using a spell slot of 5th level or higher, you can affect an additional two creatures for each slot level above 4th.

Doom of Splintered Shards

2nd-level Evocation | Sorcerer, Warlock, Wizard
Casting Time: 1 action
Range: Self (30-foot cone)
Components: V, S, M (a sharp crystal)
Duration: Instantaneous

You stab a crystal shard into the palm of your hand as you cast the spell, dealing 1d8 damage to yourself. A barrage of splinters flies from your hands. Each creature in range must make a Dexterity saving throw. On a failed save, a creature takes 3d8 piercing damage, and for 1 minute afterward it takes 1 piercing damage whenever it performs any strenuous activity, including the Attack or Dash action, from the shards that remain lodged in its body. If the creature tries to take any action that requires concentration during that time, it must succeed on a Concentration check or lose the action.

On a successful save, a creature takes half as much damage and is not subject to the secondary effect.

At Higher Levels. When you cast this spell using a spell slot of 3rd level or higher, the initial piercing damage increases by 1d8 for each slot level above 2nd, and the damage from performing a strenuous activity increases by 1.

Doom of the Baleful Rune

5th-level Abjuration | Sorcerer, Warlock, Wizard
Casting Time: 1 action
Range: 30 feet
Components: V, S
Duration: 24 hours or until triggered

When you cast this spell, a glowing rune, 5 feet in diameter, appears on the surface of an unoccupied space within range. The rune is triggered when a creature other than you that can see the rune approaches within 30 feet of it. When the rune is triggered, all creatures in range must make a Wisdom saving throw. A creature that fails its saving throw is frightened of the rune for 1 minute. The rune lasts for 4 rounds before dissipating. A creature that approaches within 30 feet while the rune is active or begins its turn within that range must make a Wisdom saving throw as if it had triggered the rune. You can approach the rune without triggering it, but if you are within 30 feet of it when the rune is triggered, you are also affected by the spell.

Doom of the Crawling

3rd-level Conjuration | Bard, Cleric, Druid, Sorcerer, Warlock, Wizard
Casting Time: 1 action
Range: 30 feet
Components: V, S, M (a living or dead scorpion)
Duration: 5 minutes

You intone a spell to summon swarming creatures of the earth and send them to engage a target creature. You swallow the body of a scorpion as you end your casting. You are poisoned until the end of your next turn.

Four **swarms of insects** appear 40 feet from the creature, surrounding the creature and equidistant from each other. The insects can be a standard swarm of insects or one of the variant insect swarms available, but all four swarms must be of the same kind. The swarms do not consider you or your companions as allies, and you have no additional control over their actions other than directing them toward the initial target.

The swarms take their actions on your initiative count, immediately after you take your turn. The swarms move 20 feet each round toward the creature that you direct them to until they fill the target's square. The swarms will move as close to the target as possible each round, pausing next to obstacles they can reach closest to the target, which may include another swarm.

If the target is killed by the insects, the swarm will change their target to you, pursuing you for the duration of the spell. If you are killed, the swarms disperse.

Doom of the Dead

5th-level Necromancy | Cleric, Warlock, Wizard
Casting Time: 1 action
Range: 30 feet
Components: V, S, M (two bones from different creatures)
Duration: instantaneous

Lines of dark power encircle a creature that you can see within range. The creature must make a Wisdom saving throw. On a failed save, up to five humanoid corpses within range are each raised as a hostile **skeleton** or **zombie** that cannot be controlled. The undead creatures attack any living creature they perceive, which can include you.

At Higher Levels. When you cast this spell using a 6th-level spell slot, the first two undead to animate are **ghouls** rather than skeletons or zombies. When you cast this spell using a spell slot of 7th level or higher, the first undead creature to animate is a **wight**, the second is a **ghast**, and the remaining ones are **ghouls**.

Doom of the Intangible Touch

5th-level Transmutation | Sorcerer, Warlock, Wizard
Casting Time: 1 action
Range: 30 feet
Components: V, S, M (a cotton ball)
Duration: Concentration, up to 1 minute

A creature of your choice within range must make a Wisdom saving throw the first time it attempts a melee attack against you or one of your allies for the duration of the spell. If the target fails this saving throw, it shifts to the border of the Ethereal Plane until the end of its next turn. The target can see only 60 feet while on the Ethereal Plane and can pass through objects on the Material Plane. If it ends its turn while occupying the same location as a creature or object, the target is immediately shunted to the closest unoccupied space when it returns to the Material Plane and takes force damage equal to twice the number of feet it was forced to move.

If the target succeeds on its saving throw, the spell has no effect on it. A target can willingly fail the saving throw.

Doom of the Oasis

5th-level Transmutation | Cleric, Druid, Sorcerer, Warlock, Wizard
Casting Time: 1 action
Range: 30 feet
Components: V, S, M (three drops of water)
Duration: Instantaneous

You send powerful waves of dark energy coursing through a living creature within range. The target must make a Constitution saving throw. On a successful save, it takes 2d8 necrotic damage and the spell ends. On a failed save, the creature becomes incapacitated, and it takes 2d8 necrotic damage at the end of each of its turns as water pours out of its mouth and eyes. The target can repeat the saving throw at the end of each of its turns, ending the effect on itself on a success.

The water that gushes forth from the target is safe to drink; particularly vicious cults of the wastes use this spell to produce drinkable water as they sacrifice their victims.

Doom of the Oracle

1st-level Enchantment | Cleric, Sorcerer, Warlock, Wizard
Casting Time: 1 action
Range: 60 feet
Components: V, S
Duration: Instantaneous

You bring down a curse upon a creature of your choice within range, intending to hasten the creature toward its death. The target must make a Wisdom saving throw. On a failed save, the next attack that hits the target before the end of the round deals an extra 1 damage. The first attack that hits the target during each subsequent round deals an extra 1 damage for each round that has preceded it: a total of an extra 2 damage at the end of the second round, and so forth, up to an extra 5 damage at the end of the fifth round, at which point the effect ends. If no attack hits the target in a particular round, it takes no extra damage at the end of that round.

Doom of the Tentacle

3rd-level Transmutation | Druid, Sorcerer, Warlock, Wizard

Casting Time: 1 action
Range: 30 feet
Components: V, S
Duration: Concentration, up to 1 minute

When you cast this spell, a creature of your choice within range must succeed on a Constitution saving throw, or one of its arms turns into a tentacle. Any item the target was holding in the transformed arm is dropped at its feet. The tentacle randomly attacks one creature within 10 feet at the start of the target's turn, which might be you or the target itself. The tentacle uses your spell attack bonus as its attack bonus and deals damage equal to 1d8 + your Intelligence modifier. The target can repeat the saving throw at the end of each of its turns, ending the effect on itself on a success. The spell has no effect on a shapechanger or a creature with 0 hit points.

Doom of the Void

4th-level Evocation | Cleric, Druid, Paladin, Sorcerer, Warlock, Wizard

Casting Time: 1 action
Range: 10 feet
Components: V, S
Duration: Concentration, up to 3 rounds

You open the area to the dark energy of the Void at the target location, which fills a 10-foot-radius sphere within range of the spell. Each creature in the area must make a Wisdom saving throw. A creature takes 2d6 cold damage and 2d6 necrotic damage on a failed save, or half as much damage on a successful one. The energy of the void expands in the second round, becoming a 20-foot-radius sphere as the void attempts to consume everything in its path. The void expands again in the third round, becoming a 40-foot-radius sphere. Creatures that begin their turns in this area, including you, must succeed on a Wisdom saving throw or take the same amount and types of damage as when the spell was initially cast.

Doom of the Vulnerable

2nd-level Transmutation | Cleric, Druid, Sorcerer, Warlock, Wizard

Casting Time: 1 action
Range: Touch
Components: V, S
Duration: 1 minute

Your hand glows with purple fire when you cast this spell. Make a melee spell attack against a creature you can reach. If you hit the target, choose two options from among bludgeoning, piercing, and slashing. The target gains vulnerability to those types of damage, and you gain vulnerability to the type of damage you did not select. If the effect of this spell ends on you or the target, the effect ends on both of you.

Doom of the Warped Skull

1st-level Necromancy | Cleric, Druid, Sorcerer, Warlock, Wizard

Casting Time: 1 action
Range: 30 feet
Components: V, S, M (a bird skull with two heads)
Duration: Instantaneous

You raise the skull of a mutated bird of the wastes as you profess your target's doom. Make a ranged spell attack against a living creature of your choice within range. On a hit, the target is poisoned and takes a −2 penalty to AC until the end of your next turn. The next saving throw the target makes before the end of your next turn is made with disadvantage.

Chapter 7
Gear & Ancient Treasures

This chapter describes the riches that can be found in the wastes, including ancient magics and lost alien technology. These powerful or rare items can be the basis for complete adventure plots.

Ancient Treasures

Treasures from long-dead civilizations are scattered throughout the wastes, waiting to be claimed by enterprising treasure hunters.

Aberrant Sextant

Wondrous Item, artifact (requires attunement)

Like a standard sextant, this tool aids navigation, using the horizon and the celestial bodies as reference points to establish the user's current position. Unlike a standard sextant, however, this device can be used to travel to another plane of existence.

To use an aberrant sextant, you must be attuned to it, be aboard a vehicle, such as a boat, airship, or carriage, and have an unobstructed view of the sky and the horizon. On planes without a sky or a horizon, you must have a clear view of the area around you. For instance, you cannot be in a ship's cabin, even if you are looking out a window, but must be on the deck of the ship or in the crow's nest. You must spend 10 minutes using the sextant to determine your location and the route to your destination. At the end of that time, you speak the name of the plane of existence you want to travel to, such as the Shadowfell or the Elemental Plane of Air, or the name of a location on your current plane of existence. A portal large enough for your vehicle and its passengers opens in front of you and remains open only long enough for the vehicle to pass through. The vehicle emerges at the desired destination, and the portal immediately closes behind you before any other creatures or vehicles can make use of it. Once the sextant is used in this manner, it can't be used again until the next dawn.

You can name a specific location on another plane of existence, such as the City of Brass on the Elemental Plane of Fire. You appear at or near that destination, at the GM's discretion. If the specific location does not exist, you arrive at a similar area (a different area that's visually or thematically similar to the target area) on that plane of existence.

Sextant Components

An aberrant sextant is made up of five main components, each a powerful magic item in its own right that functions if it is detached from the sextant. If any component is removed from the sextant, the sextant becomes unusable until all the separated parts are reinstalled. Detaching a component or reinstalling one takes 1 minute of work.

Being able to use a detached component requires attunement, and the creature attuned must hold the component to make use of its features.

Index Mirror. When it is attached to the sextant, this mirror catches the reflection of the celestial body being used to determine the vessel's position.

If you are attuned to the index mirror separately, you have advantage on Intelligence (Nature) checks.

In addition, you can use a bonus action to assume stardust form for 1 hour. In this form, your outline is hazy and you glitter like starlight, shedding dim light in a 10-foot radius. You become incorporeal, along with everything you're wearing or carrying, and you have a walking speed of 120 feet. You have resistance to nonmagical damage, and you have advantage on Strength, Dexterity, and Constitution saving throws. You move through other creatures and objects as if their spaces were difficult terrain. If you end your turn inside an object, you take 4d10 force damage.

While in stardust form, you can't speak or manipulate objects, and any objects you are carrying or holding can't be dropped, used, or otherwise interacted with. You can't attack or cast spells.

You can use a bonus action to end this effect early; if you do, choose one of the following effects:

- Each creature within 30 feet of you regains 8d10 hit points.
- Each creature within 30 feet of you takes 4d10 cold damage and 4d10 radiant damage.

Once you use the index mirror's stardust form feature, it can't be used again until the next dawn.

Horizon Mirror. When it is attached to the sextant, this mirror displays the horizon and the celestial body reflected by the index mirror.

If you are attuned to the horizon mirror separately, you have advantage on skill checks using navigator's tools.

In addition, you can cast the following spells at will: *arcane eye, clairvoyance, find the path, locate creature,* and *scrying*.

Eyepiece. Resembling a small telescope, the eyepiece is used to sight through when it is attached to the sextant.

If you are attuned to the eyepiece separately, you have advantage on Intelligence (Investigation) checks.

In addition, you can use your reaction to capture the soul of a humanoid when it dies. The soul becomes trapped within the eyepiece and remains there until you use an action to release it, after which you can capture a different soul if the opportunity presents itself. The soul can perceive its surroundings from inside the eyepiece using its own senses, but it can't move or take actions. You can communicate telepathically with the soul.

Arc. When it is attached to the sextant, the arc pivots to display the measurement of the angle between the horizon and the celestial body.

If you are attuned to the arc separately, you gain a +1 bonus to Intelligence saving throws.

In addition, you can cast the following spells at will: *detect magic, fabricate, identify,* and *mending*.

Index Arm. When it is attached to the sextant, the index arm supports the index mirror and indicates the correct measurement of the angle on the arc.

If you are attuned to the index arm separately, you have advantage on Dexterity saving throws.

In addition, you can use a bonus action to cause a blade of silver starlight to spring forth from the index arm, which serves as the hilt of the weapon. The blade can take the form of a longsword, a short sword, a rapier, or a dagger (your choice), and it deals 3d6 cold damage. You are proficient with this weapon. The blade remains until you dismiss it.

Ajna Maang Tikka

Wondrous item, very rare (requires attunement)

This beaded headpiece attaches to your hair and hangs down in the center of your forehead. When attuned to this item, you gain a +1 increase to your Intelligence and Wisdom scores, and you have advantage on Intelligence (Investigation), Wisdom (Insight), and Wisdom (Perception) checks.

Armageddon Sphere

Wondrous item, legendary

Five adamantine bands slowly revolve around the diamond sphere at the heart of this floating eldritch machine. Four of the bands bear the symbols of the elements—fire, water, earth, and air. The fifth band is emblazoned with an image of a dragon. Long ago, a forgotten civilization used spheres such as this to power flying cities, far-ranging void vessels, or planar rituals of unfathomable power. Today, the sphere can't be used as a power source, only as an evil apocalyptic weapon.

Activating the armageddon sphere requires sacrificing elementals of CR 10 or higher, feeding the essence of each creature into the appropriate adamantine band. Next, the heartblood of an Adult or older dragon must be poured onto the fifth band. Once this is accomplished, the sphere begins pulsing with the build-up of energy, and a single golden dial appears on the surface of the sphere.

You can use an action to set the dial to a number of minutes or hours (user's choice), and then set a number between 1 and 200. Once the dial is set, nothing can prevent the countdown to detonation, apart from a *wish* spell or divine intervention.

When the timer reaches 0, the armageddon sphere detonates in an explosion of force and magic out to a 10-mile radius with the following effects:

- Every living thing that is 1 mile or less from the sphere must make a DC 25 Constitution saving throw, taking 50 force damage plus 25d10 necrotic damage on a failed save, or half as much damage on a successful one. If this reduces the target to 0 hit points, it is disintegrated. All structures within this distance are destroyed, as are all nonmagical objects that aren't being worn or held.
- Every creature and living thing that is between 1 mile and 5 miles from the sphere must make a DC 20 Constitution saving throw, taking 25 force damage plus 15d10 necrotic damage on a failed save or half as much damage on a successful one. All nonmagical structures and objects within this distance take double damage.
- Every creature and living thing that is between 5 miles and 10 miles from the sphere must make a DC 15 Constitution saving throw, taking 15 force damage plus 5d10 necrotic damage on a failed save or half as much damage on a successful one. Nonmagical structures and objects within this distance take half of this damage.
- Creatures within the radius that succeed on the saving throw to survive the detonation of the sphere suffer random mutations as determined by the GM.
- All terrain within the blast radius becomes difficult terrain for 1d10 years and contains living spells, quicksand, mutated creatures, and other hazards as determined by the GM.
- Any creature attempting to cast a spell or use a magical item within the radius has a 10% failure rate for 1d4 years.
- Magical healing is suppressed for 1 year within the radius. After that duration, spells and other magical effects that heal hit point damage only heal half the usual amount.

Armor of Versatile Resistance

Armor (medium or heavy, but not hide), uncommon

While wearing this armor, you gain a +1 bonus to AC and resistance to one damage type of your choice: bludgeoning, piercing, slashing, necrotic, force, or lightning. When you finish a short or long rest, you can choose a different damage type, replacing the previous choice.

Baton of Dominance

Rod, very rare (requires attunement)

While holding this rod, you can point it at a creature and use an action to try to convince the target of your superiority. The creature must succeed on a DC 17 Wisdom saving throw or be charmed by you for 8 hours. While it is charmed, the creature must follow your commands or take 1d10 psychic damage every time it acts in a manner contrary to your instructions.

You have a telepathic link with your target as long as the two of you are on the same plane of existence. You issue telepathic commands to the target through this link without using an action. You and the target don't need to share a language to communicate through the link. If your target completes a task you assigned it and you have not issued any further commands, it acts of its own accord, defending itself to the best of its ability.

Each time your target takes damage from a creature other than you, it makes a new saving throw, ending the effect on itself with a successful save.

Once you have used the baton to charm a creature, you can't do so again until midnight of the next day.

You can use the baton to make melee attacks with a +2 bonus to attack and damage rolls. The baton is a magic weapon with the light property that deals 1d4 bludgeoning damage.

Bead of Monster Summoning

Wondrous item, rare

Each of these ocher beads is the size of a marble and weighs half an ounce. Typically, 1d3 + 1 beads of monster summoning are found together.

You can use an action to throw a bead up to 60 feet. The bead explodes on impact, and the explosion summons a miniature version of a monster that grows to its full size by the start of your next turn. Until it has grown to full size, the creature cannot be interacted with and is immune to all attacks. When it is fully grown, the summoned monster immediately attacks the target nearest to it other than you until it is slain or until 1 minute has elapsed, whereupon it vanishes in a cloud of putrid-smelling gas. The creature doesn't differentiate between your allies and your enemies, nor does it follow your commands. Roll on the following table to determine the kind of monster that the bead produces.

d10	Monster
1	manticore (CR 3)
2	winter wolf (CR 3)
3	ettin (CR 4)
4	lamia (CR 4)
5	bulette (CR 5)
6	gorgon (CR 5)
7	troll (CR 5)
8	cyclops (CR 6)
9	chaos troll (see **Chapter 5**) (CR 7)
10	hydra (CR 8)

Black Powder Popper

Wondrous item, uncommon

This pea-sized ball of paper filled with a pinch of black powder and gravel is often sold in pouches of 20, 50, or 100. When a creature within 30 feet of you makes an attack, you can use your reaction to throw the popper at its feet to distract it as the powder ignites with a popping sound. The creature must succeed on a DC 12 Constitution saving throw or make its attack roll with disadvantage.

Boutonniere of Bewildering

Wondrous item, uncommon

This cluster of tiny blue roses is ever-blooming and needs no sunlight or water. While you wear this accessory fastened to your clothing, tied around your wrist, or pinned in your hair, the world takes on a slightly hazy, sparkling quality. Everyone around you seems charming and beautiful, and you find yourself laughing and talking more than normal. You have advantage on Charisma checks, and you have disadvantage on saving throws against charm effects and attempts to influence your mind.

Bowl of Bloody Retribution

Wondrous item, rare (requires attunement)

This roughly worked clay bowl has spidery runes scratched into its exterior and interior surfaces. While you hold the bowl in your hands, you feel it radiate with malice.

When you fill the bowl with wine, add a drop of blood from a living creature that you feel has wronged you, speak its name aloud, and recite a litany of its crimes against you, its visage appears in the liquid, distorted by the ripples radiating from the point where the drop of blood hit the wine.

Your target must succeed on a DC 16 Charisma saving throw or begin to hear your voice in its ears, speaking of its crimes against you and taunting it to find you and confront you. Until you finish a long rest, your target has disadvantage on attack rolls, skill checks, and saving throws unless it is within 100 feet of you. If your target is killed while under the effect of the bowl, you gain 15 temporary hit points.

When you use the bowl, you gain two levels of exhaustion. You recover from these levels of exhaustion when you finish a long rest, when your target moves within 100 feet of you, or when your target is killed.

Bracers of the Old Gods

Wondrous item, legendary (requires attunement)

These bracers are made of pale white leather lined with pointed teeth. When you attune to these symbiotic bracers, the teeth embed themselves in the flesh of your arms. You take 2d4 psychic damage, and your hit-point maximum is reduced by the same amount. You cannot regain these hit points until your attunement to the bracers ends. The bracers cannot be removed while you are attuned to them, and you can't voluntarily end your attunement to them. If you're targeted by a spell that ends a curse, your attunement to the bracers ends, and they detach from your arms.

While you are attuned to the bracers, you have resistance to psychic damage and necrotic damage. You gain telepathy out to a range of 60 feet, and you can read, write, and speak Abyssal and Deep Speech.

The bracers hold 8 charges. While you are attuned to the bracers, you can use an action to expend 1 or more charges to cast one of the following spells (save DC 17) without the need for components: *bane* (1 charge), *enthrall* (2 charges), *fear* (3 charges), *arcane eye* (4 charges), *cloudkill* (5 charges), *contact other plane* (5 charges), *dominate person* (5 charges), or *eyebite* (6 charges). The bracers regain all expended charges at dawn. If you expend the bracer's last charge, roll a d20. On a 1, a piercing shriek fills the air, you take 6d6 psychic damage, and the bracers detach from your arm, shrivel into withered husks, and are destroyed.

Charged Candle

Wondrous item, rarity varies

When you light this candle, you activate the spell stored in it, with its effect centered on the candle. For the duration of the candle's burn time, the candle sheds bright light in a 5-foot radius and dim light for an additional 5 feet. If you extinguish the candle, the spell effect ends. A charged candle can be extinguished and relit multiple times, as long as the candle's burn time does not exceed the duration of the spell. When the burn time equals the maximum duration of the spell, the candle goes out and is destroyed.

CHARGED CANDLES

Stored Spell	Burn Time	Rarity
fog cloud	1 hour	Common
arcane eye	1 hour	Uncommon
guardian of faith	8 hours	Uncommon
tiny hut	8 hours	Uncommon
antilife shell	1 hour	Rare
private sanctum	24 hours	Rare
forbiddance	24 hours	Rare
guards and wards	24 hours	Rare
control weather	8 hours	Very rare
nondetection (all creatures within 10 feet)	8 hours	Very rare
magnificent mansion	24 hours	Very rare

Charged Crossbow

Weapon (heavy crossbow), uncommon

Instead of physical projectiles, a charged crossbow fires bolts of energy contained in the bulbs fastened to its frame. This crossbow does not have the loading property, but you must replace the spent energy bulbs after firing the crossbow twenty times, which requires 10 minutes and a set of tinker's tools to accomplish. When you make a successful attack with this crossbow, roll on the table below to determine the type of damage type the attack deals.

Charged Crossbow Damage

d12	Damage Type
1–2	Poison
3–4	Fire
5–6	Cold
7–8	Acid
9–10	Lightning
11	Force
12	Psychic

Chthorhoti Star Charts

Wondrous item, rare

Pinpricks dot these disks of thin-pressed orichalcum, creating a skyscape of unfamiliar stars. A few designs of inlaid platinum that look like alien constellations connect some of the stars.

If you spend 40 hours over a period of 30 days or fewer studying these star charts, you gain proficiency in navigator's tools if you did not already have it, and you may use these star charts to locate the cardinal directions, even underground. Additionally, you may use these charts to find the best, most direct route to their stated destination: once a day, as an action, you may make a DC 18 Intelligence check with navigator's tools. On a success, you know the shortest, most direct physical route to your destination. On a failure, you are incapacitated for the next hour as the infinite dark between the stars stretches out before your eyes. Once the star charts have been used in this way, they cannot be used again until the next dawn.

Dark Lantern

Wondrous item, uncommon

When you light this hooded lantern, it burns with a black flame that casts no light. While you hold it in your hand, you can see as though the lantern were giving off bright light in a 60-foot radius and dim light for an additional 30 feet. The lantern burns for 6 hours on a flask of oil.

Deadshot Visor

Wondrous item, uncommon

This ancient device looks like a pair of thick spectacles composed of a black glassy material and connected by an orichalcum wire to a small steel pack worn on the hip. When you wear this item, a red or green targeting reticle appears on the visor over your left or right eye, and you gain advantage on any ranged attack rolls you make with advanced weaponry such as firearms. The visor doesn't work with longbows, crossbows, or other more primitive ranged weapons.

Demonologist's Bezoar

Wondrous item, rare

This item appears as a speckled and malformed goose egg that fits in your hand. Soft down covers the exterior, making it pleasant to hold, though it is surprisingly heavy.

When you use an action to cast this bezoar on the ground, it breaks, and a demon, as determined by the table below, is summoned in that space. It remains active for 1 minute or until it's killed. If any creatures occupy the space where the demon appears, they are pushed to the closest space within 5 feet of it. The demon acts as typical for a creature of its sort and can't be controlled or commanded. The demon can't move more than 50 feet from the space in which it was summoned.

d20	Demon Summoned
1	Quasit
2–7	Vrock
8–11	Hezrou
12–15	Glabrezu
16–17	Nalfeshnee
18–19	Marilith
20	Balor

Echo Rifle

Weapon, very rare

A long, tubular firearm that is similar in shape to a trumpet, this weapon fires concentrated bursts of sound at distant enemies and makes a distinctive popping sound when used. Only a few of these marvels have ever been found in working order; most specimens are either badly damaged or missing their power sources. A functioning echo rifle can sell for thousands of gold pieces.

The echo rifle has the following statistics.

WEAPON	DAMAGE	WEIGHT	PROPERTIES
Echo Rifle	2d8 thunder	12 lb.	Ammunition, range (60/320), two-handed

A fully powered echo rifle has 20 charges, and each shot uses 1 charge. Echo rifles are solar-powered and regain 4 charges for every hour they remain in direct sunlight.

Entropy Bomb

Weapon (bomb), rare

This glass sphere is filled with swirling black gas. As an action, you can throw this bomb up to 60 feet away, where it breaks and releases the gas in a 15-foot-diameter cloud that lingers for 1 minute. A creature that starts its turn in the cloud or that enters the cloud for the first time on its turn must make a DC 15 Constitution saving throw. On a failure, the creature takes 1d6 necrotic damage and is under the effect of the *slow* spell until the end of its next turn. A creature can repeat the saving throw at the end of each of its turns, ending the effect on itself on a success.

Floating Disk

Wondrous item, rare

A 5-foot-wide disk of paper-thin, shimmering metal, this item weighs 5 pounds and can be rolled up into a tube for easy storage. When you place the disk on the ground and speak the command word, the disk rises to hover 1 foot above the ground and gains a flying speed of 60 feet. You can stand or sit on it and ride it through the air, or you can use it to carry items or other creatures, and you can mentally direct it from as far away as 100 feet. The disk can carry up to 300 pounds. If this limit is exceeded, it drops at a speed of 5 feet per round.

Fruit of Foresight

Wondrous item, uncommon

You can eat this dried pear as an action. For the next 4 hours you can't be surprised, and if you roll 9 or lower on an initiative check, you can treat the roll as a 10 instead.

Fruit of Friendliness

Wondrous item, uncommon

You can eat this honeyed date as an action. For the next 10 minutes, creatures that are indifferent to you become friendly, and creatures that are hostile to you become indifferent.

Fruit of Shielding

Wondrous item, uncommon

If a creature makes an attack against you, you can use your reaction to eat this dried apricot after your attacker has rolled, but before you know whether the attack hit you. Until the start of your next turn, you add your proficiency bonus to your Armor Class.

Fruit of Wounding

Wondrous item, uncommon

You can eat this salted and dried fig as an action. Once you do so, you add your proficiency bonus to your damage rolls for 1 minute.

Glow Bomb

Adventuring gear, rare
Weight 1 lb, 250 gp

As an action, you can throw this flask 20 feet, shattering it on impact. Every creature within 5 feet of the target space must make a DC 13 Dexterity saving throw. Those that fail take 7 (2d6) acid damage and are coated in glowing green sludge. For 1 minute, affected creatures shed dim light in a 10-foot radius. Any attack roll against an affected creature has advantage if the attacker can see it, and the affected creature can't benefit from being invisible.

A creature can scrape off the sludge by using its action and making a successful DC 10 Dexterity check or by washing it off with wine or vinegar.

Goggles of Insightful Vision

Wondrous item, legendary

These goggles have prismatic lenses with adjustable attachments of various colors and sizes. When you wear these goggles, you can use an action to activate one of the attachments. For the next 10 minutes, you gain your choice of the following benefits, effective out to a range of 120 feet:

- You can see into a plane of your choice: the Astral Plane, the Ethereal Plane, the Shadowfell, or the Feywild.
- You can see invisible creatures and objects.
- You can detect visual illusions and automatically succeed on saving throws against them.
- You can perceive the original form of a shapeshifter or a creature transformed by magic.
- You can see a faint aura around any visible creature or object within range that bears magic, and you learn its school, if any.

You can use an action to activate a different attachment and gain that benefit instead.

Hourglass of Measured Response

Wondrous item, very rare (requires attunement)

This locket-sized hourglass hangs from a fine silver chain. When it is flipped over, the cerulean sand moves from the top to the bottom of the glass with exceptional quickness.

If you have used your reaction in the current round, you can flip the hourglass over (no action required) to use a second reaction in the same round. After the second and any subsequent time you use the hourglass in a day, you must make a DC 15 Constitution saving throw, gaining one level of exhaustion on each failed save.

Hypogean Bellsphere

Wondrous item, legendary

This 20-foot-radius metal-and-crystal vessel is designed to magically travel through the ground. The *hypogean bellsphere* has AC 20, 300 hit points, a damage threshold of 15 and immunity to poison and psychic damage. It has a speed of 1 mile per hour on land, and a burrow speed of 3 miles per hour (72 miles per day). The bellsphere can hold up to 6 passengers plus 1 ton of cargo.

Description. The bellsphere is a featureless sphere inscribed with strange arcane symbols and thin, glowing tracework. Despite its shape, the craft does not roll unless acted upon by exterior forces. A circular hatch provides access to the vessel's interior. Inside, circular crystal portholes line the circumference of the sphere and magically act as windows, allowing the crew to view their surroundings. A raised pilot's chair occupies a dais in the center of the circular room, surrounded by levers, pull cords, toggles, and other strange controls. There is no other furniture in the craft.

The bellsphere has the following general features:

- The glowing magical screens provide a dim illumination.
- Air magically circulates through the sphere for 12 hours before it must be replenished from the outside.

Piloting the Bellsphere. Any creature must succeed on a DC 15 Intelligence check to decipher the controls of the bellsphere. From the pilot's chair, a creature can control the ship's speed, direction, and depth. Controlling the ship during combat requires an additional DC 15 Intelligence check to make rapid course corrections.

The bellsphere can burrow through any nonmagical, unworked earth and stone. While doing so, it doesn't disturb the materials it moves through.

While the pilot sits in the pilot chair, it has tremorsense out to a range of 60 feet. Within that range, the pilot can sense areas the ship is unable to burrow through but gains no knowledge of what the area contains.

Fueling the Bellsphere. The bellsphere is powered by the consumption of magical items. A small hatch on the side of the dais beneath the pilot's chair is large enough to hold any item a Medium-sized creature could equip or easily carry. Any magic item placed in the fueling hatch is destroyed. A common item provides power for 2 hours of operation. Each level of rarity beyond common doubles that duration, up to vary rare for 8 hours. A legendary item placed in the fueling hatch would allow the bellsphere to operate for 1 month. Placing an artifact into the fueling hatch causes the bellsphere to implode, immediately killing anyone inside it.

Implosion Arrow

Ammunition, uncommon

When you hit with an attack using this arrow, it creates a sphere of gravity 15 feet in diameter centered on the target. Each creature other than the target within the sphere must make a DC 15 Dexterity saving throw. On a failed save, a creature is pulled 10 feet toward the target, and it takes 3d6 bludgeoning damage and 1d6 force damage. The target and objects automatically fail this saving throw.

Jumping Beans

Wondrous item, uncommon

Inside a burlap pouch are 3d4 dry kidney beans. As an action, you can consume one of these beans; for the next minute, you can jump three times your normal distance.

Magic Mirror

Wondrous item, very rare (requires attunement)

This silver hand mirror is decorated with intricate etchings of birds, flowers, bats, and skulls. When you hold this mirror and gaze into it, you can cast the *scrying* spell through it (save DC 17).

While scrying with the mirror, you can cast telekinesis on one creature or object you can see within 30 feet of it. You don't need to concentrate on this effect to maintain it, but it ends if the scrying spell ends. Once it is used, the telekinesis feature of the mirror can't be used again until the next dawn.

Curse. This item is cursed. Attuning to it curses you until you are targeted by a *remove curse* spell or similar magic. As long as you remain cursed, you can't end your attunement to the mirror, and you must keep it on your person at all times. When you are attuned to the mirror, you find yourself compelled to use it as often as possible, and you are distracted by thoughts of your appearance. When you cast *scrying* through this mirror, you must make a DC 17 Wisdom saving throw. On each failed save, the mirror gains more influence over your thoughts and actions, as indicated on the table below.

Number of Failures	Effect
1	You spend your free time staring at your reflection in the mirror to the point of distraction. It takes you an extra hour to finish a short or long rest.
2	In addition to the above effect, you often compare your appearance to that of your companions, and you become jealous of any of their features that you consider superior to your own. You have disadvantage on Charisma saving throws.
3 or more	In addition to the above effects, you cannot suffer the presence of anyone you consider a potential competitor. The character with the highest Charisma score in the room, even if that character is your ally, becomes the target of your ire. You go out of your way to undercut that character whenever you get a chance. You might circulate harmful rumors, spill a drink on them at an inopportune time, or even cause them harm if it would bring them low.

Mask of the Spiderling

Wondrous item, uncommon (requires attunement)

This mask is made of molded black leather and a strange, dark-silver metal, resembling a carapace, with spider-like legs that attach it to the wearer's head. While you are attuned to this mask, you gain the following traits:

You can move up, down, and across vertical surfaces and upside down along ceilings while leaving your hands free, and you have a climbing speed equal to your walking speed. The mask does not allow you to move this way on a slippery surface, such as one covered by ice or oil.

You can communicate with spiders, ettercaps, and similar creatures.

Once per day, you can use an action to create webbing in one of the following ways.

- You can spin a spiderweb that covers an area with a radius of up to 20 feet. The webbing can support up to 500 pounds. While in contact with the web, you know the exact location of any other creature in contact with the same web.
- You can make a ranged attack with your webbing (range 30/60 feet) and try to snare a creature or an object. On a hit, the target is restrained.

A creature can use its action to break the webbing with a successful DC 14 Strength check. The webbing can also be attacked and destroyed (AC 11; hp 5; vulnerability to fire damage; immunity to bludgeoning, poison, and psychic damage). Once you've created webbing in this fashion, you can't do so again until you finish a long rest.

Personal Assistant

Wondrous item, rare

This 3-foot-tall metal construct is vaguely humanoid in shape, though instead of legs, it has three flexible wheeled appendages. Six arms ring its torso. Two of them are three-fingered hands, one is a blade like that of a longsword, one ends in a buzzsaw, one is a round collapsible shield, and one ends in two prongs with electricity sparking between them. When you speak the command word, the personal assistant hums to life. As a bonus action, you can issue it a one-word command, which the personal assistant follows to the best of its ability. It will keep following the command until it is told otherwise. A few of the commands are listed below.

Wait. The personal assistant stops moving and stays where it is.

Follow. The personal assistant follows you at a distance of 5 feet.

Defend. The personal assistant occupies a space within 5 feet of you and uses its shield to protect you from incoming attacks. You gain a +2 bonus to your AC and on any Dexterity saving throws.

Attack. The personal assistant attacks a target of your choice with its sword arm. It has a +4 bonus to hit, and its attack deals 5 (1d6 + 2) slashing damage.

Watch. The personal assistant stays vigilant and motionless and alerts you if any creatures approach. While following this command, it has a +5 bonus on Wisdom (Perception) checks.

The personal assistant has a walking speed of 30 feet, an AC of 17, 50 hp, and darkvision out to 60 feet. It can carry up to 200 pounds. It follows you unless told to do otherwise. If it takes damage, a successful DC 14 Dexterity check using tinker's tools repairs up to 10 hit points. If the personal assistant drops to 0 hit points, it is nonfunctional until it is repaired.

You may change the personal assistant's hands to different tools, as determined by your GM, with a successful DC 14 Dexterity check with tinker's tools.

Portable Span

Wondrous item, uncommon

This item appears to be a miniature model of a stone bridge. When you set it on the ground and use a bonus action to speak its command word, it expands into a 50-foot-long, 10-foot-wide stone span. The span can hold up to 5,000 pounds. When you speak the command word again, the span contracts to its miniature size and appears on the ground at your feet. After you have expanded and contracted the span, you can't do so again until the next dawn.

Portal Loupe

Wondrous item, uncommon

This brass item resembles a palm-sized, squat telescope featuring a magnifying lens at one end. A thin circle of rune-marked silver is inset into the side of the lens. As an action, the wielder can place the end of the loupe onto a vertical or horizontal surface and peer into the lens to see through a wall, floor, or door. The portal loupe can see through wood, stone, or metal with a thickness of no more than 5 feet. Using the loupe's magic to see through a barrier doesn't allow the wielder to use its own darkvision, truesight, or other method of perception.

Potion of Many Forms

Potion, very rare

This potion is pale blue and iridescent, with pink and green pearls suspended near the surface. When you drink this potion, you are affected as if by a *polymorph* spell. You change into a creature determined by rolling on the table below and stay in that form for 1 hour. Maintaining this form does not require concentration.

d100	Creature
01–06	Black pudding
07–12	Chimera
13–18	Chuul
19–24	Cloaker
25–29	Darkmantle
30–34	Death dog
35–39	Dread mouther (see **Chapter 5**)
40–44	Ettercap
45–49	Gelatinous cube
50–54	Gibbering mouther
55–59	Grick
60–64	Manticore
65–69	Otyugh
70–74	Owlbear
75–79	Phase spider
80–84	Purple worm
85–89	Remorhaz
90–94	Roper
95–99	Rust monster
100	Troll

Retching Jelly

Wondrous item, uncommon

This clear jelly compels a creature to vomit up anything covered in it. If a monster such as a purple worm or a giant toad swallows a creature or object coated in this jelly, it must immediately make a successful DC 13 Wisdom saving throw or regurgitate the creature or object. Furthermore, the creature will not try to swallow the same creature or object for the next hour.

A jar of retching jelly can coat one Medium creature or object, up to two Small creatures or objects, or up to four Tiny creatures or objects.

This unguent remains effective for 1 hour or until a creature or object that has been covered is successfully swallowed, whereupon the substance dissolves away. It can also be washed off with a single application of universal solvent or 1 gallon of alcohol.

Robot Control Circlet

Wondrous item, very rare

This thin silver circlet can be adjusted to fit snugly on a humanoid skull. While you wear it, you can use an action to take control of a **robot** (see **Chapter 5**) within 30 feet. The robot must succeed on a DC 15 Intelligence saving throw or be compelled to obey you to the best of its ability for as long as you are wearing the circlet. If you or creatures friendly to you are fighting the robot, it has advantage on the saving throw. You can affect only one robot at a time with the circlet. The item might affect other kinds of constructs at the GM's discretion.

This effect resembles that of the *dominate monster* spell, except that you do not have a telepathic link to the robot. Instead, you must tell the robot what to do by using verbal commands. The robot remains controlled by you until it is destroyed, until you remove the circlet, or until you try to control a different robot. When any of these events occur, the robot resumes its normal behavior.

Scourge of the Stars

Weapon (whip), rare

This whip ends in five strands of brown leather. Each strand is studded with shards of glass in a different color; red, purple, yellow, blue, and green. You have a +1 bonus to attack and damage rolls you make with this whip. When you hit with it, you deal an extra 2d6 damage, according to the color of the shards as determined by the table below.

d6	Shards' Color
1	Red (fire damage)
2	Purple (necrotic damage)
3	Yellow (acid damage)
4	Blue (cold damage)
5	Green (poison damage)
6	Multicolored (psychic damage). In addition, the target must succeed on a DC 12 Wisdom saving throw or become stunned until the end of its next turn.

Shielding Bracelet

Wondrous item, uncommon (requires attunement)

This metal bracelet is fashioned from a strange reddish-gold damascene metal with one or more green stones set into it. When activated as a bonus action, the bracelet generates a barrier of invisible force forming a bubble around you. While you are surrounded by the barrier created by the bracelet, all damage you take is reduced by an amount determined by the bracelet's rarity. Each variety of shielding bracelet has a maximum amount of damage it can deflect over the course of a single activation before dissipating. Once the bracelet reaches that maximum amount, it can't absorb more and dissipates.

Once you activate the bracelet, you must finish a short or long rest before you can activate it again.

Shock Shield

Wondrous item, rare (requires attunement)

This glove is made of a shiny black velvet-like material. A tarnished silver disc is affixed to the back of the glove by copper wires that run from the disc to the glove's fingertips. While wearing this glove, you can use a reaction to create a temporary field of force that grants you a +3 shield bonus to your AC until the start of your next turn. In addition, any creature striking the shield with a melee attack must make a DC 13 Dexterity saving throw, taking 7 (2d6) lightning damage on a failure or half that amount on a success.

The shock shield has 3 charges and regains 1d3 expended charges daily at dawn.

Shielding Bracelet	Rarity	Damage Deflected (Per Attack)	Maximum Damage Amount
Lesser	Uncommon	1d6	12
Greater	Rare	2d6	24
Superior	Very Rare	3d6	50

Skittering Crawler

Weapon (bomb), rare

The body of this clockwork contraption is 6 inches per side, and it is fitted with eight articulated legs. As an action, you can choose one of three activities (see below) and activate the skittering crawler by winding the key on its underside. When activated, the skittering crawler has a walking speed of 50 feet, AC 8, 5 hp, a +4 bonus on Dexterity (Stealth) checks, and immunity to psychic damage and poison damage. When the crawler finishes performing an activity, or if it is reduced to 0 hit points by any damage other than cold damage, it detonates. When it detonates, it deals 4d6 fire damage and 2d4 bludgeoning damage to each creature within 5 feet.

Crawler Modes

- **Proximity.** The skittering crawler moves directly away from you in whichever direction you choose. If it gets within 5 feet of a creature at any time during its movement, it detonates.
- **Timer.** The skittering crawler remains where you place it, and it detonates after an amount of time you choose, up to 12 hours. You can cancel this activity at any time before the crawler detonates.
- **Infiltrate.** The skittering crawler moves directly away from you in whichever direction you choose and stops at a location set by you. It then remains in place and detonates after an amount of time you choose, up to 12 hours. You can cancel this activity at any time before the crawler detonates.

Sundial of Wasted Hours

Wondrous item, very rare (requires attunement)

This bronze sundial is about 1 foot in diameter and weighs 15 pounds. The dial is notched at twelve even intervals to mark the hours, and the pointer is carved to resemble a humanoid figure in repose. The sundial always points to the correct local time, even at night or on overcast days.

The sundial has 24 charges. When you use an action to set the sundial in place, speak its command word, and expend 1 charge, you and all creatures within 20 feet of the sundial can gain the benefits of finishing a long rest after resting for only 1 hour.
When the last charge is expended, the sundial collapses into bronze dust.

Tentacle Armband of Shielding

Wondrous item, uncommon

This silver band is carved in the shape of a tentacle and encircles your upper arm. While you wear this armband, you can cast the *shield* spell once per day. The shield takes the form of a translucent barrier of writhing tentacles. After you use this item, you can't use it again until the next dawn.

Timepiece of Tralizax

Wondrous item, legendary (requires attunement)

This intricate clockwork timepiece is fashioned from a combination of electrum and brass and chiseled with minute runes. It always displays the correct time of day. Aside from that, you can use an action to have the timepiece accomplish one of the following tasks.

Rewind Time. You can undo the effects that have occurred during the previous minute to yourself and all creatures or objects within 30 feet of you once per day. All conditions, magical effects, and injuries suffered by all eligible creatures and objects during that minute are treated as if they did not occur, though the timepiece does not bring dead creatures back to life. The effect also replenishes spent ammunition and expended charges from magic items, but not spell slots or special abilities of creatures with limited uses. Affected creatures are fully aware of what has transpired, so the rewinding of time might cause them to rethink their actions.

Steal Time. You can point the timepiece at a creature within 30 feet once per day and force it to make a DC 17 Wisdom saving throw. On a failed save, the creature is frozen in time until the end of its next turn, and you gain an extra action and bonus action that you must use before the end of your current turn. While a creature is frozen in time, it is paralyzed and unconscious and cannot be harmed or interfered with in any way.

The timepiece regains its special features at dawn if you choose for it to do so. You must make a DC 17 Wisdom saving throw whenever the timepiece recharges. On a failed save, you age one year.

Tome of Enlightenment

Wondrous item, legendary (requires attunement)

This book is bound in covers of pale flesh and is marked with cuts and punctures seeping black blood. When you open the book, twisting, barbed black tentacles erupt from the pages. Make a DC 20 Dexterity saving throw (which you can choose to fail). On a failed save, the tentacles wrap around your head and plunge into your eye sockets, grasping at your brain, feasting on your memories and filling your mind with terrible and ecstatic visions. Successfully attuning to this item requires you to spend at least 1 hour communing with the tome while you are in this state. While you're attuned to the tome, you have advantage on Intelligence (Arcana) checks, your Intelligence score is 20, and you gain telepathy out to a range of 120 feet.

Curse. This item is cursed. Attuning to it curses you until you are targeted by a *remove curse* spell or similar magic. As long as you remain cursed, you can't end your attunement to the tome, and you must always keep it on your person. When you are attuned to this item, you become the preferred target of any aberrations, celestials, fiends, oozes, or undead within 100 feet of you. Additionally, you must spend 1 hour out of every 24 hours communing with the tome; if you fail to do so for an entire 24 hours, you must make a DC 20 Wisdom saving throw. On a failed save, you take 3d6 psychic damage. You must repeat this saving throw every hour until you spend 1 hour communing with the tome.

Voidmaw Bombard

Wondrous item, very rare

This item resembles a miniature mortar: a short iron tube set into a rotating metal base, small enough to fit in a pocket. If you use an action to speak the command word and throw the mortar to a point on the ground within 15 feet of you, the mortar becomes Large. The voidmaw bombard is imbued with magic. It requires no ammunition and doesn't need to be loaded. It takes one action to aim and fire the bombard. After the bombard is fired, it reverts to its miniature form and must recharge for 1 hour before it can be used again.

Firing the voidmaw bombard lobs a sphere of crackling black energy in an arc to a point you choose within 350 feet. When the sphere strikes a horizontal surface, it expands into a 20-foot-radius, 10-foot deep, magic portal full of gnashing fangs and rending claws. Any creature in the area of the voidmaw when it expands must make a DC 15 Dexterity saving throw. On a failed save, a creature falls into the voidmaw, taking 11 (2d10) piercing damage and 11 (2d10) slashing damage. On a successful save, a creature takes half as much damage and does not fall into the voidmaw.

The voidmaw lasts for 1 minute. Creatures ending their turn within 5 feet of the voidmaw must succeed on a DC 15 Dexterity saving throw or fall into the pit. A creature that begins its turn within the voidmaw takes 2d10 piercing damage and 2d10 slashing damage. It must succeed on a DC 15 Strength (Athletics) check to pull itself out of the portal.

Voidmaw Sphere

Wondrous item, uncommon

You can use your action to throw this 1-inch-diameter black sphere up to 30 feet. When it reaches that distance, or strikes a solid surface, the sphere unfolds into a voidmaw, a 5-foot-diameter opening into the Void ringed with gnashing teeth. Each creature within 5 feet of where the voidmaw appeared must succeed on a DC 15 Dexterity saving throw or take 3d6 piercing damage. For 1 minute, any creature that begins its turn within 5 feet of the voidmaw must repeat the saving throw or take the same damage. The voidmaw sphere can unfold in a horizontal or vertical orientation, and even form in midair. When the duration ends, the voidmaw is destroyed.

CHAOS ITEMS

Those who have learned to live in harmony with the environmental chaos of the wastes can harness its power to create potent magic items. In particular, dust goblin tribes and gnome communities have turned great profits after imbuing objects with raw chaos.

Amulet of Fungal Flesh

Wondrous item, very rare (requires attunement)

A palm-sized gray and black gemstone is set into delicate-looking layers of fungus that are connected to a chain of redcap mushrooms. Despite how fragile the piece appears to be, any attempts to damage it automatically fail.

While you wear this amulet, your flesh takes on a spongy, fungus-like consistency, and you gain some of the inherent traits of the mushroom folk.

- You have resistance to bludgeoning damage from nonmagical attacks.
- You have advantage on saving throws against poison and resistance to poison damage.
- If you are in an environment with naturally occurring plants or fungi, such as a grassland, a forest, or underground, you can use your action to adjust your coloration to blend in with the local plant life. If you do so, you have advantage on Dexterity (Stealth) checks for the next 1 hour while you remain in that environment. After you have used this feature, you can't do so again until you finish a long rest.
- You are treated as a mushroom folk by other creatures of that race.

Apple of Fickle Doom

Wondrous item, very rare (requires attunement)

This crystal apple has facets like a cut gemstone, each inscribed with a small glowing rune. As an action, you can take a bite of the apple and throw it up to 60 feet. To you, the apple feels real and delicious. The bite you take grants you a random magical boon or causes a strange side-effect. Moreover, the bite determines the effect the apple has on your foes, as indicated below.

The thrown apple explodes on impact and is temporarily destroyed. Each creature within a 5-foot radius of where the apple landed must succeed on a DC 15 Wisdom saving throw or be affected by the apple's magical malediction. When you finish a short or long rest, the apple appears in your pocket or backpack.

d10	Boon	Malediction
1	You magically teleport 30 feet to an unoccupied space you can see.	Each foe is teleported 30 feet in a random direction to an unoccupied space.
2	Dramatic music highlights your actions until the end of your next turn.	Each foe sings along with the music.
3	You regain 2d20 hit points.	Each foes loses 2d20 hit points.
4	A vortex of fluttering paper birds surrounds you in a 10-foot-radius for 1 round.	Each foe takes 1d4 slashing damage from nasty paper cuts from the paper birds.
5	Until the end of your next turn, your speed increases by 10 feet.	Foes' speeds are halved until the end of their next turn.
6	An apple pie appears in your hand or at your feet.	Each foe is hit in the face by an apple pie.
7	You remove one condition.	Each foes gains one condition (1 blinded, 2 deafened, 3 frightened, 4 restrained) until the end of its next turn.
8	Nearby plants or rocks yell out helpful advice to you for 1 round.	Nearby plants or rocks mock each foe for 1 round, as per the *vicious mockery* spell.
9	You turn invisible until the end of your next turn.	Next attack on each foe has advantage.
10	You become convinced that one side of a philosophical question is the correct one.	Each foe loudly lectures about a philosophical subject of interest.

Blasted Axe

Weapon (battleaxe), very rare (requires attunement)

Sharp chunks of obsidian, suspended in a hazy field of energy around a broken wooden axe haft, make up the head of this axe. When you use a bonus action to speak the weapon's command word, the suspended stones gather themselves into the shape of an axe blade atop the haft, and you gain a +1 bonus to attack and damage rolls you make with the weapon.

When you hit a creature with this weapon, your attack deals force damage rather than slashing damage, and you can use a bonus action to embed one of the pieces of the axe blade in your target. A creature that has a piece of the axe embedded in it takes 3 (1d6) force damage at the start of each of its turns. A creature can use an action to remove an embedded piece of the axe blade from itself or another creature by making a successful DC 15 Strength check. Once it has been removed, a piece resumes its place at the end of the haft.

You can use your reaction to command an embedded piece of the axe to detonate in a wave of energy. The creature the piece is embedded in must make a DC 15 Constitution saving throw, taking 21 (6d6) force damage on a failed save, or half as much damage on a successful save. Any other creature within 5 feet of the detonation must make a DC 15 Dexterity saving throw, with the same effects as noted above.

The head of each *blasted axe* consists of twelve pieces. Unless it is detonated, an embedded piece of the axe returns to hover around the haft when the creature it is embedded in reaches 0 hit points. Each time a piece is detonated, the number of pieces remaining decreases by one. When the final piece is detonated, the haft becomes a worthless piece of wood.

Chaos Extractor

Rod, legendary (requires attunement)

This rod is fashioned from dark green metal and has a retractable claw at one end and a deep purple crystal at the other. Arcane writing can be vaguely discerned along its length. When the rod is placed on a level surface and the command word is spoken, the claw extends and grips the surface, and the crystal begins pulsing with violet light.

Absorb Spells. The chaos extractor is a powerful magical device that both attracts and absorbs chaotic energy. Any spell cast within 60 feet of the rod that has the chaos descriptor is immediately sucked into it, and the spell effect does not occur. The rod can absorb 100 levels' worth of spells before it becomes full.

As an action, while you hold the rod, you can unleash some or all of the chaotic energy trapped inside it in a 30-foot cone. Every 10 levels of energy you expend converts into 1d6 damage of a random energy type from the following list.

d6	Energy Type
1	acid
2	cold
3	fire
4	lightning
5	poison
6	necrotic

A creature can make a DC 15 Dexterity saving throw and takes half damage on a successful save.

Once you have used up all the energy inside the rod, it can no longer absorb spells.

Remove Corruption. A secondary feature of the chaos extractor is its ability to remove the corrupting effects of chaos present in soil, air, and ordinary animal and plant life within a 60-foot radius. It takes the rod 1 hour to accomplish this, whereupon the area returns to its natural state or as close to its natural state as feasibly possible. Additionally, chaotic celestials, elementals, and fiends that end their turn within 60 feet of an operational chaos extractor must make a successful DC 15 Constitution saving throw or take 1d6 necrotic damage and gain the poisoned condition. A creature recovers from the poisoned condition 1 minute after leaving the area.

After you use this feature of the rod, you can't use it again until the next dawn.

Explorer's Harness

Wondrous item, rare (requires attunement)

This harness makes the work of exploration easier.

While you wear the harness, you count as one size category larger when determining your carrying capacity and the amount of weight you can push, drag, or lift. In addition, you can use a bonus action to drink a potion or perform the Use an Object action. If you are within 5 feet of a rope that can be climbed, or a ladder, or a vertical surface that has ample hand- and footholds, you can climb 20 feet up or down as a bonus action.

Fell-hunter's Spear

Weapon (spear), rare (requires attunement)

The wooden shaft of this spear is warped and gnarled. Worn leather strips have been wrapped around it, and fetishes made of animal bones dangle from its length. The foot-long spearhead looks as though it has been chipped from amethyst.

This magic spear doesn't have the thrown and versatile properties, but it does have the heavy, reach, and two-handed properties. It deals 1d10 piercing damage on a hit.

When you hit a Large or larger creature with this spear, your target takes an extra 2d6 piercing damage. If you score a critical hit, your target must succeed on a DC 15 Constitution saving throw or be restrained until the start of your next turn. Beasts and aberrations have disadvantage on this saving throw.

Friendly Penny

Wondrous item, uncommon

This copper piece has a smiling face pressed into one side. If you give it to a creature that isn't hostile toward you, you have advantage on Charisma checks against that creature for 10 minutes.

Gaoler's Whip

Weapon, rare (requires attunement)

You gain a +1 bonus to attack and damage rolls with this weapon.

This whip has 3 charges. When you hit a creature, you can use a bonus action to expend 1 charge, which releases a jolt of stupefying energy. Your target must succeed on a DC 15 Constitution saving throw or be stunned for 1 minute. A creature can repeat the saving throw at the end of each of its turns, ending the effect on itself on a success.

Everlasting Spell Scroll

Scroll, rare (requires attunement by a sorcerer, warlock, or wizard)

Each time you unroll this spell scroll, it has a random spell inscribed on it. To determine what spell the scroll holds, roll a d10 and consult the table below. The spell is cast at the level indicated on the table.

Once you cast the spell inscribed on the scroll, the scroll rolls itself up and can't be used again until you finish a long rest.

If you choose not to cast the spell that the scroll offers, you take 1d6 psychic damage per level of the spell, and the scroll rolls itself up and can't be used again until you finish a long rest.

d10	Inscribed Spell
1	acid arrow (2nd level)
2	burning hands (1st level)
3	fireball (3rd level)
4	grease (1st level)
5	ice storm (4th level)
6	lightning bolt (3rd level)
7	ray of enfeeblement (2nd level)
8	scorching ray (2nd level)
9	slow (3rd level)
10	thunderwave (1st level)

Mail of the Waste Walker

Armor (chain mail), rare (requires attunement)

This suit of chain mail is weathered and rusty. Its links are broken in several locations, and it has no matching gauntlets.

While you wear this armor, you have a +1 bonus to AC and you ignore the effects of moving across difficult terrain.

As an action, you can permanently change a 10-foot cube of nonmagical stone to a 10-foot cube of caustic mud. If the affected stone is on the ground, the area becomes muddy enough for creatures to be caught in it. Each foot a creature moves through the area costs 4 feet of movement. A creature that starts its turn in the mud or moves into the mud for the first time on its turn takes 3d4 acid damage and must make a successful DC 15 Strength check or be restrained. A restrained creature can try to pull itself free of the mud by using an action to make another DC 15 Strength check.

If the affected stone is part of a wall or a ceiling, the mud falls to the ground. Any creature in the area where the mud falls must make a successful DC 15 Dexterity saving throw or take 2d8 bludgeoning damage.

Unless environmental conditions prevent it, the mud dries after 1 hour. Once you have used this feature of the armor, you can't do so again for 24 hours.

Manychop Axe

Weapon (any axe), rare (requires attunement)

You gain a +1 bonus to attack and damage rolls made with this magic weapon. In addition, while you are attuned to this weapon, if you score a critical hit on a target, you can immediately make an additional attack with the *manychop axe* against every target of your choice within range, with a separate attack roll for each target.

Misshapen Blade

Weapon (scimitar), rare (requires attunement)

The blade of this deformed scimitar is fashioned from iridescent green metal and has a hilt made of bone. You have a +1 bonus to attack and damage rolls when you wield this weapon.

Twisting Blade. Whenever you attack with this weapon, it seems to squirm in your hand, avoiding shields and other barriers in its path. A target does not benefit from cover except for total cover and does not add any shield bonus it might have to its AC, including the bonus from the *shield* spell.

Distorting Strike. When you score a critical hit with this weapon, the target must make a DC 15 Constitution saving throw. On a failed save, the creature's limbs warp and twist, reducing its speed by half and imposing disadvantage on its attack rolls and Dexterity saving throws for 1 minute. A creature can make a new saving throw at the end of each of its turns, ending this effect on itself on a success.

Near and Far Glass

Wondrous item, rare (requires attunement)

A tapered cylinder of thick leather, tightly fastened with silver buckles, has a crystal lens mounted at each end of the cylinder, one larger than the other. A creature that isn't attuned to the glass can use it as an ordinary spyglass.

When you are attuned to the glass and you look through the smaller lens, objects you see are magnified to 10 times their actual size. When you use the glass to look at distant vistas, you can use it to cast *clairvoyance* with a duration of 1 minute, and the sensor allows seeing but not hearing.

In addition, you can view small items as though they were 10 times larger by turning the glass around and looking through the larger lens. When you use the glass in this way, you can use it to cast the *identify* spell.

Once you have used the glass to cast one of the spells it allows, you can't do so again until the next dawn.

Ring of Anarchic Control

Ring, rare (requires attunement)

This glass ring has small imperfections in its form, including small cracks and bubbles. When you cast a spell that has the chaos descriptor while you are attuned to this ring, you gain a +2 bonus on your spell attack roll, and your spell save DC increases by 2.

In addition, whenever you roll on the Chaos Magic table (see **Chapter 6**) or any similar table while wearing this ring, you can roll twice and use the result you prefer.

Ruiner's Mattock

Weapon (maul or war pick), very rare (requires attunement)

The head of this weapon is made of marble and seems to absorb light.

You gain a +2 bonus to attack and damage rolls when you use this weapon. When you hit a construct, elemental, or undead with it, the creature takes an extra 2d8 damage of the type dealt by the weapon. If you score a critical hit against a construct, elemental, or undead, and your attack deals less than 20 damage before you add any modifiers that apply, you instead deal 20 damage plus any modifiers that apply.

Shard of Hateful Wasting

Wondrous item, rarity varies (requires attunement)

Shards of hateful wasting are the crystallized by-product of planar conflicts between the forces of order and chaos. They appear on the Material Plane in areas of fierce conflict, or in locations that have experienced a ruinous magical conflagration. Seven colors of shards exist, all roughly the size of an adult human's fist.

When you attune to a shard, it melds with your body at the location indicated and, unless you choose to end the attunement, can't be separated from you while you are alive. When you trigger your shard, you take 1d12 psychic damage that can't be reduced by any means. Unless otherwise specified, triggering the shard is an action, though many of the shards have additional effects if they are triggered again within the duration. If you die as a result of taking this damage, the shard forms a chrysalis around your body from which a **gibbering mouther** emerges after 1d4 rounds. The effects of each shard have a duration of 1 minute. You can only be attuned to one *shard of hateful wasting* at a time.

Amber (Rare). This shard melds into your jaw. When you trigger this shard, your mouth widens and fills with jagged teeth. For the duration, you can use your bonus action to make a bite attack that deals 1d6 piercing damage and you become immune to poison. When you make a bite attack, you can trigger your shard again to deal an extra 2d6 piercing damage.

Blue (Rare). This shard melds into your crown. When you trigger this shard, you have advantage on ability checks and saving throws for the duration. If you make a roll of 9 or lower on the d20, you can trigger the shard again to treat your roll as a 10.

Green (Very Rare). This shard melds into your chest. When you trigger this shard, one creature that you can see within 30 feet of you must succeed on a DC 17 Wisdom saving throw or become charmed by you for the duration. If you are hit by another creature, the creature you have charmed must use its turn to move within range of your attacker and make a spell attack or weapon attack against it. If you are attacked by multiple creatures, the creature you have charmed can choose which of those creatures it attacks. Each time the creature you have charmed takes damage, it can make a new saving throw, overcoming the shard's effect on a success. If the creature you have charmed is hit, you can trigger the shard again as a reaction to give it disadvantage on its saving throw to overcome the shard's effect.

Orange (Uncommon). This shard melds into your brow. When you trigger this shard, for the duration, you gain proficiency on Intelligence (Investigation) and Wisdom (Perception) checks, as well as on ability checks you make with thieves' tools. If you already have one of these proficiencies, your proficiency bonus is doubled when you make an ability check with it. You can trigger your shard again to have advantage on saving throws against traps and natural hazards, such as avalanches.

Pink (Very Rare). This shard melds into your throat. When you trigger this shard, you have advantage on melee attack rolls for the duration and, when you deal damage, you can roll one of the damage dice twice and take the higher result. When you're hit with an attack, you can trigger your shard as a reaction to make a melee attack against the creature that hit you and deal an extra 2d8 damage on a hit.

Purple. (Very Rare). This shard melds into the base of your spine. When you trigger this shard, each creature of your choice within 30 feet of you must succeed on a DC 16 Wisdom saving throw or be charmed by you for the duration. If you take damage while the shard is in effect, each creature that has been charmed by you takes 2d12 psychic damage. If you take damage, you can trigger the shard again as a reaction to add the amount of damage you take from triggering it to the amount of psychic damage taken by the creatures you have charmed.

Yellow (Very Rare). This shard melds into your stomach. When you trigger this shard, for the duration, creatures you hit with melee or ranged attacks gain 1 level of exhaustion in addition to the damage you deal. When you hit with an attack roll, you can trigger your shard again to halve your target's speed until the end of its next turn.

Skulls of Nogg

Wondrous item, varies (requires attunement)

Named after an ogre magi warlord who terrorized the wastes for several decades and was infamous for his collection of skulls, these objects look like normal human, elf, or orc skulls constructed out of semiprecious stone. The saving throw DC for any spell cast from a skull is DC 15.

Amber Skull (Rare). While holding this yellow skull, you have resistance to psychic damage and you can cast *suggestion* from it once per day.

Garnet Skull (Uncommon). This red skull protects you from bleeding effects. While holding it, you can cast *cure wounds* (at 3rd level) from it once per day.

Iolite Skull (Rare). While holding this dark purple skull, you have resistance to necrotic damage and you can cast *death ward* from it once per day.

Jade Skull (Very Rare). While holding this greenish skull, you have immunity to the paralyzed condition and you can cast *hold monster* from it once per day.

Slinger's Belt

Wondrous item, uncommon (requires attunement)

The ostentatious gold buckle of this leather belt portrays a trio of hummingbirds in flight.

While you are wearing this belt, you can roll a d4 and add the number rolled to any Dexterity (Sleight of Hand) checks you make. Furthermore, on your turn you can draw a weapon or object, or a combination of the two, into each of your hands without using an action.

Surly Gnoll's Friend

Weapon (flail), rare (requires attunement)

The spiked end of this flail is roughly the size of a halfling's head.

While you are wielding this weapon, you add your proficiency bonus to your Charisma (Intimidation) checks. If you already have proficiency in that skill, you add double your proficiency bonus. When you hit a humanoid of your size or smaller with an attack using this weapon, you can use your bonus action to make a Charisma (Intimidation) check against it contested by its Wisdom saving throw. On a successful check, the creature becomes frightened of you until the end of your next turn. Once a creature has been frightened in this way, it is immune to further uses of this feature for 24 hours.

Tightrope Crossbow

Weapon (any crossbow), rare (requires attunement)

You gain a +1 bonus to attack and damage rolls when using this weapon. When you hit a construct or a plant creature, the target takes an additional 1d8 piercing damage.

When you hit a target within normal range with an attack using this crossbow, you can affix the head of the bolt to your target by using your reaction to speak a command word. Once the bolt is affixed, a flat plane of 1-foot-wide, slightly shimmering force stretches between the projectile and the weapon. You can affix the crossbow to an unattended object or to the ground by using a bonus action to speak a second command word.

You can walk across the plane of force without difficulty. Other creatures can walk across it by succeeding at a DC 12 Dexterity (Acrobatics) check.

A creature that has a bolt affixed to it can pull it off by using its action and making a successful DC 16 Strength check. Once the crossbow has been affixed to an object or the ground, it can be removed from that anchor point only when you use a bonus action to speak the command word again.

Vagabond's Cup

Wondrous item, uncommon

This wooden tankard is banded in brass and has a solid brass handle.

When you place your hand on the handle of this tankard and say the phrase, "Please let me wet my parched throat," it fills to the brim with liquid. Roll a d10 and refer to the Vagabond's Cup table to see what type of liquid has filled the cup. Once you have used the cup, you can't do so again for 1 hour.

VAGABOND'S CUP

d10	Beverage
1–2	Clean, cold water
3	Wine
4	Goat's milk
5	Scalding hot water that tastes of peppermint. When you drink this, you recover 1 Hit Die.
6	Vinegar
7	Ale
8	Murky brackish water
9	Bitter, hot, dark beverage. When you drink this, you have advantage on the first initiative check you make within the next four hours.
10	Mead

Wand of Bedlam

Wand, rare (requires attunement)

This wand has 7 charges. While holding it, you can use an action to expend 1 or more of its charges to cast one of the spells listed on the Wand of Bedlam table.

The likelihood of casting the spell you want from the wand increases with the number of charges you expend to cast the spell. If you expend 1 charge, roll a d10 and consult the table to determine which spell you cast. If you expend more than 1 charge, state which spell you would like to cast and roll a d10 for each charge you expend. If one of the d10 rolls corresponds to the spell you want to cast, you cast the lowest level version of that spell. If more than one of the d10 rolls corresponds to the spell you want to cast, you cast that spell as though it was cast using a spell slot equal to the number of dice rolls that correspond to its table entry, if it is possible to cast the spell using a higher spell slot.

If you expend multiple charges and none of the d10 rolls correspond to the table entry of the spell you want to cast, you instead cast the lowest level of one of the spells corresponding to one of the other d10s rolled.

The wand regains 1d6 + 1 expended charges daily at dawn. If you expend the wand's last charge, roll a d20. On a 1, the wand crumbles into dust and is destroyed. On a 20, the wand regains all of its charges.

WAND OF BEDLAM

d10	Spell Cast
1	arcane eye
2	charm person
3	color spray
4	disguise self
5	fireball
6	hideous laughter
7	locate object
8	protection from evil and good
9	shatter
10	stinking cloud

Wastelander's All-Terrain Wagon

Wondrous item, very rare

These carts are highly sought after by those who regularly travel inhospitable lands. The worn and graying wood of the cart is patched with scrap metal, wire, and some unidentifiable adhesive. All four of the wheels are steel-shod and the rear ones are oversized. The contact surfaces of the wheels are spiked, either to improve the wagon's grip on the terrain or to better crush victims beneath it. The wagon's flanks are protected by battered shields, and rusty shards of metal jut from the vehicle at odd angles to deter attackers from trying to climb aboard. Three 4-foot-long, perpetually smoking tubes stacked atop each other are affixed to each side of the wagon.

The cart has 4 charges. While seated in the wagon, one of its riders can use an action to expend 1 of the charges to perform one of the following exploits.

Levitate. The wagon and everything inside it rise vertically, up to 100 feet, and remain suspended there for 10 minutes. While levitating, the wagon can move laterally only by being pushed or pulled against a fixed object. At the end of the duration, the wagon floats gently to the ground if it is still aloft.

Spider Climb. The wagon can drive up, down, and across vertical and horizontal surfaces, as well as upside-down along ceilings for 1 hour. While this mode is engaged, a field of magical force prevents riders and cargo from falling out of the wagon.

Summon Goats. The spectral goats that pull the wagon appear in their harness and remain there for 8 hours. If the goats aren't in their harness, the wagon can only move if it's pushed. Living animals that are harnessed to the wagon teleport to the nearest empty space, unsecured and unharmed.

Water Walk. The wagon gains the ability to move across any liquid surface as if it was harmless solid ground for 10 minutes. Surfaces that can damage the wagon, such as acid or lava, do so. If the wagon becomes submerged in a liquid, it bobs to the surface at a rate of 60 feet per round.

The *wastelander's wagon* has the following statistics:

Wastelander's All-Terrain Wagon

Huge Vehicle (15 ft. by 15 ft.)

CREATURE CAPACITY 1 pilot, 1 navigator, 4 passengers
CARGO CAPACITY 1,000 pounds
TRAVEL PACE 6 miles per hour (48 miles per day)

STR	DEX	CON	INT	WIS	CHA
20 (+5)	6 (−2)	18 (+4)	4 (−3)	10 (+0)	5 (−3)

DAMAGE RESISTANCES piercing and slashing from nonmagical attacks
DAMAGE IMMUNITIES poison, psychic
CONDITION IMMUNITIES blinded, charmed, deafened, exhaustion, frightened, incapacitated, paralyzed, petrified, poisoned, prone, stunned, unconscious

ACTIONS

On its turn, the wagon can take 3 actions, choosing from the options below. It can take only 2 actions if it has no passengers, and only 1 action if it only has a pilot. If the wagon is unmanned, it can't take any actions. A creature that takes one of the wagon's actions expends their own action to do so.

Fire Cannon. A passenger or the navigator can fire one of the wagon's cannons.

Ram. The pilot can direct one of the wagon's spectral goats to ram a creature.

Move. The pilot or navigator can direct the goats to move.

Enable Movement Mode. The pilot, navigator, or a passenger can expend 1 charge to activate one of the wagon's forms of movement.

CHASSIS

ARMOR CLASS 15
HIT POINTS 100 (damage threshold 15)

CONTROL: TACK AND HARNESS

ARMOR CLASS: 16
HIT POINTS: 50

Move up to the speed of the wheels with one 60-degree turn. If the harness is destroyed, the wagon can't turn.

MOVEMENT: SPECTRAL GOAT

ARMOR CLASS: 11
HIT POINTS: 90; (−30 ft. speed per 45 damage taken)
SPEED: 60 ft.

Ram. *Melee Weapon Attack:* +5 to hit, reach 5 ft., one target. *Hit:* 10 (3d6) bludgeoning damage. If the target is a creature of Large size or smaller, it must make a DC 15 Strength saving throw or be knocked prone.

MOVEMENT: WHEELS

ARMOR CLASS: 13

HIT POINTS: 80 (damage threshold 10); −15 ft. speed per 20 damage taken

The wagon ignores the effects of difficult terrain.

WEAPON: CANNON (6; RECHARGE 6)

ARMOR CLASS: 13

HIT POINTS: 50

Ranged Weapon Attack: +5 to hit, range 90/320 ft., one target. *Hit:* 16 (3d10) bludgeoning damage. Creatures within 5 feet of the target must make a DC 15 Dexterity saving throw or take 5 (1d10) bludgeoning damage.

Wastelander's All-Encompassing Portable Lodging

Wondrous item, very rare (requires attunement)

In its compact form, this item looks like a rolled-up scroll of yellowing parchment. When unrolled, one side of the roll shows what appears to be a blueprint for a cabin.

When you use an action to unroll the parchment on the ground and speak its command word, a log domicile rapidly appears amid a cacophony of chopping, sawing, and hammering. The domicile is large enough to comfortably hold eight Medium-sized humanoids and their gear and is comprised of a common room with a fireplace and food preparation area, a dormitory holding four sets of bunk beds, and a lavatory with a basin full of ever-clean water. Attached to the lodging is a stable with stalls for eight horses and space for a cart or wagon. There are no windows or exterior doors in the domicile.

When the lodging is erected, you and any friendly creatures of your choice within 30 feet of you appear inside it: humanoids appear in the common room, and mounts appear, one to a stall, in the stable. Your vehicle appears inside the stable as well, as long as it is no larger than a wagon. While the lodging is in use, the parchment lies flat on a small table in the dormitory. To exit the lodging, simply roll the blueprint back up.

The interior of the lodging is always clean, dry, and comfortable. Environmental effects outside the lodging, such as sandstorms or volcanic eruptions have no effect on its interior, though you may have to deal with them when you exit. Dirt and debris are magically swept away each time the lodging is stored. If an object is left inside the lodging when it is stored, there's a 50 percent chance it disappears and is lost in the Astral Plane.

To exit the lodging, you must roll up the parchment and speak the command word. You and all other occupants of the lodging appear in the spaces you occupied before you entered it. Creatures that were hitched to your cart when you erected the lodging are hitched to it once again when you exit.

Wastelander's All-Environment Protective Suit

Armor (studded leather), rare (requires attunement)

This rugged suit of studded leather armor is reinforced with steel bands at the knees, elbows, neck, and stomach, and includes a close-faced helmet, gloves, and sturdy boots. It seems to be molded to the form of its wearer.

While you wear this armor, you gain the following benefits:

- You have a +1 bonus to your Armor Class.
- You have darkvision to a range of 60 feet.
- You can tap your head as a bonus action, lighting a headlamp on your helmet that illuminates as a bullseye lantern. You can tap your head again to put the light out.
- You can add your proficiency bonus to Strength (Athletics) checks.

As a bonus action, you can speak the armor's command word to seal it and gain the following features for 1 hour:

- You have an independent air supply that renders you immune to drowning and disease, as well as contact and inhaled poisons.
- You have resistance to acid, cold, and fire damage.

Once you have activated these features, you can't do so again until the next dawn.

Wastelander's All-Knowing Protective Device

Wondrous item, very rare (requires attunement)

This skullcap has a core of steel bands sandwiched between a durable boiled leather exterior and comfortable silken interior. While you wear the skullcap, you have a +1 bonus to your Armor Class.

The skullcap has 2 charges. When a creature makes a critical hit against you, you can use your reaction to expend 1 charge. When you do so, you can move 5 feet to an empty space and avoid taking damage from the attack.

You can use an action to expend 2 charges to cast *detect thoughts*.

The skullcap regains any expended charges at dawn.

Wastelander's All-Purpose Tool

Wondrous item, uncommon

This series of linked metal tubes, compartments, and flaps can be folded and twisted into several useful tools for the oft-encumbered wasteland traveler. In its compact form, it weighs 4 pounds and can easily be carried in one hand or stowed in a pack.

As an action, you can adjust the tubes and flaps to allow the all-purpose tool to function as one of the following:

- Carpenter's tools
- Crowbar
- Lamp
- Manacles
- Portable Ram
- Tinker's tools
- Thieves' tools

While using the all-purpose tool, you can use a bonus action to gain advantage on an ability check. Once you have done so, you can't do so again until the following morning at dawn.

Wastelander's All-Seeing Almanac

Wondrous item, very rare (requires attunement by a cleric, druid, or wizard)

When you open this book, loose pages seem to float out and disappear. When you examine it, however, none of the pages appears to be missing.

While this book is on your person, the following spells are added to your spell list: *augury, detect magic, detect poison and disease, divination,* and *locate animals or plants*.

You can cast these spells as rituals with a reduced casting time of 1 minute and requiring no material components. Using the book, you can cast *commune* or *commune with nature* as a ritual, but you can't do so again until dawn on the seventh day following the last casting.

Well-Rested Traveler's Boots

Wondrous item, very rare (requires attunement)

These leather boots look like they've seen a lot of use.

While you are wearing these boots, you regain all your expended Hit Dice when you finish a long rest.

Zoantharian Staff

Staff, uncommon

This staff appears to be made from black wood with a twisting design, but looking closer, it becomes clear that it is actually eight black tentacles braided together. You can use an action to speak this staff's command word and plant one end of the staff upon the ground. A magical tentacle bursts from the ground in the space occupied by one creature you can see within 30 feet.

The target must make a DC 13 Dexterity saving throw or take 2d6 bludgeoning damage and be restrained. At the start of each of its turns, the target takes an additional 2d6 bludgeoning damage and at the end of each of its turns, the target can attempt another DC 13 Dexterity saving throw, ending the effect on a success. Maintaining the tentacle's hold on a target requires the wielder to maintain concentration.

VRIL ITEMS

An ancient island people flourished for thousands of years as the first human civilization. Gifted this progress by their strange masters, the aboleths, this civilization also inherited an unearthly and primitive science-magic known as vril. Vril technology—that elusive, primitive magical force so naturally wielded by the ancients—is highly prized. New discoveries are made every day by those who mine the ancient ruins of the wastes, but the devastating effects of time have left most of these as barely worth recording. Still, as more and more technologies are unearthed and those who study them learn to replicate them, forgotten vril-powered items have begun to resurface.

HARNESSING VRIL

The key to vril technology is, at its core, a reaction between vril fluid and an arcane-infused alloy of gold and copper called orichalcum. This reaction produces volatile energy that can be channeled through various materials to produce electricity, raw force, or even vitalizing rays of energy. Without proper precautions, the technology can be hazardous, and as both materials are scarce, only the most intelligent, powerful, and resourceful can work with it.

ORICHALCUM

This mystical, manufactured metal only exists in fragments and recovered pieces, taken from ancient wrecks and ruins in the wastelands and other remote areas of the world. Orichalcum is a lighter-than-steel, extremely durable, copper-gold alloy with a reddish-gold tint once used in the manufacture of armor, weapons, and powerful items. Typically, this equates to 50% less weight.

Weapons and armor made primarily from orichalcum have the following properties:

- Heavy weapons lose the heavy property.
- One-handed weapons are considered to be light and gain the finesse property.
- Weapons with the light property gain advantage on damage rolls from critical hits.
- Most light armors do not contain enough orichalcum to change their properties.
- Medium armor loses any disadvantage to stealth.
- Heavy armor no longer has Strength requirements and loses any disadvantage to stealth.
- Shields crafted of orichalcum reduce any lightning damage their wielders suffer by 5.

Most consider orichalcum items priceless, but the value of the metal used in creation adds 3,000 gp to the cost, if one knew how to create it.

VRIL BATTERIES

These long, cylindrical glass jars contain alternating discs of copper and orichalcum suspended in a briny alchemical solution and are needed to power vril weapons and other artifacts. The jars are sealed with filigreed brass end caps with short terminals and thumbscrews that allow for the attachment of all manner of devices. Newly charged batteries contain 50 charges and attached devices consume this power at different rates. Efforts to reproduce them have thus far resulted in failure.

RECHARGING VRIL BATTERIES

One of the most closely guarded secrets among the vril scholars is how they can repair and recharge vril batteries. Without direct arcane assistance, the process is lengthy and expensive, often costing 1,000 gp to replace the metal plates and solution, called vril fluid, in a standard 50-charge battery. A vril battery requires 1 ounce of vril fluid for every 10 charges it holds. It also requires pure orichalcum and other supplies worth 200 gp.

An engineer proficient in vril engineer's tools (see below) can spend an hour per ounce of vril fluid required, using a complete set of vril engineer's tools, to recharge a vril battery. The engineer cannot gain the benefits of a rest during this time.

REPAIRING VRIL TECHNOLOGY

If an engineer wishes to repair a damaged or incomplete piece of vril weaponry or armor, they must first gather the necessary parts. Assuming a market is available to purchase such things, they tend to mimic the cost of creating a magic item of similar rarity. (The GM may modify the cost of parts needed based on how extensive the damage to the piece is.) Repairing the item itself is a long, laborious, and sometimes dangerous task, taking an hour for every 500 gp in value to repair the piece. The engineer must have access to a vril laboratory complete with vril engineer's tools, smith's tools, and alchemist's supplies. The engineer can work no more than 8 hours a day and 40 hours a week without gaining a level of exhaustion. At the end of this time, the vril item, armor, or weapon is fully functioning again. Vril artifacts cannot be repaired in this way without using a *wish* spell.

VRIL ITEMS

Examples of rediscovered vril technology run the gamut from powerful rifles that fire bursts of plasma like energy to lightning-charged shields and armor and other unusual items. Although technological rather than magical, these items should be treated as rare treasures. This section presents an assortment of example vril items.

ARC THROWER

This heavy device is slung around your shoulders, hanging near your waist. It features a massive array of orichalcum-filigreed glass tubes filled with a softly glowing blue liquid that converge on a copper tube extending a meter out the front, and the tip holds a jagged piece of crystal. One hand must operate a rear triggering mechanism, and the other supports and aims from a handle sticking out of the top while calibrating the arc emissions. The arc thrower requires two vril batteries to operate, and each use drains 2 charges from each battery. As an action, you may activate the arc thrower, which then creates a blast of arcing electrical energy originating from the crystal. Each creature within a 30-foot cone must make a Dexterity saving throw with a DC equal to 8 + your dexterity modifier + your proficiency bonus if you are proficient in vril weaponry. On a failed save, a target takes 3d6 lightning damage and is stunned. On a successful save, a target takes half as much damage and suffers no additional effects.

BOOMFIST

This heavy, articulated gauntlet of orichalcum and lead is laced with wires that terminate in copper knuckle plates. Just behind the hand of the gauntlet is a housing for a vril battery. You cannot wield a weapon in the same hand, and you automatically fail any Dexterity checks that require the use of your hand. Making a successful unarmed attack with a boomfist allows you to spend 1 charge from the installed vril battery to add 1d12 lightning damage to your normal unarmed damage. You must then wait for 1 round to do this again so that the boomfist can recharge.

CAPACITOR SPEAR

This heavy spear is made of orichalcum-laced steel and features a housing at the base of its head to accept a vril battery. This weapon functions as a normal spear.

In addition, as a reaction when you are subjected to lightning damage, you may divert half the damage suffered into the spear. For every 5 damage so diverted, rounded down, you recharge 1 charge of the attached vril battery. If overcharged, make a Dexterity saving throw with a DC equal to 10 + the number of charges overcharged. (You can add your proficiency bonus to your saving throw if you are proficient with vril weapons.) If you fail, the battery explodes, and everyone within 5 feet of the spear takes 2d6 lightning damage. The spear cannot be used until it has been repaired. Overcharged charges are lost.

DISINTEGRATION RAY

This sleek, pistol-like weapon of polished orichalcum was found sealed in a vault deep beneath what was believed to have once been a military general's estate. It was tested once by those who discovered it to devastating results. That night, the entire archaeology team disappeared along with the weapon. Its current whereabouts are unknown.

You can connect a vril battery to this weapon, and each use drains 50 charges from the attached battery. If the battery has fewer than 50 charges, the weapon does not activate, and the battery is irrevocably destroyed, all valuable parts being converted to lead. If the battery is drained to 0 charges, it is similarly destroyed. Successfully activating the weapon causes a white-hot blast of electrified plasma to spring from the barrel to a range of 60 feet. A creature targeted by this must make a Dexterity saving throw against a DC equal to 10 + your dexterity modifier + your proficiency bonus if you are proficient in vril weapons. On a failed save, the target takes 6d12 + 30 force damage. The target is disintegrated if this damage leaves it with 0 hit points.

A disintegrated creature, including everything nonmagical it is wearing or holding, is reduced to a softly glowing pile of blue ash. Only a *true resurrection* or *wish* spell can restore the creature to life. Magic items are unaffected by this ray, but any Large or smaller nonmagical object is automatically disintegrated. Huge or larger objects lose a 10-foot-radius sphere of mass originating from the point struck. This ray does not affect magical forces, such as the wall created by a *wall of force* spell.

DUAL-CHARGE RIFLE

This vril device fires wooden darts infused with vril liquid. The rifle requires two vril batteries. Each shot costs 1 charge from each battery and a wooden dart, fed by an internal magazine of eight darts. One of the batteries powers the firing mechanism and the other infuses the ammunition. The vril dual-charge rifle can infer your intent when fired, requiring a certain amount of focus, and thus the vril dual-charge rifle can only ever be fired once per round. On a successful ranged attack, the dart explodes in a spray of sparks and the target takes 2d6 lightning damage.

You may also instead shoot an ally. On a successful ranged attack, the dart infuses its vril energy into the ally, who regains 1d6 hit points. An ally who understands the nature of the rifle—and is aware of their ally attempting to shoot them with it—may use their reaction to allow the ally's attack to succeed automatically.

FULMINATOR ROD

This short bar of carved orichalcum houses a vril battery and is tipped with two reinforced copper tines. On a successful melee attack, which consumes 1 charge from the attached vril battery, the target takes 1d6 lightning and 1d6 thunder damage. The explosion of electrical energy can be heard up to 300 feet away.

ORICHALCUM PROSTHETIC

Complex clockworks have been available for a long time that could mimic the movements and responsiveness of natural appendages when driven by magic, but these rare items are only available to those with great money and resources. However, developers have found a way to link vril directly to a

NEW VRIL WEAPONS

Item	Cost	Damage	Weight	Properties
Melee Weapons				
Boomfist	1,000 gp	Unarmed + 1d12 lightning	5 lb.	Light
Capacitor spear	1,000 gp	1d6 piercing	5 lb.	Thrown (range 20/60), Versatile (1d8)
Fulminator rod	1,000 gp	1d6 lightning, 1d6 thunder	2 lb.	Light
Vril saber	2,000 gp	1d12 Force	2 lb.	Light, Finesse
Ranged Weapons				
Arc thrower	8,000 gp	3d6 lightning	25 lb.	30 ft cone, Two-Handed
Disintegration ray	10,000 gp	See description	3 lb.	Loading, see description
Dual-charge rifle	6,000 gp	2d6 lightning or 1d6 healing	10 lb.	Ammunition (range 30/90), Loading, Two-handed
Thunderbuss	5,000 gp	2d6 piercing	12 lb.	Ammunition (range 20/60), Loading, Two-handed

NEW VRIL EQUIPMENT

Item	Cost	Weight
Rejuvenation table	10,000 gp	500 lb.
Orichalcum prosthetic	1,000 gp	As limb
Vril engineer's tools (artisan's tools)	50 gp	10 lb.

conscious mind to power often beautifully crafted prosthetics. Fine woods infused with vril liquid, encased in a framework of orichalcum filigree, are crafted to match the size and shape of the lost limb. A vril craftsperson can spend 8 hours fitting and tuning one of these devices to a single creature missing a limb. Once fitted for such a device, this nonmagical prosthetic moves and behaves as the lost limb once did. It can be attached or removed as an action, and damage to it heals while it is worn as living tissue normally would.

REJUVENATION TABLE

Some scholars have discovered that vril is useful for more than triggering blasts of lightning or plasma, that it has links to the energy inside every living thing. One of the results of this discovery, for which the wealthy local patrons pay richly to develop, is the rejuvenation table. This Large casket-like device is linked via tubes and wires to a series of pumps, dials, and other strange electrical devices, including four spots to attach the vril batteries required to operate the table. One Medium or smaller creature may lie in the casket at a time. The rejuvenation table has three functions:

- You may spend 10 charges from each attached battery (40 total) to allow the user inside the casket to experience the effects of a short rest in 1 minute.
- You may spend 25 charges from each attached battery (100 total) to allow the user inside the casket to experience the effects of a long rest in 1 hour. Spellcasters that use this function retain the same spells they prepared at their last long rest.
- You may spend 50 charges from each attached battery (200 total) and irreversibly destroy the attached batteries to regrow a lost limb on a still-living creature.

THUNDERBUSS

When refining the coil rifle to a working condition, some enterprising engineers took the initial design and sought to improve upon it. Instead of using the coils to launch a ferromagnetic projectile directly, they created a crossbow-like device that used the energy of an attached vril battery to launch whatever happened to be at hand.

You must plug the thunderbuss into a vril battery to fire it. Each shot fired uses 1 charge from the battery and destroys its ammunition. For ammunition, you may use a bonus action to jam a handful of any rigid, non-combustible, nonmagical material, such as pebbles, nails, or the like, into the receiver compartment.

VRIL ENGINEER'S TOOLS

These artisan's tools include ratchets, lubricants, wire tools, and other implements needed to work with vril-powered clockworks and machinery. Proficiency with these tools lets you add your proficiency bonus to any ability checks you make to understand or repair vril technology. Also, proficiency with these tools is required to recharge vril batteries.

VRIL SABER

This intricate, hilt-like device is made of orichalcum and has a compartment that allows the housing of a vril battery. Assuming the attached battery has at least 1 charge, you may activate or deactivate the saber as a bonus action, causing a 3-foot electric-blue beam of arcing plasma to emerge from the hilt. The energy blade deals 1d12 force damage on a hit, draining 1 charge from the attached battery each time. The blade is hot enough to burn or melt nonmagical materials on contact (the details of which are left to the GM's discretion). Rolling a natural 1 on an attack with the vril saber means you've overestimated the weightless nature of the blade and struck yourself, suffering the damage.

Other Lost Technology Items

Aurora Candle

Wondrous item, uncommon

This foot-long metal tube is etched with thin blue lines that seem to shimmer faintly. One end of the tube is hollow, and the other ends in a transparent reservoir containing a swirling greenish-yellow mist. As an action, you can activate the aurora candle, firing a cloud of shimmering mist and light into the air in a 40-foot sphere. Creatures in this area must succeed on a DC 12 Wisdom saving throw or be charmed for 1 minute. While charmed by this effect, the creature is incapacitated and has a speed of 0. At the end of each of its turns, an affected creature can repeat the saving throw, ending the effect on a success.

The effect ends for an affected creature if it succeeds on its saving throw, if it takes any damage, or if someone else uses an action to shake the creature out of its stupor. Once it is used, the aurora candle crumbles to dust.

Lightning Emitter

Wondrous item, very rare

This item is a remnant of an ancient technology not clearly understood today. It resembles a copper rod topped by a glowing crystal attached by a flexible metal tube to a clamp-like device studded with crystal cocoons containing crackling lightning clouds. The lightning emitter has two main parts:

- **Conduction Harness.** The clamp-like device is large enough to fit around the torso of any Medium- or smaller-sized creature. Attaching or detaching the clamp requires an action. Two straps on the harness allow it to be secured firmly. The wielder can attach the harness to itself or to another creature.

- **Emitter Rod.** The crystal-topped emitter rod can be wielded like a traditional magic rod and requires an action to activate. The metal tube connecting the rod to the harness appears to be 2 feet long but automatically extends up to 20 feet as needed.

As an action, you can expend 1 charge and use the lightning emitter to project a bolt of lightning as a ranged weapon attack. The lightning forms a line 5 feet wide that extends out from you to a target within 80 feet. Each creature in the line excluding the target must succeed on a DC 13 Dexterity saving throw, taking 4d6 lightning damage on a failed save and half as much damage on a successful one. If the target is hit, it takes 1d10 thunder damage and 6d6 lightning damage.

Ammunition. The lightning emitter has 1 charge and recovers all expended charges daily at dawn. If the conduction harness is attached to a living creature, you can use an attack action to drain 2d6 hit points from the creature and fire the weapon again.

Mining Charge

Wondrous item, rare

This item is a fist-sized, unadorned metal sphere with a seam running around the circumference. As an action, you can twist the upper and lower halves of the sphere in different directions and throw it up to 60 feet. The sphere detonates on impact. Each living creature and unattended magical item within a 5-foot radius must succeed on a DC 12 Dexterity saving throw, taking 4d6 force damage on a failed save or half as much damage on a successful one. Stone and non-living wood (such as a door or chest) within the area is turned into fine dust.

Sentinel Orb

Wondrous item, uncommon

This fruit-sized metal sphere resembles a stylized mechanical eye with a crystal pupil. When you speak the activation word, the sentinel orb levitates to a height you choose and monitors a 20-foot-radius area for up to 10 hours. The orb sounds an alarm if any creature of Small size or larger enters the area during its watch. You can set the orb's alarm to have any volume between a soft chime and a clanging alarm. The orb monitors the area until its duration ends or you use the activation word again, whereupon the orb floats gently to the ground. Once you use the sentinel orb, you must wait 5 hours before using it again.

Shotcaster

Weapon, rare (requires attunement)

This strange weapon resembles a flattened metal barrel festooned with an array of crystals, tubes, and technology attached to a metal, hinged cuff designed to clamp on the wrist. If you are attuned to a shotcaster, the weapon looks like a fanciful metal bracer. The barrel of the weapon extends and retracts as part of an Attack action. Characters who have proficiency with martial ranged weapons have proficiency with a shotcaster.

Firing the Shotcaster. When you fire the shotcaster, it projects a bolt of energy at a target. The shotcaster deals 2d6 radiant damage, has a range of 40/120 and weighs 1 lb. The shotcaster links to your neural system as part of the attunement process, producing a number of charges equal to your proficiency bonus when you finish a short or long rest. Each shot you fire expends 1 charge.

Overcharging. As part of an Attack action, you can expend one or more additional charges while firing a shotcaster. Each charge after the first charge increases the damage by 1d6. You must decide to overcharge a shot before making the attack action.

Shrouding Belt

Wondrous item, rare

This dark leather belt is secured by an oval silver buckle set with a reddish-gold metal dial. The belt has 3 charges and regains 1d3 expended charges daily at dawn. While wearing the belt, you can use an action to turn the dial and activate one of the following functions:

- *Optical Masking Field (1 charge).* For 1 minute, light partially bends around your body. Any creature has disadvantage on Wisdom (Perception) checks made to see you. Moreover, the first melee or ranged attack made on you each round has disadvantage. However, if the attack is successful, the optical masking field ends.
- *Auditory Dampening Field (2 charges).* For 10 minutes, you can't create or make any sound. Items in your possession do not make sounds, but objects you interact with may still make sounds. For example, firing a crossbow would be silent, but the bolt hitting a target would not be.
- *Observation Scattering Field (3 charges).* For 8 hours, you can't be targeted by any divination magic or perceived through magical scrying sensors.

APPENDIX: MIDGARD LORE

While Midgard abounds with settled regions rife with political and social intrigue, with conflicts of inhabitants and the ambitions of the powerful, it also hosts warped landscapes. This appendix highlights regions of Chaos Wastes in the Midgard campaign setting.

WASTED WEST: WESTERN WILDERNESSES

Starting in the western edge of the midlands, arcane battlefields litter the west-central region of the Wasted West. The consequences of the Great Mage War means even 400 years haven't yet healed these ancient magical wounds. These are some of the most significant.

CASSILON

The former capital of the Sun Kingdom suffered badly in the blaze that engulfed it following its sack by the automata devil Bazios. Nearly 80% of the city burned, although the outer wall survived. The hill giants who fled and later returned built a smaller, ramshackle community inside the breached wall and its wells; its greatest artisans died defending the city. Refugees incorporated partially burned timbers into many new buildings, but the whole area still has great swaths of land scorched and blackened by hellfire, where nothing grows.

MOLOVOSCH

Knocked from the sky as a Great Old One sundered the Cobalt Tower, the crash of Molovosch carved a seven-mile gash leading to a deep crater, where the city skipped like a stone before coming to its final rest. The impact affected structures unevenly; some were reduced to crumpled piles of rubble while others landed nearly intact or slightly tilted. Fighting persisted, even after it landed, as surviving archmagi tried killing Ornis Ammos. Stories claim the tunnels within its earth mote still hold intact, unplundered treasure vaults of the magocracy's elite.

PILLARS OF UXLOON

Enkada Pishtuhk swore revenge after the Isonade devastated the shores of Bemmea. In revenge, he summoned Pah'druugsthlai and marched on Uxloon. Between its massive, corrupting claws and various arachnid-like spawn, over a week the city of nearly 90,000 was reduced to marble debris, open foundations, and a solitary structure surrounded by three glowing monoliths. Pah'druugsthlai refused to touch the Pillars of Uxloon, and the lonely building remains safe to this day.

WASTED WEST: GOBLIN WASTES

The result of the scorched-earth campaigns of the magocracies, the eastern regions of the Wasted West suffer from magically induced destruction. Acid rains, boneshard sleet, gravity quakes, and zombie fog contribute to creating widespread wastelands.

FLENSING GULCH

This series of interconnected slot canyons provides a shorter, less exposed route for pilgrims traveling to the Seat of Mavros. Unfortunately, these badlands suffer from intense winds capable of stripping flesh and creating soul-hungering boneshard wraiths. A nearby dust goblin tribe venerates the wraiths as ancestors, attacking anyone entering the canyons from the north or northeast. This aggression forces pilgrims to try lesser-known routes, suffering a greater risk of winds.

ROATGARD FOREST

This polluted blight also suffers from the circle of demented druids with poisoned minds, bent on restoring the forest by transforming people into trees bearing the screaming visages of the former travelers. Enabled by their fellow druids in humanoid form, the Roatgard only grows larger with each season. Whether or not this living filter cleanses the earth within the forest of the magocracies' magical pollution remains unclear, but its cruelty is undeniable.

ADDITIONAL SITES

Several discrete locales that qualify as wastes lie beyond the obvious destruction of the Wasted West.

FELLMIRE SWAMP

South of Maillon, the Fellmire expands outward a few yards a year, the result of springs tainted by a dumped slurry of failed potion-making and other experiments. This provides benefits the city's leadership values enough to leave it unremedied. First, it acts as an enormous defensive moat and buffer, making the idea of any army approaching from the south a ludicrous thought as it would be exposed to the dangerous effects of the swamp before ever arriving. Second, creatures captured from the swamp often have useful alchemical properties, creating an ever-churning industry of monster hunters.

GARDENS OF CARNESSA

Before the arcanely crafted plagues destroyed the magocracy of Caelmarath, the wizards claimed the walled overgrowth of the initial stone giant residents and indulged in a wide variety of arcane experimentation, trying to create enhanced fruits and incorruptible plant-based guardians. The spirit ancestors of those first occupants combined with the neglected magical botanicals of the Caelmarathians to create a region that shares aspects of both polluted blights and haunted marshlands. It draws the foolhardy seeking relics of the magocracy brought by fleeing refugees and intrepid explorers hoping to strike it rich despite the legion of dangers.

KHAZEPHON

The City of Baubles suffered a cataclysm of draconic origin, as the Mharoti sundered the Great Dam and unleashed a massive torrent on the community and surrounding countryside. While Ishadians rebuilt the urban landscape, the effects of the deluge still remain apparent, with suddenly eroded gullies and waterways, huge boulders, monuments, structures pushed to strange locations, and other stone formations carved into unusual shapes in a matter of moments. The water deposited all manner of items in unusual sites, and treasure hunting, as well as hunting those who have found treasure, has become common.

BATTLEFIELDS

Given the constant warfare among the polities of Midgard, battlefields are unsurprisingly widespread even beyond the Wasted West.

CLOVEN CROWN

Marking the site where a Magdar princeling attempted to enforce a poorly advised claim of rulership over the Ironcrag cantons, it also bears the marks of some of the first recorded uses of dwarven black powder on the battlefield. The site's name comes from an apocryphal tale of elite dire badger cavalry breaking the Magdar lines in a night raid, overwhelming the camp, and killing the prince before he could secure his helmet.

FIELD OF SALESH

Before Morgau and Doresh conquered Krakovia, the Field of Salesh served as a point of historical pride, reflecting Krakovian ingenuity and tactical prowess. Here a junior officer rallied troops after a general's death, luring Doreshi attackers into a false retreat and encirclement and inflicting such heavy casualties that the principalities didn't consider war to the north for several generations. It was the site of one of the first defeats of the recent campaign.

HAKON'S DEFEAT

The Scourge of the Wolfmark found the end of his reaving career at this surprisingly southern Dornitian lakeside. He had utilized Shadow fey allies to access the Processional ley line and strike deep into the Imperatrix's realm. In a turn of bad luck, what he thought to be the soft, rural belly of the Duchy turned out to be the site of the retributive muster, as imperial companies mobilized to repulse the northlanders.

SOUTHLANDS SITES

Beyond the vast, central region of the Abandoned Lands, and the slow crumbling of the Titans' empire, there exist several other wastelands that wandering adventurers may encounter.

BLACK LOTUS MESA AND YAWCHAWKA JUNGLE

Beneath the rent in reality where the Well of Urd's waters pour through lies the Black Lotus Mesa, the Great Sinkhole of Haldaheim, and the hungry shadows of the Yawchawka Jungle. While the mesa offers an undisputed example of a magically polluted blight, the Great Sinkhole demonstrates a vertical badlands, a plunging reminder of the Green Walker's arrival. The rest of the Yawchawka, outside the realms of Kush, bears the corrupting influence of the Green Walker and the vinelords.

STONE, CRESCENT, AND SARKLAN DESERTS

This broad swath of intensely dry terrain stretches across the northernmost third of the Southlands. The Stone desert is the undisputed realm of the Windlords, a barren arid expanse of hamadas, foothills, and mountains with the only dune fields existing where it meets the Crescent along the Mukupe Sahel. The Crescent is a mix of sandy ergs and rocky hamadas that start at the Mbazha Mountains and do not stop before the shores of the Middle Sea. Beyond the nourishing magical currents of the River Nuria lie the great sandy swaths of the Sarklan Desert, where sandships ply the winds and cut silty wakes from Per-Bastet to Siwal to Mhalmet.

THE RED WASTES

Beyond the provinces of the Mharoti Empire, on the border shared with embattled Ishadia and Great Khandiria, lies the badlands and battlefields of the Red Wastes.

CEMETERY CITIES

Dozens of these crumbling ruins jut from the pale crimson earth of the Red Wastes, the bones of the lost Sindu culture serving as silent monuments to the generations of warfare inflicted on the region. They house bands of ghouls born from campaigns of siege-induced starvation, shades, skeletons, looters, and refugees seeking ungoverned or unoppressed spaces. Life amid these broken locales is hardscrabble and unceasingly hazardous due to the monsters and remnant alchemical munitions.

FIELD OF WHEELING ANGELS

The most recent addition to the Red Wastes, this battlefield marks the alliance of Ishadian celestials and Khandirian juggernauts joining to check the advance of the morzas' ambitions. Yet unplundered by brazen necromancers, rotting corpses lie amid the aftermath of alchemical barrages, savage hand-to-hand combat, and siege weaponry. Smoldering husks of juggernauts and howdah-bearing elephants lie where they fell, their forms blackened and partially melted by dragonfire. Numerous impact craters litter the terrain, where angels and dragons alike plummeted to earth, sometimes locked in battle or the casualties of eagle-eyed archers and artillerists.

CAMPAIGN BUILDER
CITIES & TOWNS

A HOMEBREWER'S GUIDE TO FANTASY CITIES!

Campaign Builder: Cities & Towns provides a complete toolkit to create, expand, and enhance the cities and towns in your 5th Edition game, whether running an established or homebrew setting. From guilds to temples, and from craftspeople to criminals, this tome strengthens and expands your game's world immediately.

CAMPAIGN BUILDER: CITIES & TOWNS BRINGS YOU EVERYTHING YOU NEED:

- City character sheets to help build and track your settlements
- Guidance on all aspects of urban planning, from trade goods to architecture
- NPCs, rulers, guilds, and cults to populate your metropolis
- New character options to help urban heroes survive and thrive
- A bounty of tables, from name generators to urban encounters

START BUILDING BETTER CITIES TODAY!

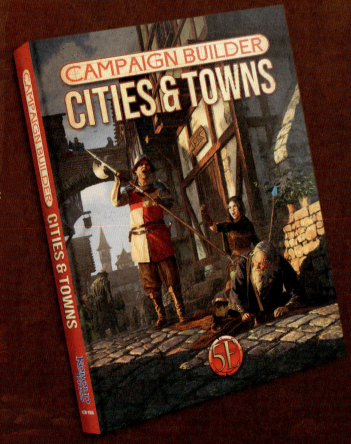

RULE THE STREETS WITH HIGH-QUALITY MAPS

Nothing screams adventure quite like the city: the hustle, the intrigue, the energy, and the unpredictability of it. And now there's no need to draw every side street and shop. Just use the *Cities & Towns Map Folio* to create the rich city experience.

The **CAMPAIGN BUILDER: CITIES & TOWNS MAP FOLIO** is a collection of maps for game masters running any urban adventure:

- 12 beautiful, full-color battle maps, including an arena, canals, cemetery, central square, city streets, docks, forest village, market, monument, plaza, ruins, sewer, and temple
- Each 24" × 36" double-sided map (8" × 12" when folded) features a 1-inch square grid, perfect for miniatures
- Specially coated for use with wet-erase, dry-erase, or even permanent markers—wipe them clean in a moment!

Kobold Press

WWW.KOBOLDPRESS.COM

Kobold Press logo is a trademark of Open Design LLC. ©2022 Open Design LLC.

A FLOCK OF OVER 400 FEROCIOUS MONSTERS FOR 5TH EDITION!

TOME OF BEASTS 3 brings you more than 400 new monsters including:

- Void knights and breakwater trolls
- Prismatic dragons and royal chimeras
- Stained glass moths and voidclaw zombies
- Breathstealers and witchalders
- Kobold drake riders and hellfire giants

Delight your players with a swarm of new, fascinating, and deadly opponents every time!

WWW.KOBOLDPRESS.COM

Kobold Press logo is a trademark of Open Design LLC. ©2022 Open Design LLC.

LEVEL UP YOUR MONSTERS

The **Tome of Beasts 3 Pawns** include more than 300 monsters from this volume, from Small to Huge! Get these creatures on the table:

- From the Adult Sand Dragon to the Necrotech Reaver!
- From Puffinfolk to Satarre Infiltrator!
- And from Black Sun Ogres to Doom Creepers!

With **Tome of Beasts 3 Lairs**, you get 23 ready-to-play adventures with encounters featuring creatures selected from *Tome of Beasts 3* to challenge heroes from 1st to 12th level.

- Visit an abandoned bardic college overrun with musical instruments come to life
- Save a druid's hidden sanctuary filled with exotic, deadly plant creatures
- An ancient, once-dormant volcano, awakened and unleashing horrors

WWW.KOBOLDPRESS.COM

Kobold Press

Kobold Press logo is a trademark of Open Design LLC. ©2022 Open Design LLC.

SMALL BUT FIERCE!

From hundreds of monsters, character options across all classes, dastardly adventures, and game design guides, Kobold Press has something for every table.

Kobold Press

SEE WHAT'S NEW ONLINE AT KOBOLDPRESS.COM

© 2023 Open Design LLC. Kobold Press and Midgard are trademarks of Open Design LLC.

Open a Trove of Wonders!

Inside *Vault of Magic*, find a vast treasure trove of enchanted items of every imaginable use—more than 950 in all! There are plenty of armors, weapons, potions, rings, and wands, but that's just for starters. From mirrors to masks, edibles to earrings, and lanterns to lockets, it's all here, ready for your 5th Edition game.

THIS 240-PAGE VOLUME INCLUDES:

- More than 30 unique items developed by special guests, including Patrick Rothfuss, Gail Simone, Deborah Ann Woll, and Luke Gygax
- Fabled items that grow in power as characters rise in levels
- New item themes, such as monster-inspired, clockwork, and apprentice wizards
- Hundreds of full-color illustrations
- Complete treasure-generation tables sorted by rarity

Amaze your players and spice up your 5th Edition campaign with fresh, new enchanted items from Vault of Magic. It'll turn that next treasure hoard into something...wondrous!

©2022 Open Design LLC. Kobold Press logo is a trademark of Open Design LLC.

OPEN GAME LICENSE Version 1.0a

The following text is the property of Wizards of the Coast, Inc. and is Copyright 2000 Wizards of the Coast, Inc ("Wizards"). All Rights Reserved.

1. Definitions: (a)"Contributors" means the copyright and/or trademark owners who have contributed Open Game Content; (b)"Derivative Material" means copyrighted material including derivative works and translations (including into other computer languages), potation, modification, correction, addition, extension, upgrade, improvement, compilation, abridgment or other form in which an existing work may be recast, transformed or adapted; (c) "Distribute" means to reproduce, license, rent, lease, sell, broadcast, publicly display, transmit or otherwise distribute; (d)"Open Game Content" means the game mechanic and includes the methods, procedures, processes and routines to the extent such content does not embody the Product Identity and is an enhancement over the prior art and any additional content clearly identified as Open Game Content by the Contributor, and means any work covered by this License, including translations and derivative works under copyright law, but specifically excludes Product Identity. (e) "Product Identity" means product and product line names, logos and identifying marks including trade dress; artifacts; creatures characters; stories, storylines, plots, thematic elements, dialogue, incidents, language, artwork, symbols, designs, depictions, likenesses, formats, poses, concepts, themes and graphic, photographic and other visual or audio representations; names and descriptions of characters, spells, enchantments, personalities, teams, personas, likenesses and special abilities; places, locations, environments, creatures, equipment, magical or supernatural abilities or effects, logos, symbols, or graphic designs; and any other trademark or registered trademark clearly identified as Product identity by the owner of the Product Identity, and which specifically excludes the Open Game Content; (f) "Trademark" means the logos, names, mark, sign, motto, designs that are used by a Contributor to identify itself or its products or the associated products contributed to the Open Game License by the Contributor (g) "Use", "Used" or "Using" means to use, Distribute, copy, edit, format, modify, translate and otherwise create Derivative Material of Open Game Content. (h) "You" or "Your" means the licensee in terms of this agreement.

2. The License: This License applies to any Open Game Content that contains a notice indicating that the Open Game Content may only be Used under and in terms of this License. You must affix such a notice to any Open Game Content that you Use. No terms may be added to or subtracted from this License except as described by the License itself. No other terms or conditions may be applied to any Open Game Content distributed using this License.

3. Offer and Acceptance: By Using the Open Game Content You indicate Your acceptance of the terms of this License.

4. Grant and Consideration: In consideration for agreeing to use this License, the Contributors grant You a perpetual, worldwide, royalty-free, non-exclusive license with the exact terms of this License to Use, the Open Game Content.

5. Representation of Authority to Contribute: If You are contributing original material as Open Game Content, You represent that Your Contributions are Your original creation and/ or You have sufficient rights to grant the rights conveyed by this License.

6. Notice of License Copyright: You must update the COPYRIGHT NOTICE portion of this License to include the exact text of the COPYRIGHT NOTICE of any Open Game Content You are copying, modifying or distributing, and You must add the title, the copyright date, and the copyright holder's name to the COPYRIGHT NOTICE of any original Open Game Content you Distribute.

7. Use of Product Identity: You agree not to Use any Product Identity, including as an indication as to compatibility, except as expressly licensed in another, independent Agreement with the owner of each element of that Product Identity. You agree not to indicate compatibility or co-adaptability with any Trademark or Registered Trademark in conjunction with a work containing Open Game Content except as expressly licensed in another, independent Agreement with the owner of such Trademark or Registered Trademark. The use of any Product Identity in Open Game Content does not constitute a challenge to the ownership of that Product Identity.

The owner of any Product Identity used in Open Game Content shall retain all rights, title and interest in and to that Product Identity.

8. Identification: If you distribute Open Game Content You must clearly indicate which portions of the work that you are distributing are Open Game Content.

9. Updating the License: Wizards or its designated Agents may publish updated versions of this License. You may use any authorized version of this License to copy, modify and distribute any Open Game Content originally distributed under any version of this License.

10. Copy of this License: You MUST include a copy of this License with every copy of the Open Game Content You Distribute.

11. Use of Contributor Credits: You may not market or advertise the Open Game Content using the name of any Contributor unless You have written permission from the Contributor to do so.

12. Inability to Comply: If it is impossible for You to comply with any of the terms of this License with respect to some or all of the Open Game Content due to statute, judicial order, or governmental regulation then You may not Use any Open Game Material so affected.

13. Termination: This License will terminate automatically if You fail to comply with all terms herein and fail to cure such breach within 30 days of becoming aware of the breach. All sublicenses shall survive the termination of this License.

14. Reformation: If any provision of this License is held to be unenforceable, such provision shall be reformed only to the extent necessary to make it enforceable.

15. COPYRIGHT NOTICE

Open Game License v 1.0a Copyright 2000, Wizards of the Coast, LLC.

System Reference Document 5.1 Copyright 2016, Wizards of the Coast, Inc.; Authors Mike Mearls, Jeremy Crawford, Chris Perkins, Rodney Thompson, Peter Lee, James Wyatt, Robert J. Schwalb, Bruce R. Cordell, Chris Sims, and Steve Townshend, based on original material by E. Gary Gygax and Dave Arneson.

Creature Codex. © 2018 Open Design LLC; Authors Wolfgang Baur, Dan Dillon, Richard Green, James Haeck, Chris Harris, Jeremy Hochhalter, James Introcaso, Chris Lockey, Shawn Merwin, and Jon Sawatsky.

Warlock Grimoire 2. © 2020 Open Design LLC. Authors: Wolfgang Baur, Celeste Conowitch, David "Zeb" Cook, Dan Dillon, Robert Fairbanks, Scott Gable, Richard Green, Victoria Jaczko, TK Johnson, Christopher Lockey, Sarah Madsen, Greg Marks, Ben McFarland, Kelly Pawlik, Lysa Penrose, Richard Pett, Marc Radle, Hannah Rose, Jon Sawatsky, Robert Schwalb, Brian Suskind, Ashley Warren, and Mike Welham.

Tome of Beasts 1. ©2023 Open Design LLC; Authors: Daniel Kahn, Jeff Lee, and Mike Welham.

Wastes of Chaos. ©2023 Open Design LLC; Authors: Richard Green, Tim Hitchcock, and Sarah Madsen.